MW00573898

A THOUSAND BLUNDERS

During the first two decades of the twentieth century, the Grand Trunk Pacific Railway played an important role in the development of the north-central corridor of British Columbia. Running from Winnipeg via Edmonton and the Yellowhead Pass to Prince Rupert on the northwest coast, the GTP was built to challenge the primacy of the Canadian Pacific Railway. The 1,500-kilometre British Columbia line, built at great cost over some of the country's most rugged terrain, was completed in 1914. But traffic on this line fell far short of company expectations, and this contributed to the collapse of the GTP in 1919.

In this book, Frank Leonard looks at the failure of the Grand Trunk Pacific Railway, focusing on the problems of the BC line. He calls into question traditional interpretations of the company's collapse by arguing that much of it can be attributed to 'a thousand blunders' made by senior and junior GTP managers. His research is based on the meticulous examination of surviving internal company documents, which provide important insights into the routine decisions that formed the basis of GTP policies.

A Thousand Blunders is a provocative account of one of the greatest failures in Canadian entrepreneurial history. Richly detailed and thoroughly documented, it makes an important contribution to the fields of railway and business history, as well as to the study of the history of northern British Columbia.

Frank Leonard teaches in the Department of History at Douglas College, New Westminster, BC.

FRANK LEONARD

A THOUSAND BLUNDERS

THE GRAND TRUNK
PACIFIC RAILWAY
AND NORTHERN
BRITISH COLUMBIA

UBC PRESS / VANCOUVER

Printed in Canada on acid-free paper ∞

ISBN 0-7748-0532-3

Canadian Cataloguing in Publication Data

Leonard, Frank, 1948-
        A thousand blunders

Includes bibliographical references and index.
ISBN 0-7748-0532-3

        1. Grand Trunk Pacific Railway Company – History. 2. Railroads – British Columbia, Northern – History. I. Title.
HE2810.G65L46 1995   385'.06'5711   C95-910652-9

This book has been published with the help of a grant from the Social Science Federation of Canada, using funds provided by the Social Sciences and Humanities Research Council of Canada.

UBC Press gratefully acknowledges the ongoing support to its publishing program from the Canada Council, the Province of British Columbia Cultural Services Branch, and the Department of Communications of the Government of Canada.

Set in Minion, Gill Sans, and Bauer Bodoni
Printed and bound in Canada by Friesens
Copy-editor: Carolyn Bateman
Proofreader: Randy Schmidt
Cartographer: Eric Leinberger
Designer: George Vaitkunas

UBC Press
University of British Columbia
6344 Memorial Road
Vancouver, BC V6T 1Z2
(604) 822-3259
Fax: 1-800-668-0821
E-mail: orders@ubcpress.ubc.ca

CONTENTS

ILLUSTRATIONS AND FIGURES

Illustrations

Figures

PREFACE

I MUST FOLLOW the example of railway labour historian Walter Licht and confess at the outset that I, too, am not a train buff. Though I had an electric train as a child, I played with it only sporadically. While I enjoyed watching with my parents the steam locomotives chuff back and forth in a West Toronto yard, I turned down the early invitation of a kind engineer to ride in one. And a cross-country trip by day coach from Vancouver to Montreal for Expo 67 led to a firm resolution to fly forever after.

My interest in the Grand Trunk Pacific Railway Company (GTP) grew incrementally during a teaching sojourn in Prince George, the largest community on the successor CN North Line. I was contemplating prospective dissertation topics, and I needed a demonstration for a local history course. By satisfying the second, the GTP aroused my interest for the first. The discovery of extensive GTP records in the National Archives in Ottawa, though far from complete, convinced me that one could illuminate much of what appeared to be the arrested development of northern British Columbia through an examination of the papers of company managers stationed thousands of miles away.

This book first saw the light of day as a doctoral dissertation for York University, and it is the examining committee members for that work whom I first thank: Christopher Armstrong, John Saywell, Gilbert Stelter, Tom Traves, and John Warkentin. Viv Nelles, the supervisor of the study, offered much good advice throughout the exercise.

Like many historians of British Columbia, I have benefitted from the advice and encouragement of Robin Fisher, Patricia Roy, and Robert McDonald. Pat opened her collection of editorial cartoons; Bob walked the grade and listened with good humour to a disquisition on the finer points of railway cuts, fills, and bridges as we spent a day motoring leisurely from Terrace to Prince Rupert. All have shared their research with me; the notes indicate my debt to each. I have also learned much from discussion and correspondence with historians across Canada and the United States who share an interest in the business of railways. John

Eagle, Maury Klein, and Carlos Schwantes, in particular, answered many difficult questions. And many 'railfans,' whose fraternity I did not join, have shown patience and forbearance in guiding me through some of the technical aspects of building and running a road.

I can only list friends and colleagues who, having read part or all of this study in its current form or one of its several past forms, made suggestions that improved the work: Robert Campbell, Don Freeman, Robert Galois, John Gilpin, Jacqueline Gresko, Gordon Hak, Cole Harris, Trevor Heaver, Logan Hovis, James McDonald, Richard Mackie, Jeremy Mouat, Allen Seager, John Thomas, and Peter Ward. The anonymous readers chosen by UBC Press and the Social Science Federation of Canada clarified my thinking and facilitated revision.

Archivists and other members of the institutions noted in the first section of the bibliography have been without exception helpful in directing me to relevant unpublished material. I wish to underline, however, the important contribution of local historians, museum workers, archivists, and librarians in northern British Columbia. None of these, of course, bears responsibility for any shortcomings in what follows. All errors of fact and interpretation that remain are mine alone.

I thank *BC Studies* for allowing me to use portions of two articles that first appeared in that journal.

I wish to acknowledge the financial support of the following institutions and agencies for research, writing, and revision: the Graduate Program in History at York University, the Social Sciences and Humanities Research Council of Canada, the College of New Caledonia, the University of Toronto/York University Joint Program in Transportation, Douglas College, the Department of Indian and Northern Affairs, and the Gitwangak Band. Time is almost as important as money, particularly when primary sources are scattered across the country. My principal employers over the past decade, the College of New Caledonia and Douglas College, have also supported my work by awarding me educational leaves.

The members of UBC Press efficiently transformed a manuscript into a book. Senior Editor Jean Wilson guided me deftly through the stages leading to publication. Acting Managing Editor Camilla Jenkins illuminated the mysteries of the editorial process. Cartographer Eric Leinberger made sense of my sometimes unclear wishes for the maps.

Judy Leonard has provided encouragement through two jobs, many moves, and much more as well. It is to her that I dedicate this book.

ABBREVIATIONS

BC Express	B.C. Express Company
BRC	Board of Railway Commissioners for Canada
CPR	Canadian Pacific Railway Company
Canadian Northern	Canadian Northern Railway Company
DIA	Department of Indian Affairs
FWS	Foley Brothers, Welch & Stewart Company
GTP	Grand Trunk Pacific Railway Company
Grand Trunk	Grand Trunk Railway Company of Canada
IWW	Industrial Workers of the World
NRS	Natural Resources Security Company, Ltd.
PGE	Pacific Great Eastern Railway Company
PNO	Pacific Northern & Omineca Railway Company

ONE

INTRODUCTION: 'A TRAGEDY RATHER THAN OTHERWISE'

On this continent wide, where our loved ones reside,
We have railways, both 'great' and 'small';
But of first-water brand, ours alone is styled 'Grand',
So the Grand Trunk leads them all!

... And we all declare, that no chief can compare,
With the chief of our road – Mr. Hays!

The great legal lights, in the fierce railroad fights,
Seem anxious to make a figure;
Let them swagger and frown in their biggest gown,
Still the Grand Trunk has a 'Biggar'!

... The Grand Trunk Pacific is an infant terrific!
Whose pranks Mr. Morse could expound;
Last winter was frightful, but he thought it delightful!
And engaged one for the year round!

... So Officers all, both great guns and small,
We gather with good cheer and toast,
... Many happy returns! and ... blessings divine
... For our loved chief and host – Chas. M. Hays.

'For the Reunion of Official Family of the
Grand Trunk Railway System'
W.H. Rosevear
16 May 1907

The road of a thousand wonders
The trail of a hundred hell's [*sic*]
The story of a thousand blunders
Is the tale the death roll tells.

The life that God created
Is mangled, torn and hurt,
By those who in their greed have rated
Humanity to be as cheap as dirt.

And ever the one's [*sic*] who are toiling
Die hard for the one's [*sic*] that rest.
The victims of a hellish spoiling
Of a system that stands accurs'd.

In a tale of a future grandeur
And the dream of a judgment day,
I stand by the sorrow and wonder
Who is great – God or Laurier.

'The Grand Trunk Pacific'
J.A. McKechnie [John Houston]
Prince Rupert Evening Bulletin
30 March 1909

THE TWO POEMS ABOVE indicate different contemporary perceptions of the Grand Trunk Pacific Railway Company (GTP), the organization that played a predominant role in the development of the north-central corridor of British Columbia during the first two decades of the twentieth century. The first ode, read at a gathering of officers of the GTP's parent corporation, the Grand Trunk Railway Company of Canada (Grand Trunk), celebrates the instigator and first president of the GTP, Charles Melville Hays. It also reflects the unwarranted optimism and assurance, 'the empire of innocence,' with which company officers approached expansion and development in western Canada under his leadership during the first decade of the twentieth century.[1] The second poem, penned under a pseudonym by a fierce critic of the company, suggests not only that rapacious railway construction practices on the west coast injured workers, but also, more generally, that GTP actions frequently hurt everyone.

This work probes the actions of the Grand Trunk Pacific that elicited the second poem and created tension with the corporate self-image expressed in the first. It investigates a series of GTP activities concerning its British Columbia line, the most expensive and least remunerative portion of the railway, from the inception of the company in 1902 to its collapse in 1919. The study does not oppose the received view that the performance of the GTP in the construction and operation of its line from Prince Rupert to the Yellowhead Pass represented a failure.[2] It regards this failure, however, not as proof of moral shortcoming but as a product of many actions, 'a thousand blunders,' which senior and junior GTP managers carried out. By examining actions on both managerial levels, the study calls into question traditional interpretations of the company's collapse. It also challenges a central tenet of what has been termed the 'Octopus school' of railway historiography: that the power of railway companies was monolithic as well as menacing.[3] By viewing local problems of acquisition and control through the prism of the company's legal department, it departs from other evaluations of the role of railway companies in townsite development in western North America.

Earlier works on the GTP have outlined the company's rise and fall. Formulated by the Grand Trunk management as a western extension to its lines in central Canada, the GTP project received the financial support of the Liberal federal government only by transforming itself into the western division of a much enlarged line across Canada. The new 'transcontinental' company began to build westward from Winnipeg in 1905 and eastward from Prince Rupert in 1908.[4] Overruns in construction costs after 1909 caused the GTP to petition the government repeatedly for additional support. The line was completed in 1914, but traffic during the war could not pay its fixed charges. The parent company's refusal to cover its subsidiary's shortfalls caused the government to put the GTP into receivership in 1919.

In 1921, W.H. Biggar, former head of the GTP legal department, defended the actions of company managers by describing the outcome of the GTP venture as a 'tragedy rather than otherwise ... But for his [Hays's] untimely death in 1912, and for the War, and resulting conditions, I believe that the GTP today would have a very different story to tell.'[5] Though academic studies have superseded polemics, explanations for the company's fall have shown a surprising tenacity. Almost without exception, students of the GTP have attributed its collapse to the circumstances to which Biggar alluded. Many historians acknowledge that decisions concerning the location of the Pacific terminus and the expensive construction standard, made under Hays's leadership, added to the burdens of the new company. However, they have subordinated these details to a discussion of his grand design to challenge the Canadian Pacific Railway Company (CPR). Central in many accounts is not the

GTP president's actual decisions, but his drowning as a passenger on the *Titanic* in April 1912.[6] By joining the newspapers in speculating on the president's secret plans to save the enterprise, historians have frequently left unexplained the transition of the company to a position where it required saving.

Hays's tragic end no doubt encouraged early, partisan evaluations of the GTP as a glorious, if flawed, final project for the heroic builder whom Laurier lauded as 'the greatest railway genius in Canada.'[7] Accounts of the interwar period, by contrast, draw on belated government investigations of the GTP president's plans and actions to support the CPR contention that the state should never have subsidized its competition.[8] Less partisan is J.A. Lower, the first student of the GTP in British Columbia, who catalogues some company actions in townsites that antagonized those who generated traffic for the railway. While recognizing Hays's role in these activities, Lower uncritically accepts the contentions of a company

CHARLES M. HAYES, Esq.
Second Vice President & General Manager
Grand Trunk Railway System   Montreal

Heroic caricature of C.M. Hays, circa 1909

publicist in concluding that the GTP experience demonstrated the president's 'foresight, will, and ... ability.'[9] Though the GTP later came under the scrutiny of the entrepreneurial school of business history, its president still received the charity due a Great Man. In his financial study of the parent Grand Trunk, A.W. Currie ties the folly of locating the GTP Pacific terminus at Prince Rupert to Hays, but concludes that the president's death represented an irreparable loss to the company.[10] Since they gained access to an edited correspondence between Hays and Grand Trunk president Sir Charles Rivers Wilson, academic historians have come to view as less benign the GTP president's actions.[11] But even Canadian National official historian G.R. Stevens, perhaps the most strident critic of Hays's direction of the GTP, perpetuates the view of Hays as a dark hero by dismissing his successors as mediocrities who lacked the ability to save the company.[12]

The second cause advanced for what one reviewer has called 'the misfortune which overwhelmed the project' is the impact of the First World War. Given 'a breathing space' to develop traffic on its new line, the GTP might have secured enough revenue to pay both its operating expenses and interest charges and thereby permitted the parent Grand Trunk to 'squeeze through.' But the war-induced 'inflationary ... spiral, sucking prices ever upward,' destroyed the potential of the just-completed line to pay its charges by building traffic. A recent popular study of the GTP rehearses both these arguments to explain the company's collapse.[13]

The lack of financial data concerning both the construction and the short operation phases of the GTP explains in part the disinclination of historians to investigate the construction and collapse of the GTP as a function of the evolution of a larger business cycle. They have also avoided econometric estimates of the promoters' *ex ante* expectations of returns.

This study draws on the perspectives and insights of the econometric studies of other railways to create estimates of costs and returns for the GTP. While not ignoring the effect of Hays's demise or the impact of the war, it contends that the transcontinental was probably never an economic venture. It suggests, however, that the actions of Hays and other company officers hastened the company's failure in British Columbia by increasing its losses. At the senior level, management decisions concerning acquisition of the Pacific terminus, construction, and labour relations created in large part the onerous financial obligations that brought on the company's collapse.

The work then moves beyond the system-building concerns of head office in an examination of company actions in several communities and railway townsites in the province. At this level, GTP activity offers a marked contrast with the findings of students of other railways. Since the 1920s, scholars have used company land department records to create institutional studies of the 'colonization policies' of several American and Canadian roads. While acknowledging that railway promoters sometimes enriched themselves through speculation in townsites, these studies maintain that the company's general intent in townsite development was to attract settlers and investors who would generate traffic for the line. The land department of an American road expressed this philosophy clearly during the 1870s. 'It is not to be supposed that railroad corporations surpass all men in disinterested benevolence, but it is beyond question that they know their own interest, and so will take some pains to help [the lot purchaser] earn a dollar whenever they can thus make two for themselves.'[14]

More recent studies of the CPR and Canadian Northern Railway Company (Canadian Northern) do not substantially change this interpretation. W.K. Lamb accepts CPR general manager William Van Horne's contention that his company discouraged outside speculators by choosing townsites 'without regard to any private interest whatsoever.' Though he admits that the CPR secured large returns from the sale of its lots in Vancouver, Lamb suggests that the company's prices, and its profits, were reasonable.[15] Max Foran is more candid. In his survey of the CPR townsite policy in western Canada, he remarks that many of the company's development decisions were geared to its own economic considerations. For immediate profits, the railway company bypassed superior locations and sometimes refused to pay municipal taxes. Nevertheless, he concludes that the CPR was generally 'consistent in its desire to build up an urban west that complemented the needs and resources of the rural economy.'[16] While historian T.D. Regehr notes that the purpose of government land grants to the Canadian Northern was to assist the railway in financing construction, he reiterates that company owners William Mackenzie and Donald Mann did not act as speculators. The land they acquired or purchased in townsites was for development of their primary interest: the railway. To make it a success, thriving towns and prosperous settlers were needed. Mann later boasted about the restraint he and his partner had exercised in townsite speculation.[17]

Relying primarily on the records of the GTP legal department, this study presents a different view of GTP townsite activity in British Columbia. While the larger white communities that the GTP created along its British Columbia line certainly fit into historian H.S. Stromquist's typology of urban centres as 'railroad towns,' their stagnation or decline after an initial period of spectacular growth stemmed as much from the activities of company officers as it did from commercial disadvantage.[18] Unlike most nineteenth-century transcontinentals, the GTP secured no general land grant to finance building. Driven by Hays's demands for immediate returns to cover part of the costs of construction, the company achieved some apparent successes on the strength of townsite lot sales in British Columbia, which improved the balance on the company's land department books.

Impressed with this apparent gain, historian Margaret Ormsby implies that the GTP was a late participant in the 'Great Potlatch,' a series of British Columbia government land grants and subsidies to railway companies during the last two decades of the nineteenth century.[19] Sharing the general admiration of muckrakers for the business acumen of railway companies, Martin Robin contends that the GTP laid 'rails of steal' [*sic*] by cleverly acquiring terminus land 'for purely speculative purposes.'[20] The most recent survey of British Columbia history recognizes that the company lost significant rents from its townsite activities to the provincial government and outside promoters.[21] But for a railway company with limited land holdings, however profitable, the generation of traffic was crucial. Within railway communities, junior officers frequently committed the resources and prestige of the GTP to policies that antagonized local residents and damaged concerns that could have provided valuable traffic for the line.[22]

THESE EVALUATIONS of company actions, at both a system and a local level, imply strategies for success that the GTP did not adopt. The prescription advanced here for the successful working of a transcontinental railway accepts as an axiom the contention of standard texts on railway construction and finance: that expenditure on construction must be tied to realistic estimates of the resulting income from traffic.[23] But it also draws on Harold Innis's scattered comments on the operation and impact of railways in British Columbia. In his first monograph, Innis compares the CPR to a transcontinental bridge that required a particularly expensive abutment on the Pacific slope. During its early years of high costs and limited earnings in British Columbia, the CPR concentrated on the development of more remunerative local main- and branch-line traffic rather than through or transcontinental traffic. For the operation of the CPR Pacific slope line, then, Innis implies that success meant simply controlling expenditure and limiting losses that were covered by returns from more profitable sections of the line.[24] For the construction and operation of its lines in the Kootenay region in the southeastern corner of the province, Innis elaborates the CPR's strategy. By establishing a low tariff that encouraged mine owners to ship their ore, the CPR elicited extensive local traffic that reduced the railway company's overhead costs over long stretches of otherwise non-revenue-producing territory and relieved in part the cost of settlement.[25] The most recent overview of railway development in British Columbia sees this ability to generate traffic (or capture it from competitors) as the key to the success of the Canadian Pacific and the failure of both the Canadian Northern and the Grand Trunk Pacific.[26] For Innis, however, the success of the CPR in British Columbia as well as on the prairies also advanced 'the dominance of eastern Canada over western Canada.'[27]

The owners of the Canadian Northern, the last transcontinental to enter British Columbia, also attempted to encourage traffic along a section of the line requiring greater construction expenditures and offering much less local traffic than the prairies. In his detailed study of the enterprise, Regehr asserts that the 'development of local traffic resources was certainly very much a part of Mackenzie and Mann's British Columbia plans.' To generate freight, they purchased the Dunsmuir Colliery on Vancouver Island, built a huge sawmill at Fraser Mills near Vancouver, and invested in numerous hardrock mining and fishing enterprises. These activities would, one of the Canadian Northern officers claimed, have produced enough traffic by 1920 to make the British Columbia section pay not only its operating expenses but also its fixed charges.[28]

'Not following the CPR example' may embrace the causes of the GTP failure as a unit, but it does not offer explicit measures of failure for the different components of a large, complex organization such as a railway company. Though he concentrates on success in his studies on the evolution of the managerial structure of American corporate enterprise, business historian Alfred D. Chandler, Jr., also suggests functional standards of failure. For senior managers who allocate the resources of the enterprise, one can characterize as failure those acts or decisions that cause the concern not to do better than costs. Not doing better than costs, after all, represents the ultimate, if not the immediate, explanation for the GTP's slide into receivership in 1919. But the GTP records that survive, described below, allow estimates of the consequences for the consolidated balance for only a few of the company's actions in British Columbia. Rarely can one measure on the balance the impact of the activities of junior company officers who did not determine policy. Chandler implies that junior managers fail when they commit or omit acts to the detriment of those resources allocated by their superiors.[29] This study suggests that for the GTP, one can also characterize as failure those acts or omissions that increased the company's net deficit or reduced the company's net gain.

In several accounts of the corporate organization of American railway companies during the later nineteenth century, Chandler offers an insight that can be applied to the organization of the GTP.[30] Clearly an advocate of the divisional organization most closely associated with the Pennsylvania Railroad, Chandler briefly outlines the centralized departmental system, the '"natural" form of organization' of British railways that the New York Central haphazardly adopted. On the longer American lines, he contends, the departmental system led to problems in delegating authority. Accordingly, nearly all the roads in the United States carrying traffic over long distances came to use the divisional organization.[31]

After Hays became general manager of the parent Grand Trunk in 1896, he shifted the British-owned railway company toward a divisional administration.[32] He did not replicate this organization in the GTP, however. With headquarters in the Grand Trunk's Montreal building on McGill Street, the GTP senior managers created a separate organization for the transcontinental that also distinguished it from both the CPR and the Canadian Northern.[33] While Hays, as the GTP president, was responsible to shareholders (i.e., the Grand Trunk London Board) and communicated frequently with the Grand Trunk president, he assumed the effective direction of the company. GTP agents and officers who appeared in western Canada soon after the transcontinental project was launched were organized in departments that apparently enjoyed little independence. As construction began in 1905, the office of the land commissioner, which would manage and sell the company's land holdings and townsite lots, was created in Winnipeg. With the completion of the

Prairie Section in 1909, the GTP transferred from Montreal to Winnipeg the offices of general manager, chief engineer, and assistant solicitor, the junior officer in the legal department. But while the GTP lawyer in Winnipeg responded to instructions from the general manager, he was responsible to the general counsel in Montreal. The GTP also did not act on the Winnipeg lawyer's suggestion to create an office in Victoria to do the company's legal work in British Columbia. Although the amount of legal work in the West compelled the company to promote its western officer to solicitor and appoint another assistant solicitor in 1910, it kept both officers in Winnipeg and hired legal agents to do much of its court work in Edmonton, Vancouver, Victoria, and Prince Rupert. Hays explicitly refused to delegate authority to the solicitor in Winnipeg on the grounds that only he and the general counsel understood from their origin 'questions of a serious character, or affecting relations with the government.'[34]

The reluctance of the senior management to delegate authority extended beyond the legal department. 'Like many other very able men,' remarked Rivers Wilson, Hays was 'disinclined to delegate any portion of his authority, or even to encourage initiative in his subordinates.'[35] The surviving files of several departments indicate that the GTP had no intention of shifting any of the offices that supervised construction and operation of the Mountain Section to British Columbia, as the CPR had done in the 1880s. Although the company established an office of general superintendent in Prince Rupert in 1910, two years after it had embarked on construction on the Pacific coast, it appears that the officer had limited authority to act outside the immediate confines of the terminus.

Not only the administrative structure but also the organizational memory of the GTP lagged behind many American roads. The document folders of the surviving GTP files reveal that the company adopted the vertical file storage methods that American enterprises had employed a decade earlier. Interdepartmental correspondence indicates, however, that each GTP department had a unique, and incompatible, document notation and filing system. Many offices, including the legal and land departments in Winnipeg, used traditional, arbitrary numerical filing systems that could be accessed only through a single name/subject-number index, presumably located in the respective office. Only the engineering department had adopted the railway version of the Dewey decimal designation system, which an American commission on business efficiency declared invariably saved a large company both time and money.

Most striking was the incompatibility of the file system at the legal department branch office in Winnipeg with that of its head office in Montreal. Frequent notations concerning file tracing on interoffice correspondence suggest this vestige from the nineteenth century hindered control as well as communication.[36]

The small number of GTP managers during construction suggests two levels of activity and authority. Senior company officers included the president, general manager, and other vice-presidents. Junior officers included the solicitor, land commissioner, and general superintendent in Prince Rupert. Until 1907, the GTP agent resident in British Columbia was not a company officer. During the construction period, the GTP had few officers who fit Chandler's description of middle managers. Perhaps only the chief engineer and the general counsel supervised the work of other managers and reported to senior executives.[37]

This study draws on both Innis and Chandler to elaborate T.D. Regehr's contention that the GTP operated as an instrument of metropolitanism.[38] The argument in the following chapters that the company's impact on the north-central corridor was metropolitan is double-edged. Certainly the illumination of a particular set of external influences emanating from GTP offices in Montreal and Winnipeg in the creation and evolution of communities along its British Columbia line challenges the claims of A.F.J. Artibise. Along with other proponents of boosterism, he exaggerates the role of local elites in urban development in western Canada.[39] Indeed, the ubiquity of the GTP in the region suggests Martin Robin's important, if vague, notion of a 'company province whose output, rate of growth, and social organization depended upon the rise and fall of large corporations.'[40] A close examination of the activities of the GTP along the 'company corridor' reveals, however, that junior officers, particularly those in the Winnipeg legal and land department offices, frequently did not forward the interests of the metropole, whether it be the shareholders in Britain or the GTP senior management in Montreal. Rather than order or success, contradiction emerges as the dominant theme of the activities of the GTP in the development of northern British Columbia. If, as American historian Maury Klein suggests, badly managed roads are representative of most railway development in North America, the Grand Trunk Pacific certainly deserves attention as a case study.[41]

The ordering of chapters follows from the two levels of activity by GTP managers in British Columbia set out above. The following three chapters concentrate on the actions of senior managers in matters that affected the entire line. Chapters concerning the acquisition of a Pacific terminus, the elements of construction, and labour relations investigate company decisions that in large part determined the first cost and the fixed charges of the British Columbia line. Chapter 4, on labour relations, also bridges management perceptions from a system to a local level by discussing in some detail the company's response to challenges to authority in Prince Rupert.

The next four chapters (5-8) focus on company actions in a series of communities in the province. The survival of significant company files, discussed below, determined in large part the uneven geographical distribution of the accounts that follow.[42] For these communities the files reveal that officers of the Winnipeg legal department often assumed responsibility for making decisions on which the success of the company's local projects depended. Chapter 5 reviews the multifarious company actions in the largest community, Prince Rupert. It illuminates contradictions in both GTP development and trouble-shooting activities at the Pacific terminus. The study then turns to the company's stumbling efforts to acquire Indian reserve land in the interior for right-of-way and townsites. The last two chapters of this section contrast the company's 'achievement' in eliminating opposition in the second community on the British Columbia line, Prince George, with its dismal failure to recognize and secure valuable traffic for the line in the Hazelton district.

The penultimate chapter returns to a consideration of the entire British Columbia line with an examination of the operations of the company after completion. It presents estimates of traffic and returns for the line for the period 1914-19. It then outlines the bumbling attempts of the company to operate the largest industrial enterprise on the line outside the railway proper, the Prince Rupert drydock. The conclusion assesses the activity of both levels of management.

THE MAJOR SOURCE for the study is the surviving files of the GTP legal department branch office established in Winnipeg in 1909, which have been deposited in the National Archives. While most of the files concern specific legal problems along the line, particularly in the railway townsites, one can also locate material on the larger questions of location, construction, and, less frequently, operation. These records invite, indeed require, an examination of the problems of railway development from the perspective of the junior as well as the senior company officer.

It is difficult to place the GTP legal department in an appropriate North American context because surprisingly little has been written about the role of house counsel, the lawyers and legal departments within railway companies or other large concerns.[43] This lacuna stems in part from the concentration of both legal and business historians on legislation and judicial decisions concerning railways rather than on the majority of disputes between economic interests that never reached the courts.[44] The closest examination of legal activity on behalf of an American railway company focuses on a separate firm on retainer rather than on house counsel proper. The resulting studies isolate the general attorney for the Southern Pacific Company subsidiary lines in Texas from the wider range of SP activities in the state.[45]

The careers of two renowned Canadian railway lawyers of the early twentieth century, R.B. Bennett for the CPR and Z.A. Lash for the Canadian Northern, unfortunately provide few benchmarks for measuring the activities of their GTP counterparts because their activities transcended their respective employers. To find more useful comparisons for GTP lawyers D'Arcy Tate, W.H. Biggar, and H.H. Hansard, which the following chapters suggest excelled neither in law nor in business, we need to remember the names, and peruse the files, of other 'forgotten' lawyers who served the railway companies and little else.[46]

While the GTP apparently did not create a manual that set out the duties of the legal department, an examination of the surviving files suggests that it performed two types of tasks. First, it had to secure a host of authorizations from government departments and agencies for construction and operation of the road. To obtain federal government funds for construction, for example, the legal department routinely forwarded four sets of plans for consideration by two, and sometimes more, bureaucracies. In addition, the British Columbia government required two sets of plans. To channel the flow of paper to the appropriate institution at the correct time was no mean task, and the company department sometimes omitted an element in the procedure that resulted in costly delay.[47]

But the legal department also had another role. In 1915, a GTP solicitor remarked that 'in order to advance ... [the company] has done and must necessarily ... do things which have brought us [the GTP] into conflict ... trusting ... that matters would be righted afterwards through the Legal Department.'[48] It was this perception of the legal department as troubleshooter that GTP counsel brought to conflicts concerning the railway company in communities along the line. Thus, many files of the legal department that go beyond routine contractual matters illuminate the actions of the legal department intended to deflect or neutralize opponents of the company.

Even within these limited areas, however, there are important gaps. Many files concerning the company's initial activities in British Columbia, which the head office in Montreal created, were not transferred to Winnipeg. After 1915, the head office apparently took over many of the outstanding legal matters, so that discussions in the Winnipeg files frequently come to an abrupt end. But for the period 1909-15, the legal department files contain material from virtually every company department. An examination of the relevant files of the GTP corporate records, the office of land commissioner (land department), and scattered files of the secretary, engineering department, and the Hays-Rivers Wilson correspondence noted above overcomes in part both the limitations and the bias of the legal department files. These records and sources beyond the railway company are briefly reviewed in the bibliography.

While the surviving records invite an investigation of certain aspects of company activity, they discourage the study of other elements. Though the hand-written minutes and annual reports of the GTP and GTP Development Company, the corporate name for the land department, have survived, both the dearth and unreliability of financial data there have circumscribed a precise analysis of company expenditures in British Columbia during and after construction.[49] Second, information in the legal department files does not provide an adequate base for the creation of community studies. Thus, the chapters concerning townsites deal largely with company actions to secure returns and eliminate opponents and the judicial evolution of some of these actions.[50]

Throughout this book, I have used the terms 'GTP management' and 'GTP managers' in a functional sense to describe those who organized and promoted the GTP project since 1902. The first item in the GTP Directors' Minute Book is a copy of the petition to Laurier in November 1902 for the Grand Trunk western extension. Some members of the management, led by Hays, assumed formal titles as officers of the Grand Trunk Pacific Railway Company at its first shareholders meeting in August 1904, almost a year after the federal government passed an act to incorporate the company. Others, such as Grand Trunk president Rivers

Wilson, had a formal connection with the GTP only as directors.

I have sometimes emphasized the separate perceptions or calculations of the parent company concerning its transcontinental subsidiary, particularly before the GTP was organized, by using the term 'Grand Trunk management.' The two formally distinct management groups shared an important identity, however. Hays retained his office of general manager of the Grand Trunk until late 1909, when a corporate reorganization of the parent company allowed him to become president of that concern as well. His successors in the GTP presidency also held the office of president of the Grand Trunk.

TWO

'IN A HOLE': ENTRY INTO
BRITISH COLUMBIA, 1902-12

WHAT LED THE GTP to embark upon construction of a line across British Columbia, one which entailed enormous fixed charges? Part of the answer, ironically, is that it believed it had secured a concession that would offset much of the construction cost. Though the company's agenda for land and townsite acquisition emerged concurrently with its plans for construction, the GTP's early acquisition of its Pacific terminus determined not only the location of much of its line across the Pacific slope but also the timing of construction.[1] This chapter investigates the motives underlying the company's original undertaking with the federal government to build across British Columbia. It then examines the GTP acquisition of its terminus land as an expression of the company's calculation that the success of the transcontinental in the Pacific province turned on a subsidy from the provincial government over and above that secured from the dominion. This calculation led the GTP president to commit the company to premature construction on the west coast.

The negotiations during the period 1902-4 between the Grand Trunk Railway Company of Canada and the federal government, which established the terms of construction for the company's transcontinental subsidiary, the Grand Trunk Pacific Railway Company, have been examined at length in two recent studies and need not be treated in detail here.[2] Both G.R. Stevens and R.M. Coutts contend that Charles M. Hays, general manager of the Grand Trunk and first president of the GTP, largely ignored the concerns of Grand Trunk president Sir Charles Rivers Wilson and the more cautious members of the company's London board in committing the parent company to a much enlarged project that had little chance of economic success. But in their concern to demonstrate the folly of the eastern half of the new line, which now crossed the entire country, Stevens and Coutts eschew an examination of the motives that had earlier led the company to propose an extension to the Pacific coast.[3]

The surviving Hays-Rivers Wilson correspondence makes clear that the primary motive in the Grand Trunk management's decision to build a western extension was the company's desire to capture a share of the Northwest's rapidly expanding wheat exports and its market for products from the central Canadian manufacturing districts that the railway company currently served. To justify this new 'policy of aggression and extension,' Hays offered a model for the Grand Trunk – the Atchison, Topeka & Santa Fe Railway Company. Emerging from receivership in the 1890s, the Santa Fe had become a profitable operation by the turn of the century. For Hays, the key to the American road's new prosperity had been its rapid westward expansion to capture traffic. The Grand Trunk must also 'take some means of fastening [the grain traffic] to us.'[4]

Hays apparently had little trouble persuading the Grand Trunk president of the advantages of a prairie line. But the parent company's London board expressed 'apprehension of the GTP earning enough to make up the interest on the Mountain Section,' if construction began on that portion of the line connecting the prairies with the Pacific coast before the completion of the Prairie Section and connection of the link to the Lakehead. Accordingly, Rivers Wilson wished to relegate the Mountain Section to the end of the construction schedule for the extension. Indeed, the federal government regarded the Grand Trunk request for a separate mortgage on the Mountain Section as an indication that the parent company might attempt to evade its obligations to build this part of the line.[5]

Following the Santa Fe example, Hays believed that the Grand Trunk's extension must also cross the Pacific slope. But why build across northern British Columbia? CPR and Geological Survey of Canada expeditions had established accurate geographical and geological information about the region some twenty-five years earlier. In 1877, CPR surveyors had inspected the four river valleys that the GTP would later select as the major conduits of its route – the Skeena, Bulkley, Nechako, and Upper Fraser. Appreciating the northern route's apparent advantage for capturing the Asian trade, CPR chief engineer Sanford Fleming ignored his surveyors' comments on the high cost of construction and contended that a line through these valleys was practicable. But after a lengthy survey in 1879, federal geologist G.M. Dawson decided that the region west of the Rockies bracketing 55° latitude held little immediate economic potential for railway development. 'For the development of ... revenue,' a consulting engineer concluded, 'there can scarcely be a doubt that this route ... would be found inferior to [a more southerly route].'[6]

Passed over by the CPR, the northern valleys had attracted only a few white trappers, prospectors, farmers, and travelling missionaries by the turn of the century. Living beside or beyond the complex Native societies of the region, this small minority could not transform the valleys into a corridor. In 1900, a Hudson's Bay Company official lamented that it was still impossible to send mail directly from New Caledonia in the interior to Port Simpson on the coast.[7]

Unfortunately, we must turn to Hays's statements after the fact to suggest how the GTP president regarded this apparently unpromising territory and convinced the Grand Trunk board to build across it. These later statements indicate that Hays believed the British Columbia line he proposed would pay its costs in two ways. Like all promoted lines, he expected that this railway would encourage settlement and economic activities along its length, which would in turn generate traffic. But because of its location and standard of construction, the line would also serve as a fast land bridge between points that already produced traffic and thereby capture through business from other roads.

Maintaining that the proposed railway would stimulate local economic activity, Hays transformed the findings of the CPR expeditions that had dismissed the northern route. Early in 1904, the GTP president declared that the company's information on timber, coal, and other mineral resources along the line, taken from these very sources, guaranteed a 'good traffic from the time of commencement of operations.' To win over doubtful Grand Trunk shareholders, he declared that the company's decision to build across northern British Columbia 'simply confirm[ed] the judgment [of the CPR survey] of fifteen or twenty years ago as to the desirableness of the route and the character of the country.' After a hasty inspection of the lower Skeena River in August 1904, he predicted confidently that the construction of the railway would lead to the rapid development of large deposits of coal and stands of timber.[8]

More well known is Hays's belief that the Grand Trunk's new line would capture a rapidly growing Asian trade. With a terminus in northern British Columbia, the GTP president maintained, 'vessels in the Asiatic trade ... can land there [at the GTP terminus], unload their cargo and have it far inland. While the same vessel is going down around Vancouver Island to reach the Canadian Pacific terminus in Vancouver.' The insight that a terminus location on the north coast would provide the GTP with an advantage in sailing time to Asia was not original; Hays probably drew it from a prospectus of the Trans-Canada Railway Company, a promotion that had sought government subsidies since 1895 for a northern line from Quebec City to Port Simpson.[9] But Hays conjured a trade that would seek this advantage: 'The [GTP] line will be the shortest one between the East, China, Japan, and all of that country to which we must look for our future development ... There are many of you here today who will live to see the Grand Trunk Pacific hauling as much of its grain towards the Pacific for consumption in China, Japan, and that great territory, as will be hauled in an eastern direction.' Such views would inform GTP promotion of both its route and its Pacific terminus, as the map of Prince Rupert's zone of influence illustrates. For his efforts to make good these grandiose predictions, Hays later received an award from the Japanese emperor.[10]

Somewhat less dramatic was Hays's claim that the GTP would serve as a land bridge between Alaska and the continental United States: 'When the Panama Canal opens, America will turn their attention to Alaska and it will open up quickly. I want to be ready for that rush. Prince Rupert will be the nearest port to the country, and we shall be able to offer them a direct, easy rail route between ... the eastern manufacturing states and the door of the [Alaska] country.' Hays was only extending the practice of shipping goods in bond between American points, which had long provided a significant amount of traffic for the parent Grand Trunk.[11]

How these observations and predictions combined in Hays's advocacy of the British Columbia line is unclear. His hasty return to the Grand Trunk from the more prestigious position of president of the Southern Pacific in 1901 might suggest that he could not adapt to the conditions, nor perhaps understand the calculations, for running a western road.[12] Perhaps Hays actually believed a preposterous claim that construction of a second main line across northern British Columbia would immediately produce an astounding growth in net receipts. By early 1904, though trade was not developed nor traffic assured, the GTP president proclaimed himself a 'believer in the earning capabilities of the Mountain Section.'[13]

Hays's advocacy of the British Columbia line stemmed not only from his imaginative predictions of traffic: it also rested on returns he

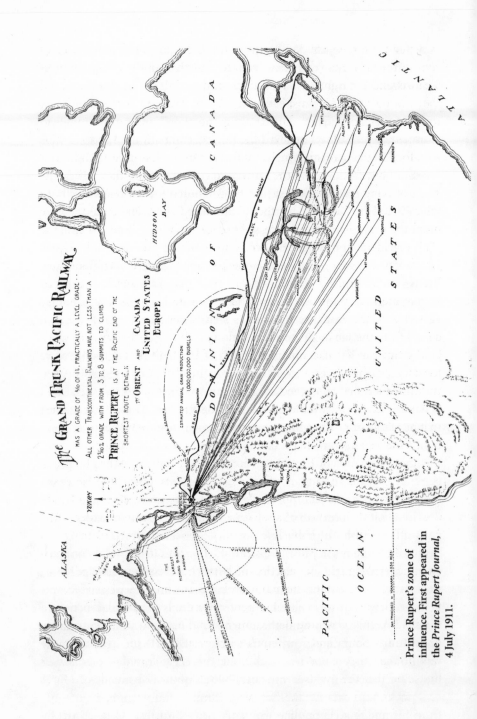

The Grand Trunk Pacific Railway

HAS A GRADE OF 4/10 OF 1% PRACTICALLY A LEVEL GRADE.

ALL OTHER TRANSCONTINENTAL RAILWAYS HAVE NOT LESS THAN A 2½% GRADE WITH FROM 3 TO 8 SUMMITS TO CLIMB

PRINCE RUPERT IS AT THE PACIFIC END OF THE

SHORTEST ROUTE BETWEEN

THE ORIENT AND

CANADA
UNITED STATES
EUROPE

Prince Rupert's zone of influence. First appeared in the *Prince Rupert Journal,* 4 July 1911.

expected from townsite development along the line. From the outset, of course, the GTP managers had realized that the railway company must acquire land for right-of-way, sidings, and buildings. But they attached more importance to prospective townsites, the 320-acre parcels surrounding each of the 200 stations along the main line from Winnipeg to the coast. In 1905, Hays believed the railway company could acquire this land for $10 per acre, making its total expenditure less than $1 million.[14]

But how, then, should the railway company develop these holdings? The surviving records suggest that Hays ignored the experience of both the CPR and the Canadian Northern in western Canada and emulated once more the example of two western American roads. In land matters, the GTP president first sought advice from Santa Fe president E.P. Ripley, whose activities concerning westward expansion he had so openly admired. Persuaded by Ripley's account in late 1903 that the American concern had created an 'immensely profitable' townsite business, Hays quickly agreed with the Santa Fe president's suggestion that the GTP create a company to pursue townsite activity along its line. But the Santa Fe was a land grant road; it had obtained much of the land that it marketed as townsites as a bonus for its construction during the 1870s and 1880s. Thus, it did not require an immediate return from the land it acquired. As a Santa Fe vice-president informed the GTP secretary, 'There is no attempt to make large sums from the sale of these townsites, but rather to upbuild the country and serve the general interests of the railway company.'[15]

On the matter of the disposition of land, more to the GTP president's liking was the report of an engineer-promoter on the Nebraska townsite operations of one of the Burlington lines. This gentleman declared that the creation of a separate townsite company shielded company officers from the inevitable hostility of local interests suffering as a result of company decisions to locate the line and townsites. With judicious advertising and the selection of 'better businessmen,' sales of townsite lots went smoothly. The major problem, the promoter confided, was to deflect rivals in town development. 'Hundreds of speculators are on the field, keenly watching developments and eager to pounce on every opportunity. Safety and economy lies in forestalling them, in acting more rapidly than they do.' When such policies were followed, the promoter predicted that the townsite operation would return dividends of 24 per cent per annum over twenty-five years.[16]

In framing GTP policy on land and townsites, Hays evidently

selected elements from both American roads. In a memorandum in October 1904, the president proposed the formation of a subsidiary land improvement or development company that would control all GTP property outside that required for the operation of the railway itself. As well as right-of-way, it would 'obtain the townsites at no greater price per acre and so give the town company the profit that the growth of the towns along the line would eventually produce in the increased value of land and especially at the towns.' Following the Santa Fe example, Hays maintained that the railway company's control would permit the 'location of the station sites in such a way as to control the growth of the towns.' But the arrangement would confer on the railway company an even more profitable advantage, 'the ability on [the GTP's] part to regulate a matter which would otherwise be subject to the influence of parties who would obtain property along the line.' Such a notion could quickly be extended from physical layout to economic hegemony. That the return from townsite lot sales rather than the sale of agricultural land would apply in particular to the company's operations in British Columbia is suggested by his review in the same memorandum of the company's acquisition of land in that province and his prediction that the most important townsite on the entire line would be the terminus on the Pacific coast.[17]

The corporate records also cast doubt on Stevens's contention that GTP general manager Frank Morse was responsible for this shortsighted townsite policy that alienated many. In fact, Morse sought to bring the GTP to the Santa Fe practice of integrating townsite sales into the operation of the railway by concentrating on creating a nucleus in each community, a nucleus that would provide traffic for the road rather than touting boomtowns. Hays, emulating the example of the Burlington and others, however, demanded a more immediate return. 'I am exceedingly anxious that we should, at the earliest date possible, recoup ourselves for the total expenditures made to date in connection with the purchase of lands including Prince Rupert townsite.' An immediate, high return on townsite lot sales 'would establish a very strong basis for our issue of bonds which should then sell at a good price and furnish us capital for additional development purposes ... We can undoubtedly secure more purchases for our lots at the outset than we can the second or third year after we have been in operation.'[18]

Thus, Hays regarded townsites not as a step in the long-term development of traffic for the line, but as a quick method to generate capital for 'additional development,' i.e., construction. Any attempt to decrease or divert that return would be regarded by the company as a threat to its existence. On the prairies, where much of the land was already alienated, the company would follow the Santa Fe system of dividing proceeds with the owner of a prospective townsite.[19] In British Columbia, however, the largely uninhabited land promised larger returns if the company could secure complete control. Nowhere would this be more important than on the coast.

Hays first had to obtain the sanction of Grand Trunk president Rivers Wilson, who had remarked in 1903 that the land in British Columbia was 'of little value.' Early in 1905, Hays convinced his superior by suggesting that 'a very large profit' could be made at a Pacific terminus where property was acquired at 'low price.' On other lines, a few individuals had benefitted from the advantage of knowing where the line would go. For the GTP, however, 'there is no reason ... why this should not be a source of profit for the railway company itself. There is a great advantage to the railway company in being able to ... direct the development of the town in an orderly and systematic manner and so that the interests of the company in connection therewith are protected.'[20]

Under the terms of the GTP incorporation act, the railway company could hold shares in a company that dealt in land. Accordingly, the GTP incorporated the Grand Trunk Pacific Town and Development Company in August 1906, later shortened to GTP Development Company, with an authorized capital of $5 million.[21]

For the GTP's townsite development policy to produce returns in British Columbia, the company had to secure a substantial property largely held by the Crown. When company managers realized that, from the federal government at least, they would not receive a land grant, they mounted a protracted campaign to tie construction of the transcontinental across British Columbia to a substantial subsidy from the province.[22] In December 1902, Hays indicated to Premier E.G. Prior that the company would require a second 'railway belt' across the province to build to the coast.[23]

The company had little reason to expect such an award, however. Although successive provincial governments had long sanctioned conditional grants of large tracts of land to railway promoters to encourage the extension of a rail network across the mountainous territory, this practice had recently come under attack. Since 1900, British Columbia governments had distanced themselves from land granting. In part, this move stemmed from a recognition that the old policy was inefficient; few of the promoted railways that received land grants were actually built. But political pressure probably played a greater role in the change. Allegations of corruption in land granting played a part in bringing down the last two so-called personal governments. The 'Columbia and Western scandal,' the CPR acquisition of land allotted to another concern it had leased, was excoriated in both Conservative and Liberal newspapers during the summer of 1903. Such general condemnation indicates a widespread disenchantment with the whole land grant system for railways.[24]

What is striking about the GTP's early relations with the government of British Columbia was its refusal to recognize that the local government could no longer encourage railway development by generous land grants. Even though reaction in the press and Assembly had compelled the ministry of James Dunsmuir to repudiate a land grant to the Canadian Northern during the summer of 1902, Hays blithely indicated to his superior only that the GTP could expect more than the meagre bonus of $5,000 per mile that the legislature had grudgingly substituted for the land grant. What had, in Hays's version, really thwarted the efforts of the Canadian Northern to obtain greater assistance from the government was the arrival in Victoria of Grand Trunk officers in December to lobby for the company's project![25]

The first result of the company's campaign was promising. After assiduous work by GTP vice-president William Wainwright, the company's chief lobbyist, Premier Prior returned to the old tradition and promised 'a large land grant to any company that will build through to the coast. We have not got very much money, but we have lots of land and will readily help any company that will help us develop it.' He even indicated that the GTP might receive the land grant denied to the Canadian Northern. This statement led Hays to assure his president that he was 'counting with a considerable degree of certainty' on a subsidy from British Columbia.[26]

Prior's undertaking only encouraged more antagonism in British Columbia toward further land granting, however. In late February, a Vancouver business journal contended that 'B.C. should remember that they control absolutely the only Pacific coast outlets, and every new Canadian transcontinental line must come hat in hand begging permission for use of one or other of these outlets, and before their request is granted, they should be made to pay all the privilege is worth.' The stance of Prior's successor toward the GTP suggests that he acted on this insight. When Richard McBride formed the first Conservative government in June 1903, his party had added the prohibition of bonuses to railway companies to its platform.[27]

Even before fighting his first election as premier, McBride signalled his determination to obtain Pacific construction of the GTP without a land grant. In August 1903, the provincial cabinet requested the federal government to insert an amendment in the GTP contract that required 'in the interests of the Province, that the location and construction of the Mountain Section should begin at the western terminus of the Grand Trunk Pacific line on the Pacific Ocean, and proceed continuously and uninterruptedly to the easterly limit of the Rocky Mountains.'[28]

This clear expression of the intent of the new premier made little impression on the GTP, however. The railway company's agenda remained straightforward: to obtain from McBride what Prior had promised, a large land grant. At the end of 1903, Hays requested that the premier grant the railway a 200-foot right-of-way and 20,000 acres per mile for the length of the road in the province in return for construction of *one-half* of the British Columbia line from the west end, i.e., the Pacific coast. McBride's outright rejection of this demand led Hays to conclude only that British Columbia was fearful that the GTP might postpone indefinitely the extension to the coast, not that the government had turned away irrevocably from the practice of land granting. This novel interpretation certainly did not depend on the premier's communication that the government would consider concessions only for an undertaking to commence construction from the Pacific coast. And McBride's denunciation of the Canadian Northern land grant was now a matter of record in the *Canadian Annual Review*.[29]

Despite McBride's refusal, the Grand Trunk management still counted on the province to grant a significant subsidy in land. In the spring of 1904, the provincial government's London agent reported to the premier that Rivers Wilson still 'would prefer a land grant to anything else.'[30] Although the province renewed its request to the federal government for an amendment requiring Pacific construction, McBride realized that the GTP had 'absolutely no intention of touching B.C. until they have to.'[31] To encourage the company to 'touch B.C.' sooner, he facilitated the GTP acquisition of terminus land at Kaien Island.

From the company's negotiations with the province for a general land grant, we must now turn to the first phase of its acquisition of terminus land. Unlike the other northern transcontinentals, the GTP was compelled to acquire land for its Pacific terminus on Kaien Island in two separate transactions.[32] This was necessary because an Indian reserve on the west side of the island placed the company's desired terminal land under federal as well as provincial jurisdiction. The outcome of these two transactions would determine in large part the fortunes of the railway company in British Columbia.

Both the chronology and the significance of the events surrounding the company's first acquisition, its purchase of 10,000 acres on Kaien Island from the provincial government in 1904, have been obscured because the major source for these events, the Legislative Assembly's investigation of the transaction in 1906, emphasized elements of political scandal rather than the motive and methods of the GTP. This obsession with ministerial indiscretion has also distracted students of the GTP. Perhaps the only general conclusion that emerges from these studies is that after allowing outsiders to locate the terminus, the GTP purchase of the first parcel on Kaien Island represented one of the company's few astute actions in British Columbia.[33]

A review of the inquiry proceedings and other scattered sources suggests, however, that the company itself made this crucial decision not on engineering or operating considerations but on Hays's demands for townsite returns. In this evaluation of location factors, the company simply followed the example of other transcontinentals.[34] The GTP president dismissed the two harbours that west coast newspapers most frequently proposed, Port Simpson and Kitamaat [Kitimat], the former for its proximity to the Alaska boundary, the latter for 'its great depth and difficulty in obtaining anchorage for vessels.' Since Kaien Island was not only close to Alaska but also fronted by a harbour of great depth, these explanations are not convincing. From the company's viewpoint, the real drawback of these sites was the high price of settled land, which would cut into the returns Hays had stipulated.[35]

In contradistinction to the claims later advanced during the inquiry, the GTP did not simply wait for speculators to select a harbour for its Pacific terminus. During the autumn of 1903, Hays hired a New York engineer to make a trip to the Pacific coast where he 'secured considerable information as to Coast topography,' and reported his findings

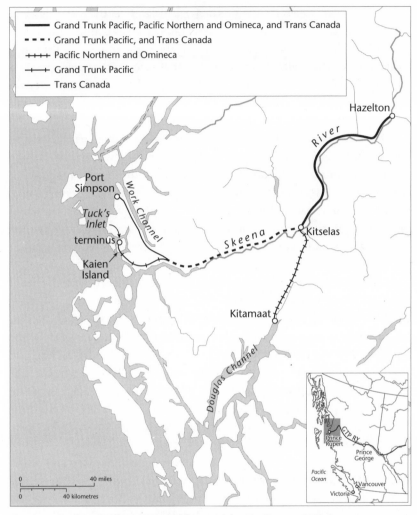

Figure 2.1 **Projected railway routes and prospective terminuses, 1900-5**

directly to the president.[36] Although this report has not survived, it probably prompted the company to send harbour engineer James H. Bacon to
inspect Tuck's Inlet late in 1903.

   Hays had repeatedly stated to Rivers Wilson that the characteristics
of the harbour would be the prime factor in the selection of the terminus. On this standard, the advantage of Tuck's Inlet was by no means
clear. As every brochure and newspaper article later proclaimed, the inlet
contained a deep harbour that required no dredging and was screened

from the prevailing westerly winds by Digby Island. Yet the inlet's fjordlike qualities increased the cost of wharves and, even the company publicist admits, hindered anchorage.[37] Nevertheless, after making a thorough inspection late in 1903, Bacon decided that Tuck's Inlet was the most suitable location for a terminus on the coast. Thus, the critical decision was made not by a promoter's agent, but by a company officer, undoubtedly aware of the GTP president's requirements.[38]

Hays then encouraged American railway contractor Peter Larsen to form a syndicate to negotiate with the provincial government early in 1904 for the purchase of Kaien Island – the land fronting the inlet that he desired for a terminus – because he believed McBride's condemnation of bonusing would cause the province to raise the price if the purchaser were the company.[39] Because Larsen desired contracts on the new transcontinental, Hays could ensure that the contractor would turn over the property to the company. The syndicate's Victoria lawyer, E.V. Bodwell, persuaded the government that the province would benefit from what was an act of bonusing.[40] Rather than oppose the GTP, McBride demanded an assurance that the company was behind the syndicate. Hays was only too happy to oblige by the end of April with a telegram to Bodwell that was passed on to the government: 'Will be glad to have you act on Mr. Stevens [Grand Trunk chief engineer J.D. Stephens] communication in regard to Lima Harbour [Tuck's Inlet and Kaien Island] in such ways as to fully protect our rights for the time being, and until definite plans can be determined without, however, committing us irrevocably.'[41]

On the strength of this undertaking, the cabinet passed a secret order-in-council binding the government to issue a crown grant for 10,000 acres, which Bodwell could select from the vicinity of Tuck's Inlet, reserving one-quarter of the townsite and waterfront for the province. The order also stated that Bodwell represented the GTP and acted under its instructions. It gave the lawyer nine months to obtain a formal commitment from the GTP; otherwise the entire property would revert to the government. For a terminus property larger than that of the CPR in Vancouver, the company paid only $10,000. That the GTP followed closely, if it did not determine, the formulation of the order is suggested by Hays's private pronouncement to the lands commissioner that terms were satisfactory.[42]

Documents in the GTP corporate records allow us to adumbrate some of the immediate consequences of the purchase. For his efforts in locating

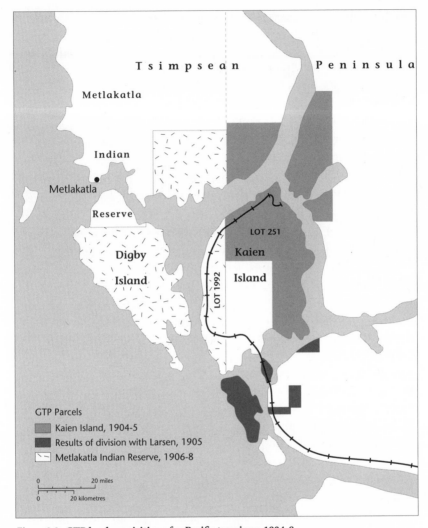

Figure 2.2 **GTP land acquisitions for Pacific terminus, 1904-8**

and securing the terminus, the company undertook to pay Larsen a bonus of $55,000. In March 1905, Larsen waived the undertaking, declaring he wanted only the goodwill of the company. Since his contracting firm obtained most of the contracts on both the Prairie and Mountain Sections of the new transcontinental, this benevolence proved a valuable asset indeed. But Larsen also received almost $30,000 in place of the bonus.[43]

Before it committed itself to locating the terminus on Kaien Island, the railway company determined to acquire more land in the district, which it expected to market at great profit as the limits of the terminus expanded. By controlling the limited land approaches to Kaien Island, the company could also safeguard its investment from speculators who would extort a high price for right-of-way.

Accordingly, in July 1904, the railway company directed James Anderson, Larsen's agent, to obtain additional crown lands adjacent to the 10,000 acres, which he would then divide with the railway company. GTP engineers expected that the new railway line would be located only on property the company currently controlled. The first projected line from Tuck's Inlet followed the eastern shore of Kaien Island, crossed to the mainland at the obvious narrows of Galloway Rapids, and hugged the coast for twelve miles until it reached the Skeena River Valley. Aware of this projected route, Anderson staked six lots along the mainland coast for some five miles as well as two islands south of Kaien Island.[44]

By February 1905, Anderson had applied as Larsen's agent for crown grants for eight parcels including the islands comprising 3,200 acres. After the government accepted the application, the railway company undertook to divide the spoils with Larsen. In July 1905, in Bodwell's Victoria office, agents of the two interests came together, compared the lots claimed, and divided them into two packages of equal size for selection by flip of a coin. One package contained the mainland lots facing Galloway Rapids and the two islands. The other included a large mainland lot, Lot 446, south of Kaien Island through which a line hugging the coast must traverse. E.G. Russell, agent for the GTP, won the toss and selected the first package.[45] For a payment to Larsen of $26,510, less than $17 per acre, the company had acquired the first suburbs for its terminus.

When Anderson made a trip north in March 1904 to survey precise parcels of land for the original purchase of 10,000 acres, however, he covered both sides of Tuck's Inlet with stakes lettered 'GTP,' an obvious indication of the company's intentions. Consequently, in the same month, G.T. Kane, a Vancouver millwright, took up six transferable grants of 160 acres each from South African veterans and filed for 960 acres and a 160-acre preemption on Kaien Island. Lands Commissioner R.F. Green attempted to return Kane's application and deposit with the ludicrous explanation that Kaien Island was part of the Tsimpsean Peninsula on which a provincial reserve had been established in 1891. Kane responded with a series of court actions from 1904 through 1909. The attorney general's dismissal of one of these actions in early 1905 pleased the company.

But since the grounds for denial were suspect, the leader of the opposition took up Kane's charges in the House early in 1906.[46] By alleging irregularities in the transfer of crown land to the railway company, he compelled McBride to strike a legislative committee, the Kaien Island Investigation, to deal with the matter.

Committee member and opposition leader J.A. Macdonald distracted later students from the role of the GTP by exaggerating the independence of the syndicate, which he described as a 'band of adventurers.' More perceptive was his charge that the government had overstepped a Land Act amendment of 1891 that expressly forbade the practice of bonusing railway companies.[47]

The majority report of the four Conservative members of the committee responded that the government had been dealing with the GTP almost from the outset. Their finding that the Tsimpsean Peninsula reserve embraced Kaien Island was no more convincing in the report than it had been in the proceedings. But the most important conclusion of the majority report was its support for the government's contravention of the Land Act's prohibition of railway land grants. The attorney general even refused to use the term in defending the government's actions. By sharing returns with the province through the reconveyance of one-quarter of the townsite, the GTP secured what was in effect a land grant.[48]

The company also obscured its role in the affair. The principal witness in the inquiry, Larsen employee Anderson, exaggerated his role and ignored the actions of Bacon and other GTP officers and agents. Now appointed legal agent for the railway company as well as the syndicate, Bodwell refused to produce documents. And the GTP general manager who oversaw the day-to-day negotiations in 1904 begged off appearing on the excuse of pressing business in Montreal. That McBride's opponents later charged that the government had violated the constitution for a gang of speculators indicates how successfully the company had shielded its actions from scrutiny during the investigation.[49]

The closing of the investigation without serious damage to the government meant that the company had also apparently preserved its windfall. If one includes the settlements with Larsen and Anderson, the company had acquired 10,000 acres surrounding its terminus for $5.20 per acre, much less than it would have paid elsewhere. With such a low cost, the GTP could preserve the returns Hays expected from townsite development.

With its purchase of Kaien Island in May 1904, the company had secured a valuable concession from the provincial government. The British Columbia premier had already signalled that he expected the company to begin construction from the coast in return. In April 1904, a Conservative senator inquired whether the federal government intended to insert in its new bill, which ratified revision of the contract with the Grand Trunk, a stipulation concerning Pacific construction.[50]

Though Liberal Senate leader William Templeman turned away the question with a reference to CPR construction on the west end without such a stipulation, McBride was adamant. To counter claims concerning the increased expenditure of construction on the west end, the premier argued that the west end line could be supplied as cheaply from Vancouver as the east end was from Winnipeg.[51] When the amended contract came before the Senate, the Conservatives tried again. This time they proposed an amendment specifically requiring Pacific construction. It was left to Templeman to express the company's position: 'If you build a road from Port Simpson to the Rocky Mountains, that road by itself will not do much good. It will not have very much traffic. Its traffic will depend largely upon the prairie section, and looking at the thing purely as a matter of business, I think it desirable that the prairie section should be completed rather in advance of the mountain section.' The Liberal senator declared, however, that since the Conservative amendment reflected public opinion in British Columbia, he would support the amendment if it were possible to revise the contract a second time. Yet he could not imagine the GTP transporting *all* its supplies across the continent from Winnipeg. Since such a strategy would be 'utterly ridiculous,' he declared that 'the company would be bound to commence work on the Pacific Coast.'[52]

Although the Liberals voted down the Conservative motion, the GTP quickly denied this apparent commitment for Pacific construction, stating that it was too early to set a date for construction at either end of the road. Some days later, Templeman gave notice for a similar amendment that would require GTP construction from the Pacific coast within two years. If, as the Liberal senator had claimed, the Conservative motion would have jeopardized the contract, then his own amendment would also certainly do so.[53]

Though the company had secured a valuable concession in the Kaien Island purchase, Hays still expected the British Columbia government to offer much more, 15,000 acres per mile, for an undertaking to build from the west end. But Templeman's amendment, if passed, would eliminate the incentive for the government to agree to the railway company's terms. Hays asked Laurier to mediate. Apparently the prime minister suggested that Hays send Templeman a letter of intent, which would leave the 'coast clear, and the amendment [revised GTP charter] will do as it is.' The GTP president complied by drafting a private letter that was clearly intended to persuade Templeman to withdraw his amendment. While Hays noted that the company must first complete its surveys and select a harbour, he declared that 'so soon as the progress of the surveys in British Columbia will permit, construction will be commenced from the Pacific Coast to the end of the road and be carried on continuously in an easterly direction.'[54]

Hays's letter had the desired effect: Templeman withdrew his amendment without revealing the GTP commitment. The senator's later explanation that the Department of Justice had convinced him to withdraw the motion rings hollow indeed. But while a Tory paper declared that the GTP had strangled Templeman's intentions, the *Victoria Daily Times,* which the minister controlled, began to hint broadly that McBride would deliver a large land grant to the GTP when in fact the province could now resist. The first part of the contention probably stemmed from rumours about the Kaien Island purchase; the second certainly referred to Hays's letter of intent to Templeman.[55]

GTP attempts to disguise its commitments were not helped when the minister of marine, undoubtedly coached by Templeman, declared in August that the GTP would commence construction simultaneously on the coast and at Winnipeg. They were completely destroyed when Templeman melodramatically read out Hays's letter during an October election rally in Victoria.[56] For the Liberals, the revelation had the desired effect: all six British Columbia ridings returned Liberal members. But now the company saw its commitment to Pacific construction revealed to the provincial government.

With the Kaien Island purchase, the GTP had achieved an important goal and preserved the opportunity to enlarge the government subsidy before it embarked on Pacific construction. As construction on the west coast could not realistically begin until the GTP had completed its survey and obtained Ottawa's sanction for its route, the railway company had a period of two years to bargain for more concessions, particularly on that part of the line that had the greatest potential to generate immediate income, the terminus.

Again, it is striking how the GTP misjudged the situation. While McBride's majority was not large, and the Liberal members of both the federal and provincial houses as well as the Liberal press sought opportunities to discomfit him, many Liberals were also committed to compelling the GTP to build from the coast without an additional subsidy. When the railway company conformed to the 1904 order-in-council and formally announced its intention to establish its terminus at Kaien Island in February 1905, many were convinced that McBride had already been too generous. Yet despite press reports that popular opinion as well as Liberal members were against another subsidy, Hays expected that McBride's 'weak and uncertain' government could be turned as easily as the personal governments of his predecessors.[57] Thus, General Manager Frank Morse travelled to Victoria early in 1905 not only to commit the company to establish its terminus, but also to compel the government to grant another land subsidy.

Evidently, the evolution of provincial policy concerning railway land grants over four years and three ministries did not persuade the GTP management to modify significantly its original demands. While the company no longer demanded 20,000 acres, the land grant in the Canadian Northern agreement repudiated by the government in 1902, Morse now submitted two draft bills calling for the government to grant 15,000 acres per mile of construction as well as a 200-foot right-of-way. These lands would be exempt from provincial taxation for an unspecified number of years. Beyond Prince Rupert, the GTP would not have to share its townsites with the province. For a line that would eventually traverse 677 miles within the province, such a grant entailed more than ten million acres. At the government's lowest price, $1.00 per acre for wild land, the grant was worth more than $10 million. Better land within the blocks, of course, could be sold for $2.50 or $5.00.[58]

When the Conservative Victoria *Daily Colonist* charged that Morse's demands proved that Hays's letter of the previous year was a political deception, the general manager became impatient and issued a statement lamenting that 'the people of British Columbia have not signified a desire to co-operate with us to the extent of giving assistance ... that would justify at this time our taking up the subject of early construction at this end ... It is, however, for the people of British Columbia to say whether or not they can afford to make it possible.'[59] Such a position clearly departed from Hays's letter of intent. A disgruntled Tory warned that if the government accepted the GTP demands, 'we at once constitute ourselves an everlasting mark for every unscrupulous subsidy grabber who may be foisted upon us by the Dominion government.' The *Daily Colonist* agreed, exhorting the government to 'accept defeat rather than surrender to demands which are immoral from every point of view.'[60]

But Morse still believed that the government would eventually accept the GTP demand. In early March, the general manager marshalled his arguments for McBride. He declared that Pacific construction would be more expensive than building from the east: 'It would not only be more expensive for us, in the way of getting in labour, supplies, and material to the front, but we will, for a considerable period, have a large amount of money invested in property on which we will be paying an interest charge, and on which we will have absolutely no return, i.e., there will be no local business upon the line, and it cannot be used as a through line until connected with the line from the East.'[61] Morse explained that GTP estimates depended on the more economic strategy of building from the east. Only if the government would accord the company the privileges set out above could the company defray the additional cost and undertake Pacific construction. To put additional pressure on the premier to accept these demands, he also hinted broadly at the company terms in an address to the Victoria Board of Trade.[62]

Once again McBride rejected the GTP demands completely. But even before he received the formal response, Morse declared that if the terms were rejected, the company would act independently. Three days later, the general manager informed McBride that the cabinet's refusal 'permanently disposes' of the matter of Pacific construction. This abrupt conclusion led to questions for Templeman in the Senate about the origin of Hays's letter. Even the federal minister of railways attempted to persuade the company to reverse its stand. That the minister had no success indicates that Morse spoke not of his own accord but at Hays's direction. The GTP president informed Rivers Wilson that though Morse had not reached a 'satisfactory' conclusion, the railway company would drop the matter only for the time being.[63]

If the GTP could not obtain a land grant under its own name, it would do so through another charter, the Pacific Northern & Omineca Railway Company (PNO). In July 1904, Hays obtained options from a syndicate of Victoria businessman for a moribund railway charter from Kitamaat harbour to the junction of the Skeena and Copper rivers and then up the Skeena to Hazelton. The company took over the PNO only after the provincial government had refused its request for a land grant for its own line. A few days after receiving the government's refusal on the GTP land subsidy, Morse undertook to pay double the agreed price of $60,000 for the syndicate's properties if the promoters could persuade the government to grant the PNO 15,000 acres per mile. A draft bill calling for the exchange of the cash bonus for the land grant the GTP desired was evidently drawn up by the same solicitor who drafted Morse's bill in 1905.[64]

Given the hostility of the McBride government toward land grants, the promoters of the PNO had no more luck than the GTP general manager in securing the bonus. But they cajoled the government into transferring to the GTP a cash subsidy intended for the PNO for the 120-mile portion of its projected line between Kitselas and Telkwa, which traversed the same route as the GTP. And the GTP had a bill passed in the federal house for the purpose of obtaining the small federal subsidy granted to the PNO by granting the latter company running rights over its main line. The proclamation of this act meant that the GTP could collect the subsidies promised to the PNO by both the federal and provincial governments by construction of its main line, in effect a triple subsidy. Only after construction had begun on the west end along the PNO route did Templeman and the provincial Liberal leader demand that the federal government at least curtail its subsidy to the PNO.[65]

WHILE THE GTP's acquisition of Kaien Island turned on the company's uncertain relations with the British Columbia government, its attempt to secure part of Metlakatla Indian Reserve to enlarge its Pacific terminus holdings engaged both the province and the dominion. Selective publication of documents by both governments has led many historians to view the acquisition as an element in a federal-provincial conflict over title to the Indian reserve.[66] For the most part, the published documents diminish or ignore a desperate corporate drive to secure what company managers expected to be lucrative returns from land that would be sold as townsite lots. This policy led the company to commence Pacific construction.[67]

Even before the GTP had reached an understanding with the provincial government for the purchase of 10,000 acres in May 1904, the company evinced an interest in acquiring part of the extensive Indian reserve of the Tsimshian bands surrounding the villages of Metlakatla and Port Simpson. For the company, that part of Tsimpsean Indian Reserve No. 2 on the west side of Kaien Island represented an essential addition to the first acquisition. Although the first published map of GTP holdings at its terminus featured a railway line along the eastern, landward side of Kaien Island, the company prepared a plan for its line to the mainland along the western, seaward side of Kaien Island as soon as it secured an undertaking to purchase the adjacent land from the province in 1904. Even before architects had laid out the city of Prince Rupert, E.G. Russell, the company's British Columbia agent, advised the general manager that the GTP 'yards and ... wharves must be out along this Indian land.'[68]

Because the land in question was part of a reserve, the company first approached the federal government. In April 1904, Hays asked the Department of Indian Affairs (DIA) to determine the price of Indian lands in the district as it would play a role in the decision to locate the terminus. The following month the company expressed an interest in 7,000 acres of the Metlakatla reserve on the north side of the harbour, which the GTP 'would like to obtain should it decide to locate upon Port Simpson.'[69]

Taking steps to complete the Kaien Island purchase from the provincial government apparently monopolized the company's attention on the coast for the next six months. When it sought to enlarge its holdings, it again looked to Bodwell, the lawyer who had brokered the company's original purchase on Kaien Island. As a veteran charter hawker at the provincial capital, Bodwell was aware of the province's claims in a complex, long-standing dispute with the federal government concerning reversionary interest, the title of crown land removed from an Indian reserve.[70] His initial approach on behalf of the company to Lands Commissioner Green in February 1905 demonstrates that he, at least, recognized that provincial actions could hinder transfer of title to Indian reserves, if not determine it. The GTP would undertake to purchase the province's interest in the west Kaien Island portion of the reserve, which the company now required 'for the railway yards, coal, docks, etc.' As it was, the GTP legal agent argued, the reserve land was worthless to the province. Following the arrangements in the Kaien Island purchase, the GTP would convey back to the province one-quarter of the additional property, but it wished to hold its three-quarters as an undivided parcel since it would be devoted exclusively to railway service. Of course, Indian title would have to be extinguished first. The agent implied that the province could expect only a moderate price for such an encumbered title.[71]

Following General Manager Morse's hard line in the ongoing land grant negotiations with the province, Bodwell then extended the GTP request to 5,000 acres of the reserve, but insisted that the railway company expected to pay in total no more than it had for the earlier property, i.e., $1.00 per acre. Consequently, the company must settle with the dominion for the Indian title before paying the balance to Victoria. McBride responded carefully, promising priority to the company if the Natives removed, but forgoing setting a price. But Morse, now disappointed at not obtaining a general land grant and, in fact, misunderstanding the proper designation of the reserve in question, barged into the negotiations and berated the premier. He also advised McBride to defer to Green on the matter since the minister had demonstrated that he understood the requirements of the company in the Kaien Island purchase. Morse concluded that the premier had already promised to sell the reserve to the company at the same price as in the earlier transaction. When these impertinent suggestions elicited no positive response, the general manager likened the railway company to a cow and warned that it would not give milk unless treated kindly.[72]

Morse then delayed the execution of a corporate undertaking to locate the terminus on Kaien Island as a lever to obtain provincial acquiescence. But this delay endangered the original purchase, and the company capitulated and made formal undertaking on 1 August with the reserve matter still in abeyance. Even the deputy superintendent of Indian Affairs, who had resisted British Columbia's claims of reversionary interest, now admitted that the GTP had to obtain the relinquishment of title from the province before the reserve land could be used as a terminus.[73]

But the company turned away from Bodwell's apparently unproductive negotiations with the province and the advice of the federal department. In April 1905, the GTP had initiated an application to the Department of Indian Affairs to acquire portions of the reserve on west Kaien Island and Digby Island across the harbour. Circumstantial evidence suggests that Russell, the GTP agent on the spot who had been successful in acquiring suburban lands around Kaien Island for the company, convinced Morse during the fall of 1905 to take a more direct route by 'securing Indian rights first.'[74] Neither Morse nor Russell were lawyers, and the general manager had already demonstrated his inability to understand the notion of reversionary interest.[75] Since the company had not yet assigned one of its solicitors to review GTP activities in British Columbia, the only informed source of legal advice on the matter was Bodwell who was on retainer and did only as he was instructed.

In November, the GTP advised the DIA that it preferred a company agent rather than a department official to negotiate with the band for the sale of the land it required. Upon reaching Metlakatla early in 1906, Russell simply informed the local Indian agent that 'the management has decided to use Kaien Island [parcel purchased in 1904]; and they would require Digby Island, Tsimpsean Peninsula, and [west] Kaien Island.'[76]

About the negotiations with the band itself, little has survived. The GTP agent spent a week in negotiations with the Metlakatla band, the small Coast Tsimshian band that had held the southern half of Tsimpsean Indian Reserve No. 2 since 1888.[77] Russell and the band settled on a price of $7.50 per acre as a compromise between the original GTP offer of $5.00 and the band demand of $10.00. The company would acquire west Kaien Island, most of Digby Island, and a part of the Tsimpsean Peninsula north of the harbour; the three parcels later surveyed as 13,567 acres. After obtaining for the band an additional $1,500 as compensation for loss of gardens, the local Indian agent concluded that it was an excellent bargain from which Native people could use every cent in repairing and furnishing their houses. He accepted the deal subject to the approval of the DIA. Anglican Bishop F.H. Du Vernet presided over the signing of the provisional agreement for surrender on 7 February 1906.[78]

On one matter, the railway company encouraged the DIA to alter the Indian Act to satisfy the demands of the band. Although the current law concerning surrender permitted a down payment of no more than 10 per cent, the provisional agreement called for one-half of the proceeds of the sale to be divided immediately among adult band members. When the department suggested reopening negotiations to reduce the down payment, the company asked for 'the agreement [to] be given effect in some other way.' On 15 June, the minister responsible introduced an amendment to the Indian Act that authorized the terms of the Metlakatla agreement by increasing down payments for surrender to 50 per cent.[79]

More intractable than the regulations for surrender was the resistance of the British Columbia government to the company's prospective purchase. The federal government, probably at the instigation of the GTP, now requested the province to waive its reversionary interest in what the Toronto *Globe* described as another 'gold mine' for the GTP. Echoing the arguments of the GTP proposition of 1905, the federal government maintained that the purchase would afford 'a great benefit to both the Dominion and the province generally as well as enhancing the value of ... the remaining portion of the reserve [to which British Columbia might still claim reversionary interest].' But news of the provisional sale of the reserve came as the provincial government was embroiled in the Kaien Island Investigation. The *Vancouver Daily World* suggested with malice that the ministers of the provincial government 'should sit at the feet of savages to learn how to deal with railway sharpers.' Fabricating the name of the chief who had allegedly secured the settlement from the GTP as 'Ver-Dan [sic],' the paper proposed that he should take over the lands portfolio from his namesake.[80]

Given the long-standing grievances of the provincial government concerning federal administration of Indian reserves in British Columbia and its recent difficulties over the Kaien Island sale, McBride's cabinet found the federal request to waive its reversionary interest in the reserve obnoxious. In May, the cabinet rejected the proposal, declaring that one of the reasons for the sale of part of Kaien Island to the GTP was to enhance the value of the province's reversionary interest in precisely the adjacent Indian reserve the company sought to purchase.[81]

Apparently unaware of the province's case in the dispute, the new GTP solicitor for western Canada, D'Arcy Tate, declared in May 1906 that the company and the federal government could complete the transaction even without the concurrence of the province. But after reading the federal department's analysis of the dispute, which the deputy minister had sent him in confidence, the lawyer reversed course. He first conveyed Superintendent-General of Indian Affairs Frank Oliver's warning that if the company completed the purchase, the provincial government would 'endeavour to hold us up.' However, the company's corporate undertaking in August 1905 to locate the terminus at Kaien Island made the minister's suggestion for resolution – to threaten to remove the terminus – impossible. Two weeks later, Tate concluded that the dominion could not give good title and advised that it would be 'unwise now to acquire any part of the Dominion title before we have settled with the province as the latter would be in a position to demand what ever price they might see fit to ask.' But Morse feared that cancelling the provisional sale would allow the band to demand a much greater price than the one that Russell had negotiated in February, and he ordered his solicitor not to jeopardize the company's advantage. Thus, Tate declared that the railway company would accept patent without recourse and instructed the DIA to proceed with the surrender. The railway company soon executed an undertaking to this effect. In mid-August, the department's British Columbia superintendent held a council with half the adult members of the Metlakatla band, and a formal surrender following the terms of the February undertaking was drawn up and executed. Although the decision of the band was described as unanimous, it was not taken until 2 a.m. after several meetings. The $10,000 that the superintendent had brought for immediate distribution was apparently not employed. An order-in-council ratifying the surrender was approved on 21 September. Shortly after, Hays boasted that the acquisition of the reserve land now placed '25,000 acres of land under the control of the Company, completely encircling the harbour.'[82]

When the department informed the GTP that it would issue a patent on payment, Morse, ever one to cut a sharp deal, decided to pay the full amount, $103,202.50, immediately, which would save the company the cost of the survey before payment. 'Force them to pay for survey as they cannot issue patent without survey.' Only several months later did a GTP solicitor discover that the patent could be issued without a survey.[83]

In January 1907, the question of the GTP purchase came up for debate in the House of Commons. The Conservatives maintained that if the land on the reserve would soon be worth $100 to $1,000 per acre as a Liberal had boasted, the Department of Indian Affairs had in effect robbed Native people by not reserving one-quarter of the grant for the original owners as the provincial government had done in the earlier sale. One member charged that 'they [the Liberal government] would not allow the Grand Trunk Pacific, poor, little, inferior corporation that it is, poverty stricken, without any rights and franchises to speak of, to go single-handedly to the provincial government and do its own work on a fair business basis. They must intervene and send their invitation [the April 1906 order-in-council] – equivalent to a command.' The minister was forced to counter with the argument that when the federal government acted, the land belonged to Natives and not the province.[84]

In the middle of February, the *Globe* announced that McBride would dispossess the GTP of its newly acquired lands at Prince Rupert. The new provincial attorney general, W.J. Bowser, declared that no alienation would be permitted. On 26 February, the British Columbia government declared that the dominion government had no right or power to make a grant or lease. Along with portions of two reserves in the southern part of the province, the 13,567 acres of the Metlakatla Indian Reserve 'now belong to and should be claimed by the province.' On 19 March, the British Columbia government passed a second minute specifically claiming the surrendered portion of the Metlakatla Reserve, and a provincial constable served an eviction notice on the company the following week.[85] In desperation, Tate suggested to the Department of Indian Affairs that it cancel the sale and give the company a 999-year lease 'to assure us the undisturbed possession of the lands.' But the deputy minister of justice declared that such an action would not negate the surrender.[86]

Even though E.G. Russell, now directing GTP construction operations on the reserve, stubbornly maintained that his course of ignoring the province's claims was correct, he could suggest only that the 'legal Dept should go to work on this subject with vigour and care to determine every point in the Ry favour.'[87] But Morse had already turned away from Russell. In early 1907, the general manager, probably at Hays's suggestion, swallowed his pride and resumed correspondence with McBride. He reiterated that the acquisition of the reserve was essential if the company were to carry out its plans to build a model terminal city. Morse indicated, however, that the GTP would now accept the province's position on reversionary interest, and invited him to a meeting in Montreal with the GTP management to 'clear our title ... so that there be no cession of work in British Columbia.' At the meeting, Morse produced a sheaf of telegrams to demonstrate how the GTP management had distanced itself from Russell. This corporate rejection apparently led Russell to commit suicide a week later.[88]

Though the company had paid the entire price of the reserve to the department in December 1906, it had persuaded the department to hold back forwarding even the first instalment to the Native people in order to delay completing the formal alienation of the reserve. By the end of April, the band was becoming restless at the delay in receiving the first payment. The local Indian agent informed the department that the band held him personally responsible. Some band members had already expressed support for the ideas of Squamish chief Joe Capilano concerning the exclusion of whites from Indian land. Further delay, the Anglican bishop telegraphed the minister, would be disastrous.[89] Yet Morse pleaded with the department to hold back payment to Natives, and thereby alienation of the reserve, until the imminent agreement could be secured. On 10 May, though the company had no agreement, Tate informed the department that an arrangement had been worked out and allowed the initial payment to be disbursed to the Native people.[90]

During the meeting in Montreal on 17 April, Morse blustered to McBride that if the premier would not settle with the GTP, the railway company would withdraw its forces from the province and delay construction on the Pacific. But it was clear to everyone, as one of McBride's colleagues observed, that the province now had the GTP 'in a hole.' Tate admitted that the company should have settled with the province first. Proceeding on the 'business principles' the premier so admired, the general manager undertook to acknowledge and then purchase the reversionary rights that the province claimed in the reserve.[91]

Two days later, Morse conceded a great deal more. The GTP would purchase the reversionary right of British Columbia in the reserve for $1.00 per acre, and then allow the province to select one-quarter of the land on the same terms as the Kaien Island purchase. But the most important new condition was that the company would 'commence construction from western terminal not later than 1 March 1908, build then [eastward] to Summit [of Rocky Mountains], work [to] proceed continuously.' Several days later, McBride explained the scope of this victory to R.G. Tatlow, his finance minister. That both Hays and Morse now acknowledged the reversionary right McBride thought excellent since he believed the provincial case might 'be suspended for many years to come' if the matter went to the courts. As well as one-quarter of the new parcel, the government would obtain a windfall of some $30,000 as acknowledgment of reversionary interest. Most important, however, 'we should certainly be entitled to the credit of having secured for our country, first, construction from the western terminal, second, purchase of all necessary commodities in our own markets, and last the commencement of operations within a fixed period.' In all, it was a 'business-like' arrangement that could be defended as such.[92]

While this was a good bargain indeed, the members of McBride's cabinet at home decided that they could extract even more. Taking exception to an announcement at a Grand Trunk shareholders' meeting in London that the company now owned the reserve land at its terminus, Tatlow, acting premier while McBride was in Britain, believed there was something suspicious in the deal and informed the premier that his cabinet now demanded one-half the new parcel. When Morse made a formal offer in May, the cabinet rejected it, stating that it would only accept an arrangement in which the province received one-third of the waterfront and one-half of the land as well as a price of $2.50 per acre for the entire parcel. Tatlow even wanted the province to claim the one-half of the parcel the company had already purchased.[93]

Why did the cabinet increase its demand? And why had the GTP now conceded what Hays had carefully protected in 1904 and Morse had bluntly refused in 1905? Probably resentment played some role in the cabinet's actions. Observing that the company claimed control of the disputed land long before the GTP made any concrete proposal, Fred Fulton, the commissioner of lands, charged that the GTP recognized British Columbia only when it protested. Now, 'the public will blame us if we do not make the best deal.' Even if the government charged the railway company $5.00 per acre for the reversionary interest, the reserve was 'practically a gift. If we keep half, the GTP will still get $3,000,000.' The minister would change his position for only one concession. 'The only consideration would be if we bind them to commence construction in B.C. Is this worth $3 or 4 million to Us?'[94] It is extraordinary that the minister regarded 6,700 acres, one-half of the reserve land in question, much of which was separated by water from the townsite proper, worth $3 or $4 million.

What is more surprising is that the railway company officers apparently shared this belief since they agreed to Pacific construction to obtain this land. Indeed, one source suggests that the company would have regarded the minister's estimate as very low. In the fall of 1907, the GTP corporate secretary calculated the returns the company expected from the sale of all its Prince Rupert holdings. The sale of one-half of the property as lots with a twenty-five-foot frontage, the remainder in one-acre parcels, would produce a return of $21,336,000. Even with the subtraction of the province's quarter, the company would still secure a return of more than $16 million. Undisputed title of the reserve lands, three-fifths of the GTP holdings in the area, would bring the company more than $9.6 million, almost the value of the land grant that Morse had demanded in 1905 as the price of Pacific construction.[95] The company, of course, did not reveal its calculation of returns to the provincial government.

In the face of these additional cabinet demands, the GTP management balked. Morse returned to his old style, complaining to the premier that 'we have accomplished nothing satisfactory with your government.' Insisting on the original agreement, Hays declared that the company had offered 'extraordinarily liberal terms ... having regard to the exceedingly slight claim you have for any consideration on the ground of reversionary interests.' This challenge simply brought a careful response from the premier that he had always informed the GTP officers that he spoke only in a personal capacity concerning the negotiations.[96] But even as Tate cobbled together an opinion to justify renewed GTP resistance to the province's 'most inconsistent and extortionate claim,' the solicitor recognized that 'for the necessity of securing the right to immediate possession of the land and the uninterrupted prosecution of our work,' the company would have to concede.[97]

This realism made an agreement possible. When Tate visited Victoria during the fall of 1907 as the new GTP negotiator, McBride spelled out the conditions for a general settlement, which he loftily described as a policy toward the GTP based on 'equitable business principles.' The government, the premier declared, desired to be friendly with the railway. The province had never any intention of opposing the GTP's construction, but if the company took sides with the dominion, i.e., resisted the province's claims to reversionary interest, the provincial government could justify in the eyes of the people its refusal to further the ends of the railway company. Indeed, such a misguided course would lead to the loss of the concessions the railway company had already negotiated.[98]

Though the solicitor boasted to his superiors that he would accomplish 'a great deal,'[99] he secured few improvements on the province's 'extortionate' demands, which the management had decried during the summer. The company settled for the same 3:1 division as in the Kaien Island purchase. In addition, it would pay the province $2.50 per acre, and agreed to reconvey to the province one-quarter of the waterfront. Tate evidently expected to make these concessions; even before he received the government's proposals, he advised Morse to accept reconveyance and payment. 'Additional payment not large when we consider the immense development probable. Also have good effect on certain members of the cabinet and help us in other negotiations.'[100] On the issue of reversionary interest, GTP vice-president William Wainwright's breathless announcement that the company would 'go to the limit to cooperate' was not inaccurate. The general agreement was signed on 29 February 1908 and passed the Legislative Assembly without amendment during the following week.[101]

Although the GTP had conceded much, the company's Ottawa lob-byist maintained that the agreement was better than he expected: 'We are in far better position in the Province of British Columbia than we could have hoped for many years if our negotiations had fallen through and lit-igation had ensued ... It is expected that Prince Rupert will grow very much faster than any development that has taken place on the Pacific Coast by the opening up of transcontinental railways.' The response of the senior management was just as optimistic. Shortly after the bill became law, Morse exclaimed to McBride that he was delighted that the 'complication' had at last been settled.[102] The GTP had finally out-stripped the CPR in one element of railway development, the size of its land holdings at the Pacific terminus.

THAT HAYS STILL HANKERED after a general subsidy from the province is apparent in GTP proposals the company made to McBride in the two years following the master agreement. Unable to secure an open land grant for construction of its main line, the company resorted to a ruse. To break the hold of speculators on crown land in the north, the com-pany now generously offered to organize a colonization syndicate. While the company specified neither the number of settlers it would import nor the price it would charge them for land, it was clear on its own requirements to cover the high overhead charges: one million acres at the nominal price of $1.00 per acre with a further reserve to be transferred when required. Recognizing this for what it was, McBride brusquely turned the proposal down.[103]

The company also attempted to exploit its last remaining lever with the province, its charter for a line from Fort George to Vancouver granted by the federal House in 1906. Early in 1909, in the midst of rumours con-cerning a provincial subsidy for the Canadian Northern British Columbia line, Tate sought a guarantee that the GTP line would receive an equal grant. But the company destroyed the credibility of the project by suddenly shifting the northern terminus of the line from Fort George to Tête Jaune Cache to preempt the Canadian Northern route to Vancouver. Although it scrambled to shift the line back to Fort George after the federal minister of railways rebuffed its bald attempt at route piracy as 'a wanton waste of money,' the damage had been done. After the British Columbia government campaigned on its guarantee to the Can-adian Northern later in the year, Hays demanded a similar guarantee for the GTP branch of $35,000 per mile because it would 'open up a section of country of more importance than that traversed by the Canadian Northern.' But McBride chose to regard his campaign undertakings as a block to additional government support for the GTP project. Tate concluded that there was 'nothing to be gained by insisting upon something we know we cannot get – attempting to force an impregnable situation.' The company would have to remain satisfied with a vague promise from McBride that he would be liberal with the GTP request 'at the proper time.'[104]

But Hays was impatient. And if some of McBride's ministers admitted that the 'South' line would open more new territory than the Canadian Northern, perhaps the premier might be more amenable to supporting an independent corporation; 'its identity (though it might be suspected) not to be known as directly connected with the Grand Trunk Pacific.' After the president failed once more to secure McBride's support for the GTP project in September 1911, apparently because he would not relinquish control of rates to the province, Hays allowed D'Arcy Tate, the GTP solicitor who had put together the master agreement, to approach the premier with an 'independent' proposition. With Foley Brothers, Welch, and Stewart, the principal contractor on the GTP Mountain Section, Tate created a construction proposal that gave the province control of rates. But Hays retained effective control by insisting on a traffic arrangement that routed all through traffic originating on the branch line, even that near Vancouver and thus closer to the rival CPR, over the GTP, and allowed the GTP a monopoly in the supply of materials and labourers for construction of the line.[105]

For an enterprise that wished to secure a return on the heavy expenditure of construction, these were onerous, probably impossible terms. Yet contractor J.W. Stewart paid Tate $500,000 and 25 per cent stock of the new company to secure them. Unaware of the principals' private arrangements and unable to comprehend the consequences of the GTP conditions, McBride blithely awarded the new firm, the Pacific Great Eastern Railway Company, a bond guarantee of $35,000 per mile early in 1912. Touting the project as the first step in linking the south with the Peace River country, the premier handily won the next election.[106]

Thus, shortly before his death, Hays apparently secured the provincial subsidy for the GTP system in British Columbia that he had been seeking since 1902. The GTP would now have its 450-mile branch constructed largely at the expense of the provincial government, and the fixed charges would not further burden the company. But the contractors of the branch line evidently chose to take their profits during construction, in part because of the conditions Hays had imposed on operation. When the GTP was completed in 1914, the PGE had less than 120 miles in operation. It would not generate additional traffic for the GTP main line until many years after the company's collapse.[107]

The entry of the GTP into British Columbia was not auspicious. Apparently unaware of time required to generate traffic on a new line across the Pacific slope, Hays undertook to build to the coast before completing a more remunerative line on the prairies. His insistence on large returns from townsite sales led to the selection of Kaien Island as the GTP terminus. The company's gross overestimate of the returns from terminus lot sales in turn supported the president's squabble with the province for additional land, much of which the company would never market. Most damaging for the GTP, then, was Hays's concession of Pacific construction in 1907 to secure these lands. Even if the terminus property had realized the company's wildly speculative estimate, the return would not have covered the GTP expenditure for its line across the entire province or even for the west end alone. After the company embarked on Pacific construction in the following year, it sought yet another subsidy in the guise of a colonization syndicate but was rebuffed. Finally, the company secured a substantial subsidy from the province in 1912 for a major branch line, but imposed conditions that contributed to the branch's failure to deliver traffic to the main line.

During the company's negotiations with the provincial government in 1907, a vice-president made a bleak evaluation of the British Columbia line: 'There was no likelihood of the Mountain Section paying its fixed charges for a long time to come ... It is on a very different footing to the Prairie Section where revenue would be derived immediately.'[108] Of course, the GTP management did not repeat this prediction in shareholders' reports or publicity pamphlets. But as Morse had warned in 1905, the west end ran up huge expenditures with no prospect of returns from traffic until the transcontinental was completed. The repeated attempts of the GTP to secure immediate returns and complete control in the development of Prince Rupert and other communities along the line in British Columbia suggest that the management chose to wrest its return from the townsites before investors realized that meagre traffic would destroy the GTP British Columbia line as a 'live proposition.'

THREE

'BANGING RIGHT THROUGH ON A STRAIGHT LINE': CONSTRUCTION

THE PROGRESS of construction, particularly when the line traverses difficult territory, has long occupied a prominent place in many accounts of railway development. Triumph over natural barriers provided a graphic setting for nineteenth- and early twentieth-century celebrations of the indomitable power of railways and their captains.[1] The most influential view of the construction of the GTP in British Columbia remains the tendentious contemporary accounts of British journalist Frederick Talbot, who travelled over the uncompleted line from Edmonton to Prince Rupert in 1910. In two books and a stream of articles, this unofficial company publicist justified the slow progress of the Mountain Section to British investors by presenting a 'first-hand, face-to-face impression of the obstacles that reared up at every foot advance which had to be broken down by sheer physical effort or ingenuity.'[2] Because Talbot evidently perused selected GTP documents and recorded fragments of conversations with some of the company's officers, later historians have borrowed data from his works almost without question. They have, for the most part, also accepted his unreflective Whiggism, and offer little beyond what an American scholar has described as 'anecdotal history, with the emphasis on personalities, colourful and melodramatic events, and the triumphant completion.'[3] These laudatory accounts elicited an opposing view of construction from those who regarded the owners and managers of the project as robber barons. But though the muckrakers and their more restrained academic successors have suggested other motives for building the railway, they have not substantially revised our understanding of the nature and problems of construction of the GTP.[4]

From works in both these traditions, one can construct a simple narrative of the construction of the GTP in British Columbia. Crews began work on the main line near Winnipeg in 1905 and pushed west to Edmonton in 1908. In the following year the first contract was let on the east end of the Mountain Section, the 830-mile portion of the road from Wolf Creek, Alberta, to the Pacific coast. The end of steel, however, did not cross the British Columbia border until November 1911. In the meantime, the railway company began construction eastward from Prince Rupert on the west end in the spring of 1908. Heavy rock work in the Skeena River Valley and a continual shortage of labour slowed the pace on this end, and the end of steel only reached the Hazelton district, 180 miles inland, at the end of 1912. In April 1914, the ends of steel were joined near Fort Fraser, 373 miles east of Prince Rupert and 457 miles west of Wolf Creek, but the line did not open for commercial service until August. By 1916, the government inspector certified the global cost of construction of the Mountain Section, including land and interest charges, as $93,307,184 or more than $112,000 per mile. Although several earlier works maintain that the construction of such an 'expensive' line across the mountains brought on the company's collapse, no one has investigated the reasons for the high cost.

For systems such as the CPR, for which detailed financial data survive, cost-benefit analysis of construction permits an escape from narrative and offers some striking contrasts with the GTP calculations for its Pacific slope line.[5] They indicate that for the GTP, which all accounts suggest produced an inadequate rate of return throughout its existence, the question becomes how the company failed to control its expenditure. Whatever its analytical strengths and empirical weaknesses, the cost-benefit approach requires specific accounting data on construction and on economic activity after completion of the line, something that is not available for the GTP.

Two other studies provide some useful propositions on which to create an examination of GTP construction. In his discussion of Canadian Northern strategy, T.D. Regehr elaborates the finance and construction primer axiom that railway companies could not recover costs when they failed to tie the route and standard of construction of new lines to the immediate traffic requirements of the regions the extensions traversed.[6] In a provocative account of the rent-seeking behaviour of railways taken over by governments, H.A. Innis argues that the relatively easy prospect of building on government guarantees led GTP officers to establish a high standard of construction, which immediate traffic on the road would not support. He also remarks that the financial structure of the road without the support of land grants occasioned high fixed charges and produced a lack of resilience to survive the long period of slow traffic development.[7] While the following examination challenges Innis's assignation of responsibility for the standard, it suggests that the GTP management's fundamental miscalculations about traffic and the opportunity to build chiefly at government expense in the short term caused the company to accept high expenditures that ultimately caused the enterprise to collapse.

Since most engineering records of the company have been destroyed, it is impossible to write a complete construction history of the GTP in British Columbia.[8] Drawing on scattered records that survive in the departments and agencies of the federal government, the following study concentrates on relations between the GTP and the federal government, the major guarantor of construction. After setting out the financial arrangements that supported construction, this chapter advances a hypothesis for the railway company's acceptance, if not proposal, of the high standard of construction. It then demonstrates how the management's unrealistic traffic predictions encouraged engineers to accept overruns that brought on conflict with the representatives of the federal and provincial governments.

The agreement that the Grand Trunk made with the federal government in 1903 for construction of the GTP line created separate financing arrangements for the Prairie and Mountain Sections. The Grand Trunk acquired all GTP common stock with a face value of $25 million. After the parent railway company secured significant changes in 1904, the revised contract limited the Grand Trunk's immediate obligations on the Mountain Section to a guarantee of one-quarter of the sum, which was expected to cover the cost of construction. The government guaranteed the remainder. For the Mountain Section, there was no ceiling on the size of the government guarantee of three-quarters of the cost, and the company would pay interest only on its own one-quarter share for seven years. It could extend this limitation of interest payments for three additional years although the payments would now be added to its debt. In 1905, the company secured its share of the expected cost of construction by selling 4 per cent sterling bonds, which matured in 1955.[9]

As the major guarantor of the GTP's construction bonds, the federal government sought to regulate the new railway carefully. In the 1903 contract, it required the company to submit to regulation from both the Department of Railways and the newly created Board of Railway Commissioners. Following the established precedent for railways chartered and subsidized by the federal government, the contract required the company to obtain the sanction of the government for its plans and specifications. In practice, the company had to obtain approval from the officials of the Department of Railways and Canals. But the contract also required that to obtain government funds for construction, the company had to present estimates 'to the satisfaction of the Government periodically from time to time.' Since the contract did not set out a method for the release of funds under the guarantee, the Grand Trunk had to cover the entire expenditure on the preliminary elements of construction, primarily surveys, for the GTP west of Winnipeg, much to the company's displeasure.[10] Though the Grand Trunk had secured an increased government share for the financing of the Mountain Section, nervous shareholders in Britain wanted more concessions. To convince them to ratify the revised contract, GTP president C.M. Hays misrepresented the terms and claimed that after its guarantee of one-quarter of the principal, the Grand Trunk would face no charges on the Mountain Section for ten years.[11]

In the spring of 1905, as grading was about to begin, the railway company reached agreement with the government on the size and method of the sale of securities by both parties to cover the expected cost of construction. A clause in the government mortgage instrument provided that a special inspector would review and certify monthly company progress reports before releasing appropriate funds. Specifications, the amount and quality of materials used in construction of the road, were accepted by cabinet in May 1905. Shortly after the onset of grading, Hays submitted a form for government inspection of railway company expenditure and requested that an officer be designated as a conduit for government funds.[12]

Reviewing Hays's request, Collingwood Schreiber, the Department of Railways engineer, insisted that an inspector for the government must not only check company statements of expenditure against the company's books but also ensure that the expenditure 'fairly represents the reasonable value of the work done.' This concern for husbanding the government's contribution to the enterprise, as well as his experience in supervising the construction of the CPR twenty years earlier, persuaded the finance minister to appoint the engineer as government inspector for the project.[13]

To carry out the financial check of company statements, Schreiber had department auditors examine the expenditures on each monthly certificate against company books in its Montreal headquarters. The inspector also placed engineers on every section of the road, who sent him monthly reports on the activities of company engineers and the contractors to ensure that expenditures represented reasonable value.[14] Consequently, in order to obtain government funds for construction, the railway company had to submit copies of all its proposals and estimates to both the railways department and the inspector's office. Only after Schreiber certified the company statement of expenditure would the cabinet pass an order-in-council allowing disbursement of the government share of funds to cover the statement. To receive government funds, then, the company had to obtain Schreiber's sanction.

But the government also insisted that the company submit to another regulatory regime by making it subject to the provisions of the new Railway Act. Passed shortly before the GTP bills in 1903, the act created the Board of Railway Commissioners for Canada (BRC), an independent tribunal of railway experts set up to relieve a cabinet committee overwhelmed by the task of adjudicating the myriad claims and disputes arising from the construction and operation of railways.[15] Under the new act, the railway company required ministerial approval for its route, i.e., its proposed line in general terms. But after obtaining this sanction, the company also had to submit its location, i.e, its precise plans, profiles, and reference book for a particular section of the line, not only to the minister but also to the new agency for independent consideration. In addition, the company required BRC sanction for its station locations and any obstruction it created in navigable waters.[16]

As the following chapters will show, while the company dealt successfully with both the department and the board during the early stages of construction of the Mountain Section, it eventually entered into conflict with them. The company's conflicts with Schreiber concerning aspects of the cost of construction of the Mountain Section are examined below. Later chapters examine the company's relations with the BRC in a series of disputes concerning GTP actions in several of the communities established on the British Columbia line.

Although students of the GTP have long acknowledged that the standard or design of the line was an important factor in the railway company's failure, they have largely avoided an examination of both its origin and its effect on the construction of the Mountain Section. The 1903 contract called for the company to construct and equip the Western Division 'to a standard not inferior to the main line of the Grand Trunk Railway Company of Canada between Montreal and Toronto, so far as may be practicable in the case of a newly constructed line of railway.' Although not stated in the contract or the specifications, the parties regarded the major elements of this standard as .4 per cent ruling gradient, 6° curvature, the use of eighty-pound rails, and concrete and steel bridges over large rivers. Such a standard was far above pioneer roads at this time.[17] For example, the Intercolonial had a gradient of 1.75 per cent, sixty-five-pound rails, and many timber structures.

Historians have followed company statements, pamphlets, and publicists in assigning responsibility to the GTP management for this standard. In 1908, Hays justified the most expensive element in the standard, the low gradient, as a condition for high-speed, safe travel on the new line. The building of the Mountain Section with 'prairie grades' would give locomotives on the GTP line a gross hauling capacity seven times that of the CPR. Although he admitted that construction on such a standard required immediate 'generous expenditures,' Hays expected that the immense economy in operation would return the interest cost of the additional expenditure ten times over. Shortly after this interview, several GTP pamphlets added a table illustrating Hays's assertions that the low gradient produced superior hauling capacity and, implicitly, guaranteed the success of the GTP when it entered competition with other roads. Given these statements from company sources on the advantage of the standard, it is perhaps not surprising that Talbot credits Hays with the origin of the standard. The GTP publicist maintained that the GTP president, desirous to 'make the first cost the last cost,' convinced the government to accept the standard.[18] Later writers have assumed rather than proved that Talbot's contention is substantially correct.

A review of the Hays and Laurier Papers and the debates in both the Commons and Senate concerning the contract does not reveal who proposed the standard or when, exactly, it was established. Clearly, both the Grand Trunk and the government had accepted it when they signed the contract on 29 July 1903. But during the period November 1902 to July 1903, none of the surviving petitions of the Grand Trunk to the government mentions this standard. After two months of detailed negotiations, the Department of Railways engineer responded to a request from the finance minister by estimating the cost of the GTP 'as a road of ordinary character ... with maximum grades of 1 per cent.' Surely he would not have made such an estimate if the railway company had indicated that it wished to build the road according to the Montreal-Toronto standard. Two sources suggest that the railway company's original intentions were more modest. A pamphlet published in 1903, probably by the Grand Trunk, observed that while the railway company would adhere to a .5 per cent gradient on the prairies, it would push a much less expensive road of 1.75 per cent through the mountains. And according to a railway commissioner, early GTP surveys also reported this gradient.[19] Indeed, Hays's estimate in February 1903 of $50,000 per mile, significantly lower than Schreiber's estimate of $67,000 per mile for a road with a 1 per cent gradient, suggests such a modest standard.

Although the Liberals said little in Parliament about the standard, the finance minister made the following suggestive observation. 'As to the Western division, the standard is to be remarkably high ... I do not think *we* could have selected in the Dominion a better standard than this [emphasis added].' Of course, W.S. Fielding may well have meant that the government *and* the railway company selected the standard. But for the Winnipeg-Moncton section of the road, we know that the first suggestion to follow the standard of the Western Division, i.e., to improve the standard from 1 per cent gradient to .4 per cent, came from a Liberal MP. Perhaps a similar political whim led the government negotiators to propose, and the Grand Trunk negotiators to accept, the Montreal-Toronto standard for the Western Division. This hypothesis concerning the origin of the standard is supported by the contention of the Grand Trunk president in 1909 that the 'high standard of perfection, with attendant high rate of expenditure, was imposed upon us ... by the Canadian government.'[20]

Previous examinations of the GTP have not attempted to assess the effect of the standard on the cost of the road. In its analysis of the Eastern Division, the National Transcontinental Railway Investigating Commission implied that most of the cost overrun stemmed from this fundamental flaw, but admitted that it had not calculated the extra costs entailed by the superior standard. As part of the Royal Commission on Railways in 1917, the valuation report of the GTP Mountain Section noted only that 'the general limits adopted for grades and curves probably greatly increased the expense. Had an undulating grade been adopted, with more curvature, the line would have cost much less.'[21]

Steam shovel and dinky engines cut and haul rock from the railway yard on the Prince Rupert waterfront, circa 1910. A great deal of expensive 'solid rock' excavation was necessary to build the railway terminus.

More recent examinations of the line have not been more specific. If one is to evaluate the factors advanced for the collapse of the GTP, however, one must attempt to estimate the role of the standard in determining the cost (and cost overruns) of construction. What follows, then, is a comparison of the components of the actual standard described above with the more modest standard Schreiber applied to the Mountain Section in his estimate of 1903.

The most important factor in the comparison, the effect of the gradient and curvature on cost, is also the most difficult to estimate. The major cost in creating a road with a particular gradient and curvature stems from the quantities of excavation, the amount of material removed from cuts and placed in fills. Even for the actual standard, a complete record of quantities of excavation has not survived. But since we have the final cost of the elements of construction, i.e., elements of the Montreal-Toronto standard, a comparison of quantities of excavation required by the actual standard and Schreiber's 1903 estimate for construction of a 'road of ordinary character' across the same territory would allow us to compute the difference in cost of the two standards.

While contemporary textbooks on railroad construction contain tables relating gradient and curvature to excavation, they offer no practical examples that embrace the length and variety of terrain of the Mountain Section. The key to the estimate in the following table, a suitable comparison of quantities for grading and tunnels, lies in a supplementary comparison of the 1917 Royal Commission on Railways. While the valuation data on both the GTP and the Canadian Northern suggest only an appropriate price for construction *given* the standard, an appendix compares excavation quantities of the CPR and Canadian Northern lines along the same or opposite sides of the Fraser and Thompson river valleys from Vancouver to Kamloops (245 miles). On this section, the gradient of the Canadian Northern equals that of the GTP, i.e., .4 per cent eastbound, while the CPR's gradient is somewhat inferior to Schreiber's, i.e., 1.3 per cent v. 1 per cent. The maximum curvature of the Canadian Northern exceeds the GTP by 2 per cent; the CPR exceeds Schreiber's curvature by 1°30'. To 'improve' the CPR line, I have ignored the preponderance of 'heavy' grading in Canadian Northern quantities by making an unweighted comparison.

In 1909, Schreiber calculated the difference in the cost of laying sixty-five-pound and eighty-pound rails on the GTP grade. I have

Table 3.1

Comparison of cost of standards in Mountain Section

Component construction	Cost actual standard ($ millions)	Reduction in standard (actual = 1.00)	Cost Schreiber's standard ($ millions)	Saving ($ millions)	Estimate Cost actual / Cost Schreiber's
Grading (includes overclassification)	45.5	.72[a]	32.8	12.7	
Tunnels	2.5	.55[a]	1.4	1.1	
Rails, switches, fastenings	5.6	.89[b]	5.0	.6	
Bridges, embankments (+ Fraser Crossing)	6.1 (+1.7)	.30 (1)[c]	1.8 (+1.7)	4.3	
Total	61.4		43.2	18.2	
Other construction items constant	16.9		16.9		
First cost (without land or interest)	78.3		60.1	18.2	1.30
				18.2 +10%[d]	1.34
				18.2 −10%[e]	1.26

a Comparison of CPR excavation to Canadian Northern excavation in Fraser and Thompson river valley
b Schreiber's calculation of cost difference in laying 65 lb and 80 lb rails
c National Transcontinental Railway Investigating Commission estimate for substituting wooden bridges for steel and concrete bridges
d Upper limit of cost increase
e Lower limit of cost increase
Sources: Canada, Royal Commission to Inquire into Railways and Transportation, *Report;* Canada National Transcontinental Railway Investigating Commission, *Report;* NAC, RG 43, vol. 306, file 4402-General

applied the same ratio to the cost of other components in the construction of a steel line, such as switches, brackets, and fasteners. The comparison for the substitution of wooden bridges and trestles for steel and concrete bridges and embankments, and trestles filled with material during construction, comes from the National Transcontinental Railway investigation. The reduction factor of .30 exaggerates the actual difference in cost since some rivers and chasms in the Mountain Section required steel and concrete structures no matter what the standard. I have therefore assumed that the most expensive structure in the Mountain Section, the Fraser River crossing at Prince George, would be built with no reduction of cost even if the road were constructed at the more modest standard.

With such crude devices for reducing quantities, one must allow a substantial margin of error. With a 10 per cent margin of error, the comparison indicates that construction according to the Montreal-Toronto standard instead of a standard 'of ordinary character' resulted in an additional expenditure of between $16.4 million and $20 million on the Mountain Section. If the cost of all other items remained constant, the standard raised the first cost of construction by 26-34 per cent.[22]

The comparison suggests that the construction according to the superior standard was the most significant factor in the increased construction cost of the line above the first estimates of both the Grand Trunk and the government in 1903. Two other factors not considered in the comparison produced additional increases, however. Whereas the comparison assumed that unit prices for materials and excavation remained constant, both increased during the course of construction. While material prices, particularly for steel rails, rose most dramatically before the completion of the Prairie Section, unit prices for excavation rose after 1908. Increased quantities of excavation and slower construction of concrete and steel bridges also delayed completion and thereby advanced interest charges on construction.

Why did the GTP accept, if not propose, construction at such a standard that resulted in onerous fixed charges? Hays's declaration that later returns from low operating expenses justified initial generous expenditures, cited above, obscures a more fundamental reason: the company's omission of the high standard as a factor in its estimates. It has been suggested the company's original estimate in February 1903 was based on a 'road of ordinary character.' For the bond issue of the company and the government in 1905, the company submitted another estimate in which the cost per mile for the Mountain Section, $50,000, remained unchanged even though the road was now required by contract to be built according to the Montreal-Toronto standard. Before submitting the estimate, Hays explained to Rivers Wilson that the company's expectation of the total cost of the Mountain Section had not changed. Nevertheless, the company inflated its estimate to $34.5 million, presumably by extending the length of the Mountain Section, and then adding a

15 per cent contingency of $5.1 million. Even with this cushion, the company's estimate of total cost was still less than $40 million. Hays assured the Grand Trunk president that a guarantee of $10 million 'should cover' the company's one-quarter share of construction. That the company sold securities worth $9,963,000, only 54 per cent of its proportional share of the value of the government bonds, demonstrates that it had not yet revised its calculations of the total cost. The GTP president's belated claim in 1914 that the company had urged a larger limit in the original bond issue financing the Mountain Section was an unconvincing lie.[23]

WHEN THE GTP began work on the west end of the Mountain Section in 1908, costs had already risen significantly during the construction of the Prairie Section. Why, then, did the company continue to prosecute the work? Like their colleagues on the National Transcontinental, 'erroneous assumptions' by the GTP engineers concerning the volume of traffic on the new road led the company not only to select an uneconomic route but also to tolerate large cost overruns.[24]

Before examining the route decision, however, something must be said about the survey on which it was ostensibly based. As the government inspector noted, the economic success of the GTP depended on a judicious selection of a pass through the Rocky Mountains since it would determine in large part the route and length of the GTP line from Edmonton to the Pacific coast. Both Hays and Talbot maintained that the company spent hundreds of thousands of dollars on an exhaustive survey of all possible routes before settling on the Yellowhead Pass ahead of the Canadian Northern.[25] Other sources suggest, however, that the survey was erratic and unsystematic.

It was certainly not ordained that the GTP would build through the Yellowhead. The company's charter specified only that the GTP build to the Pacific coast 'by way of either the Peace River Pass, or the Pine River Pass, or such other Pass in the Rocky Mountains as is found most convenient and practicable.'[26] During the first two years of the surveys, the railway company conformed to the terms of the charter and directed most of its activity toward the Peace and Pine River routes. Before the onset of surveys, the federal finance minister indicated that the railway would select the Pine River Pass. Reflecting the railway company's expectations, Laurier quoted selectively from the CPR surveys of the 1870s to boost the Pine Pass and dismiss the Yellowhead: 'In place of a bleak sterile country, the line by the Pine River route would traverse an area of remarkable fertility – the fertile belt or wheat-producing country, extends nearly 300 miles further to the west, before the Rocky Mountains are reached, than by the route over the Yellowhead Pass: a corresponding reduction being made in the breadth of sterile country to be crossed in the Rocky Mountains.'[27] The only surviving report of the survey in March 1904 supported the Pine River route because it traversed 560,000 acres of arable land east of the Rocky Mountains while the longer route to the Peace traversed only 20,000 additional acres.[28]

During this period, company engineers passed over the Yellowhead Pass, apparently on the strength of an unfavourable report in 1903 by the company's western agent, E.G. Russell. A reconnaissance map dated March 1905 indicates that GTP survey parties had not yet traversed the Yellowhead route to Fort George. In the same month, Hays lamented that little progress had been made on surveys on the western side of the Rockies.[29] Only after his appointment as GTP chief engineer in July 1905 did B.B. Kelliher take the remarkable course of reviewing the Canadian Pacific profiles of the Yellowhead route made in the 1870s. He promptly decided that a .4 per cent gradient in both directions from Edmonton to the coast could 'very easily' be obtained and began an intensive survey of the Yellowhead route. Under the direction of division engineer C.C. Van Arsdol, GTP engineers during the following year located a practicable route with a .4 per cent gradient with the exception of twenty miles eastbound at Tête Jaune Cache.[30]

Although the railway company had settled on the Yellowhead Pass at least two months earlier, Kelliher presented the survey results only in November 1906. In a formal report to the general manager, obviously meant for wider distribution, the chief engineer concluded the route to the coast via the Yellowhead was 'incomparably the best available.' Kelliher apparently took the unusual step of making his case on engineering grounds alone. 'The present condition of the territory between Edmonton and Prince Rupert show no local traffic advantage on either route as against the other, that would justify a lengthening of the main line or above all any increase in the lowest rate of gradient available via the Yellowhead Pass.'[31] An examination of his calculations reveals that this decision departed from contemporary railroad practice where 'economics,' i.e., the estimate of potential traffic, was the primary factor in determining location.[32]

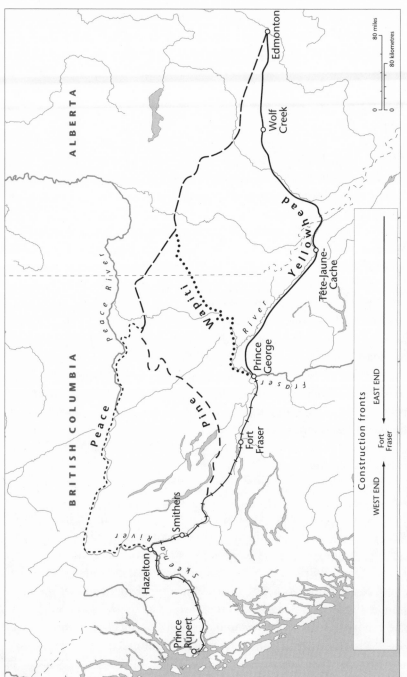

Figure 3.1 GTP Mountain Section alternative routes, 1906, and selected communities, 1913

For the route from Edmonton to Prince Rupert via the Yellowhead, a distance of 955 miles, Kelliher offered the following estimate:

Cost grading (and bridges) per mile	$30,100
Cost tracks, buildings, etc., per mile	$14,000
First cost per mile	$44,100
Total first cost (955 miles)	$42,115,500[33]

Such a calculation is striking because the cost per mile is significantly lower than the GTP 1903 estimate of $50,000 per mile. Since prices for labour and material, notably steel, had risen during the construction of the Prairie Section, the calculation must have been based on a much smaller quantity of excavation. Indeed, a consultant hired by Hays doubted the accuracy of the small quantities of rock excavation that appeared in later GTP estimates. Beyond the underestimation of quantities that the low grading cost suggests, the comparison of the Yellowhead route with alternative routes through the Peace River, Pine River, and Wapiti Passes indicates how traffic prediction allowed the engineers to accept much higher construction costs. Kelliher claimed that the surveys demonstrated that the three alternative routes were not only longer but also steeper. Only on the matter of curvature were they more desirable than the Yellowhead. In his comparison for each alternative, he set out the 'excess,' an estimate of the cost of each factor in operating times above its cost for the Yellowhead route. While the estimate of excess construction cost depended on the same calculations as the Yellowhead, the other factors, excess distance, rise and fall, etc., capitalized the operating expense in overcoming these factors on the rival lines. The operating expense, of course, was a function of expected traffic.

The preceding chapter has indicated Hays's rosy views on traffic on the British Columbia line. Probably at the prompting of the 'believer,' GTP engineers in 1905 based their calculations on operating expenses in the Mountain Section on an expected traffic of sixteen daily trains. In his calculations for the route decision, Kelliher reduced the number of daily trains to fourteen. This figure exceeded the current number on the CPR main line on the prairies by 40 per cent; it doubled the average number over two subdivisions on the CPR Mountain Section for 1906-8. Yet Hays regarded the estimate as 'very moderate and conservative.'[34] On this base, Kelliher calculated the following excess for the Pine River route over the

Yellowhead. With the exception of first cost, all the remaining factors were a function of the traffic estimate. For fourteen daily trains, each mile of distance that could be saved by selecting the Yellowhead over the Pine River route, i.e., the excess, represented $103,400. Of the total excess, 72 per cent stemmed from the traffic prediction.

Not only did the excess calculated in this manner encourage the selection of the Yellowhead by increasing significantly the cost of alternative routes, but the calculation also required engineers to expend on the construction of the selected line *any amount less* than the excess on the alternative line.[35] Thus, while Kelliher estimated that each mile of the Yellowhead route would cost $44,000, the excess on the Pine River route allowed a further $16,736 per mile (56 per cent of grading; 38 per cent of total first cost) to be spent. With this cushion, engineers could contemplate an enormous cost overrun without alarm.

The excess in 1906 was calculated on fourteen daily trains. By 1912, GTP engineers, following the example of the Union Pacific, automatically calculated the excess on the basis of twenty daily trains, 25 per cent more than the greatly expanded traffic over the CPR mountain subdivi-

Table 3.2

GTP estimate of excess for Pine River route, 1906

	Yellowhead Pass route (955 mi.) ($)	Pine River route (1,046 mi.) ($)	Excess of Pine River route over Yellowhead ($)
Construction cost	42,116,500	46,651,600	$4,536,100
Operating cost for 14 daily trains, capitalized Pine River route			
Excess			
91 miles	0	9,409,400	9,409,400
3 pusher engines	0	1,050,000	1,050,000
1,750 ft. rise and fall	0	1,092,000	1,092,000
Credit			
1306° less curvature	104,180	0	−104,180
Total operating cost	104,180	11,551,400	11,447,220
Total	42,220,680	58,203,000	15,983,320

Source: NAC, RG 43, vol. 306, file 4402-EYP, pt. 1

sions.[36] By this time, government inspectors realized the calculation was inappropriate, but did nothing to change it.

The company had not completed its survey of the passes routes before it sought the sanction of the minister of railways for its plans in the Mountain Section. In December 1905, GTP assistant solicitor D'Arcy Tate filed a route map showing four alternative lines (Peace, Pine, Wapiti, and Yellowhead) and asked for approval of all the routes. He explained that the company took this unusual move to 'preserve ... the first right of selection of such one of the passes ... as may, after detailed surveys, be found most convenient and practicable.' Not surprisingly, Schreiber rejected this blanket proposal as too vague and demanded to review all information that the company had obtained in the surveys. This provoked GTP general manager Frank Morse to claim that no company had run as many miles of preliminary survey as the GTP. It is more probable, as a GTP lawyer later alleged against another company, that the route was 'nothing more than a line drawn on a map for the purpose of securing priority.'[37]

After the GTP engineers had made their decision on the calculations described above, Tate filed a route map for the Yellowhead Pass in September 1906. Schreiber again demanded that the company provide the results of surveys of the other passes so that he might determine if it was the most feasible route. The inspector explained to Laurier that government approval of the GTP choice would extend by 100 miles the length of the new railway's Mountain Section and thereby increase government liability, as the $30,000 per mile limit to the government guarantee had been removed for this section.[38]

In September 1906, Morse ordered Tate to take an unusual step and file location plans and profiles immediately for the Edmonton-Yellowhead portion of the proposed line even though the government had not yet approved the route map. Since the general manager had learned that the Canadian Northern was preparing to file plans, he wished to protect the GTP to the fullest extent. As Morse predicted, the Canadian Northern submitted its route map from Edmonton to the coast via the Yellowhead to the government on 22 October 1906, although it had apparently drawn it up sometime in 1905.[39]

In late September, the GTP general manager approached Schreiber personally and requested that the engineer aid the railway company in securing the pass. Schreiber agreed to 'do what he could to further [Morse's] views,' but again demanded the results of surveys of the other routes in order to 'pass intelligently on the more feasible route.'[40] To meet Schreiber's demand, Kelliher issued the formal report on routes discussed above. In conveying the report to Schreiber, Morse admitted that the GTP surveys had produced practically the same result as Fleming's surveys of the 1870s, but expressed the hope that 'the conclusion drawn from these documents will impress you as it does us.' It obviously did. Stating that the prime object was 'to secure as short a line across the Continent as may be practicable with grades kept down to a low point thus enabling traffic to be handled at a minimum of cost,' Schreiber recommended that the minister approve the GTP route application.[41]

There was still the matter of the Canadian Northern application. On 12 November, Morse urged the minister of railways to approve the GTP route map and location plans quickly since the company required a long lead time to make arrangements for work. With the upcoming parliamentary session expected to be busy, the general manager expressed the fear that the House might delay the company. On 24 November, an order-in-council was issued sanctioning the GTP route.[42]

After Tate ascertained that the route order had passed cabinet, he saw Schreiber and persuaded him to recommend that the government also approve seven location plans comprising a 284-mile section west of Edmonton, including twenty miles west of the Yellowhead summit. Two days later, Tate reminded the minister that he should implement the approval of the route map by approving the location plans immediately. In early December, Morse urged Schreiber to speak to Laurier about passing the order. The order-in-council was issued on the following day, 8 December.[43]

A few days later, Schreiber informed the rival company that the location plans it had submitted were drawn to the wrong scale and extended only to the Yellowhead Pass instead of to the Pacific coast. On the present scale, they could not be compared with the location plans of the GTP to ensure that they did not overlap with the GTP line whose location plans had already been authorized. He concluded that unless the plans were submitted in proper scale, a formal hearing before the minister would be 'a mere waste of time.' Though a Canadian Northern solicitor contended that these 'trivial objections ... put the Department in a rather farcical light,' the Canadian Northern application was rejected on 17 December, Schreiber claiming that the company had submitted a 'crooked line' that crossed and recrossed the line of the GTP.[44]

Such a decision prompted controversy, of course. The GTP allowed the railways minister to borrow its plans so that he could prepare for criticism in the House.[45] Canadian Northern officers chose to regard the decision as a political one, however, and company promoter Donald Mann protested strongly to Laurier. The Canadian Northern, through the charter of an attached project, was tied to the Yellowhead by a subsidy granted in 1903, and had coal deposits there. In addition, the rival company had not been informed of the GTP intention to build through the same pass. Mann concluded that he would like to see the GTP authorization revoked and his company's application confirmed.[46]

Hays was ready with his reply. The GTP president maintained that the terms of the GTP charter in no way limited the GTP to the Pine or Peace Passes and claimed that the company had spent thousands of dollars to locate 'the shortest, most direct and economical line for operation of a transcontinental railway.' He conceded that the GTP would not monopolize the pass; indeed, it could not by act of Parliament.[47]

Thus, the GTP secured the most important element of its route across the Mountain Section. Unlike the company's attempt to secure approval for a 'branch' from the Yellowhead to Vancouver in 1909, the evidence does not support Regehr's claim that the company's primary motive for selection of the Yellowhead route was to drive the Canadian Northern out of the pass.[48] Coordination between the engineering and legal departments facilitated the application's authorization by both government department and regulatory agency. By exerting influence to hasten approval of the route decision, company officers obtained first choice of line through the pass, which they regarded as an important advantage.

GTP PUBLICIST TALBOT praised fulsomely not only the strategic acumen of the GTP management but also its methods for building a superior line. Most contemporary magazine articles on construction of the Mountain Section, including those in engineering journals, resemble the GTP pamphlets that the authors probably used as a major source.[49]

Three appraisals of the line deserve attention, however. In April 1909, Hays hired H.A. Parker, former chief engineer of the Rock Island Railway, to carry out an independent appraisal of the Mountain Section. To make a personal investigation of the condition and the prospects of the line, the engineer travelled across the largely uncompleted Mountain Section in May and June. In his report to the GTP president, Parker lauded the

G.T.P.

1st Passenger Train From Prince Rupert.

Mile 33. June 14, 1911.

F. Button Photo
Prince Rupert
No. 2-38

GTP inaugural passenger train traversing the first one hundred miles opened on the west end, June 1911. This view of the road seems to support Hays's boast that the company had located 'the shortest, most direct and economical line for operation of a transcontinental railway.'

company's engineering staff for locating a gradient of .4 per cent, but he suggested that in some areas the line should be built cheaply and then improved when steam shovels could be easily transported to the front. He also observed that the company practice of letting contracts for grading sections much longer than 100 miles resulted in an increase of unit excavation prices due to inaccessibility of the wilderness end. By confining activity to 100-mile sections at each end of the line, he claimed that it might be possible to reduce unit prices by 15 per cent. Unfortunately, Parker did not cost out the effect of the lower unit prices in his own estimate of the road. He noted only that his estimate was $51 million, presumably including the Prince Rupert terminus.[50] Maintaining that too many decisions were delayed by the bureaucracy at the head office of the engineering department in Winnipeg, Parker also advocated giving division and residency engineers more freedom in the field. To this suggestion Kelliher retorted that central decision-making not only ensured that the standard of construction met the specifications, but also aided residency engineers who for the most part were not performing adequately.[51]

The appraisal of Thomas Macnabb, a CPR engineer who inspected the almost completed line in the summer of 1914, was blunter. He concluded that the design was too good for the traffic the line would attract. His photographs of many slides and washouts led the CPR chief engineer to conclude that for a number of years maintenance charges on the GTP line would be enormous, contradicting Hays's claim that it would have low operating expenses. In an admittedly unsystematic valuation, Macnabb estimated the cost of the work he saw on the Mountain Section, including the Prince Rupert terminals, as $52 million. This low figure suggests that much of the GTP expenditure was wasted.[52]

Consulting engineer J.B. Berry, who inspected the GTP line for the Grand Trunk Arbitration in 1921, echoed Macnabb. Comparing some features of the road to those of the Chicago, Milwaukee & St. Paul, another recently completed transcontinental that was headed toward collapse, the engineer criticized the 'bad practice' of hauling steel and concrete 'to the front in advance of their own trains' for initial construction of bridges. He pointed to low gradients and permanent structures as the important elements of a standard 'too high for that time and place and population and traffic.'[53]

The first cost overrun concerning the Mountain Section actually increased the accounting cost of the prairie leg. The GTP chief engineer did not accept Schreiber's interpretation of a clause in the 1903 contract that called for the location of the dividing line between the Prairie and Mountain Sections at the 'eastern edge of the Rocky Mountains.' After making an inspection of the region during the summer of 1907, the government inspector had maintained that the dividing line should be located 140 miles west of Edmonton. It was in the interest of the GTP, however, to have as long a Mountain Section as possible since there would be no limit on the government's 75 per cent guarantee for that leg as opposed to the limit of $13,000 per mile for the Prairie Section. Accordingly, Kelliher followed Hays in contending that the line should be designated at Edmonton to compensate for 290 miles of GTP construction east of the town, which had exceeded the prairie estimate. Although the contract called for arbitration in case of disagreement, Hays demanded an immediate settlement to prosecute the work west of Edmonton, and the company settled on a compromise dividing line at Wolf Creek, 120 miles west of Edmonton. In their haste to settle, the company officers limited the government guarantee to $1.56 million for the Edmonton-Wolf Creek section, which ultimately cost more than $5 million.[54] This was a serious blow to keeping the fixed charges of the line at a manageable level.

An examination of the activities of Foley Brothers, Welch & Stewart Company (FWS), principal contractor for the GTP on the five grading contracts that traversed the province, reveals that the contractor increased the cost of construction in several ways. Here, we shall investigate the return it obtained from the railway company on the grading contracts. A review of scattered records of the railway company, the contractor, and reports of the federal government inspector provides some indication of the role of FWS in increasing the cost of construction for the company, particularly on the agency contract, the final contract spanning 415 miles between Aldermere on the west end and Tête Jaune Cache on the east end.

To appreciate the unusual features of the agency contract, something must be said about the nature and outcome of previous contracts between the contractor and the GTP. Under the corporate name of Foley Brothers, Larsen, & Co., Timothy and Michael Foley of St. Paul and Peter Larsen of Helena, Montana, had won contracts from the GTP for the grading of the Lake Superior Section in 1905 and the Saskatoon-Edmonton leg of the Prairie Section in 1906. Larsen's efforts to facilitate the sale of 10,000 acres on Kaien Island and its environs to the GTP certainly did not harm relations between the contractor and the railway company. With the death of Larsen in 1907, the company reorganized and, under a new corporate name, brought into the partnership Larsen's associates Patrick Welch, a railroad contractor from Spokane, and John W. Stewart, a Canadian who had started contracting in the 1890s. Winning contracts during the following decade from not only the GTP but also the CPR, the Canadian Northern, the Pacific Great Eastern, and several American roads, the firm became the largest railway contractor in North America.[55]

A comparison of the prices for excavation and clearing on the five GTP contracts in British Columbia in Table 3.3 reveals no obvious change in prices during the construction of the line. When one excludes the prices in the first contract on the west end, which required much heavy-rock work and tunnelling along the steep, fjord-like banks of the Skeena River, a pattern of rising prices on each successive contract emerges. The contractor, of course, defended the rising prices as a reflection of higher labour costs. But the following chapter suggests that FWS did not significantly increase the wages of its construction day labourers in British Columbia during the period. Railway company officers also did not defend the assets of the GTP by extracting the lowest price possible from the contractor.

Negotiations for grading the line in the Mountain Section commenced even before the completion of the GTP's agreement with the British Columbia government in 1908. An FWS price list for 24 February 1908, included in Table 3.3, suggests that FWS was prepared to grade the first hundred miles on the west end for prices not significantly higher than those obtained in the prairie contracts. Yet in the following month, the GTP awarded the contract at unit prices 7 to 22 per cent *above* those which FWS was prepared to accept. Such an increase in price forced the GTP to pay FWS an additional $1.4 million for the work on the first contract, the final cost of which was $6.8 million. It was therefore not surprising that the contractor requested that the GTP chief engineer not publicize the prices that were accepted. Although the FWS undertook to complete the section by November 1909, it did not finish the contract until the end of 1910, a delay of fourteen months. No penalty was levied against the contractor for the delay.[56]

As work on the first contract progressed, Stewart made an offer in

GTP inaugural passenger train stopped on the Skeena River bank, 1911.
The rock-fill roadbed in the river was expensive both to construct and to maintain.

Table 3.3

FWS tenders and FWS-GTP grading contracts in British Columbia, 1908-11

Sequence of negotiations and contracts	Excavation			Grubbing $/acre
	Solid $/cu. yd.	Loose $/cu. yd.	Common $/cu. yd.	
1. West End				
FWS price list, 24 Feb. 1908	1.40	.45	.28	375
Prince Rupert-Copper River				
Contract, 19 Mar. 1908				
Prince Rupert-Copper River	1.50	.55	.32	400
2. West End				
Stewart tender, 18 Aug. 1909				
for 'gap' between ends of steel:				
in 3 seasons (end 1912)	1.45	.60	.32	
in 4 seasons (end 1913)	1.35	.55	.28	
Contract, 5 Nov. 1909				
Copper River-Aldermere	1.35	.55	.28	300
3. East End				
Contract, 21 Jan. 1910				
Miles 100-179, Wolf Creek West	1.45	.55	.30	
4. West End				
Contract, 31 July 1910				
Prince Rupert waterfront	1.35	.55	.28	300
5. 'Gap' (Aldermere-Tête Jaune Cache)				
FWS demand for 'gap,' 11 Oct. 1910	1.35	.55	.35	300
FWS tender, 15 Aug. 1911				
in 3 seasons	1.40	.60	.32	
Agency contract, 19 Aug. 1911				
(maximum)	1.47	.63	.34	

Sources: Minnesota Historical Society, Foley Brothers Records; NAC RG 30, vol. 3355, file 1622

August 1909 to grade the 'gap' between current contracts on the east and west ends, a distance of 550 miles. He presented alternative prices to complete this work in three or four seasons.[57] Given an opportunity to hasten completion at admittedly higher prices, the railway company opted instead for a lower pace of construction at lower prices. But the GTP let only the next 136 miles on the west end (Copper River to Aldermere) because it was negotiating with the government for an extension beyond 1911 for completion of the line.[58] With the exception of loose rock, the unit prices were substantially lower than those accepted for the first contract, in part because the next section involved less rock work on the banks of the Skeena. The final estimate of $8,240,542 for the second contract led FWS to complain that it had not made an adequate profit on the work. Yet in January 1910, FWS agreed to extend the first contract on the east end of the Mountain Section to Tête Jaune Cache at much lower prices.[59]

As these contracts were completed, the railway company had to make a decision about the final contract for the 'gap.' In October 1910, Stewart declared that the high price of labour would make a higher unit price for excavating common earth necessary if the contractor were to make even a small profit on the last contract. But he also allowed that FWS would be willing to do the work on a percentage basis, an element in contracting on the NTR Eastern Division for which the company had been criticized.[60] In August 1911, FWS made a formal offer with unit prices close to its 1909 offer for completion in three seasons. Its estimated date of completion was the end of 1914. The railway company, faced with going to Parliament for more support, now required a more rapid completion. Hays first considered building the entire contract on force account, i.e., at premium rates, but Schreiber vetoed such a course. The government engineer did, however, accept the second GTP suggestion that the contract be let on a percentage or cost plus basis.[61] Accordingly, FWS and GTP signed a memorandum of agreement in which FWS acted as an agent for the railway company rather than as a contractor. FWS would hire and pay subcontractors to do the work and take 5 per cent of the actual prices it paid subcontractors. Although the prices set out in the FWS tender of August 1911 were to be maximum unit prices, FWS would hire subcontractors to perform the work at the lowest possible price, regardless of the maximum figures. For work which exceeded the unit prices, FWS would receive no commission.[62]

Thus, the agency contract contained no maximum unit prices, although it referred to them, and it relied on FWS to keep costs down. The GTP solicitor was astute enough to realize that the memorandum of agreement did not enforce the maximum unit price and drew up a complicated addendum to permit the GTP to object to any work the company thought could be done for less. But, as the GTP engineer later observed, FWS was in effect taking charge of construction.[63] For a promise to keep prices below those that the GTP had found unacceptable in August 1911, the railway company undertook to pay FWS the unit price and 5 per cent more. While most of the agreements with the subcontractors contain prices that, even with the FWS commission of 5 per cent, were slightly lower than the maximum unit price, there was no incentive on the part of FWS to inspect closely the cost of the work. With the attendant 5 per cent commission, the price the GTP paid FWS for excavation of loose rock on several subcontracts frequently exceeded the maximum unit price.[64]

Complete quantities of excavation have not survived for the agency contract, so it is impossible to determine total cost according to various prices. On commission alone for supervising the grading contract, FWS made more than $1.3 million. This figure does not include revenues that the principal contractor obtained from renting equipment and selling goods to subcontractors at a return of 10 per cent.

In 1910, FWS bid not only to grade the remainder of the GTP line but also to build the concrete substructures for steel bridges across the major rivers. In July it won a contract to do this work with a basic price for concrete piers of $15.00 per cubic yard.[65] Later that year, FWS balked at completing the gap at prices then acceptable to the GTP, and the substructure contract evidently lapsed. When FWS obtained the agency contract in 1911, rather than perform the substructure work itself, it sought a subcontractor. In August 1912, it accepted a tender from the Chicago firm of Bates and Rogers with a concrete price of $17.00. However, the contract was never executed because of 'a legal interpretation of the conditions of the tender.' Thus, as a government inspector later concluded, the railway company allowed the subcontractor to work for a year without a legal contract.[66]

In September 1913, FWS drew up a new contract with substantially higher prices, including $19.50 for concrete. For the total work of the subcontractor, the change increased the price from $1,830,140 to $1,999,449, a difference of $169,309. On this extra amount, of course, FWS made its 5 per cent commission of $8,400. Just as significant was an arrangement where Bates and Rogers charged FWS (and ultimately the GTP) 65¢ per ton/mile to move its plant to the site. For freighting its plant to Fort George by scow, Bates and Rogers thus charged a rate of $205 per ton, whereas the most expensive charge by river steamers was currently $70 per ton. The change allowed Bates and Rogers to charge an extra $273,000 for freighting its plant to Fort George.[67] Thus, FWS's alteration of the contract in favour of the subcontractor resulted in an additional expenditure by the GTP of more than $500,000.

The extant records concerning one section of the road in British

Columbia illuminate not only the ideas of the engineers who made the location decision, but also how that decision led to cost overruns. Even though the GTP had selected and obtained government sanction for the route along the upper Fraser River from the west side of the Yellowhead Pass to Fort George district in 1906, it remained for the engineers to locate exactly an appropriate line along this difficult valley. During the following two years, engineers ran surveys. Early in 1909, the GTP applied for government sanction in two parts for its location 110 miles west of Tête Jaune Cache. This was granted in the same year.[68] When a GTP residency engineer for Mile 93-139, British Columbia, returned to the valley in 1911 ahead of the grading crews, however, he discovered that the approved location, 'high' on the south side of the valley, was vulnerable to slides from cut banks and gumbo, and ran an alternative line 'low,' closer to the river. He concluded that the revised location would be straighter, shorter, and would eliminate an expensive tunnel at Mile 139 in 'wet sliding ground.' Such a location would save $1.5 million in first cost. Not only would the low line be cheaper and safer to maintain, it would also facilitate the handling of local traffic since it was closer to the farms and logging camps on the valley floor.[69]

The local government inspector supported this revision but Kelliher evidently rejected the proposal. Both the GTP division engineer and the residency engineer resigned, charging that the chief engineer was supporting the existing line to please the contractors since it required more excavation.[70] A formal investigation was necessary, and Schreiber sent out an engineer who inspected only the first thirty miles west of Tête Jaune Cache. A comparison of the first cost and capitalization costs follows.

Capitalization was simply another name for the 'excess' discussed above in the calculation concerning route. What is striking about the calculation is the comparison of capitalization and first cost. Though the consultant noted that the GTP had a 'moral obligation to reduce distance and curvature,' even he admitted that capitalization based on twenty daily trains was unrealistic. It exceeded the GTP estimate used in the route decision of 1906 and almost doubled the prospective cost of alternative routes for purposes of comparison. Such excessive capitalization allowed the consultant to reduce the difference in cost between the revised and existing lines of $481,000 (37 per cent of the first cost of the existing line) to $160,000. Since the contractors had already excavated material worth $200,000 from the existing line at the time of the report,

Table 3.4

GTP estimates of cost of alternative locations, Tête Jaune Cache Westerly, Miles 0-30, 1912

	High (existing) ($)	Low (revised) ($)
First cost (excavation, grading tunnels, riprap, etc.)	1,285,000	804,000
Capitalization (20 trains daily)		
Extra distance	–	224,338
Extra curvature	–	114,397
Extra grade (minor)	–	13,832
Extra grade (ruling)	60,757	
Total	1,336,691	1,176,281

Source: NAC, RG 43, vol. 307, file 4402-YHP

the saving after capitalization is eliminated.[71] When the line opened, the actual traffic, estimated as eight trains per week, made comparison based on such capitalization absurd.

Although Schreiber was aware of the problem, he recommended that the minister support the existing line. It is ironic that the tunnel at Mile 139, against which the residency engineer advised, was abandoned after 800 feet had been driven at great expenditure and replaced by an extra mile of track, much to the chief engineer's chagrin.[72] On the high side of the valley, the line was also subject to more frequent slides of 'flowing mud,' which led in part to the overrun.

As a preceding section has indicated, the GTP let contracts according to rates for excavations of different types of rock or soil. While the unit prices for excavation moved upward after the second contract in British Columbia, they remained tied to definitions or classifications of the different types of material set out in the specifications for the Western Division approved by the government in 1905. Kelliher claimed that the engineering department had considered the experience of 'many large systems' before establishing its definitions. The three classifications were 'solid rock,' masses greater than a cubic yard that required blasting; 'loose rock,' masses less than a cubic yard that could be removed by pick and shovel, though not by ploughing; and 'common excavation,' all material that did not fit the first two categories.[73]

While FWS paid its major subcontractors various prices in the

Slide at Kidd, Mile 138, BC, 1914. A common product of weather and indurated clay or gumbo.

agency contract, the average price per cubic yard was $1.30 for solid, 52¢ for loose, and 32¢ for common. But in the drive toward the Rockies on both ends, grading crews came across a particular form of 'stiff blue clay in various degrees of hardness.' Since it could dissolve in water in fifteen minutes, it moved frequently in wet weather, knocking out the footing of wooden trestles. But in cold dry weather, it sometimes became as hard as rock. A government inspector noted that it could only be removed with difficulty with shovel and mattock; a steam shovel was more efficient. Where these were not available, blasting was necessary. But since it could usually be dissolved, the blue clay fell under the classification of 'common excavation.' At rates for common on both east end and west end, the subcontractors could not make a profit on its excavation.[74]

Although it was technically a form of indurated clay, one of the materials listed under 'loose rock,' Kelliher claimed that this 'clay rock' definitely did not fit the existing specifications. Here the GTP engineers ignored the experience of the CPR, which encountered blue clay or gumbo in the Selkirk Mountains in British Columbia in the 1880s.[75] Complaints by subcontractors prompted the first GTP response at the end of 1910. In the first contract on the east end of the Mountain Section, the GTP engineers simply changed the classification of gumbo from 'common' to 'loose rock.' When Schreiber discovered this, he claimed that classification must follow the specification and branded the GTP change as 'sheer nonsense.' Kelliher defended his engineers, stating that the GTP would 'not pay any contractor more for his work than he is entitled to.' A GTP division engineer in Jasper, however, justified the change in classification by explaining that close adherence to the specifications departed from the government's liberal policy east of Winnipeg.[76]

As the problem remained relatively minor for grading during 1911, nothing was done about the matter at that time. In spring of 1912, however, grading crews on the east end working along the Fraser River west of Tête Jaune Cache encountered large amounts of the blue clay. Both the company and the government now accepted the necessity for a new ruling, and in July 1912, Kelliher and Schreiber inspected a blue-clay cut at Mile 58, British Columbia. Schreiber admitted that heat or pressure had transformed part of the clay into shale rock, but would only allow a specific proportion of clay to be classified in this manner. The GTP chief engineer claimed that the government inspector had conceded that all blue clay might be classified as 'solid rock.' 'No railway company of repute ever awards contracts for less than they think the work can be executed with reasonable profit to the Contractor, and no contractor will undertake to do work for less than he thinks it will cost.'[77]

Both the company engineers and the inspectors admitted that contractors could not remove blue clay for the rates GTP paid major subcontractors on the agency contract for 'common' or even 'loose rock.' In August 1912, a government engineer observed that it was practically impossible 'to determine where loose rock ends and solid rock begins.' He suggested that a special rate between 'loose' and 'solid,' $1.00 per cubic yard, be established to deal with the problem. Other inspectors also suggested rates of between 80¢ and $1.00.[78] Yet while the GTP engineers evidently shared the inspector's perception that present rates were inadequate, they solved the problem in a different way by classifying most of the clay as 'solid rock.'[79]

For a 150-mile section of the grade along the Fraser River, the GTP engineering department reported excavation of quantities of solid rock by the end of 1912 that exceeded twenty-fold an estimate made by Kelliher in 1911. This effectively doubled the final cost of grading. In January 1913, an inspector observed that this reported excavation included a suspiciously large estimate of 'solid rock.' But the GTP engineering department refused to reveal how it arrived at these proportions. This led Schreiber to complain that the GTP engineering staff were 'running riot,' and he refused to certify amounts on the estimates that he claimed arose from 'overclassification.' In February, the government engineer ordered his inspectors to disregard samples from the most recent cuts, which contained 'solid' and 'loose rock' at a ratio of 3:1, and classify strictly according to definitions in the specifications, not upon the cost of the work.[80]

But the railway company now faced demands from the contractor. A division engineer in Fort George noted that under the present classification all estimates would show the contractor behind on his work. Consequently, the GTP engineers accepted the contractors' classification. When Schreiber deducted from the monthly certificates amounts that stemmed from overclassification, Kelliher attacked his action as a high-handed procedure.[81]

Directly, GTP president E.J. Chamberlin went over Schreiber's head to the railways minister, Frank Cochrane. Since Schreiber's deductions now totalled more than $600,000, the railway company experienced difficulty in paying its contractor, which in turn paid the subs. Chamberlin confessed that the company was 'now in great want of funds.' The minister agreed to pay the deductions provided the company put up security if an arbitration went against it. While the president accepted the offer, he angrily added that the company had already furnished $5 million at the outset of the 1905 agreement with the government and that should be sufficient. The minister was evidently not convinced, having 'no means of knowing if GTP are holding back from contractors large amounts.'[82]

The railway company now presented testimony from its principal contractor. In early February, FWS partner Stewart complained that the refusal of the government to pay the GTP estimates meant that FWS could not make final settlements with the contractors on sections that were completed. Without a final estimate (payment for most work), the contractors refused to move ahead to work on other sections of the line. Indeed, Stewart mentioned that one of the largest subs refused to move west to Fort George and was planning to pull his plant off the work. No matter what solution was reached, the unsettled state of affairs had already retarded progress very materially. While the complaint was addressed to the GTP, since it had guaranteed protection to FWS in the agency contract, such notice allowed the railway company to argue that the government's policy caused the stationmen and subs to leave work. By letting things drag along, the government would set the work back a year, and the railway and the government would eventually have to pay extraordinarily high prices in excavation prices and freight charges to bring the construction plants back into the country.[83] In early February, Cochrane submitted to cabinet a proposal to postpone all deductions until the end of May 1913, by which time the chief engineers of the company and the government would have worked out a satisfactory settlement. On 31 March, the proposal was issued as an order-in-council. In early April, Schreiber issued a certificate of $1,308,870 to cover the sums that had been deducted from the company's accounts.[84]

Kelliher now admitted that his staff had not followed the specifications to the letter and had overclassified. With prices of 50-58¢ for loose rock, the subs were losing heavily and would not continue. The company maintained that it must pay for the value of the work. But Kelliher did not want to raise prices in the contract since that would cause an increase in the subcontracts for the final sections of the line, which were not as difficult. He proposed rather that the government audit the books of the subcontractors and make good their losses. However, a government auditor noted that while the contractors' books were in order, present losses might very well turn into profits when one considered their current supply accounts.[85]

When an agreement was not reached by the end of May, Schreiber returned to withholding the monthly certificate, and the GTP was again caught short of funds in early summer. While a GTP vice-president claimed that the new government loan of $15 million would secure its expenditures from June on, he admitted privately that the railway company was now 'hard-pressed.' Cabinet passed two orders to extend the postponement to the end of 1913.[86]

The subcontractor that sustained the greatest loss, Siems-Carey, now resorted to excavating clay by steam shovel at the price of 'solid rock.' To increase its return, the subcontractor also began to classify even common earth this way. Defending this irregular procedure, Kelliher offered glibly the irrelevant observation that the principal contractor, i.e., FWS, was ultimately employing the shovel. This remark led Schreiber to repeat his denunciation that the GTP was running riot.[87]

In November 1913, the GTP engineering department abandoned any pretence of cooperation with Schreiber's office. Kelliher angrily proclaimed that the 'government had nothing to do with any contract the Ry Co. might see fit to make or the prices they agree to pay.' He intended to allow the contractors $1,000 profit per mile, and he instructed his engineers to accept such a classification from the contractors. There was, of course, no independent check on the contractors, as an investigator later remarked. Kelliher admitted that he arranged the classification to pay the cost of the work.[88] By the end of December, the contractors had submitted estimates containing $4.9 million for overclassified material. When Schreiber again withheld certificates in 1914 after the expiry of the last cabinet postponement order, an official of the Department of Finance informed the GTP that the government intended to 'release a substantial part in view of progress on construction account.'[89]

In February 1914, the cabinet issued yet another order to postpone deductions. In the meantime, Schreiber sought a rationale for a prospective retreat from his adherence to strict classification. When the deputy minister of justice declared that the company could vary prices even if it could not change classification, the statement proved adequate both for the railways minister and the inspector. On 28 April, the cabinet passed an order allowing an increase in clay prices on the grounds of Kelliher's statement that he had made such an arrangement with the contractors. Such an order must have been hard to swallow for Schreiber, since Kelliher had declared that he had undertaken to pay the contractors solid rock prices for the clay in 1912 with the inspector's approval if not quite at his suggestion.[90]

While it was probably inevitable that the railway company would have to pay more than the price set out in specifications to persuade the subcontractors to excavate large amounts of this troublesome material, the 5 per cent commission FWS secured on all excavation increased the cost of the overrun. More disturbing is that through much of the final year, the GTP ceased its supervision of the major subs, which must have encouraged them not only to overclassify but also to increase amounts. Even if the railway company had paid the subs $1.00 per cubic yard for all the clay, a rate that all the government inspectors in British Columbia advocated, the company would have saved $2,749,531 over submitted estimates. Kelliher probably secured the profits of the contractors; the chief engineer certainly increased the fixed charges for the railway company.[91]

The company had no more success extracting construction funds from provincial undertakings or obligations. The engineering showpiece of GTP railway construction on the Pacific slope was the Fourth Crossing of the Fraser River in Fort George district. Twelve steel spans eventually carried the line 2,658 feet into the new GTP townsite of Prince George. The centrepiece was the 100-foot lift span that a GTP engineer boasted was the most modern in Canada.[92] What made the bridge even more noteworthy, and expensive, were two twelve-foot roadways that bracketed the railway line.

Long before the line reached the Fort George district, GTP officials were looking for ways to reduce company expenditure on the major structures in British Columbia. When the provincial government approached the company about a combination railway-highway bridge at Fort George, Kelliher responded that the 'company would consider very favourably the idea,' and suggested a similar undertaking for the Nechako crossing near Fort Fraser. The GTP president made clear that the government must pay for the entire construction and maintenance of the highway portion. The provincial minister of public works, perhaps enthused by his government's recent electoral victory on the platform of building the Pacific Great Eastern Railway to connect with the GTP, decided that the combination bridge project was 'advisable for cost and public' and directed his officials to proceed. The deputy minister committed the government to the project set out by the company, only requesting plans for authorization.[93] In July 1913, Kelliher sent the government plans for a six-span structure including the lift bridging the east channel of the Fraser. The chief engineer added that he expected a pile bridge to carry the line and highway from an island near the centre of the river to the west bank, but plans for that section were not complete. The deputy minister certified and returned the GTP plans without comment.[94]

Late in the year, however, Kelliher made a personal inspection of the site and discovered that a pile bridge could not withstand the ice flows already playing havoc with the temporary construction bridge. He decided to extend the steel and concrete structure across the entire river. Early in 1914, Kelliher stated the government share would now be $420,000, the company expending $1,255,000.[95]

This information prompted the government to inform the GTP that it was cancelling the agreement 'as [there was] absolutely no traffic at that point to warrant any such expenditure.' Compared to the government bridge at New Westminster, which contained seventeen piers and cost only one million dollars, the company's estimate of the highway portion of the Fourth Crossing was extravagant. While the government was willing to spend $100,000, the sum the GTP required was out of the question. GTP general manager Morley Donaldson franticly telegraphed that materials had been ordered on Kelliher's estimate and that no change was possible now. After touting the value of the bridge for the PGE as well as for the territory east of Prince George, he concluded that 'it should be a calamity should the combination bridge not be carried out.'[96] His prediction included, of course, the GTP treasury.

GTP solicitor H.H. Hansard contended that the company had acted on good faith and 'cannot afford to bear so large an expenditure for a public work which is no part of its railway undertaking.' But the deputy minister was adamant that the addition of seven spans without consultation voided the earlier agreement, implying that the change unduly inflated the government's share. The government later contended that it had intended to spend no more than $150,000. To demonstrate that the company demand was 'out of all reason,' the deputy minister asked a consulting engineer to provide independent estimates of the cost of the highway portion. The consultant's estimate for the highway portion of the original design with wooden trestle was $188,230, and for the revised bridge $268,474.[97]

In December 1914, Hansard claimed that the change in bridge structure did not require prior government approval. He added that the completed lift bridge represented a goal of the government that it could never have achieved for the arbitrary sum of $150,000. Declaring that the company was within its rights, the solicitor demanded that the government pay the sum the company had expended. In the spring of 1915, the GTP blocked the highway portion of the bridge 'pending settlement of the dispute.' But the company had little leverage with the provincial government, and Hansard was reduced to dunning Attorney-General Bowser, pleading that reimbursement was of 'utmost importance to the [GTP] treasury.'[98]

Bowser turned the request aside with the observation that it was a serious matter in the present financial condition, out of all proportion to requirements. Hansard replied in August that the GTP was out of pocket for the money expended on a public work for the benefit of the province. 'We are not justified, even if we could afford it, in donating any proportion of this cost.' Finally, to avoid violence on the bridge, the government agreed to pay $150,000, and the company opened the roadway.[99]

The GTP was only able to extract a portion of the remainder in 1918 by refusing to fulfil its obligations to pay for sewers in Prince Rupert. When presented with a bill for $169,750, Chamberlin refused to deal with it until the province had settled the bridge dispute. Roughly splitting the difference between the GTP estimate ($420,000) and the government's ($268,000), the parties settled on $350,000, and the government finally paid its obligation later that summer. By cancelling its indebtedness in the sewer dispute, the company received only $30,250 for a significant expenditure made more than five years earlier.[100]

One other factor remains to be considered, the additional costs of construction from the Pacific coast. During its negotiations with the British Columbia government before 1908, the GTP management had made much of these costs. Of the three elements in the cost of the GTP Mountain Section, that Pacific construction affected, supply and labour expenditures undoubtedly rose while interest charges probably declined. Unfortunately, no company or government estimate of these costs has survived.

Following Morse's complaint in 1905, historian John Eagle points to the added expense of sending materials from eastern Canada via the CPR to Vancouver and then by water to Prince Rupert. To alleviate this burden, the GTP shipped some of its rails from mills in Nova Scotia around the Horn directly to Prince Rupert.[101] More significant was the cost of labour on the west end. With reported costs per day above east end labour decreasing from 43 per cent in 1908 to nil in 1913, one would expect total labour costs on the west end over five years (1908-13) to be on the order of 100 per cent more than the cost for similar work done on the east end if the differential declined at a uniform rate. Yet royal commission valuation of the Prince Rupert-Smithers Section, the western 227 miles that represented 27 per cent of the entire length of the Mountain Section, represented only 34 per cent of the valuation of the Mountain Section. Shortage of labour on the west end probably kept down the expenditure on higher wages and supply costs.

Most important was the effect of Pacific construction on the interest charges and the construction schedule for the British Columbia line. If we assume that all the inputs at the west end could have been transferred to the east end, then there would be no change in completion date, no change in interest charges. However, the following chapter indicates that the company had difficulty supplying its existing force on the east end. It was highly unlikely that the GTP and its contractors could have organized a front with twice the number of men. If we assume that the railway would not have been built more rapidly from the east end, only the eastern third of the line through British Columbia would have been completed by 1914. For completion in 1920, the six construction seasons required on the west end, interest charges would have increased significantly. Thus, Pacific construction might have saved the company more in interest charges than it lost in added labour and supply costs.

With construction so far from completion on the east end at the outbreak of war, however, the company might well have convinced the government that construction be halted for the duration and that it operate only to Prince George where the PGE was expected to arrive from Vancouver. Such a decision would have delayed or prevented the expenditure of $35 million on the construction of the west end. Pacific construction eliminated the justification for expenditure delay, which Rivers Wilson had sought in 1903.

WHAT HAS BEEN DISCUSSED ABOVE is not a complete examination of the cost overruns in the construction of the Mountain Section. In a commentary on the royal commission valuation, for example, a government engineer noted that submitted engineering and legal expenses for the Mountain Section, $5,355,479, exceeded the valuation by 35 per cent.[102] However, no data have been discovered to evaluate or explain how the increase occurred.

When one turns to other railways built over mountainous territory during the same period, the cost increases on the construction of the GTP do not appear exceptional. In 1914, one of the partners of the Canadian Northern admitted to McBride that the increased cost of his company's British Columbia line left him 'dumbfounded.' In a study of construction costs on several American railroads west of the Rocky Mountains, the *Railway Age Gazette* noted that the average cost of grading alone 'in heavy mountainous country' was $120,500 per mile.[103] With significantly higher unit prices, the corresponding average cost of grading alone on the Mountain Section of the GTP was $57,700 per mile. Table 3.5 indicates that several other contemporary roads experienced increases in construction costs similar to, or greater than, the GTP. One must be wary of reading too much into this comparison since the accounting procedures were different for each road. It is not clear whether the reported cost after construction for the other roads represents a 'first' cost, i.e., construction cost alone, or a 'general' or global cost including land and interest charges. Nevertheless, the comparison suggests that the cost increases on the construction of the GTP Mountain Section were not unique. None of the other roads recovered their costs before 1920; the construction increases played an important role in their failures.

As certified by Schreiber, for the entire GTP main line, the 'final' first cost, i.e., construction cost alone, was $109,828,588; for the Mountain Section alone, $78,269,721. Using the valuations of segments of the road found in the royal commission, one can estimate the first cost of the British Columbia line as $70.4 million. Excluding the added cost of labour and supply for Pacific construction, the sum of the cost increases and overruns on the Mountain Section discussed above, $27.4 million, represents 35 per cent of the first cost of the Mountain Section. In addition, the location of the Mountain-Prairie Dividing Line resulted in an immediate additional charge of $1.6 million to the Prairie Section. While not as spectacular as those for the National Transcontinental, the increases and overruns on the GTP Mountain Section went far to create the fixed charges that the company could never overcome.[104]

Table 3.5

Comparison of cost increases on construction of railways

		Initial estimate ($1,000/mile)	Estimate after location ($1,000/mile)	Cost after construction ($1,000/mile)	Increase $\dfrac{\text{Cost after construction}}{\text{Initial estimate}}$
GTP Mountain Section 832.5 miles					
(company	*First*	50	66	88	1.76
figures)	*General*	50	66	114	2.28
(government	*First*	67	70	94	1.40
figures)	*General*	67	70	112	1.67
Canadian Northern Pacific 499 miles (main line only)		—	50	70	>1.40
Western Pacific 925 miles (main line)		41	—	86	2.09
Chicago, Milwaukee & St. Paul Pacific extension 1,399 miles (main line)		32	43	71	2.21
National Transcontinental 1,804 miles (main line)		27	63	88	3.26
Pacific Great Eastern 480 miles		25[*]	57	84[**]	3.36

 * Estimate for predecessor company, Vancouver, Westminster & Yukon
 ** Cost for 348 miles only

Sources: Canada, Royal Commission to Inquire into Railways and Transportation, *Report;* Canada, National Transcontinental Railway Investigating Commission, *Report;* T.D. Regehr, *The Canadian Northern Railway: Pioneer Road of the Northern Prairies, 1895-1918* (Toronto 1976); A.M. Borak, 'The Chicago, Milwaukee and St. Paul Railroad: Recent History of the Last Transcontinental,' *Journal of Economic and Business History* 3, 1 (Nov. 1930):81-117; W.C. Odisho, 'Salt Lake City to Oakland: The Western Pacific Link in the Continental Railroad System' (PhD diss., History, University of California 1941); B. Ramsey, *PGE: Railway to the North* (Vancouver 1962)

Table 3.6

First cost, GTP, 1916

	Actual ($)	Estimated ($)
Mountain Section	78,269,721	
BC Line		
As .81 (length		
of Mountain Section)		63,398,474
As .90 (weighted in		
valuation)		70,442,748
Prairie Section	31,558,867	
Total main line	109,828,588	

Source: Canada, Royal Commission to Inquire into Railways and Transportation, *Report*

What this chapter has also shown is the disinclination of the GTP engineers to eliminate or control those increases. Ignorance or complacency toward cost increases went far beyond the engineering department, however. Faced with construction of the Mountain Section on the Montreal-Toronto standard with the government's original three-quarters guarantee of no more than $30,000 per mile, Hays blithely assured Rivers Wilson in 1903 that the road could be built at an average cost not exceeding the subsidies.[105] As Innis suggests, the GTP management, bedazzled by the prospect of building largely at government expense, at least in the short term, took few steps to control its construction expenditure. By 'banging right through on a straight line,' i.e., by locating and building its line to the Pacific coast with little 'regard to the traffic that was in sight,' the company had, according to a government engineer, created an extravagant railway 'about one hundred years too soon.'[106]

FOUR

'TOO GOOD OR TOO FAT FOR THE JOB':
LABOUR RELATIONS

AN EXAMINATION of labour relations during the construction of the GTP line in British Columbia reveals a variation on the theme of company attitudes toward the costs of building. Though the GTP and its contractors placed steam shovels and dinky engines on the construction fronts, men with picks, shovels, and barrows still did most of the grading.[1] From the management perspective, a sound labour relations strategy could have reduced the estimated expenditure of $50 million on the construction of the British Columbia line, undoubtedly the largest input.[2] Since the 1890s, American railway companies had established personnel departments and implemented some of the principles of scientific management and industrial betterment. The CPR had already imported some of these techniques, if only for its shop employees.[3] In the early years of the twentieth century, labour on the GTP, as in other large corporations, represented a problem that company officers attempted to solve. But the GTP response to its particular labour problems was not only backward but also wasteful. It probably increased final construction costs.

To examine the GTP stance toward its construction workers departs from the subject of most academic studies of railway labour in North America. Only for the running trades and shopmen have historians so far systematically assessed the role of management, along with other factors, in determining working conditions.[4] In accounts of the navvy, by contrast, students in Canada have long been content to draw on anecdotes and scattered data across the country to create a profile of the blanketstiff, rather than undertake a detailed examination of the worker in a particular system or region.[5] Like the Native peoples in histories now regarded as suspect, such an approach implies that railway construction labourers were largely undifferentiated and driven by the same considerations in every location.[6]

Generalization is an essential part of any historical investigation, but conditions differ over time and place. So do managers as well as their workers. A close study of 'the circumstances directly found, given, and transmitted from the past' under which, in this case, GTP managers laboured promotes a more sophisticated understanding of the actions of both boss and worker.[7] The following examination of some aspects of labour relations during the construction of the British Columbia line illuminates ambiguities in the management agenda for its workers.

Even such a limited study goes well beyond the scattered remarks on labour relations on the GTP in several genres. With the exception of company publicist Talbot, students of the GTP have largely ignored labour.[8] Those with interests in the working class have usually subordinated an examination of labour relations on the GTP to an account of the larger strike on the Canadian Northern in 1912.[9] While local histories sometimes imply that the nature of station work or the pricing of goods at the contractor's store offered possibilities for exploitation, they more frequently relate anecdotes concerning the navvy's predilection for booze and whores.[10]

The apparent cause for the lack of studies on navvies is the dearth of sources.[11] The records of the GTP legal department, the major source for an examination of other aspects of GTP activity in British Columbia, say little about working conditions or industrial disputes on the construction of the line. Yet labour newspapers, proceedings of two royal commissions, and the payrolls of part of the work force allow a more ambitious study than those noted above. After outlining the size of the work force and suggesting reasons for its high turnover, this chapter examines the management perception of the labour shortage, its attempts to import Asian workers, and its response to challenges to its authority and demands for greater expenditure on wages.

How many men built the line? Again, the destruction of the company's engineering records makes difficult an accurate response to this important question. Table 4.1 draws specific counts from the reports of government inspectors and contractors and rounded estimates from local newspapers. Although tentative, the table suggests a number of observations. First, the railway company and its contractors probably had difficulty supplying a force of more than 3,500 men at either end, particularly after the fronts moved beyond the environs of Prince Rupert and Edmonton. Continual complaints of supply shortages at both ends make implausible

'GTP construction days.' This view captures both the old and the new approach to railway building in British Columbia.

the claim of company opponents that upwards of ten thousand men were building the line in British Columbia at the height of construction.[12]

Second, the size of the work force changed significantly at both ends. On the east end the pattern of change suggests a swell of navvies preceding and accompanying the steady westward movement of the end of steel. On the west end, however, the erratic growth stems largely from widespread desertion and several strikes. But the table obscures the organizational units that in large part determined both wages and working conditions. On the GTP grade, construction work was divided among three different organizations: the railway company proper; the contractors; and stationmen, groups of men who worked as subcontractors. Of the three, company day labourers, ranging between 8 and 15 per cent of the work force, usually secured the highest wages and best camps.[13]

As the following sections set out, the company continually complained about the shortage of labour, particularly on the west end. The causes of the shortage, high turnover and inadequate replacement, stemmed from workers' appraisals of wages and working conditions. For company employees, one can track wages through a semiannual sampling of surviving payrolls.[14] A government agent's report in 1909 and an admittedly partisan newspaper account during the 1912 strike provide some comparative data on contractors' day labourers.[15] For the stationmen, unfortunately, one must rely on scattered testimony and anecdote. A review of wage rates on the west end for the first two groups suggests

Table 4.1

Number of construction workers on GTP line in British Columbia, 1906-14

	West End	East End (BC only)	Estimated total
1906 August	49 (Kaien Is.)	—	50
1907 August	98	—	100
1908 November	1,835	—	1,850
1909 April	2,600	—	2,600
1909 June	3,051	—	3,100
1910 November	2,160	—	2,200
1911 April	1,680	15	1,750
1911 August	2,112	1,387	3,500
1912 February	1,277	1,576	2,900
1912 July	2,772	1,900	4,700
1912 August	1,400 (strike)	2,000	3,400
1913 February	2,500	3,100	5,600
1913 November	3,100	3,342	6,500
1914 April	2,100	2,400	4,500

that those who worked a full month were able to meet a labour leader's calculation of the minimum monthly wage for supporting a family in Prince Rupert. Wages for most jobs did not rise after 1909, however.[16] Even during the construction workers' strike on the west end in 1912, the company did not choose to advance the rates of its own wage earners to encourage them to resist the promises and threats of the strikers. Thus, the claim of GTP managers that they were continually raising wages has no foundation among the railway company's own employees, in any case.

Even though the wages on the west end were usually described as 'very good,' the prospect of higher wages on the Alaska Railroad drew workers away from Prince Rupert after 1908.[17] The consequences of management's failure to offer competitive wages is more clearly shown in the following comparison of rates over distance in 1913. During the summer of 1913, the members of the British Columbia Royal Commission on Labour established the following 'normal' rates for railway construction.[18] From these rates, one can construct a crude gradient indicating that wages varied with the distance from 'civilization.' By 1913, there was no significant difference in wages between the two ends. These data also reveal that the Canadian Northern offered higher wages than did the GTP on the east end. Not surprisingly, the GTP general passenger agent complained that large numbers of labourers, transported at company expense to Tête Jaune Cache, deserted to the rival project in the same district. But instead of raising wages to the level of the Canadian Northern, the GTP solicitor advised that 'the only way to get these men to the front is to have them locked up in cars under sufficient guard to keep them there.' He proposed instead railway company constables who would arrest men who endeavoured to escape.[19]

More significant than wage rates in prompting dissatisfaction, however, were camp conditions. Largely controlled by the contractors, the provision of food, shelter, and medical services varied from camp to camp. The GTP general manager had confidently predicted that the navvy on the GTP line would enjoy food 'very superior both as to quantity and quality,' and dwell in 'comfortable quarters [with] due attention paid to sanitation.' Labour newspapers and testimony before the royal commission suggest, however, that contractors in British Columbia more frequently provided food 'unfit for a dog' and bunkhouses 'so filthy that a self-respecting pig would refuse to die in one of them.' Even supporters of the company during the 1912 strike admitted that medical services

Table 4.2

Wage rates on contract day labour for railway construction, summer 1913

West End				East End
GTP				GTP
Prince Rupert	Hazelton District	Fort Fraser	Prince George	Tête Jaune Cache
$3.00 (8-10 hours/ day)	$3-3.75 (10 hours/ day)	$5.00 (engineer)	$3-4.00 (10 hours/ day)	$2.75-3.00

Canadian Northern Railway

$3.25

Source: BCARS, GR 684, vol. 4, file 26

were inadequate. While justifying the conduct of the contractors, provincial government sanitary inspectors burned several camps that had contracted typhoid.[20] With its exorbitant markups for commissary goods and crude attempts to hold workers in the camps by issuing time checks instead of cash payment, the principal contractor, Foley Brothers, Welch & Stewart Company (FWS), earned the derisive label of 'Fool 'em, Work 'em and Starve 'em.' Uncompetitive wages and intolerable camp conditions produced a high turnover on the 'Overall and Tobacco Railroad.' One worker reminisced that for every man working, one was coming to the camp, and one was leaving.[21]

While the preceding chapter has indicated that the GTP and its principal contractor sometimes clashed over the estimates and prosecution of the five grading contracts on the line across British Columbia, they invariably acted in unison in labour relations. The company let contracts that called for the contractor and his agents to pay fair wages, provide decent and safe working conditions for labourers, and assume legal responsibility for any shortcomings in these matters.[22] But since the railway company had to step in for contractors who defaulted, company officers attempted to minimize cost and nuisance for the company by propping up the contractor. This goal produced an identity of interest between the GTP and at least the principal contractor in disputes with labourers. Although the GTP did not, for the most part, set wages and

'Passengers, first class, open-air express; ride now, pay later.' A wag's description of these navvies in front of a subcontractor's building at Tête Jaune Cache, circa 1913, suggests the managerial strategy to import replacement labourers, as well as worker disillusionment with the result.

establish camp conditions that provoked the disputes discussed below, the GTP president, general manager, legal department, and engineering department all supported the contractor's management rights in these matters. This is most apparent in the company response to demands for compensation for injuries on the job.

Even before the advent of construction in British Columbia, the GTP management realized that it would embark upon 'extremely hazardous construction through British Columbia,' i.e., construction that would entail a high number of accidents among the members of its labour force. And this prediction was accurate. While principal contractor John W. Stewart claimed that construction on the GTP actually produced fewer accidents than on any other contract, a Swedish consul advised his countrymen not to work for the GTP because of the number of accidents.[23]

In 1908, the GTP legal department received from a prominent solicitor in Vancouver an opinion on the provincial law concerning workers' compensation. Most odious for the railway company was Section 5, which stated that 'the Undertaker [of a project] was liable for injury to workmen under a contractor.' Indeed, the general effect of decisions in British Columbia courts entitled workers to compensation whether they were careless or not. The lawyer suggested that injured parties would be 'very apt to look to Ry. Co. itself rather than to take any chances of failure to secure payment from the contractors.' Such a practice made it imperative, he concluded, that both the GTP and contractors acquire liability insurance. Local insurance agents, obviously desirous of obtaining the GTP account, concurred. 'Laws in this province are very severe. When employers are sued; they have little chance of escape, especially big companies.'[24]

The legal department accepted these bleak evaluations of the liability law. One solicitor lamented that it 'practically amounts to a scheme of insurance for employees for which the company receives no consideration.' It might even be an encouragement to suicide. But though the legal department worked in concert with the solicitors of other railway companies for relief from such a draconian law, it did not recommend that the company create a liability insurance scheme. GTP assistant solicitor D'Arcy Tate argued that the company had no need for expensive insurance since the standard GTP contract contained a clause indemnifying the company against all claims of negligence made against the subcontractor. The solicitor also rejected compelling contractors to take out liability insurance.[25]

Of course, one way to escape suits was to coerce workers into waiving their rights under the law. Accordingly, FWS forced those who required paid transportation to Prince Rupert to sign a waiver that included the following clause: 'In consideration of advanced fare and the offer [of a wage of $2.50 per day], I hereby release FWS from all liability for injuries to person or property whether caused by the negligence of its servants or employees or otherwise.'[26] But Tate believed that the company had little to fear even from workers who had not waived their rights. Such a conclusion probably stemmed from one other point in the Vancouver lawyer's opinion on the British Columbia liability law. He had observed that the company would not be liable for injury stemming from 'serious misconduct or neglect of the workman.'[27] Such a remark suggested that the legal department could husband the company's resources most efficiently by resisting all claims, not only against the company, but also against contractors, on the ground that the employee had contributed to the injury. Tate thus acknowledged that an employee's claim of damages against FWS for loss of leg and arthritis in the remaining knee could be transferred to the GTP, but rejected the claim on the advice of a local agent who maintained that the employee had arthritis in both knees before losing a leg. The file suggests that the employee was unsuccessful in his suit.[28]

In most of the cases heard in Prince Rupert, the standard argument of the railway company's legal agents was contributory negligence, which freed both the contractor and the GTP of any responsibility in the accident. When a brakeman was knocked off a car in a freight yard and lost a leg, the GTP agent immediately convinced the employee while still in shock to sign an account of the incident including a statement that no one was to blame. When the injured man protested that the account was garbled and complained that his wages had been cut the same day, the agent made much of a vague promise by the superintendent that the GTP would find employment for him after he recovered. This undertaking said nothing about the wage.[29] The denial of responsibility also characterized the department's actions in holding back the payment of a deceased worker's salary to his widow, denying compensation to the family of a clerk who was killed helping a GTP client beyond the terms of employment, and rejecting the claims of a worker injured by a falling roof on a project that the railway company directly supervised.[30]

One can illuminate the attitude and actions of the legal department in an examination of the case of Joe Prégent, a GTP labourer crushed to death between a floating pile driver and a dock in Prince Rupert in October 1910. At the inquest, the construction foreman admitted that the pile driver had not whistled before moving and that Prégent could not hear his warning shout. But all Prégent's workmates signed identical affidavits that warning was given, and the coroner found no grounds for company negligence. Claiming that he had lost his only support through the death of his son, Prégent's father in Montreal nevertheless pressed for compensation of $3,000. The company expected this request but dismissed it as a pretence on the part of acquisitive solicitors. When the elder Prégent resorted to the courts in desperation, Chamberlin instructed Tate to see that the company's interests were protected.[31]

During the spring of 1911, Prégent's lawyers pressed for an arbitration, but the GTP's counsel opposed such a move. After the GTP legal agent committed a legal error that made arbitration probable, Tate authorized another Prince Rupert lawyer, L.M. Patmore, to make an immediate, much smaller settlement on the advice of the Prince Rupert general superintendent. When the old man refused to accept an offer of $1,500, Tate arranged for agents to spy on the man to discover the amounts the father had received from his son. To coerce the claimant into accepting the offer, Patmore then cited a recent court ruling that stated that non-resident dependents were not entitled to benefits from workers' compensation, and threatened to have the case dismissed. By August, the GTP had compelled the old man to reduce his claim to $1,000. Although Tate had authorized payment of $1,000 as a settlement, Patmore forced Prégent to accept $850. Both lawyers joked about the old man's insecurity and his reluctance to pay his own solicitor.[32] Thus, for Patmore's fee of $65, Tate had secured the company a saving of $2,150 as a settlement. He had shepherded the company's limited financial resources, and Patmore had obtained recognition from Tate as the most competent lawyer in Prince Rupert. A successful defence of parsimony toward the labourers resulted in liberality toward the helpful lawyer. Shortly after this case, Patmore became the new GTP legal agent in Prince Rupert.

In the short term, the company was successful in fending off large settlements for accidents.[33] By defending without hesitation the position of the contractors in these disputes, however, the company in effect assumed the responsibility for working conditions and labour relations, which it sought to place on the contractors. The legal department's success in resisting compensation demands only increased for bitter litigants and their comrades the attraction of those who challenged the company's authority.

Even during the first construction season on the west end, the labour shortage attracted the attention of senior managers. Although the local FWS superintendent boasted that the contracting company was getting the 'cream of labourers,' principal contractor Stewart admitted that his firm required 1,500-2,000 additional men, but with every boat landed, 25-50 per cent quit. At the end of the year, Collingwood Schreiber, the chief government inspector, remarked to the federal railways minister that the force was inadequate to finish the contract on the west end in a reasonable time.[34]

The year 1909 promised better things. Responses to a Department of Immigration survey of all major railway construction during the spring indicate that the wage of $2.50 per day that FWS offered in Prince Rupert was among the highest in Canada. By April 1909, the FWS local superintendent observed that the work force had grown to 2,600 but claimed that the company would require twice that number if it obtained the adjacent contract on the west end.[35] Labour disputes, discussed below, disturbed both the GTP and its contractors in Prince Rupert later in the spring, however. To recruit replacements for navvies who struck or quit, FWS had to place duplicate orders with Vancouver employment agencies and advertise daily wages of $3.50 to $4.00 in Seattle newspapers. The government inspector observed that FWS had only been able to obtain men by paying 'more than [it] can afford for navvy work.' Progress of construction depended on the supply of labour, but 'there does not appear to be a class of men in British Columbia available who are willing to work at railway construction in the wilds of the Rocky Mountains.' He belittled those who rejected railway construction work as 'too hard' and preferred to walk the streets of British Columbia towns. To complete the railway in four years, Schreiber claimed that the contractors must obtain immediately a work force of 25,000. The perceived shortage also prompted GTP president C.M. Hays to declare that completion of the line on time required 'more men of the right kind.'[36]

At the beginning of the 1910 construction season, the shortage of labour on the west end became acute. In May, a subcontractor in Prince Rupert declared that only a relaxation of immigration restrictions would allow FWS the 3,000 men it required. In July, a GTP vice-president pleaded with the immigration department to relax regulations so that GTP subcontractors on the Pacific could get half the men they require.[37]

The visible shortage of labour led to renewed speculation among all parties on its cause. Concerning construction on the west end, Hays remarked in Vancouver in June that 'the only thing that worries us ... is the scarcity of labour. Where do all the men who come out to the coast go to? The contractors are always complaining, and yet as I came through this time, every coach of every train bound west was packed.' A Prince Rupert newspaper fumed that the Canadian worker had 'grown too good or too fat for the job.' Schreiber averred that the slow construction works resembled nothing so much as 'a hen's little scratching, and all through the scarcity of labour.' He confessed he did not know 'what's the matter with labour in B.C. On the Prairies there is good labour available, but for some reasons it cannot be got in this province.'[38]

At the end of August, the GTP general manager declared that work on the west end was 'not getting along at all,' in part because the cost of labour was much higher than on the prairies. Grand Trunk chairman Alfred Smithers suggested the cause. In an interview in Victoria, he deplored the rise in the cost of labour because it led to an enormous overrun in the cost of construction. It was now impossible to get half the men wanted for construction work even at a wage of $3.00-3.50 per day. While he admitted that the company might have offered higher wages in the past, he maintained that navvies were 'getting more than their fair share today.' Yet the company still lacked 5,000 men.[39]

In September 1910, Stewart formally declined to commit the FWS plant to the construction of the last contract, the 415-mile gap between Aldermere in the west and Tête Jaune Cache in the east. He cited the difficulty of hiring men for camps even at $3.00 per day and claimed that work was progressing so slowly on the second west end contract that the company would lose money. In Prince Rupert, Hays declared that the labour shortage was 'the real problem all the time now.' While the GTP president still expressed a preference for white labour, he now revealed that 'we will take every kind of labour we can get.'[40]

Within these interviews and statements can be found the GTP president's most revealing comments on the reasons for the shortage of labour on the GTP west end. After the British Columbia premier had rejected a request for grants of homesteads to GTP labourers, Hays lamented that 'nothing could be done to accelerate the tardy pace of construction.' But Hays was not always so small-minded. The president had evidently read some of the government reports concerning deplorable camp conditions and was aware of the complaints. '*If* the camp conditions were not adequate,' Hays mused in an interview, the railway company would improve the conditions 'and so secure all the labour we want.' At least once he realized that the railway company could alleviate, if not eliminate, the shortage of labour. But he retreated from even this hypothetical formulation and disputed reports that the company did not provide suitable accommodation, good wages, and the best food. He regarded navvies as 'a class who like to be where they can spend half their time in palaces of amusement, and such resorts are not to be found in the interior.'[41] Thus, the fault for the labour shortage lay not with the railway company, but with the navvies. This view informed the company's actions toward labour.

At least one contemporary recognized the railway company's role in the labour problem. The *Edmonton Journal* maintained that the labour shortage stemmed from 'circumstances over which Hays and Smithers have absolute control and which they could amend merely by issuing the orders.'[42] But the company officers adhered to the views of the president and, for the most part, regarded the GTP's problems with labour as the fault of labourers. This perception prevented managers from reaching the obvious solution, the improvement of working conditions. Accordingly, the GTP was still short of men as late as the construction season of 1913. In May, the chief engineer reported that 2,000-3,000 additional workers were needed to speed work on closing the gap between the two ends of steel in British Columbia.

Rather than increase wages or improve camp conditions to attract more white workers as the Edmonton paper advised, the company remained intent on building the line at pay rates as close as possible to the ones envisioned in 1903. By 1909, wages had risen dramatically by more than 30 per cent, complained the Grand Trunk president. If white workers would not work for such inflated wages, the company would employ 'any kind of immigrant.' Though the company also sought labourers from Russia, the obvious alternative was workers from China or Japan, and Hays had requested the import of Asian labour even before construction began in British Columbia.[43]

But this solution entailed a conflict with the British Columbia government. By the early 1900s, after the federal government had disallowed

several provincial attempts at exclusion, a series of provincial governments had settled on a policy of obstruction to Asian immigration. It was
not surprising, then, that the first formal reaction of the provincial government under Premier Richard McBride to the GTP project was a
request in August 1903 that the prohibition of Asian labour be inserted
into the company's charter.[44] When the Laurier government ignored this
request, the premier forwarded the minute again in March 1904, claiming that its 'considerations are of so important a nature and affect the
interests of British Columbia so deeply.'[45]

    During the negotiations for Kaien Island, the railway company had
steered clear of the anti-Asian agitation that troubled the province. But
in November 1906, General Manager F.W. Morse asked his solicitor to
interview the federal minister of labour on the subject of importing
Japanese labour for the GTP. In December, GTP agent E.G. Russell held a
meeting in Vancouver with Saori Gotoh, director of the newly formed
Canadian Nippon Supply Company, whose aim was to import Japanese
labourers for work in Canada. To aid Gotoh in convincing the Japanese
government that he could secure a contract from the GTP, Russell wrote
out the following declaration. 'Upon the subject of Japanese labour for
general and railway work in Northern British Columbia, I would say
5,000 men will undoubtedly be required ... There could not be any objec-
tion to giving an exclusive right to supply Japanese labour required.'[46] At
the hearings of the Royal Commission on Oriental Labourers held in
Vancouver the following year, a GTP officer claimed that Russell had
overstepped his authority in making even such a general statement since
only Morse could execute an agreement to engage Asian labour. But the
GTP's approach to the Department of Labour in November indicates
that Morse's declaration that 'no arrangements had been made' expressed
only the result, not the intent, of the railway company's actions. While
the commissioner's conclusion that the GTP had not entered into a formal agreement for Japanese labour was accurate, more perspicacious was
the observation of a former BC attorney general that the GTP's rejection
of a formal agreement 'may not have proceeded from any desire not to
employ or to promote Japanese immigration into this country, but to the
fact that they [GTP] do not need labour at this particular time.'[47]

    Russell's statement produced more immediate difficulties for the
railway company, however. The GTP was not Gotoh's only customer; he
had already made arrangements with both the Dunsmuir coal interests

and the CPR. To draw these contracts Gotoh had engaged Conservative lawyer W.J. Bowser, who evidently became aware of Russell's statement.[48] On the day before the provincial election in February 1907, the Conservative *Vancouver Daily Province* ran a front-page story with the sensational headline 'Fifty Thousand Japanese for British Columbia.' The article, an unacknowledged account of a speech Bowser would deliver to a rally in Victoria several hours later, alleged that the GTP had poured money into Liberal coffers to elect a new government that would not only accede to company demands for the Metlakatla Indian Reserve adjacent to Prince Rupert, but also no longer pass immigration and labour bills hindering the import of Japanese navvies. If the Liberal government were elected, the article warned, the GTP would import 50,000 Japanese labourers in the following year, and even worse, settle them along the line after construction was completed. While Bowser fulminated against secret agreements in which Russell's own construction firm would erect huge barracks for Japanese labourers who would then be hired innocently by the GTP, he produced no evidence to support this claim.[49]

Such a scenario was probably not far from the wishes of the GTP management, but the surviving documents on the matter are ambiguous. The files of the legal department contain no agreement with Russell's construction company. Bowser probably made the charge because Russell had apparently contacted the Liberals during the election even though head office instructed him to stay out of the campaign. Whatever his action, it incurred McBride's animus. After the election, McBride informed Morse that 'the attitude of some of your representatives in this country created the impression of a feud.'[50] Russell, of course, denied all the allegations, and the Liberal *Victoria Daily Times* attacked the article as a 'roorbach,' but this information did not circulate widely on election day. The Conservatives won a smashing victory including all five seats in Vancouver, at least three of which the Liberals had expected to take.[51]

Even though the company shortly replaced its agent, it now faced a provincial government that had won an election in part by alleging that the GTP wished to import Asians. Any agreement between the GTP and the provincial government must now address directly the question of Asian labour. Although the GTP persuaded the government not to insist on a formal ban of Asian labour within the general settlement that the two parties signed in February 1908, it obtained this concession only by giving the government a formal undertaking on the matter. On the day the agreement was signed, a GTP vice-president gave McBride a written undertaking that in the construction of the railway within British Columbia, 'white labour shall be exclusively employed unless otherwise permitted by the Lieutenant-Governor in Council.' At the end of the year, the railway company executed a more formal document under company seal in which the ban on Asian labour was extended to the railway company's contractors, agents, servants, and assigns.[52]

The examination of GTP engineering department payrolls for Kaien Island in Table 4.3 indicates that the undertaking to ban Asian labour had little effect on hiring practices in at least one important case. By the end of 1907, the Prince Rupert *Empire* charged that the number of Japanese labourers had grown to 125, over a third of the island's population.[53] Questioned about this practice at the proceedings of a royal commission in November 1907, a GTP agent admitted that both contractors and the railway company itself employed Chinese and Japanese at Kaien Island. He explained that the Asians had simply 'drifted in' and were doing only 'menial work ... round the table and cleaning dishes.' Such a description ignored the Japanese employees who usually worked as axemen. GTP harbour engineer J.H. Bacon bluntly declared that 'it is the policy of the railway company to place no restrictions whatever on the contractors as to the character of the labour that they shall employ.'[54] After the GTP made the undertaking, Asians continued to find regular employment with the company. A cursory examination of other payrolls suggests the GTP continued to hire Chinese regularly as cooks for both engineering parties and, less frequently, construction gangs, up to 1912 on the west end.

For two years after the ban, the railway company insisted that its hotel in Prince Rupert employ at least a token Asian work force, as a possible precedent for a larger force for railway construction itself. By refusing to

Table 4.3

Asian surnames on GTP engineering department payrolls, Kaien Island, 1906-9

	May 1906	Aug. 1906	Feb. 1907	Aug. 1907	Feb. 1908	Under-taking	Aug. 1908	Feb. 1909
Total surnames	31	49	186	89	81		98	179
Chinese surnames	3	4	13	7	5		7	3
Japanese surnames	0	0	9	16	19		5	10

Source: NAC, RG 30, vols. 6864, 7050

forsake Asian help, the GTP violated the terms of the 1908 undertaking in a public manner, and probably prompted the British Columbia government to withhold the issue of the hotel's liquor licence. Only in the summer of 1910, at the insistence of a local licence commissioner, did the GTP insert into its licence application an undertaking to eliminate Asian employees. It received its licence immediately.[55]

Leaving junior officers to deal with the problems of the labourers that the company and its contractors had secured, the GTP senior management expended much effort over the next four years in repeated attempts to convince the provincial government to revoke the ban. Using as a pretext the studied remarks of Schreiber on the labour shortage, Hays would approach McBride at the height of the construction season and propose that the company, without endangering the rights of white workers, might import Asian labourers under bond. With the same regularity McBride would turn down the suit. These rejections caused much wringing of hands and remarks about damage to the company, but the managers returned the following season.[56] At the height of the strike on the British Columbia line in 1912, E.J. Chamberlin, now president, informed McBride that FWS could not obtain Austrians or Italians for west end work. If the ban was not revoked, Chamberlin predicted that completion would be delayed for at least one year. But when McBride reiterated that his government still opposed the wholesale importation of labourers, the company apparently gave up.[57]

THE COMPANY had failed to secure its preferred solution to the labour shortage. It now remains to investigate how the GTP responded to demands from the workers the government compelled it to employ. Though it did not sustain a significant loss, the company's record in turning back the challenges to its authority in Prince Rupert during the early years of construction was mixed. Its response to a major strike in 1912, however, probably delayed completion of the line.

While the conditions on the grade were weighted in favour of the employers, it did not mean that the railway company could automatically win every conflict with its workers. In a pair of disputes in Prince Rupert in 1909, the company had to deflect regulatory agencies as well as the concerns of provincial and federal politicians to maintain its hold on its suspect labour force. Dissatisfaction with contracts and pay rates also led to a legal challenge from a group of stationmen and a walkout of day labourers in March. If the railway company did not act carefully, appeals to both the federal fair wage clause and the 1908 general settlement might set very damaging precedents for a much larger number of workers.

The origin of the first dispute supports sociologist Edwin Bradwin's observation that stationmen could sometimes take advantage of a sub-contractor. Early in February 1909, a dispute concerning liquor occurred in the boardinghouse of Fred Peterson, one of the FWS subcontractors working east of Prince Rupert. The contractor decided that one of his cooks was to blame and summarily fired him. A station gang that had worked for the subcontractor since July 1908 hired him immediately as a teamster, however. When the gang refused to release him, and his replacement boardinghouse cook threatened to quit in consequence, Peterson dismissed the gang. Although Peterson offered to give them their estimate (payment for all work completed) or pay them off at $3.00 per day, they refused and brought an action in the county court at Prince Rupert. In March 1909, the jury found with the plaintiffs, giving the station crew both its estimate and damages amounting to $7,548. But Peterson had run a debt of $16,600 with FWS on an earlier contract in Manitoba, and the principal contractor intervened quickly to assert its prior claim, under the Creditors' Relief Act, to approximately $8,000 in tools and supplies at the Peterson camp. For six months' labour and damages, the station gang received only $939.50.[58]

Not content with the result, the stationmen approached the GTP's most vocal critic in Prince Rupert, John Houston. Taking up their cause, the *Empire* editor observed that the contractor, as 'practical railway builders,' had a system that was 'good for FWS, however poor it may be for the men who do the work.' Although 'speciously framed-up contracts' rendered contractors judgment-proof against the legitimate claims of stationmen, the editor predicted that 'public opinion will smash them [the contractors] just as they smashed the poor stationmen.' In the following weeks, Houston compared FWS prices for station work to much higher rates obtained on the Alaska Railroad.[59] Such charges attracted attention. On 5 April, a Conservative member referred to Houston's articles in the House of Commons and demanded that the claims be satisfied. In a complaint to the Department of Labour, Prince Rupert labour leader Patrick Daly noted that many men had been cheated of their returns for six months' work and consequently, 'the court and lawyer's office is a regular trail.'[60]

Acting on the question in the House, Schreiber declared that the Prince Rupert judgment vindicated the stationmen and refused to issue additional monthly certificates for the government share of GTP construction until the matter was settled. Though the GTP general manager responded that the decision concerned merely the claim of a subcontractor rather than the rights of employees, Schreiber would not budge.[61]

The government inspector's insistence on making good the judgment posed additional problems for the GTP. The division engineer explained that the prospective profit by which the jury calculated damages depended on blasting material, which should have been hauled to an adjacent fill, into the river. Such deliberate waste violated a clause in FWS contracts with all subcontractors and would encourage other stationmen to waste fill. Principal contractor J.W. Stewart charged that the stationmen had simply defaulted while in debt to the company. 'If we make a practice to allow stationmen to throw up their contracts whenever the notion strikes them and then pay them wages, we will have an endless amount of trouble.' He attached a legal brief on the Peterson case, and complained that it was unacceptable for FWS to pay every time stationmen 'get tired, simply quit, go to Rupert, and bring an action.' The FWS brief concluded that 'the only men who are kicking along the line about not being paid are stationmen, who take their work by contract in the hope that they can do better than by day labour, but, unlike other contractors, they are not prepared to accept the bad with the good.'[62]

In mid-May, the general manager sought an opinion from W.G. Biggar, the general counsel for the GTP. Biggar argued that the federal fair wages clause in the 1903 contract had been superseded by the 1905 mortgage agreement, which contained no such clause. Even if the clause were still applicable, it should not apply in a dispute of subcontractors rather than actual day labourers who have not been paid wages. Schreiber was evidently not impressed by the distinction; while he made no comment to his minister, he intimated to Laurier that correspondence about the 'contractors' failure to meet claims of workers' gave 'a clear vision of the case.'[63]

The stationmen sought other avenues to pressure the railway company. Their counsel, besides winning a judgment in a Prince Rupert court against the subcontractor, wrote William Templeman, now MP for Prince Rupert and British Columbia's representative in the cabinet, that FWS had in effect flouted the law. 'Foley [Welch & Stewart] pays for it if

Foley pleases, when Foley does not please, the stationmen can go to blazes!' Declaring that the 'ignorant man certainly deserves some protection,' the lawyer demanded legislation to prevent contractors from exploiting the workers in this manner.[64]

Templeman was less impressed by the legal merits of the case than by its political implications. He angrily wrote the railways minister that though the 'trouble' was not his, 'I shall have to shoulder it, whether I will or no, because I shall be then looking for votes.'[65] However, it appears that on this matter, the GTP and FWS prevailed against both Schreiber and Templeman, since the Prince Rupert newspapers contain no account of a settlement for the stationmen. In July, Schreiber began to issue certificates once more.

The second dispute arose from the activities of Patrick Daly, a carpenter who arrived in Prince Rupert in 1908. Daly clearly was ambitious. He intended to organize under the banner of the Industrial Workers of the World (IWW) not only Prince Rupert workers but also 'the entire continental railroad by starting at one end.' Since Daly believed that the GTP would 'work every conceivable means to ... keep wages down,' he sought political allies. In February 1909, he wrote to the local provincial member that neither the GTP nor FWS was paying the prevailing rate of wages in the district, which he claimed was $3.00 per day. The MLA, though a member of the Liberal opposition, declared that it was 'in the power of the government to see that the matter is made right.'[66]

This promising reply apparently encouraged Daly and other leaders of the local Workingmen's Association to challenge the wage rates of both the GTP and its principal contractor. On 8 March, most of the day labourers walked off work for one of the FWS subcontractors claiming they required more wages. The local government agent, William Manson, discovered that while 54 had a rate of $2.50, 41 received only $2.25 per day. The association maintained that these men, mostly 'Montenegroes [sic], must be kept up, otherwise English speakers would suffer.' When the FWS superintendent in Prince Rupert realized that Manson's hostility toward the lower rate made the current FWS position untenable, he promptly offered to raise the minimum wage to $2.50. Daly persuaded the men to refuse unanimously.[67]

When the railway company rejected the labour organizer's demands, Daly lodged a formal complaint with the federal Department of Labour that the GTP permitted its contractor to flout the fair wage clause of its

1903 contract. Besides referring to the specific dispute with the subcontractor, he claimed that the contractors' reckless care of their employees
endangered all working men on the GTP. To stir up racist feeling to support his case, he also enclosed copies of agreements to work for fifteen
East Indians who had paid employment agencies for the chance to work
on the GTP.[68] Houston then advanced this strategy. In early April, the
editor persuaded the Board of Trade of which he was president to strike a
committee to investigate fair wages in Prince Rupert. Following the
Empire's bald hint that wages of $3.00 to $3.50 per day had 'always been
paid' in the district, the Board of Trade passed a motion stating that
$3.00 per day represented a fair wage. Daly praised the decision as the
first of its kind to support the interests of manual labourers.[69]

The railway company effectively countered these actions, however.
After luring large numbers of men to Prince Rupert as replacements with
advertisements of wages of $3.50 to $4.00 per day, it blacklisted the strikers. When one labour leader urged men on an adjacent contract to join
the strike, police immediately arrested him. Although Daly claimed that
the strike had spread to 1,000 workers, there is no evidence in the federal
Labour Gazette, the Department of Labour files, or the local newspapers
that the strike grew.[70]

The GTP also prepared for the government inquiry. When the
Department of Labour approached the GTP concerning Daly's complaint, the chief engineer offered an elaborate defence. He extolled the
excellent organization that FWS had for taking care of its employees.
While he admitted FWS had paid $2.25 per day, he claimed that average
wage was more than one-third above the corresponding rate on the east
end. Before the advent of the railway, the engineer observed, most of the
workers in local canneries and sawmills were 'cheap Chinese and Japs.' By
claiming the GTP was responsible for bringing the majority of white
labourers to the district, he foiled Daly's attempt to raise the anti-Asian
issue. An investigation would show, he concluded, that the contractors
were honestly meeting their obligations.[71]

Principal contractor Stewart used the dispute as another opportunity to press the government for lower wages. Picketing had forced FWS
to meet incoming ships outside Prince Rupert in a launch to take men
directly up the Skeena to the railway camps. When FWS had taken the
contract, the company expected that $2.50 would be a maximum wage;
with a minimum of $3.00, FWS costs would increase by 20 per cent. He

suggested that such a raise would compel the company to build the rest of the line from the east end. Kelliher went further and declared that with such exorbitant wage demands and interference of labour agitators, it would only be a matter of time before the contractors were faced with a general strike. The GTP needed the freedom to import strikebreakers from any source to counteract this threat.[72]

McBride responded to the company stance by requesting a report from Manson on the labour situation of the GTP in Prince Rupert. Though Manson observed that wages on the GTP did not cover the high cost of living in Prince Rupert, he recommended only that the GTP or its contractor should not reduce wages under existing conditions.[73] With feigned displeasure, Chamberlin allowed that the GTP 'would have to make the best of it [Manson's recommendations].' He took one more opportunity to remind the premier that the advance Daly advocated would seriously interfere with further contracts.[74] The company had deflected the intervention of the provincial government.

It also turned back federal intervention. In July, the Department of Labour sent a fair wages officer, J.D. McNiven, to investigate Daly's charges. While neither McBride nor Schreiber accepted completely the GTP version of labour relations, clearly McNiven did. He stayed in the area for less than one week, and issued a report in September. Like Manson, he was granted access to FWS payrolls in Prince Rupert. Although he was aware of the judgment concerning the stationmen, McNiven claimed that Daly could produce not one specific case of any real grievance concerning workmen not being paid their wages. He observed that most of the men in the camps were unable to speak English, but dismissed complaints from those few who could as trivial. He rejected as the fair wage the rate advocated by Daly of $3.00 in sewer construction because it did not include a board charge of $7.00 per week. Thus, the civic workers were receiving less in real terms. Since there was a labour shortage, he recommended that some latitude should be allowed in the fixing of the minimum rate. To bolster this view, he noted that the Board of Trade had rescinded its fair wage motion of $3.00 per day on 19 July. He concluded that current wages were 'fair and reasonable and should not be interfered with.'[75] Such observations might suggest that an increase of the minimum rate was warranted to retain labour; the railway company regarded it as a justification to keep it at the same low level.

Thus, in a tight labour market, the GTP managed to restrain the

Battle of Kelly's Cut, April 1911. The contractors look down from the high ground on the strikers in the foreground.

income of both stationmen and day labourers. Such a dubious achievement may well have preserved the company's current construction balance as well as the profits of FWS, but it hindered the completion of the railway because the company could never obtain enough labourers.

THE BATTLE OF KELLY'S CUT, the violent end to the street-construction workers' strike in Prince Rupert in 1911, was the most dramatic labour conflict in northern British Columbia before the war. Court records and newspaper accounts indicate that the Prince Rupert Industrial Association, the successor to the Workingmen's Association, led construction workers out on strike against private street contractors in February 1911 when the latter refused to match the wage rates that city council established in January for municipal crews. During March, other workers flocked to join the Industrial Association, and its membership grew from several hundred to more than 1,000. Over the objections of both the contractors and city council, the Industrial Association supported the strikers by a levy on members who continued to work for 40¢ per day. Strikers picketed and harassed those who continued working, and at least one private contractor suspended operations. When the private contractors imported strikebreakers, the Industrial Association struck municipal jobs as well in early April. In the late afternoon of 6 April, a riot broke out at the cut of private contractor McGinnis and Kelly between the strikers on the one hand, and police, contractors, and their supporters, several of whom served as special constables, on the other. While both sides made good use of stones and pick handles during the struggle, gunfire seriously wounded several strikers. After several hours, the police routed their opponents and quickly arrested the leadership of the Industrial Association, seizing both its hall and its records. Although the authorities released the association leaders shortly for lack of evidence, they transported and tried fourteen strikers in Victoria. Only a handful were convicted, but the contractors had defended the old rate and broken the strike.

The willingness of the street contractors to raise wages after the conflict as well as the acknowledged discipline of the strikers during the dispute casts doubt on the received explanation that the riot stemmed exclusively from the actions of the direct combatants.[76] While labour historians have rehearsed the strikers' claim that the violent confrontation issued from a conspiracy to break the strike, they have not established a motive, beyond universal capitalist malevolence, for such behaviour.[77] Since the dispute pitted the Industrial Association against private street contractors, it is not surprising that students of the conflict have ignored the railway company's role. But only when one considers the goals of the railway company in this dispute does a plausible motive for the actions of the opponents of the strikers appear.

By the summer of 1910, work on the grade had moved from the environs of Prince Rupert more than 100 miles up the Skeena River to the Kitselas tunnels. Since large ships bringing labourers from outside could dock only at the Prince Rupert wharves, the railway company and its contractors continued to enter the Prince Rupert labour market in search of men to replace those who left the grade. As the shortage of men on the west end become ever more acute, the railway contractors found themselves now competing with the city and private contractors for construction workers. If work in the city offered navvies not only 'civilization,' i.e, the opportunity to avoid camp conditions, but also better wages, the difficulty of the railway company in recruiting and retaining men on the grade would increase and hinder the progress of construction.[78]

Thus, the GTP had a vital interest in the wage levels that its prospective competitors offered manual labourers in the city of Prince Rupert. The interests of the company and the railway contractors in this matter were defended by Alderman Vernor Smith. Elected to the second city council in January 1911, Smith came to the city as the superintendent of FWS at the Pacific terminus. His opposition to the demands of city workers stemmed in part from personal experience. The *Prince Rupert Optimist* charged that he had operated a particularly obnoxious bunkhouse on the grade up the Skeena. His time, the newspaper predicted, 'would be bought and paid for by the GTP.'[79]

When the Industrial Association struck the private contractors, Smith called a secret meeting of council in early March in the absence of the mayor to discuss the threat to law and order. To protect life and liberty, argued the alderman, 'cost was of consequence.' The result of this secret meeting was a request to the Naval Service to dispatch the cruiser HMCS *Rainbow* to Prince Rupert to suppress any illegal action with its heavy guns. The cruiser did not arrive, but the unusual request suggests the hostility of some council members toward attempts by construction workers to win higher wages. At the outset of the dispute between the Industrial Association and the private contractors, the council had formally declared its neutrality. But when the strikers picketed the wharves to inform incoming workers of the situation with signs proclaiming 'Don't be a scab; be a man!' Smith urged his contracting colleagues to 'starve the ——— out.'[80]

But there was an additional incentive for the GTP and its supporters to break the strike. On 22 March, the membership of the Industrial Association passed the following resolution: 'That every member of the [Association] who has the franchise shall use it against the GTP assessment settlement if the plebiscite on that issue takes place before the strike is over, in order to cause the businessmen trouble and lessen security for business carried on.'[81] As Chapter 5 sets out, Hays had struggled with a recalcitrant city council during the summer of 1910 to reach a settlement regarding an assessment dispute concerning GTP lands on the waterfront. To compel the council to accept his terms, he stopped all GTP development in Prince Rupert in September 1910. By 1911, the delay in development of the waterfront, construction of a drydock, and building of a major hotel had convinced most of the local business community that the continued growth of the city, and preservation of their investments, depended on the resumption of GTP activity. One result of this perception was the election in January of a new city council more amenable to the wishes of the company. Thus, the undertaking to veto a settlement from an organization that currently included 339 voters in a city where 550 constituted a majority in the last election represented not only a challenge to the railway company's agenda but also a threat to the economic survival of the business community.

Although the *Optimist* rhapsodized that the riot elicited a 'spontaneous rallying of the entire British population of Prince Rupert to the side of law and order,' circumstantial evidence indicates that the response was planned. Throughout the day when the riot occurred, 'prominent citizens' gathered at Kelly's Cut to support those who wanted to work. That the police chief was aware that something unusual would happen on that day is suggested by the fact that he assigned seven special constables to the day shift. At no time before or after did he assign more than three special constables to any shift.[82]

The Industrial Association secretary appealed to the minister of labour for an investigation into the firing on a peaceful procession, but Mackenzie King evidently preferred the evaluation in an on-the-spot telegram from the city engineer. Justifying the violent suppression of the strikers, the engineer explained that 'paid agitators ... who themselves got off with their whole skins ... pushed Bohunks, ignorant of our language, into the fight.' Perhaps the minister did not realize that the message time indicates that the telegram, which contained not only a summary of the origin and development of the strike but also an account of its outcome, was sent before the police had routed the strikers and made their final arrests.[83]

While complaints in the labour press and scattered accounts of federal and provincial investigations indicate that the GTP management made few attempts to improve camp conditions after the disputes of 1909, no large disturbance occurred on the grade itself until the middle of 1912. But as the IWW strike on the Canadian Northern petered out, the Wobbly *Industrial Worker* of Spokane predicted that GTP navvies would join the struggle. In July, an IWW organizer claimed that these labourers, with grievances similar to those driving the navvies on the Canadian Northern to strike, were on the verge of revolt.

Although contractors were quick to claim that outside agitators engineered the conflict, the working conditions established and defended by the GTP officers prompted the strike. In mid-June, inspectors of both the federal and provincial governments made critical reports on the camps.[84] Although the actions of the provincial sanitary inspector to clean up camps were probably intended to undercut some of the workers' grievances, it did not prevent delegates from the two IWW locals, which had appeared at camps on the west end, from submitting a set of demands to all contractors on the GTP. The most important of these was a nine-hour day with a minimum wage of $3.25, improved food and board for $1.00 per day, and IWW control of the medical fees for the construction of union hospitals.[85] When the contractors rejected these demands out of hand on 18 July, the IWW struck on 20 July.

Newspapers sympathetic to the railway company claimed that the IWW had succeeded in mounting a strike only because it threatened honest men with teams of rifle-toting agitators who would sweep through the camps and clear out those who resisted. Hoping to repeat the strategy used in the breaking of the Canadian Northern strike, the provincial police superintendent ordered the Hazelton detachment to arrest and deport any IWW member found carrying arms or causing trouble. But the local detachment chief reported that the contractors' claim concerning gun-carrying IWW members was patently false, and that strict order was maintained at camps. Later in the month, police dropped charges of intimidation against IWW camp delegate W.A. Thorne, the only Wobbly who appears to have migrated from the Canadian Northern strike, because of lack of evidence. Two weeks after the strike had been called, there was 'no disorder of any kind'.[86]

Even the *Vancouver Sun*, a new Liberal daily with connections to contractor Stewart, reported that 2,000 day labourers had heeded the strike and that only 700 stationmen continued to work. But after downing tools, most of the strikers began to tramp out of the construction zone toward Prince Rupert. Realizing that the empty camps invited the contractors to fill their places with scabs, IWW members explained that 'if we want to win, we have got to strike ON the job instead of OFF it.' If the 'sharks,' the employment agencies, could transport scabs to the camps, the company and its contractors could break the strike.[87]

But it proved impossible to hold the strikers in the camps. While strikers on the Canadian Northern could simply squat beyond the contractors' camps on the Fraser and Thompson and receive supplies from the CPR trains chugging along the opposite bank, there was no alternative system for transporting food to the men in the valleys of the Skeena and Bulkley. During the summer months, the wagon road from Skeena Crossing to the head of the Bulkley valley was a river of mud. Even using the completed section of the GTP line, the contractors had experienced difficulty moving provisions to the forward camps. Indeed, the *Empire* accused the contractors of provoking the strike so that they would not have to pay the cost of supplying the men during the summer season of 1912.[88]

One element of the strike much contested by the newspapers was the number of workers who walked off the job. Here as elsewhere, the agency that was supposed to make a systematic analysis of the strike, the federal Department of Labour, obtained contradictory evidence. In early August, the secretary of the IWW in Chicago informed the department that the strike affected only 800 labourers. Almost three weeks later, an FWS official admitted that the strike had affected 2,800 workers directly and 700 indirectly. Noting that 1,000 men had already left the district for other parts of the country, however, he claimed that the strike had ended on 15 August. All that the department correspondent in Prince Rupert could provide was that the strike had drawn 1,000 men to the environs of the GTP terminus by the middle of the month.[89]

A review of newspaper accounts indicates that of the 2,772 workers on payrolls from the bridge camps below Hazelton to the grade camps near Telkwa, approximately 1,400 quit their work. The crews of the railway company proper and stationmen, fearing they would lose their past labour if they did not complete their contracts, remained in the camps. The claim that workers on the east end also joined the strike, issued from Prince Rupert and repeated in the Vancouver papers, is implausible. Although the IWW trumpeted that 10,000 strikers on this section had halted construction completely, the police records show no disturbances of any kind. The police records also refute the report in one Vancouver paper that militia units were rushed into this section to halt an exodus and protect property.[90]

Although the IWW representatives from the grade camps had met at Skeena Crossing, more than 160 miles upriver from the coast, the strike leaders evidently decided that its headquarters must be located in Prince Rupert, to which the majority of the strikers tramped. From mid-August until mid-October, the leaders published on the *Empire* press the *IWW Strike Bulletin* to inform not only the strikers but also those who came to Prince Rupert looking for work about the GTP.[91]

At the outset, the company and the contractors had little success in replacing workers who left. When ships landed replacement workers, strikers infiltrated and persuaded them not to go upriver. The local IWW secretary asserted that it was impossible for the contractors to secure non-unionists. When a ship landed 50 workers on 29 August, for example, the strikers claimed they persuaded 34 to join the strike. The leadership issued instructions for live wires in the coast cities both in Canada and the United States to picket employment agencies that attempted to secure scabs. When the replacement workers reached the camp, they frequently deserted in any case because of the abominable conditions.[92] The IWW also won the tolerance, if not the support, of the city for its cause. The strikers set up tents near the waterfront at the 'IWW Hotel' and survived on donations, strike funds sent from workers in other areas, and fish they could catch. As in the Canadian Northern strike, no drinking was permitted in the strike camp, and order apparently prevailed.[93]

But the refusal of the IWW to enter into a confrontation with the GTP also had its disadvantages. In August, the *Strike Bulletin* admitted that 'we must have money to feed and shelter these men.' The following month, the IWW secretary in Prince Rupert complained that though his men were now entitled to the same support they had always given to other strikes, the contributions from other unions were 'not all they could be.' Since the alarmist stories of violence had no substance, the strike attracted relatively little attention in the commercial press after the first few weeks. Because workers usually sent donations to more dramatic conflicts, lamented a Wobbly editor, 'a quiet strike is entirely lost sight of.'[94] For the IWW convention in September in Chicago, the Prince Rupert local sent a delegate along with 100 strike tags. The local secretary informed the convention that the workers now relied on clams as a steady diet and needed money for spuds and punk. 'What are we to do during the three months that elapse between the flounder and the mackerel season?' The delegate nevertheless informed his fellow Wobblies that the strike had been a success.[95]

It was the lack of publicity, the weak financial support, and the separation of the strikers from the city that the GTP and FWS determined to exploit. Since outright confrontation with strikers on the Canadian Northern had proved expensive for the contractors, the new strategy was simply to ignore the strike. Accordingly, the FWS superintendent in New Hazelton exaggerated the demands of the IWW at the outset of the strike. He acknowledged that a considerable number of day men had quit but claimed that all camps had returned to work. At least one party accepted this partisan report that the strike had ended on 15 August; the federal *Labour Gazette* published this item in its September number.[96]

Another company response was to mount an inspection trip of the work shortly after the outset of the strike by principal contractor Patrick Welch and GTP chief engineer Kelliher. In Prince Rupert, Welch opined that a wage of $3 per day was 'pretty good,' and threatened once more to abandon all construction on the west end. When workers on a small waterfront contract refused to join the IWW strike, the newspapers made light of a 'phantom strike.' The contractor also dangled the bauble of commencement of large terminal works, which had hitherto been postponed.[97]

Although the city council had decided not to intervene, the presence of such a large number of unemployed men caused consternation. On 11 August, a special meeting was held to inform the citizens about the strike. The following evening, council voted 5-4, the mayor casting the deciding vote, to approach FWS with an offer to serve as negotiator with the strikers. But when the mayor contacted Vernor Smith, now FWS superintendent in New Hazelton, he replied that the principal contractor 'did not recognize the strike as existing' and, like Welch, threatened to abandon the work on the west end. Although one alderman demanded that the Canadian government compel the railway company to honour its commitment, the council abandoned its effort to negotiate.[98]

On 21 August, the GTP president arrived in Prince Rupert with government inspector Schreiber and made a quick tour of the line as far as Skeena Crossing. Chamberlin expressed his disappointment at the delay in construction that the disturbance had occasioned and predicted that it would delay completion for one year. He praised the efforts of those still on the job, especially Italian labourers, and announced that the company was 'prepared to give employment to 2,000 men if they could be got.' To counter the claims that the company had encouraged the delay in settlement, the president explained that every day of delay added to the fixed debt of the road. It was therefore not in the GTP's interest to contemplate anything that would slow construction.[99]

Just as useful was the judgment of the representative of the Canadian government, who had not hesitated to castigate the railway company before. While Schreiber was no friend of the contractors and continued to criticize GTP construction activities, on the matter of labour relations his statements displayed a belief that little had changed in Canada since the building of the CPR. While acknowledging that 1,500 had left the grade even before the strike was called, Schreiber charged that the IWW had forced the men to quit work. He maintained that the contractors were paying a fair wage, 'supplying good food, and yet the demand is for higher wages.' He claimed that the contractors had 1,000 men working on the line and that many old employees were returning. He also attacked a newspaper report that men were on the beach at Prince Rupert, maintaining that most workers again preferred to take their meals at the contractors' camps. Schreiber was convinced that the contractors bore no grudge for the current trouble since they allowed men to claim their pay at a moment's notice. That Schreiber simply repeated an imaginary tale of woe from contractors, as one worker charged, is supported by his sham inspection of the camps from the rear platform of a private car. The government engineer's evaluation did not flatter the intelligence of western Canadians, noted the *Empire* editor, since he simply attacked foreigners who refused to work for nothing.[100] A Vancouver MP charged that the railway company had only temporarily removed the objectionable features of its camps for the visit of the notables. The company's new demands for labourers, particularly Italians, to replace the strikers meant simply that the GTP would now resort to the 'American system of importing "dagos," as next best to Asiatics.'[101]

Another company tactic was the vilification of the strike leaders. In a lengthy report, a correspondent in Hazelton charged that the IWW chiefs were dishonest. They had absconded with $5,000 in dues from the dupes on the line. They had also offered to guarantee subcontractors an uninterrupted supply of workers for 50¢ per week per man. After dismissing all complaints concerning camp conditions, the correspondent also presented a series of figures taken from contractors' books suggesting that the average day worker earned more than $50 per month even after all charges for board and commissary had been deducted. Even the most strident critic of the IWW in Vancouver, the *Sun*, admitted that correspondents on the line were sometimes self-interested and unreliable.[102]

While the Prince Rupert *Daily News* had not received income from GTP advertisements as had the *Prince Rupert Journal*, it had no love for the strikers since its proprietors had supported the contractors in the Battle of Kelly's Cut in 1911. Although it admitted that the toilers had grievances, it observed that railway contracts were not 'rosebuds for lily-handed labourers.' In any case, Prince Rupert did not share the conditions of the camps upriver. It castigated the strike as a kind of contagious leprosy. 'Memories of the last strike [1911] make only the most rabid agitator eager to repeat the experience; even the worst-paid worker would be better to keep on working; by striking, the selfish-souled labourer loses.' Although it conceded that there was 'something like a strike,' it rebuked the Board of Trade for sending a letter requesting maintenance of law and order. When the wives of two hotel keepers started a subscription to support hungry strikers, it described it as an obvious ploy by those who could not depend on decent businessmen alone to attract the drinking trade.[103]

Attacking the strikers or their supporters in the city would not relieve the shortage of workers on the grade, however. Directly after the strike commenced, FWS contracted with a Vancouver employment agency to ship workers to Prince Rupert. Although the agency employed professional strikebreakers from the United States to shepherd the men past the pickets in Prince Rupert, it initially enjoyed little success.[104]

The key to breaking the strike was importing large numbers of men from outside the country. Accordingly, the railway company and its con-tractors now sought men from farther afield by placing ads in papers in New York, Omaha, and St. Louis. Throughout the working season, the Canadian government had flouted its own immigration regulations and allowed southern Europeans into the country at the behest of Canadian Northern owners Mackenzie and Mann and FWS. Probably the GTP or FWS persuaded the minister of the interior to extend the relaxation of immigration regulations for British Columbia for the month of September.[105]

During the strike, the GTP revised its policy several times toward transporting men to the end of steel. In early August, Chamberlin promised that the railway company would assume half the travel cost of those who wanted to work on the GTP. Toward the end of October, the GTP advertised that it would absorb six-sevenths of the transportation cost to British Columbia from Boston. One witness for the royal com-mission even claimed that the company brought in men from Boston and Montreal for free. Certainly, the company's absorption of the travel costs increased the inducement for men to go to both ends of the line to work, and both the disgruntled strike committee and a delighted subcon-tractor implied that it attracted 'plenty of men.' Once the replacements arrived at the dock in Prince Rupert, the company used both threats of legal action for trespass and manherders to insulate them from the pick-eters. When one replacement attempted to join the strikers, a Canadian government official asserted that he was shot.[106] The IWW secretary derided those who ran the gauntlet of picketers on the dock and reached the grade camps upriver to begin work as 'mental and physical wrecks ... paralytically drunk, doped and deadened.' But his attack on current prices for goods upriver in a contractor's commissary suggests that the union was no longer able to intercept most scabs at the waterfront.[107]

On 9 January 1913, the IWW voted to call off the strike. While it claimed that substantial improvements in working conditions had been made, it admitted that the railway company and the contractors had not conceded its original demands. To extol the educational value of the strike was small consolation for the workers who had participated.[108]

THE GTP HAD WON the strike, but only at the loss of much of the 1912 construction season on the west end. By following Hays's example as an 'unyielder' in its attitudes and actions toward construction workers on both ends of the Mountain Section, the railway company and the principal contractor held down labour costs in 1912 and, presumably, in 1913 since there was no significant change in pay rates. In 1914, wages began to decline because of the surplus of labour. But the consequences of the strike illuminate the flaw in the GTP labour relations strategy since it began the west end in 1908. Even before the 1912 strike, indifferent pay and terrible camp conditions caused many to leave and slowed the pace of construction. As the *Empire* observed, for a railway to complete less than 200 miles of track in more than four years was a disgrace.[109] During the 1912 strike, even the GTP president implied that management's refusal to change its labour relations damaged the company because it slowed construction. We have no reason to doubt Chamberlin's evaluation that the strike delayed completion of the line by one year. Schreiber, after all, had made similar statements. And such an evaluation, while it permitted company officers to shift responsibility for slow construction to the strikers, may have understated the delay.

A larger estimate of avoidable delay issued from the Royal Commission of Railways and Transportation, part of the belated federal government response to the great losses incurred by both the Canadian Northern and the GTP. As part of a valuation of the GTP line, an American railway expert concluded that 'sound construction practices' would have allowed the GTP to complete its British Columbia line in four years. Chapter 3 has suggested that the failure of the GTP and its contractors to retain a work force of adequate size to prosecute the work, particularly on the west end, resulted in additional fixed charges from the delay in completion. Using the commission's method of calculation with a 4 per cent rate, the interest charges from 1908 to 1914 (six and a half years, seven construction seasons) on the 'first' cost of construction of the Mountain Section amounted to $20.4 million.[110]

This calculation invites a counterfactual argument. Suppose that to avoid the strike in 1912, the GTP had acceded to workers' demands, the most quantifiable of which was a pay rate of $3.25 per nine-hour day. This pay rate represented an increase of 47¢ per day over Manson's calculation of the average wage of $2.78 for contract day labourers on the west end in 1909. For the remainder of the work, labour costs for wages of the existing work force *on both ends* would increase by approximately $1.6 million. Of this expenditure the company would guarantee one-quarter, the government, three-quarters. An improvement in camp conditions would have required an additional outlay, of course.

If the additional expenditure on wages had been made *before and during* 1912, so that the work that produced the existing first cost had been completed by the end of 1912, i.e., six months longer than the commission allotted, the reduced interest charges would have lowered the net global cost of construction by $4.5 million. If one accepts Chamberlin's more modest estimate of avoidable delay, the same outlay *before and during* 1913 would have allowed the GTP to complete its line across British Columbia by the end of the 1913 construction season. Such a completion date would result in a net saving on final construction cost of $1.2 million.

These estimates do not recognize other benefits for the company that early completion might have produced. Of course, the interest charges would not vanish if the Mountain Section had opened for traffic in late 1912 or 1913. But with one or two years of hauling to and from Prince Rupert before the outbreak of the war, the GTP might have been able to attract the shipping lines that bypassed the terminus after August 1914, in part because they did not wish to ship to a new port during wartime. This additional revenue would have at least lowered the operating ratio and perhaps allowed the company to pay part of its fixed charges. Even after 1912, its ability to borrow money on the London Stock Exchange would have been enhanced.

There is no evidence, however, that GTP officers ever considered the long-term benefits that might accrue from a more flexible and conciliatory labour relations policy. For the GTP, the construction labourers it was compelled to employ were as tainted as the meat its contractors sometimes offered men in the camps. As one GTP contractor in the Rockies complained, 'Now we have to ask men to work for us and ask them to stay with us. They are indifferent to good treatment, show no interest in our works, and are ready to go on strike or leave us when they think we need them most.'[111] With such a perception, company officers regarded any expenditure to improve working conditions as a waste of money. But a labour relations strategy built on such a one-sided view inevitably led to management frustration and damaged the company in the long run.

FIVE

'A FRAIL LITTLE CITY':
PRINCE RUPERT

The development of a terminus on the Pacific coast frequently played a crucial role in the fortunes of the transcontinental railway system in North America. Since the location of the port in large part determined the railway's route from the Rockies to the coast, the company's selection and development of its terminus shaped not only the pattern of trade but also the growth of settlement over large portions of the Pacific slope. But before obtaining any return from traffic at the terminus, the company had to make a heavy initial expenditure to clear space and erect structures for the transfer of goods between railway car and ship. While immediate returns from traffic were less attractive than those generated from long-settled Atlantic ports, the company could extract substantial real estate revenue from the blocks of land that it usually acquired in exchange for designating a site as its terminus.[1]

Though studies of transcontinentals consider at some length the company's selection of and construction to a Pacific terminus, few devote space to the nature and extent of company activities at the terminus after selection.[2] Urban historians and geographers have attempted to fill this lacuna, but their works eschew a sustained analysis of the actions of the company throughout the city. Historian Norbert MacDonald's recent studies of the impact of the CPR on Vancouver, for example, offer a careful account of the company's astute manipulation of its property but largely ignore its concerns in the evolution of the port.[3] Studies elsewhere suggest that complex and sometimes contradictory motives drove railway companies in terminus development, but do not systematically examine sources that might elucidate this behaviour.[4]

A comparison of GTP activity in Prince Rupert with these urban studies of railway impact is difficult because of the latter's focus on the city rather than on the company. From this choice follows a disinclination to treat the company as anything more complex than a monolithic force. The reluctance of these scholars to examine significant unpublished company records concerning the port reinforces the view of the company as a single, independent variable in terminus development. This view of the company also informs and limits most studies of interior communities on railway lines on the Pacific slope.

If one shifts the focus from the city to the railway company, the GTP experience at Prince Rupert suggests three overlapping phases. The first phase, acquisition, embraced the activities surrounding the selection decision and the negotiations with the federal and provincial governments and the Metlakatla band, which ended in the confirmation of the company's holdings in the general settlement of February 1908. The second phase, development under company control, began with the arrival of the first work party on Kaien Island in May 1906 to construct wharves, railway yards, and clear the townsite. This period came to a close in May 1909 with the successful townsite lot auction. In the third phase, the company transferred its municipal responsibilities to the newly incorporated city and concentrated on the upbuilding of the terminal facilities, which led it to create the port in the first place.

Chapter 2 examined company activities during the acquisition phase. The number of company officers in Montreal, Winnipeg, and Prince Rupert that concurrently formulated and carried out GTP policy at the terminus vitiates a chronological ordering of the two later phases. While not ignoring the different circumstances of the company during each phase, this chapter divides company activities in Prince Rupert according to President Hays's formulation of GTP townsite policy: the provision of immediate returns and the protection of company interests.[5] These stipulations had determined in part the calculations of the company concerning the acquisition of the terminus; the same demands informed much of the company's activities during development. Under the first head, the chapter reviews the company's design for the townsite, its struggle to secure the waterfront, its uncertain attempts to market its property, and the fate of three major projected investments: a hotel, waterfront development, and a drydock.

Under the second head, the chapter investigates the company's response to what a Grand Trunk general manager had earlier termed 'the evils of competition.'[6] A review of the company's response to a challenge from a populist reveals that the GTP could use its superior resources and connections to overcome individuals who sought to share or impose a limit on company returns. For some company officers, however, a desire to dominate the terminus superseded the original economic objective to maximize returns. To elucidate the evolution and consequences of this contradictory behaviour, the chapter examines in greater detail the company's complex conflict with the city council. The GTP turned back this claim to returns only by creating or accepting delays whose cost exceeded the value of the original challenge.

Much has been written about the striking design of Prince Rupert. In a province that demanded checkerboard plans by law, the curved streets of the city, illustrated in Figure 5.1, come as a pleasant surprise. Indeed, a recent report commissioned by the city's heritage advisory committee praises the layout as the city's major aesthetic asset 'with national and perhaps international historical significance.'[7] One can better view the origin and evolution of the town plan as an expression of the company's desire for both a model and a profitable terminus. While one should not dismiss the company's frequent public and private declamations to establish a model city, the large initial investments that such a model required would postpone returns. Only if the plan yielded an extra profit would such a delay be acceptable.

Hays awarded the contract for designing the new city to the Boston landscape architect firm of Brett, Hall & Co. in 1907, possibly as a belated wedding gift, since its senior partner, George D. Hall, had married one of his daughters in 1906. Arriving at Kaien Island in January 1908, Hall quickly decided that the ridges and ravines on the north shore of the island made conventional town plans unsuitable and required instead a design 'original and adaptable to the unusual topography.' While the division of the townsite into sections on different planes with nearly parallel axes may well have been original, the plan's most arresting feature, the use of curved streets to define and frequently connect the sections, stemmed from a dated American terminus design.[8]

The probable source of inspiration for the curved streets and the large reserves for parks, schools, hospitals, and civic buildings was the work of the architect's mentor, F.L. Olmsted. One of the founders of the City Beautiful movement and designer of several railway town plans in the Midwest, Olmsted accepted a commission from the Northern Pacific Railroad in 1873 to draw up a plan for its new Pacific terminus, Tacoma.

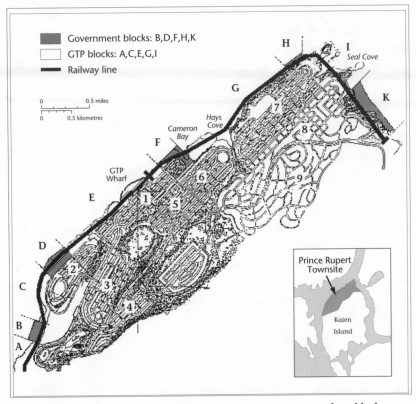

Figure 5.1 **Prince Rupert Townsite showing GTP/BC government waterfront block division, 1908**

For the American company's townsite on the hills sloping into Puget Sound, Olmsted proposed an undulating series of curved blocks, which the astonished inhabitants compared to bananas, melons, and sweet potatoes. The sweep of a single rail line around part of its perimeter to a small wharf represented the plan's only concession to the intent of the townsite's owners. Rejected as impractical by the directors of the Northern Pacific in the 1870s, these elements of the Olmsted plan reappeared in the Prince Rupert design, which the GTP touted as 'an ideal city plan ... that has ... developed all the practical advantages to traffic, [and] considered carefully the circumstances of business, homes, and sanitation.'[9]

For company officers, however, the Brett-Hall design represented the 'most practical lay-out' because it could be manipulated to maximize returns and enhance the company's control of the townsite. Aware that the company's desires might compromise the integrity of their plan, the architects insisted that the curved blocks should be divided only into deep lots of 100 feet with fifty-foot frontages to avoid the construction of dark, narrow buildings. For the auction of May 1909, however, the company rejected its architects' counsel and divided all its blocks into lots with twenty-five-foot frontages. British town planner Thomas Adams later observed that the GTP decision to create lots with such small frontages facilitated land speculation and inhibited the construction of adequate housing for workers. At the time of the auction, the division prompted complaints that the company was gouging.[10]

Unlike the striking street layout, the modern Prince Rupert waterfront obscures the railway company's development role. Wedged between the city's bluffs and a decaying wharf, which docks only fish boats and the occasional cruise ship, the small railway yard and unimpressive station do not suggest the waterfront's importance in GTP plans before 1920. Yet a review of the surviving files of the engineering and legal departments concerning Prince Rupert suggests that some officers regarded the location of the railway yard as the only element of importance. To GTP harbour engineer J.H. Bacon, it was imperative that the company retain effective control of the entire waterfront. He argued that the topography of Kaien Island forced the railway yards to be laid out along the waterfront. Even there, the cost of cutting the bluffs and filling out into the water would exceed the combined costs of the GTP yards at Fort William, Winnipeg, and Edmonton. He continued: 'It is essential from a railway point of view that a terminal railway yard should be in an unbroken stretch with each unit so placed that the flow of cars from one unit to the next be continuous ... The waste in the operating of an expensive and inadequate terminal system will be felt not only in Prince Rupert ... but will extend through the entire length of line.' General Manager F.W. Morse was blunter. 'The railway company's requirements [at the waterfront] are paramount, the townsite secondary.'[11]

Hall had applauded the 'genuine desire of the railway officials from President Hays down to plan for a model city ... locating railway yards and wharves so as best to serve the city.' But the company expected the architects, as 'practical men ... working as they are with our Engineering Department, [to] provide ... the necessary land for railway facilities.' The architects obliged by locating the axis of the townsite so that a rail line along the waterfront would effectively encircle it. In place of the natural growth proceeding inland from the waterfront, the architects substituted planned growth parallel to the waterfront.[12] Since townsite inhabitants would have to cross the rail line to reach the harbour, the company believed it might return the waterfront to a kind of closed camp, which it had surrendered when it settled its differences with the provincial government.

But to dominate the waterfront in such a manner, the company had to recover the part of the waterfront that it had conceded to the provincial government in February 1908, perfect its title to both the foreshore and adjacent water lots, and control all access from land and sea. This desire to secure a kind of hegemony on the waterfront and regulate all activity there informs much of the railway company's activity in Prince Rupert.

It will be remembered that in the general settlement of February 1908, the company undertook to reconvey to the province not only one-quarter of the Prince Rupert townsite lots but also one-quarter of the waterfront. With first selection of 1,000-foot-long waterfront blocks, the government could limit the GTP to only 3,000 feet of continuous waterfront by choosing blocks in the middle of the company's projected railway yard. But the plans of company engineers and the architects had convinced the general manager that an unbroken waterfront of 6,000 feet was 'absolutely necessary to the proper development of the terminal.'[13]

Armed with a set of complex proposals to mask this goal, GTP solicitor D'Arcy Tate set off to Victoria in June 1908. When Premier Richard McBride balked at the company demand, Tate read portions of the architects' reports and revealed preliminary plans to convince the government that the townsite's success depended on the company's acquisition of ample space for terminal facilities. The lawyer arranged a junket to Prince Rupert and used the on-site inspection to bring round two ministers, but he still could not convince the premier.[14]

A report by an independent inspector appointed by cabinet apparently carried greater weight than Tate's remonstrances. The inspector admitted that the GTP harbour engineer provided most of his information on the matter, and the report largely repeated arguments that Bacon had made earlier. The cost of building a yard at Prince Rupert was greater than anywhere else, and any obstruction the government provided would greatly harm the service the company could provide. Instead, the inspector suggested that the government trade its right to blocks near the centre of the townsite for a solid block of 12,000 feet on the northern tip of the island beyond the railway company's projected terminal and then require the GTP to extend its line. But by granting the GTP an unbroken 18,000-foot waterfront along the townsite, the report allowed critics to charge that the company would 'practically cinch Prince Rupert as [the CPR had done] in Vancouver.'[15]

In late July, Tate rehearsed the inspector's arguments for cabinet. McBride was still not satisfied, however, and wished to postpone a decision until he could present the company's proposal to his caucus next spring. In desperation, Tate offered a final concession. If the government would not settle for its entire waterfront north of the GTP terminal, the GTP harbour engineer would allow the government what he regarded as the most desirable waterfront along the entire townsite, a 1,500-foot break at Cameron Bay between the company's proposed passenger yard and the main yard. But the GTP would require a much enlarged right-of-way across the break to accommodate eight tracks to its main yard north of the break.[16]

This concession allowed McBride to maintain that the government had held the railway to the terms of the original settlement, and he immediately accepted it. On the following day, Tate drew up an instrument in which the GTP acquired 24,000 feet of waterfront, two blocks of which exceeded 6,000 feet. The company also obtained an expanded right-of-way through all government blocks, including the 1,500-foot break between the railway's two long blocks. In return, the GTP undertook to extend its line three miles beyond its terminal around the north end of the island to Block K, the government's longest block. Although Morse grumbled that the company should have done better, he emphasized to Hays that the projected yard layout had not been compromised.[17] And the local newspaper grudgingly recognized the company's accomplishment. When the settlement came before the Assembly the following spring, the editor complained that 'the provincial government could not have got less had there been but one man engaged in looking after the interests of both the government and the railway company, and that man [GTP] Harbour Engineer Bacon. Never before has there been so much bolsuter [*sic*] on behalf of the people and so little gained for them ... These men [the government] have blundered badly.'[18] It appeared that the GTP had restored its hold on the waterfront, which it lost in the general settlement in February.

Leases in the townsite had already produced some returns; company officers expected them to generate even more on the waterfront. Even before the GTP had secured its portion of the waterfront in the division with the provincial government, the company let its first lease on waterfront property to Foley Brothers, Welch & Stewart Company for $3,000 per annum. In early 1909, Bacon reported that applicants for leases on the GTP portion of the waterfront were continually pestering him. By late 1912, the company had issued leases for portions of the GTP wharf to seven concerns and for portions of its northern block at Seal Cove to two fishing companies. While officials in the freight department pointed out that waterfront leaseholders would generate traffic for the system, even they maintained that the company must receive a substantial immediate return. Although harbour business was much smaller, the GTP set lease rates similar to CPR rates in Vancouver.[19]

When challenged by McBride for accepting money for leases on the waterfront reserved for railway purposes, Tate contended that the company's patent to the waterfront property placed no restrictions on the owners. But wharfage entailed the use of not only the land abutting the water but also the corresponding water lot, the foreshore, and the sea bed extending from the high water mark to the harbour head line. Since the waterfront property the company had purchased from both the provincial government and the Indian reserve extended only to the high water mark, it was essential to acquire the corresponding water lots to defend the validity of the leases and assure control of access. Only with title to this other portion of the waterfront could the company compel recalcitrant leaseholders to pay their rent and conform to its other policies. Even before the waterfront division, the company realized it must secure the foreshore from the federal government.[20]

But the company's first application in 1907 to acquire water lots for the entire waterfront of its property surrounding Tuck's Inlet achieved little with the federal Department of Marine. The chief engineer of the department protested vehemently against conveying practically 100 miles of coastline to the company 'for merely speculative purposes.' Even after the company had obtained indefeasible title to its land above the high water mark in 1909, the engineer regarded the application as an objectionable attempt to outdo the waterfront monopoly that the CPR had obtained in Vancouver.[21]

The company responded by reducing its application to less than ten miles along its townsite and the western shore of Kaien Island. GTP chief engineer B.B. Kelliher expected that the company would build railway yards and wharves along the entire length; already the company had received enough requests for leases to fill the area. The minister, while acknowledging that the GTP would receive favourable consideration for water lots fronting its terminal facilities, decided to adhere to the department's precedent in Vancouver and only grant water rights under lease. Accordingly, the department engineer used an inspection trip to Prince Rupert to argue that the company be granted water rights only at the two wharfs it had already constructed.[22]

Six months later, the company submitted a third application for the water rights on lots abutting only its own four waterfront blocks, less than four miles, as well as its right-of-way over the provincial government's Block F. The department engineer recommended acceptance providing the company pay an annual rent based on a valuation of $10 per foot, same as in Vancouver.[23]

Though Vice-President W. Wainwright hounded the deputy minister, the department delayed in drawing up the award. By mid-summer, Wainwright even argued that the delay in issuing the lease, and not the GTP policy in response to the assessment dispute with the city, prompted the company to stop all railway work in Prince Rupert.[24] So anxious was Tate to ensure that the company's goals concerning the length and cost of the water rights were met that he came to Ottawa in early August to prod the department in drafting the complex order. When the minister refused to put through the order without a sizeable rental, Tate acquiesced. Accordingly, cabinet passed the order on 11 August 1911, awarding the GTP water rights for 21 years for its four waterfront blocks and the right-of-way over Block F for an annual rental of $6,840. Tate fumed that the minister might as well have set an annual rate of a million dollars.[25]

When the Marine Department refused Wainwright's application for a reduction early in 1912, the GTP made use of other levers. In its case for nominal rent, the company claimed that the 1903 contract entitled it to the free grant of water lots. The Department of Justice concurred but added a significant proviso: 'that such a water lot is in the judgment of the government reasonably required for the use of the company in connection with its operation.' The minister of railways would make this decision.[26]

Besides its legal brief, the company also employed a cruder argument. Although it had earlier undertaken to provide free lots for a customs house and post office in Prince Rupert, it now required the federal

Department of Public Works to pay $100,000. On settlement of the rental dispute, the company would surrender the deeds. This stratagem initially persuaded local MP H.S. Clements to intercede on the company's behalf and suggest a compromise of a water lot rental of $100. But the company's determination to withhold the deeds 'until the foreshore rental has been made right' stirred up public indignation in the city.[27]

The judicial proviso noted above offered an avenue for the expression of civic ire. In June, the Prince Rupert City Council passed a resolution against the granting of additional water rights to the GTP, and Clements urged that beyond the company's immediate requirements, 'every foot ... ought to be preserved for the city.' Minister of Railways Frank Cochrane inspected the site and decided the company should receive water rights to Block E alone, since it would fulfil GTP requirements for years to come.[28]

On the strength of this evaluation, the government offered to cancel the 1911 lease and substitute a lease for $1 per annum for Block E only. But the government informed the company that it would not recognize the leases that the GTP had granted on other lots if they included buildings on the foreshore. This declaration apparently prevented the company from collecting rent from its leaseholders, and a GTP engineer in Prince Rupert remarked that much money was lost. Faced with this prospect, the GTP general freight agent, C.E. Dewey, advocated that the railway company maintain its claim to the water lots of the four GTP blocks and Block F even if it meant paying $6,840 per annum, since the annual rent from current leaseholders in Block E alone almost covered that sum. If the railway reduced its lease to the water lot fronting Block E, the government would attempt to control the rest of the waterfront. For both immediate rents and later returns from traffic, 'the most valuable asset we can have is to control as much of the waterfront as possible.'[29]

But the company's heavy-handed attempt to intimidate the government by withholding the deeds to the lots for the customs house now produced another threat. The action infuriated not only the local MP but also Robert Rogers, the new Conservative minister of public works who quickly found a method to return the favour in kind. At a meeting of officials of Marine and Public Works in December 1912, the minister declared that the railway company should not be granted the foreshore ·whether it owned the riparian rights or not. The minister then made use of the regulations in the Railway Act. By not obtaining Public Works' approval for construction of wharfs and track on made ground, the company had violated its provisions. In early December, the local public works engineer ordered all work on wharfs and railway yards to stop until the company obtained the department's sanction. GTP solicitor Hugh Hansard instructed his engineer to continue work until he was legally stopped. But the lawyer admitted that the GTP eventually had to obtain departmental approval for structures that would obstruct navigable waters. While the GTP obtained Railways and, after much argument, BRC approval for its line north of the terminus, it was unable to secure the approval of Public Works.[30]

Rogers fumed that it was 'a crime to hand over the entire control of the waterfront to the GTP.' Something had to be done to allow concerns to locate on the waterfront 'or commercial prosperity [would] be killed.' The solution was the preposterous declaration of Prince Rupert as a public harbour at the time of Confederation, which made the federal government rather than the province proprietor of the foreshore. Even though Hansard quickly demonstrated that Prince Rupert did not fall into this category, and Rogers implicitly acknowledged this by regretting the provincial government's 'serious mistake' in handing over its rights, an ambiguous opinion from the Justice Department allowed him to push an order through cabinet reserving a water lot 2,000 feet long in the middle of the GTP Block E for use of the Department of Public Works.[31]

While the company could overturn the order in court, lengthy proceedings would deprive the GTP of the revenue from all the leases it had already let. Accordingly, the company made a dramatic concession in a proposition for settlement of outstanding disputes with the federal government on the waterfront. If the government would relinquish its reserve on the 2,000-foot water lot, cancel a water lot lease to a recalcitrant fish company in Block I, and sell the GTP the water lots it had only leased in 1911, the company would transfer to the government a 1,500-foot waterfront block for the city wharf at the south end of Block E as well as the adjacent water lot. This offer was tempting enough to persuade both Marine and Public Works to withdraw their objections to an outright grant. The government passed an order in April 1914 approving all works of the company and undertook to draw up a quit claim to the blocks.[32]

Block I on Seal Cove required special care to resolve a dispute with the largest leaseholder on the waterfront. In 1910, the Canadian Fish and Cold Storage Company, in which Canadian Northern owner William

Mackenzie held a large interest, announced its intention to build the largest cold storage plant in North America at Prince Rupert. When the GTP set a rate on $4,172 per annum on a lease of 4.2 acres, Cold Storage declined to execute the document. In 1912, the company agreed to reduce the rent but demanded that the fish company route its freight on the GTP.[33] Because the local fish company manager brought the dispute to the minister of marine, Hansard determined to extract the entire rental arrears as a penalty. Cold Storage responded by applying for a lease for the water lot on which it had built not from the GTP but from the federal government. The GTP's repeated denials of the public harbour did not deflect Roger's department from its intention to grant the lease.[34]

The ongoing dispute had not prevented Cold Storage from shipping fish south to Vancouver on GTP steamers pending the completion of the railway. The firm now refused to pay its freight bills. Although the GTP had reached a tentative agreement with Cold Storage in December 1913, Hansard received instructions to 'get after these people' by initiating ejection proceedings despite the freight department's plea to settle as soon as possible.[35]

Since the GTP had obtained its order-in-council in 1914, Mackenzie conceded that the parlous state of the fish company's lease required a settlement. But he was able to delay issue of the government's quit claim to the GTP for several months while he dickered for a lower rental. During this period, the company demanded that Cold Storage advance the entire cost of a spur to the plant, as it claimed that unsettled conditions made it no longer able to finance the deal. Although Cold Storage agreed to this unusual condition and requested that the spur be installed immediately, Hansard would not go ahead until other legal elements had been settled. While the GTP freight agent realized that the failure to put in a spur immediately would result in a serious loss of traffic to the system, Hansard insisted that nothing be done until the company accepted the GTP terms. A GTP vice-president dismissed the company's failure to connect immediately with Cold Storage as 'a temporary misfortune' and predicted that 'their extra expense in shipping other than via our Line is ... sufficient to cause them to seriously consider the cleaning up of the existing difficulties.'[36]

The railway company's acceptance of Cold Storage's request for a fifty-year lease of the lot led the government to issue the quit claim for the GTP water lots. The rental dispute was quickly settled, and the GTP completed the spur in April 1915.[37] But even though the quit claim had been issued, it did not yet have the force of law. In order to extract rent from other recalcitrant leaseholders, it was necessary to obtain the sanction of the provincial government for registration of the quit claim in Prince Rupert. Unless the GTP would transfer a parcel of land on Digby Island, this government determined to delay registration. During the next two years, the GTP could take no action to collect back rent from leaseholders or evict squatters. Only after the advent of a Liberal provincial government in 1916 was the quit claim registered.[38]

Thus, almost ten years after its original application, the GTP finally perfected its title to the water lots abutting the waterfront blocks that it had selected in 1908. While the registration of the waterfront blocks had taken only nine months, the acquisition and registration of the adjacent water lots had dragged on since 1911. During that time, the GTP had lost revenue from current leaseholders, been unable to enforce its traffic clause, and had not provided accommodation for other businesses wishing to locate on the waterfront. From 1913 onward, businessmen complained continually about the refusal of the company to grant leases to those businesses that sought them.[39] Attacked by both citizens and outsiders for hoarding the waterfront after 1911, the company simply had no waterfront it could lease until 1917. The tortuous process of perfecting its title to the water lots did great damage not only to the port but also to the railway company.

To entice investors to contribute to the development of the new Canadian seaport 'made to order,' the railway company and other individuals and firms with interest in the city's growth mounted an extensive publicity campaign. While most of the productions were both predictable and unimpressive, one brochure boosted Prince Rupert with artistry and imagination. The product of local businessmen in 1910, *Prince Rupert and the Dawning Empire* first captured the investor's eye with a cover in brilliant hues showing a GTP train bursting through a mountain chain with the dawn to illuminate the bustling Prince Rupert waterfront. With well-chosen photographs, the pamphlet briefly touted points so laboriously rehearsed in other works: an ideal location, excellent harbour, rich hinterland, and model design made certain the city's prosperity. To emphasize that the GTP would make the city 'a funnel kept bright by a continual flow of grain, crops, field, forest, mine and sea,' the authors presented a striking bird's-eye offshore view of the British

Columbia coast with Prince Rupert at its centre and the railway line stretching back across the mountains. No other pamphlet rivalled its design or its persuasiveness.

By contrast, GTP efforts to boost the town were pedestrian. Suggestive of its lack of imagination was its choice of a name for the new terminus, certainly one of the most important elements in the publicity campaign. Despite its development on an island surrounded by tidal rapids, the company apparently gave no thought to the retention of mellifluous and appropriate Tsimshian name *Kai-en* ('foam'). Instead, it sponsored a contest in 1905 to choose a name that was 'distinctively Canadian.' From the 12,000 entries, which ranged from Port Laurier to Scotch Thistle City, company officers selected 'Prince Rupert' even though the namesake had no connection with the Pacific coast. Ignoring the fact that the entry violated contest rules, they expressed concern only about the namesake's 'immoral' character.[40]

As part of a contemplated prospectus for shares in the GTP Town and Development Company, company officers compiled in 1907 a ponderous list of Prince Rupert's advantages. With the finest harbour on the Pacific coast and low freight rates, which the superior construction of the railway assured, the terminus, maintained secretary Henry Philips, would 'take advantage of Oriental traffic.' But the entrepôt would also prosper from local main line traffic by becoming 'the natural outlet to the enormous forest and mineral wealth of North British Columbia, which is only awaiting the advent of the railway for development.' He also admired its location for capturing the northern halibut and salmon fisheries. While his most imaginative contribution, the wildly speculative calculation that the company would obtain a return of $14.5 million even after reconveying one-quarter of its holdings to the government, was never published, the other claims appeared in both the direct and indirect productions of the GTP.[41]

In 1908, the GTP hired American journalist Cy Warman as a publicist. The company first directed Warman to Prince Rupert. His visit to the area resulted in a stream of articles in Canadian, British, and American journals. The GTP Passenger Department issued one of these pieces, 'At the Tip of the Rainbow,' as a pamphlet. In fulsome prose, he described the port's 'widening harbour where black whales frolic within a stone's throw of the docks.' After opining that the region's fishing potential would soon turn Prince Rupert into a 'Gloucester of the

Pacific,' Warman even defended the city's oft-maligned climate. The rain came from 'tempering tides, whose current cradles the warm chinook winds which are the breath and life of this Northern Empire.' Only a knocker would use his observation concerning great tidal changes to predict the heavy expense of wharf construction.[42]

Hays desired a more detailed, attractive rehearsal of the terminus's advantages. But the six editions of the pamphlet entitled *Prince Rupert ... The Pacific Coast Terminus of the Grand Trunk Pacific Railway*, which the company issued between 1909 and 1912, are remarkable only for their lack of interesting and original material. Probably put together by Warman, the pamphlets contained large passages lifted from more lively efforts. Of the eleven pages of text in the first edition in 1909, for example, almost nine were taken without citation from other works. With few exceptions, the arguments advanced in the first edition did not change appreciably through the series. Several of the photographs of rudimentary development in 1909 remained in the 1912 edition as examples of the landscape of a mature city. Only Hays's insistence that the pamphlet contain a reproduction of the Brett-Hall town plan and a map of the environs, which highlighted GTP holdings in British red, saved it from being discarded.[43]

Before the 1909 auction, the pages of the first local newspaper, the *Empire*, provided the most widely read source of information about the city. But the company officers did not care to cooperate with its irascible editor who frequently married his enthusiastic boosting with savage attacks on GTP management of the townsite. Accordingly, the company placed legal notices and timetables of steamship sailings in the paper but little else. As soon as the rival *Prince Rupert Optimist* appeared in the summer of 1909, the company promptly switched its custom. The following year it made contributions toward the establishment and maintenance of a third paper, the *Prince Rupert Journal*, whose editor undertook to 'do what [he] could to help any project that has been put forward [by the company].' Because the *Journal* frequently ran vapid stories and toothless interviews 'entirely in the interests of the GTP,' it never escaped the criticism of the other two as a company mouthpiece.[44]

While the company's intent was similar to that of the local real estate shills who brayed about the duty of the investor to 'get in' while prices were low, it would require a lighter hand than Warman's to convince British investors that the company's new terminus was a 'golden city.'

Perhaps the only effective element of the GTP campaign came from the books and articles of the company's unofficial publicist, Frederick Talbot. Preceding chapters have indicated his success in propagating a sunny view of GTP construction and labour relations. But his creation of a discovery myth for Prince Rupert represents his greatest achievement. While Talbot related the advantages of the port set out above, he presented a fanciful account of the company's decision to locate its terminus at Tuck's Inlet. Because an admiralty chart incorrectly located a rock in the fairway of the harbour, other investigators had bypassed the inlet. But Hays 'somehow was attracted by Tuck's Inlet. It appeared to exercise an irresistible magnetism.' After a visit, the GTP president, 'impressed with the possibilities and outlook,' personally ordered the survey that determined the fairway was unobstructed. The results of the survey led the company to locate its terminus at this spot. Talbot thus transformed into a crucial expedition the largely ceremonial directors' inspection of the Kaien Island property four months after the company had undertaken to locate its terminus there. That no later study of the GTP, scholarly or popular, has exposed this fabrication indicates Talbot's persuasiveness.[45]

Beyond the occasional item in the *Journal*, the railway company engaged in little direct promotion of the city after 1912. It may be that the flood of publications from other individuals and institutions in that year convinced company officers that its efforts were superfluous. But the cessation of publicity corresponds roughly with the completion of the company's second lot sale. When the economic downturn and the war made further sales improbable, the company continued its silence.

During the war, the only source of published information beyond the local newspapers was an extended municipal report in 1916. While claiming that growth would continue in Prince Rupert, it admitted that building and construction had been halted temporarily. But even during this period of decline, the pamphlet tied virtually all the advantages of the city except climate to railway activity.[46] In the arguments of its promoters, Prince Rupert had become very much a railroad town.

While the architects were preparing a design for the terminus in 1908, both the railway company and the provincial government began to consider ways of selling their respective interests in the property. Although the company preferred to sell the lots of both parties in the townsite, it agreed to a joint sale under the direction of McBride's Conservative realtor, C.D. Rand.[47] GTP land commissioner George Ryley followed the wishes of the BC chief commissioner of lands in accepting a public auction but suggested that the company adopt the terms the CPR advertised in Vancouver: one-quarter down, the remainder within three years. To prevent broke purchasers from erecting shacks on the property, he recommended a building requirement of $2,000 on lots in the centre of town.[48] The most influential individual in the formulation of company policy on this matter was the GTP chief engineer. Remarking that the expenses of preparing the plan and clearing the townsite had 'run up to a very considerable extent,' B.B. Kelliher urged immediate sale of the business section and the two southern residential sections. While the hidden expenditure of lot grading might be left to the unsuspecting purchaser, the engineer realized that the company and the government must take on the heavy task of grading the streets. In October, the government indicated that the company could sell lots in May 1909. That same month the partners agreed to spend $200,000 for the initial laying of plank roadways and sewer pipe.[49]

With the platting completed early in 1909, the company prepared to divide the lots with the government in a ratio of 3:1. The architects had advised that as well as location, selection should depend on the propinquity of the lot to the street grade since this would reduce the purchaser's expenditure. With the landscape architect's help, Bacon went to Victoria to divide lots in Sections 1-8 with the government on 1 March. From 9,139 lots, the railway company chose 6,854 and the government 2,285. The architect reported the railway company's selection was good in every section and received $1,000 for his services.[50]

Expecting the sale to take place on the terminus ground, the Prince Rupert Board of Trade and the Conservative Association sent letters to Hays and McBride outlining the suspiciously extensive accommodation the few local hotels could offer to prospective investors. But the company and the government, realizing that the majority of probable buyers lived outside the area, decided to sell 1,200 lots each at an auction in Vancouver. While the request ostensibly came from the provincial cabinet, Hays accepted with alacrity and ordered the private sale of lots immediately after. As a sop to the disappointed residents, the president undertook to allow approved residents who had erected buildings to reserve their lots. The sudden shift of the auction location, the *Empire* fumed, was a fine example of 'GTP fancy work for vested interests.'[51]

After beating down the government realtor's commission from 2 to

1 per cent of gross sales, Hays sent him to Prince Rupert to fix upset (minimum) prices on the lots. To increase interest, the company helped him arrange an excursion for 'all good fellows' to look over the property before bidding in Vancouver in May. Perhaps because cabinet members wisely declined the offer of free passes, *Empire* editor John Houston dismissed the excursion as a 'cheap trick of a small-time hustler.'[52]

When Rand arrived in Prince Rupert in late April, he reported that the residents had all turned pessimistic and 'attempted to convince us of the undesirability of the property.' To combat Houston's influence, Rand placed ads in which he accused the editor of using 'sledge-hammer editorials' to knock prices into the 'sub-cellar.' But the rough shape of much of the property compelled the valuators to fix upset prices much lower than they had expected.[53]

Many buyers did not share the reservations of the valuators, however. Before the auction, local realtor T.D. Pattullo declared that 'the more I look at the resources of this place, the more I like them.' Expecting prices to treble after the completion of the line, he intended to buy a big block of property. Though it would not equal Vancouver, 'Prince Rupert will be a Hammer, 50,000 [people] and up.'[54] During the auction sale in Vancouver, 1,500 frantic investors bid up lots far beyond the upset prices. For example, two lots in the business district with a combined upset price of $6,750 sold for $10,600. After five days, the company and the government had sold 2,400 lots for more than $1.1 million. By October, the company had sold 4,600 lots for more than $1.9 million. Even the premier joined the rush. As an anonymous member of a syndicate, McBride purchased a share of property that yielded a profit of at least $9,300 in two dividends by 1910.[55]

The enthusiasm of the lot buyers was not shared by everyone. Later that year, a Toronto businessman complained that 'the GTP had everything so completely organized to keep everything for themselves that he did not see any chance of an outsider making anything at present.' By snapping up property on the projected main street, Second Avenue, speculators forced businesses to locate further away from the waterfront. Houston commented that by purchasing lots at four times their actual worth, outsiders would delay for three years the boom that Prince Rupert deserved. And by the fall, even Ryley admitted that speculation drove the Prince Rupert real estate market.[56] A resident American engineer later captured the mood of investors in a letter to his parents. 'People are coming into this country rapidly and if they wait somebody else would get ahead of them. Everything here is an anticipation and many people overestimate and think everything will be all right as soon as the railroad is completed.'[57]

For once Hays resisted the promise of a quick return and held the company's remaining lots off the market for two years. By the fall of 1911, however, the president had ridden the speculative wave long enough, and he decided to sell more of the company's holdings. This time the company would not share the return with the government or the government's auctioneer. Instead, he ordered that the auction be held in Prince Rupert under the direction of the local representative of the Development Company, his brother David H. Hays. The broker sold 583 lots in Section 2 in the company auction for $597,660.[58]

The second sale suggests that the president was not an adept speculator. Though the company now secured a return per lot 2.39 times that of 1909, this increase lagged behind the advance in property values for the city as a whole. The provincial government did much better. The following year the province sold 242 lots in several sections for $1,192,475, an increase of 8.67 over its 1909 return per lot. Although the local agent implored Ryley to join the government and sell more lots, Ryley decided that the GTP should wait until the following spring. But in 1913, the completion of the sale in Prince George engaged his attention. By the time he considered another sale in 1914, the market had collapsed and he was already seeing frequent defaults on purchased lots.[59]

Although the GTP had turned a handsome profit on townsite lot sales, it could have realized more by following the timing of the provincial government in marketing its property. While the returns per lot far exceeded the early calculations, which led to a company valuation of the Prince Rupert properties at $21 million, the GTP's disinclination in 1912 and inability thereafter to market its property ensured that it could never secure yields approaching the huge return the management had calculated in 1907. In addition, the high prices the company and the government obtained slowed the settlement of Prince Rupert and persuaded many owners to walk away from their properties in later years.[60] In this case the company was a victim of its own success.

ALTHOUGH COMPANY EXPENDITURES in Prince Rupert after acquisition of the land were largely directed to the extraction of an immediate return, three other projects that the company initiated after the 1909 lot auction appear to contradict this contention. Sharing the attitudes of the contemporary leaders of many American roads, the GTP managers looked with favour on the creation of visible monuments to their activities. The proposed construction of a chateau hotel, an integrated extension of the wharfs and railway yards, and a 'monster drydock' would not only support the company's somewhat traditional claim that its terminus was a city beautiful; it also allowed the company to advance the more fashionable claim that, like the Pennsylvania and the New York Central, the company was creating a terminus that, like its system, would become a model of efficiency.[61] But while the conception of the three projects owed much to a common managerial striving for corporate grandeur, the outcome of these schemes was closely tied to GTP calculations for minimizing expenditure, which would not produce an immediate return.

Of these ancillary projects, only the hotel has attracted attention because of its architect, Francis Rattenbury, the designer of the CPR Empress Hotel and second Legislative Buildings in Victoria. The architect had purchased extensive land in the Bulkley Valley three years before the company made its formal route decision. In 1906, he designed the first GTP hotel in Prince Rupert, the gabled Prince Rupert Inn, which was completed the following year.[62]

But for a port the company claimed would rival Vancouver, something grander was needed. Accordingly, Hays gave Rattenbury a commission in 1911 to design a much larger structure at the centre of the business district. During the following two years the architect drew up a series of plans for a chateau hotel that, in the grandest version, reached twelve stories with two wings, contained a false dome, skylights, and fountain complete with bronze figures, and offered 450 rooms finished in oak, mahogany, marble, and ornamental plaster. The cost of this luxurious structure, twice the size of the Empress, would exceed $1 million.[63]

That the architect's design responded to the company's vision of grandeur is indicated in a wash perspective of the hotel, station, and steamship terminal that the company probably commissioned in 1913 as part of an impending advertising campaign. Here, Rattenbury's three magnificent structures, largely in the Beaux-Arts style, adorn a vast eight-track passenger outlet and a wharf that could accommodate the largest ocean liners of the time.[64]

Grandeur was not the only motive for the project, however. As part of the settlement of an assessment dispute with the city council in 1911,

Perspective of Rattenbury design for GTP hotel, station, and steamship terminal, 1913

the GTP had undertaken to construct a major hotel. The award of the commission to Rattenbury simply publicized its commitment. But with the railway far from complete, the company would not expend resources on this project without a substantial additional subsidy. The excavation for the hotel, which commenced in the fall of 1913, was an inexpensive way of suggesting that the company actually intended to build the structure. Although a railway trade journal claims that excavation was completed, the company legal files suggest it was only begun. Complaints in the local papers concerning this 'empty hole' support this view. In December 1914, the GTP hotel manager admitted that the company still had not commenced construction of the hotel.[65]

The commissioned wash perspective indicates that the hotel was one element in a larger plan of waterfront development. In 1913, Chamberlin commissioned Virgil Bogue, a San Francisco engineer who had created a grandiose civic design for Seattle, to draw up a development plan for the entire harbour. The engineer presented a plan for waterfront and railway terminals 'co-ordinated to each other,' which would 'provide for one of the most extensive railway systems in the world' and 'a vast over-seas traffic in addition to an ever growing coast-wise commerce.' Where Vancouver currently had an aggregate wharf and quay frontage of 27,000 feet, Bogue projected for the GTP development a frontage of more than 35,000 feet.[66]

Unfortunately, the plan contains no indications of cost. Estimates of fill for various elements of the waterfront suggest that the initial cost of site preparation alone ranged from $560,000 to $610,000. Whatever the total cost, the company was unsuccessful in convincing the government to accept the Bogue plan and increase the subsidy to the company for terminal development to include this new cost.[67]

Though the company ostensibly accepted the engineer's conclusions that the development would create 'the opportunity of the railway, a great asset,' it did nothing to fulfil the plan. After the president admitted late in 1914 that the GTP could not 'contemplate for the present, or in fact for some time to come, the carrying out of the final lay-out,' company engineers quietly abandoned the plan.[68]

Outside of the yards and wharfs of the terminus proper, the construction and operation of the Prince Rupert drydock represented the company's largest single expenditure in British Columbia. Unlike the hotel and the Bogue plan, the company actually completed this project. The different outcome of this venture stems from its success in obtaining a government subsidy for a substantial part of the drydock. But the subsidy did not prevent the GTP from committing significant errors in planning and development. This section examines the origin and construction of the dock; the company's attempts to operate the dock during the war will be discussed later.

If Prince Rupert were to challenge Vancouver's supremacy on the Pacific coast as the premier Canadian port, it must have all the attributes of a port besides the facility to transfer goods from land to sea. Beyond the construction of the wharves, probably the most important aspect of port development was the presence of a facility for repairing and building ships. Consequently, when the federal finance minister first introduced a resolution concerning aid in the construction of drydocks in March 1908, Hays persuaded him to extend the contemplated subsidy to an unusual floating dock he had in mind for Prince Rupert.[69]

Two American naval architects advised the president that in a harbour with tidal changes of 25 feet, a recently developed pontoon system for lifting ships would be cheaper and more flexible than the traditional basin design. Since this new design could be accommodated in the company's Block G on the harbour waterfront, it would also encourage the government to transfer the water lot in front of the property. Because the works would be far from other fabricating sources, they recommended construction of as much of the dock as possible on the site.[70]

While the architects calculated the cost of a dock capable of lifting 18,000 tons at $1,676,000, the company submitted to the Department of Public Works, the federal department in charge of the subsidy, a revised estimate of $2,264,516.36 for a dock that would lift 20,000 tons. But the increase did not disturb the chief engineer of the department who noted that the 'dock will certainly be of great benefit and public utility to vessels in the coasting trade.' Even when an official discovered that the GTP estimate for the steel pontoons was $37 per ton where wood cost $50 and steel $65, the department engineer decided that the company's estimate, though 'no doubt very low, must be considered as correct.'[71]

Not everyone was so enthusiastic. Observing that the proposed GTP development was more suitable for woodworking than metal fabrication, the consulting engineer of the Canadian Naval Service expressed concern about the lack of a foundry for heavy metal repairs. But though the Naval Service recommended that payment of the subsidy should depend on the GTP complying with the requirements of the Naval Service for metal-working equipment, the order-in-council for awarding the subsidy declared that these requirements were 'not ... deemed essential for the efficient working of the dock and may be left to the Company to carry out if they think advisable.'[72]

By early 1911, Vice-President Wainwright claimed that everything had been settled and pressed for an order. When the minister wanted another check of the estimates, Wainwright convinced the department to pass an interim order of acceptance without a final calculation of the subsidy. In the final order-in-council, the government granted the company a subsidy of 3.5 per cent for 25 years on an estimate of $2,094,455. At the end of November the government and the railway company signed an agreement that put the order into effect. Because the company apparently ignored the subsidy act's proviso of completion before payment, Chamberlin gloated that the agreement allowed the company to complete its railway terminal, presumably at government expense.[73]

Early in 1912, the company's dock designers delivered an illustrated lecture that was quickly published. Although the architects declared that the plant would support the 'full equipment of blacksmith's tools,' they did not include in the description a foundry, tools, or facilities for fabricating steel plates. But they did attract much attention with an illustration

GTP Prince Rupert dock lifting 18,000-ton Great Northern steamship *Minnesota*. The GTP coastwise vessel, *Prince Rupert*, is in front of the dock for scale.

depicting the largest ship in trans-Pacific trade, the Great Northern's 18,000-ton *Minnesota*, in dock alongside the much smaller GTP *Prince Rupert*. The illustration, which appeared with the caption 'Monster Dock' in newspapers across the country, gave many the impression that the dock could not only refit metal ships but also make major repairs and even build them.[74]

Although site preparation commenced during the summer, the company did not let contracts for the piers and superstructure until the following year. The American construction firms that the company selected could not fulfil their contracts, however, and transfer of the contracts and settlement of a lien consumed most of 1913. Work on the structures did not begin in earnest until early in 1914.[75]

During construction the company experienced a serious problem with the availability and demands of labour. In April 1914, workers complained that the GTP was not adhering to the current wage clause in the subsidy agreement. The company or its contractors paid carpenters 45¢ per hour instead of $5.00 per day and labourers 30¢ per hour instead of $3.60 for eight hours. Although a government investigator on the spot supported the complaint, Chamberlin rejected the demands as 'exorbitant IWW rates fixed by organizers.' Only when Public Works notified the company that failure to comply with the report would be regarded as a breach of the subsidy agreement did the company conform. Early in 1915, the company agreed to pay electricians the current wage when the department again threatened to withhold the subsidy.[76]

Despite these setbacks, the company maintained that work on the dock was progressing steadily. Late in 1914, the GTP local superintendent noted that the October payroll for construction had been $18,000 and predicted that the dock would be completed in June 1915. One year later a booster could still exclaim that 'whenever I feel I need a little bucking up ... I just go over and take a good look at the drydock.' But by the end of the year the superintendent admitted that the dock was 'hardly ready.'[77]

By July 1916, the GTP had expended $2,800,645 on the dock, $600,000 more than the government had undertaken to subsidize in 1911. Although the dock lifted its first ship in September 1915, the company apparently lacked the wherewithal to continue and closed the dock in December.[78]

Thus, in the expectation that it would secure seven-eighths of its expenditure from the government, the company accepted for its dock design a plan suspect because of its incapacity to undertake heavy metal repairs, submitted for subsidy an estimate ignoring the cost of basic materials, and delayed payment of the subsidy by dragging out construction for years. Its bumbling attempts to operate the dock during the war years will be examined in the penultimate chapter.

OF THE CONFLICTS the company entered to protect its authority and its returns in Prince Rupert, the most well known remains the protracted dispute with John Houston, publisher and editor of Prince Rupert's first newspaper, the *Empire*. While none of Houston's private papers has survived, notes in scattered company files as well as the columns of the *Empire* reveal how the GTP finally won the 'War between the Scotch and the Whites,' the dispute with Houston that has passed into community folklore.[79]

Mayor of Nelson during the 1890s, Houston had developed a hatred for the CPR and never missed the chance to excoriate the railway company. As a prominent member of the Legislative Assembly during the Dunsmuir era, Houston had supported a motion to cut off provincial aid to railway companies. Barred from cabinet in 1903, probably because Premier McBride wished to placate the CPR, Houston appeared suddenly in Prince Rupert in the summer of 1907 with a small printing press and the intention of starting a newspaper.[80]

The first response of GTP harbour engineer James Bacon led to the 'war.' Apparently aware of Houston's antipathy to railroads, Bacon impounded the press in a small shed on the wharf. But Houston had his newspaper printed in Victoria, and the first number of the *Empire* arrived in Prince Rupert with a lead story that the GTP discouraged newcomers. Faced with an open challenge, Bacon denied Houston a permit and threatened to evict him for trespassing. He also cut off an essential source of revenue for the paper by convincing the local government agent to prohibit the insertion of legal notices in the *Empire*. But Houston persuaded the provincial lands commissioner to reverse the decision. By applying to the general manager for permission to open shop, Houston called into question the casual permit system Bacon controlled.[81]

The early numbers of the paper frequently attacked GTP policies for developing the terminus. In September, Houston described railway managers as 'little tin gods to whom all the people along the line of railway must bow down to for permission to engage in business.' If the GTP continued to hamper the efforts of individuals through its permit system, the company would 'retard and prevent the upbuilding of even a small city.' After two months of printing what a contemporary journalism survey described as 'spicy' views, Houston proclaimed that his newspaper in exile for a community of 500 had sold more than 10,000 copies.[82]

Having assured the financial base of the paper, Houston liberated its physical plant and directly challenged the authority of the GTP. In the middle of September, he swore a warrant charging the company with illegal sequestration of the press. When a police constable rejected Bacon's request to protect the warehouse, the GTP harbour engineer ordered employees to throw Houston off the wharf for trespassing. The constable convinced these worthies to break down the door of the shed and carry the press back to the police tent where Houston turned out his first local edition.[83]

Hays did not approve of such heavy-handed tactics, which could only increase the *Empire's* subscription. Arriving at Prince Rupert after the liberation of the press, the GTP president ordered Bacon to cease his harassment and granted Houston a permit to erect a building at the company's pleasure. It appeared Hays would turn an opponent into a friend as the editor lauded the president's promise of 'a free field to every one that has muscle and no special favours to anyone that has money.'[84]

But Houston was not content to operate at the company's pleasure under the permit system. Before liberating the press, he had located along with John Knox two mining claims, the 'Cariboo' and the 'Grand Turk Fractional [*sic*]' on the northeast corner of the Indian reserve beside the railway company wharf. After filing the claims with the government agent in Port Simpson, the editor declared that he now held title to land through the provincial government and no longer accepted the authority of the company. Decrying the GTP policy of a closed townsite as foolish, he invited others to build on the mineral claims and predicted that the new community of 'Knoxville' would soon have a population that rivalled the official GTP townsite.[85]

Urging the McBride government to extract a good agreement from the company early in 1908, Houston now felt secure enough to write the following satire of a future meeting of Prince Rupert city council.

John Pillsbury, Assistant Superintendent of the GTP, notified council that no salt water must be removed from the harbour without the written consent of the railway company. Referred to committee on Trusts.
... Police Report. The next serious case was that of a man who was caught

red-handed staking a mineral claim on the Indian Reserve ... There was no difficulty in securing a conviction – 21 years of hard labour. Another man who attempted to erect a tent on land belonging to the railway company was sentenced to six years with hard labour and thirty lashes. J.H. Bacon, manager of the GTP, for running over three children with an automobile, was severely censured.[86]

Although Pillsbury's son claims that Bacon enjoyed these exchanges, there is little proof in the engineer's correspondence with both head office and the provincial government. On 27 October, Bacon wrote McBride that the sole object of the claims of Houston and Knox and six others was to 'hold up rightful owners of the land,' and demanded that the government cancel the claims.[87]

The company realized that Houston's position depended on the protection of the British Columbia government at the same time as the province was asserting its right to the reversionary interest in Metlakatla Indian Reserve. Accordingly, GTP solicitor Tate inserted in the general settlement a clause providing for the extinction of all mineral claims with the registration of plans for the townsite. Morse gloated that 'as soon as we obtain approval, squatters' rights will be wiped out.' But the squatters' shacks erected under Houston's writ delayed the company from completing its survey and acquiring title for the land. In response, Bacon barred lumber for buildings on the mineral claim from landing on the GTP wharf.[88]

By the fall of 1908, the company completed its survey and registered its townsite plan. It was now inevitable that the company would acquire the province's reversionary interest and evict the squatters. Bacon's complaints even persuaded the lands commissioner to assist the company in expelling squatters.[89] But Houston apparently did not realize the precariousness of his position and continued to champion a community at the terminus united by its opposition to the GTP: 'No person in Prince Rupert has a pull, for most of the people here are here against the protests of the local officials of the GTP Ry ... Once people act contrary to the wishes of the autocrats of a railway company, they are not shown many favours.' While his campaigns against Asian labour and his crusade for the working man attracted much support, his attempt to link the provincial police with liquor sales alienated not only the hotel owners and local constables but also many prominent residents he required to continue to withstand the railway company.[90]

Not anxious to be seen as the pusher, the company quietly took care to exclude Houston from the lots it reserved for Prince Rupert residents before the 1909 auction. Unable to purchase the lots on which his building stood, the editor protested that when a 'man who has put in one to three years pioneering is shown no more consideration than a man who never was in the townsite, it is a hell of a way to start building a town.'[91] He abruptly sold his newspaper for $10,000 and left. By separating Houston from his powerful patron, the provincial government, the company had at last rid itself of a formidable, if erratic, opponent.

THE LEGAL DEPARTMENT's insouciant response to municipal incorporation produced the most spectacular challenge to GTP returns at the terminus. Early in 1909, Tate had persuaded McBride to ignore an incorporation bill inspired by Houston on the technical ground that it did not have the support of the only local landowner at the time, the railway company. Faced with another hostile incorporation scheme from the new property owners after the auction, the GTP solicitor travelled to Victoria in January 1910 to defend the company's interests in deliberations on incorporation that the government intended to inaugurate later that year. The GTP had requested cabinet to insert in the act a series of concessions, the most notable of which was the requirement that street grades conform with the GTP townsite plan. But Tate's most important task was to secure in legislation 'the observance by the future municipality of any arrangements entered into by the Province and the company prior to incorporation ... especially [financial] obligations which should naturally be assumed by the municipality.' Though the GTP solicitor persuaded cabinet to insert the specific concessions in the incorporation act that the company desired, his work was sloppy. By overlooking the threat of municipal taxation, which Houston had clearly advocated earlier, Tate allowed the new city council to challenge the company on assessment.[92]

Since the municipal assessment dispute, the most glaring example of GTP interference in the governance of Prince Rupert, generated much controversy for more than a year, it is not surprising that a number of historians have attempted to analyze it.[93] Indeed, it is fortunate that the local newspapers daily chronicled, or at least speculated on, the evolution of the conflict because the most important company file apparently has not survived.[94] The three papers, along with the minutes of city council

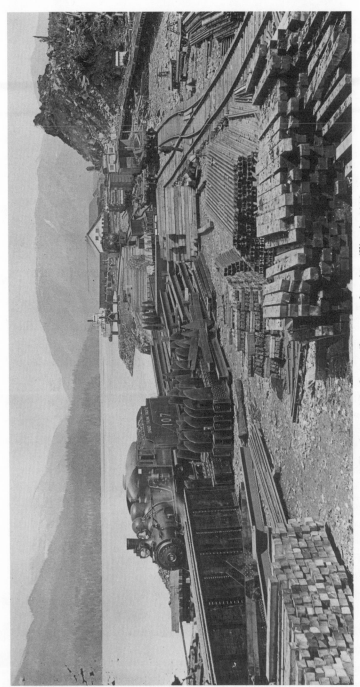

The centre of GTP waterfront property, assessed by the municipal council at more than $7 million in 1910.

and several premier's files, reveal the methods and suggest the costs of the GTP victory.

In 1907, the British Columbia government had awarded municipalities the right to tax railway property within city limits. Recognizing this threat to company returns, the GTP legal department had sought to insert an exemption clause in the general settlement of 1908, but the provincial government rejected the request. Because the Prince Rupert incorporation act allowed an appeal against assessment, Tate believed that the company could protect its returns and voiced no protest about municipal assessment. Before incorporation, the assessor, who the provincial government had already appointed, apparently valued some GTP lots lightly; the total valuation of lots held by the GTP Development Company was $242,320, a moderate sum given the number of lots the company still held within the city for future sales. But the property held for railway purposes by the railway company proper, the yards along the shore, was assessed at $7,049,180, or more than $20,000 per acre.[95]

Although this assessment was filed with the local registrar toward the end of March 1910, the local GTP officer did not register a formal protest by the close of the court of revision. Tate later claimed that the GTP land commissioner in Winnipeg did not receive the notice of assessment in sufficient time to appeal. When the GTP general manager E.J. Chamberlin arrived in Prince Rupert early in May, he discovered the valuation and complained that the city had imposed on the railway company the entire assessment burden.[96] Yet no evidence indicates that the company made the assessment an issue during the first civic election in May 1910.

When Chamberlin met Tate in Victoria the following week, they argued before cabinet that the 'figures were indeed so gross ... that legislative action must ... be taken to correct them.' But the GTP could not secure from the government an exemption similar to that enjoyed by the Canadian Northern. If the company could not move the provincial government, it would intimidate the new city. The general manager recommended that the company discontinue all work in Prince Rupert until the matter was resolved.[97]

To satisfy McBride's desire for an amicable settlement, Hays met Prince Rupert's first mayor, Alfred Stork, in Vancouver in June. Suggesting as a precedent the company's arrangement with Fort William, which granted exemption and $300,000 cash, the GTP president demanded a complete exemption from taxation for fifteen to twenty years. He suggested that a committee arbitrate the matter. But he also employed Chamberlin's strategy and threatened to discontinue work on all railway projects in the city, including the drydock.[98]

The Prince Rupert city council, however, was in no mood to compromise. Because the city had contracted for several expensive undertakings – waterworks, sewers, street grading, and the telephone system – council decided unanimously that it would not alter the assessment despite the president's threat to halt railway work. When newly elected alderman Pattullo, as head of the finance committee, levied a rate of fifteen mills on the assessment, the company received a bill for its railway property of more than $105,000. Although several aldermen indicated the dangers of such a high rate, Stork and Pattullo argued that the city required it.[99]

Hays retorted that the current assessment of railway property in Prince Rupert exceeded the combined assessments of Grand Trunk property in Montreal and Toronto. Declaring that 'the GTP has had nothing at that point [Prince Rupert] which it has not paid for and paid for handsomely,' he challenged the council to offer inducements for further railway company expenditure. To the provincial government, GTP officers expressed themselves more bluntly. Describing the assessment as 'practically a confiscation of our property,' Chamberlin declared that neither the drydock nor the proposed hotel, 'equal to the best on the Pacific Coast,' would go ahead while the city 'persecuted the company.' While Tate moderated Hays's angry insistence on complete exemption, the solicitor clearly revealed the GTP perception of its terminus: 'It is not the people who make Prince Rupert – it is the Company. Let the people remain and the Company withdraw, how long would property values be maintained? Why should the Company have to pay for something which is brought about by itself and its enterprise?'[100]

When Hays arrived in Prince Rupert at the end of August, he twisted arms in a private meeting with Stork, Pattullo, and the city solicitor. The president first warned that the company would move the proposed drydock to Porpoise Island, effectively sidetracking the city from what was expected to be a major source of revenue. But Hays's threat to shift the railway terminus to Port Simpson after more than four years of GTP development of Kaien Island was preposterous. More ominous, because it was practicable, was his hint that the GTP would halt construction permanently on the west end, where it had so often complained about the price of labour, and build the rest of the line from the prairies to the coast. When this intimidation failed, Hays complained to the press about the 'unreasonable assessment of railway property.' He concluded that 'our case may not be sustained in court, but we will not go ahead with improvements or the hotel until we get a nominal rate of taxation.'[101]

When the GTP party reached Victoria, its members continued to attack the council. In a general discussion of the railway, Grand Trunk chairman Alfred Smithers offered the following observation: 'Take Prince Rupert ... which owes its very existence to the Grand Trunk Railway. They told us that we were getting large dividends and that they were going to exact all sorts of unheard of taxes.' In a later conversation meant for terminus residents, the chairman explained that 'to any fair Rupertite, the demand of the city must seem like highway robbery.' He then asked whether the council were all socialists. With headlines trumpeting the award of hotels and docks to Victoria and Seattle, the conclusion was obvious for one newspaper. 'Wise citizens [of Prince Rupert] know that we are but the creation of the GTP.'[102] The reporter might have changed the phrase to creature.

These complaints encouraged all three local newspapers to attack the council. The *Empire* castigated the council as disloyal agitators. Fed by GTP advertising, the *Journal* pleaded for a drastic decrease in the GTP assessment. Such an action was proper for a city that 'must be what is known as a one-corporation town.' The *Optimist* warned that 'this company can very easily stop development for the next two years without materially embarrassing the transcontinental trade, but it would be disastrous for local business.' That the council recognized the importance of newspapers in the campaign is indicated by the purchase of the *Optimist* by a group of investors including Pattullo in October 1910.[103]

When an alderman remarked at a town meeting that Hays had mentioned the sum of $6,000 per annum as a reasonable tax, businessmen rushed to send a telegram to the president asking for negotiations. Chamberlin replied that the citizens should formulate and submit a proposition in accord with Hays's demands. Despite the mayor's plea to maintain the railway assessment, members of the Board of Trade quickly drew up a new valuation of railway property that reduced the assessment from $7,291,500 to $1,726,500, and the 1910 levy from $105,000 to $25,897.50.[104]

The GTP then apparently encouraged another institution to apply financial pressure. In October, the local manager of the city's bank informed the council that the Bank of Montreal would withhold all further funds from the city until the dispute with the GTP was settled. Pattullo and Stork, however, were defiant and declared independence from the bank. In passing a motion concerning the sale of debentures in London, Pattullo exclaimed that 'the GTP does not own the country; the country owns the GTP.' Although the bank relented and eventually offered $500,000 to continue improvements, the railway company was in no mood to let the council escape. Hays stopped the advertisement of city shares on the London market with a threat to make the dispute over the assessment public. The *Optimist* ridiculed this threat as a bad blunder, but there is no evidence that Prince Rupert was able to market its debentures until the dispute was concluded. In that sense the threat was effective. The company also refused to allow the new GTP steamships to be registered at Prince Rupert.[105]

On 26 October, Hays responded to the Board of Trade's offer of settlement. While he agreed to turn over all of the properties to the city that the company had previously promised, he would not accept the rate of 15 mills even on the reduced assessment of $1,726,500. In order to proceed with the development, including the drydock, the president demanded a flat annual tax of $5,000 on railway property for twenty years. The company's intent, the GTP solicitor remarked, was to maintain an unyielding pressure: 'If, and so long as work is suspended, the Company control the situation, and can secure an equitable settlement, but just as soon, and to the extent that work is resumed or undertaken, so far is our position and our ability to force a settlement reduced.'[106]

Shortly after Hays's response, McBride intervened directly in the dispute. In early November, the cabinet visited Prince Rupert and held an interview with the city council. While the premier assured the aldermen that the government would not 'force matters in favour of the company,' he suggested that the city follow the government lead by not demanding a great deal of revenue from the GTP to enter the province. By reading portions of a GTP letter that compared the Prince Rupert assessment with those in central Canada, he implied that he accepted the company's protest. His belief that the city was 'entitled to grant exemption from taxation for ten years' put him firmly in the company's corner.[107]

As both the council incumbents and its opponents geared up for the second municipal election in January, Tate arrived in Prince Rupert in mid-December. Council presented an offer to the solicitor. If the company would turn over all the parcels of land in the city that it had undertaken in previous agreements, the city would reduce the assessment to $2 million and assess a flat tax of $25,000, i.e., 11.25 mills, for a period of ten years. Such an offer effectively destroyed the council's earlier stand concerning the necessity of a uniform rate. But since Hays had demanded more, Tate rejected the offer out-of-hand. Even when the council indicated 'semi-officially' that it might reduce the levy to $20,000, the lawyer stood firm.[108]

Although the *Optimist,* now controlled by the Pattullo group, attacked the premier as 'the member for Grand Trunk Pacific' and the Conservative mayoral candidate, MLA William Manson, as 'McBride's boy,' it became painfully clear that the incumbent city council would not achieve a resolution of the problem. The Conservatives, the *Empire,* and the *Journal* advocated the council's dismissal on the grounds that it was unable to effect a settlement. Despite Pattullo's warning that the GTP had given the city a 'shakedown,' Manson defeated the Liberal candidate by 429 to 324, and only Pattullo remained on council to represent the views of the now departed Liberal members who had opposed the GTP.[109]

When Mayor Manson warned that voters would reject any settlement the company imposed, Tate charged that the new council was more hostile than the old. Since both Hays and Chamberlin were still determined not to move, the solicitor required that the entire council endorse a settlement before it was ratified by the electorate. In March, Tate went further: 'The GTP is a mighty corporation; Prince Rupert, a frail little city dependent upon the completion of the GTP for its lifeblood. If the City does not come a few notches yet, the GTP will not turn another sod on the construction of the line from the mountains to the seaport.' Although Tate repudiated the newspaper account of this threat, the publicity apparently served its purpose. On 16 March, council came several notches and offered a tax of $15,000 for ten years.[110]

Chapter 4 has indicated how the company disposed of the largest group of voters who opposed a settlement of this order by provoking the Battle of Kelly's Cut. For its second assessment in May 1911, the city reduced the railway property assessment from $7,291,500 to $2,819,500. Under the new banner of the Prince Rupert *Daily News,* the Liberal paper observed that 'either the railway is to be congratulated on a light assessment or consoled with for a remarkable shrinkage in the value of its property. It smacks a good deal of robbing Peter to pay Paul.' To discourage backsliding, the company refused to replank a central boardwalk and prohibited the city from dumping garbage off the GTP wharf. Faced with a rat epidemic, Manson and the council remained compliant.[111]

In early June, Hays returned to Prince Rupert and signed the March settlement. While one alderman allowed that he was 'tickled to death,' the president reiterated the company's final demand: 'Now that the situation at Prince Rupert has been adjusted, you may rely upon our Company putting forth every effort to get the work covered by the agreement under way speedily as possible, with a view to securing its early completion. In undertaking our work, we confidently expect the co-operation of the City.' Although the company had forwarded $30,000 by the end of the month to pay for the first two years of the agreement, Hays refused to resume work until the settlement was ratified.[112]

With the plebiscite set for September, the company solicited favourable comments on the settlement. Perhaps because the *Journal* was too closely identified with the GTP, an interview with one 'Grouch' appeared in the *Empire*. 'I do believe your settlement with the Grand Trunk was a great one. If I could control 500 votes, I would cast everyone of them in favour of ratification of settlement.' In the meantime, Grouch cancelled his subscription to the *Daily News*. On the eve of the vote, the *Journal* thoughtfully reminded voters that while it would 'not attempt to stampede citizens ... future railway construction, and implicitly, future prosperity of the city of Prince Rupert depended on it [ratification].' On 4 September, the citizens passed the bylaw by a vote of 418 to 44. While the *Journal* trumpeted the return of capital, the *Daily News* lamented that the outcome represented 'a victory for those who traded on the fears of the merchants and the workingmen that the GTP would squeeze the life out of the town.'[113]

The final levy of $15,000 per annum suggests that the legal department had secured an equitable arrangement midway between Hays's demands in October 1910 and the council offer in December 1910. But for $5,000 per annum, the difference between the council's 'semi-official' offer in December and the final settlement, the railway company had blocked development from 15 December 1910 to 4 September 1911, almost nine months. One might argue that the delay served the GTP's interest since it slowed company expenditure of capital on a terminus that would produce little return until the completion of the transcontinental. It might well have been in the company's long-term interest to use the dispute as a pretext for withdrawing permanently from construction on the west end. But the settlement and the company's resumption of work demonstrates that the GTP management did not wish to withdraw permanently at this time. If Hays's primary objective was to stop rather than delay expenditure, he would not have forsaken his demand for complete exemption; indeed, to prolong the dispute, he should have demanded a bonus similar to what the company had received at Fort William. On the GTP motive in this dispute, one must take the management at its word: the company blocked development to halt what the management perceived as 'highway robbery,' an unjustified limit on company returns. To secure Tate's 'few notches,' the company halted development for nine additional months and incurred interest charges and other costs on its works far in excess of $50,000.[114] The legal department had completed its narrow task and preserved what appeared to be an important return. But the president and general manager must have made the elementary calculations on the resulting interest charges. The company had smashed the opposition but alienated council and an important group of Prince Rupert citizens. To defend its returns, it sustained a significant overall loss. In this case, the fault can be placed nowhere other than with President Hays.

Following the examples of the CPR and Northern Pacific, the GTP expected to secure from its terminus a large immediate return on its privileges as well as on its property to cover the cost of construction of terminal facilities. By imposing an impractical plan on the townsite, the company increased the number of lots it could sell, but it hindered the economic development of the city. A campaign to perfect title to large portions of the waterfront distracted the GTP from attracting traffic-generating concerns to this crucial economic space before the completion of the railway. Indifferent advertising and poor timing probably decreased the return it could have extracted from lot sales before 1913. And with its deteriorating financial circumstances after 1912, the GTP did not complete most of its major investment projects.

By July 1914, the company had received 87 per cent of the proceeds from purchasers of GTP townsite lots. While the return of $2.3 million handily covered the construction cost of the terminal facilities, the balance did not begin to pay for the GTP's huge expenditure on the drydock.[115]

Although the GTP Development Company books, which did not include terminus or drydock charges, showed a healthy profit, the company's attempts to maximize immediate returns at its terminus resulted in a significant overall loss.

The record of the GTP at troubleshooting in Prince Rupert was no more impressive. The overwhelming superiority of its resources for struggle, its legal and technical expertise, and its influence with some members of the federal and provincial governments, allowed it to beat off a challenge for returns from a populist newspaper editor. But the GTP's protracted dispute with the municipal government reveals the desire of company officers to assert a kind of corporate hegemony, to dominate territory in the face of opposition from governments, competing businesses, and many of the region's inhabitants. Like the attempts of the Grand Trunk to limit access on the Toronto waterfront during the 1870s and 1880s, this illogical behaviour was ultimately self-defeating.[116] It did not maximize economic returns and it alienated residents and politicians whose support the company would later require to survive the period of low earnings after completion.

SIX

'A HOLD-UP BUSINESS':
ACQUISITION OF INDIAN LANDS

THOUGH THE GTP provided sporadic employment for some Native people, the company's most significant interaction with Native communities along its line in British Columbia was its acquisition of Indian reserve land. The most important acquisition of reserve land for the company's fortunes, Metlakatla, has been discussed in Chapter 2. The surviving documents concerning that taking say little about GTP attitudes toward or relations with the Native people, however. From the company's acquisition of land in 23 other Indian reserves in British Columbia, this chapter examines two cases: the GTP actions to secure the Fort George and Kitsumkalum.[1] Though the first case merits examination because it created the base for Prince George, the second city along the British Columbia line, the survival of company documents concerning both episodes, a rare occurrence, determined their selection. A review of these cases, using the records of the company's legal and land departments as well as more frequently consulted sources – federal and provincial government files, missionary documents, and newspapers – suggests that the GTP experienced a series of setbacks in obtaining Indian land. Frederick Talbot, British publicist for GTP, pointed to the 'cunning of the red man' to prolong or abort negotiations by introducing 'an obscure issue [that] brought matters to standstill.' Indeed, he lamented, 'the same difficulty has prevailed throughout the length of New Caledonia traversed by the Grand Trunk Pacific.'[2] But the 'obscure issues' that hindered company acquisition frequently did not arise solely from Native opposition. The provincial and federal governments more often represented a greater obstacle to the company's wishes. Where the GTP sought Native land for lucrative townsites, rival development concerns also deflected company plans. Only when their land was not desired by other white concerns or interests did the Native people become a significant obstacle to GTP goals, at least in the surviving correspondence of company officers.

This thesis departs from the works of both railway historians and anthropologists. Those who welcome the coming of the Iron Horse too frequently rehearse the role of American roads in military conquests during the 1860s and 1870s. In the Canadian case, the celebrants chronicle the placating or intimidation of chiefs that leads mysteriously to the establishment of rights-of-way across reserves.[3] Several works, however, consider more critically railway alienation of Indian land.[4] These studies indicate that a fifty-year tradition of corporate covetousness informed GTP actions toward Indian land, and invite the elaboration of a discourse of capitalist dispossession that could embrace the GTP.[5] Their narrow focus on company-government negotiations, however, hinders comparison with GTP perceptions of and actions toward Native people.

With a primary interest beyond railways, anthropologists and ethnohistorians have begun to describe how the railway acquisition of land contributed to the marginalization of Natives. The evolution of Native land claims in British Columbia over the past decade has produced a spate of reports assessing the damage the GTP and other railways inflicted on Native communities.[6] But a focus on these damages has led the author of the first published study on GTP relations with Native people to dismiss or obscure the significance of company actions beyond their negative effect on the band.[7] This chapter illuminates the 'specifics of that [GTP] railroad history' that eluded an expert witness at a recent land claim trial.[8] It contends that in attempting to overcome the barriers to Indian land – governments, rival development concerns, as well as Natives themselves – the GTP managers committed both strategic and tactical errors that harmed the company.

Where the provincial government presented the major obstacle to the company's acquisition of Metlakatla, the actions of rival development concerns posed the greatest threat to the company's acquisition of Indian land at Fort George. Perhaps because the GTP activities at Fort George did not cause the two levels of government to publish any documents, the railway company's difficulties in securing this reserve have not been recognized by historians.[9]

The Fort George district drew its name from the fur trade post established by Simon Fraser in 1807. During the first years of the twentieth century, the Hudson's Bay Company post journals for Fort George indicate that company servants, trappers, and travelling Oblate priests comprised the majority of whites in the district.[10] Only after the announcement of the GTP route across British Columbia in 1907 did whites begin to enter the district in significant numbers. By 1910, promoters had established rival townsites west and south of the reserve and marketed them energetically as terminal sites not only for the GTP but also for half a dozen paper railways.

The largest community in the district, a Carrier Indian band, occupied Fort George Indian Reserve No. 1, established in 1892 at the confluence of the Fraser and Nechako rivers. In 1910, the band held three other reserves besides No. 1 and numbered 144 persons in 29 families. Band members made their living primarily by trapping and were described as 'well-off when fish and furs are plentiful.' The entry of white trappers into the region at the turn of the century endangered the band's livelihood; the influx of railway construction workers some years later saw trapping and fishing decline rapidly.[11]

The company's original intent was to lay out a townsite across the northern part of the reserve and the land immediately west of it. When the owners of the western lots demanded $75 per acre, the company revised its plans to embrace the entire reserve.[12] After going over his maps, GTP chief engineer B.B. Kelliher concluded:

> If Divisional Yards will be constructed at Fort George, and they can only be constructed by acquiring the Indian Reserve, I believe that there will be in the future a town built up at that point. The buildings, station grounds, etc., must, of necessity be all in the Indian Reserve and located on the northerly portion of it. The southern portion of the Reserve is also excellent for a townsite, consisting of a plateau of about 50 ft. above the railroad.

Scant attention was paid to the residents. The engineer observed that the Native people occupied only a small portion of the junction; therefore, most of the desired land was vacant.[13]

GTP solicitor D'Arcy Tate first suggested that the company expropriate the entire reserve of 1,366 acres under the authority of the Railway Act on the ground that the whole parcel was 'so small' it would all be necessary for railway purposes. This was a foolish suggestion from an experienced railway lawyer. Tate should have realized that the extent of the railway grounds, even for a divisional point, could not surpass the size of the

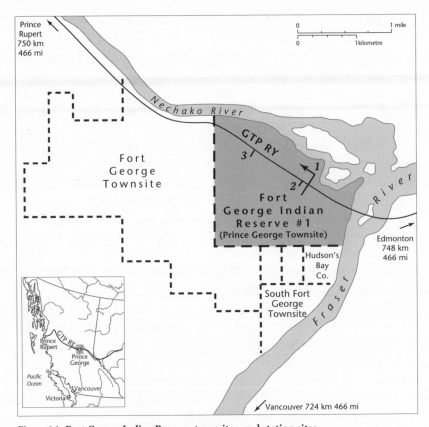

Figure 6.1 **Fort George Indian Reserve, townsites, and station sites**

1   BRC ruling, 5 March 1912. The GTP must build *west* of this line, 3,500 feet *west* of
    river bank.
2   GTP location, 24 January 1913 (George Street), 6,715 feet east of Fort George Townsite,
    331 feet west of 1912 ruling
3   BRC order, 14 May 1913 (Maple Street), 3,000 feet east of Fort George Townsite

projected railway yards for the Pacific terminus at Prince Rupert. Kelliher
soon realized that only a small part of the reserve would be used for railway
purposes and pointed out Tate's blunder: 'We cannot, of course, develop
any railroad plans for a divisional terminal that would occupy 1,366
acres and subject it to any reasonable criticism ... As it is the intention
that this land would be used for a townsite, should it not be acquired by
the Town and Development Company and not by the Railway Company?'[14]
Tate agreed to secure the land by negotiation rather than by statute.

    Since it had settled with the provincial government in early 1908, the
company expected to eliminate the major obstacle in this acquisition that

it had faced at Metlakatla. Though the general settlement did not specify how the company would acquire land in the interior, Premier McBride apparently promised Hays at that time to look favourably on additional GTP applications.[15]

Consequently, in making the company's initial application to the federal Department of Indian Affairs (DIA), Tate offered to purchase only the interest that Native people and the dominion government enjoyed in the land and then negotiate with the provincial government for its claim as had been done with the Metlakatla Reserve. The application encountered a different obstacle, however. A department official replied that the application could not be considered until the department had resolved the dispute with British Columbia concerning reversionary interest.[16]

After six more months, Tate was able only to suggest reversing the order to purchase. The railway company would first acquire the reversionary interest of the province and then negotiate with the dominion government for its interest. The GTP solicitor concluded that 'our engineers are most anxious that they should not be delayed in order that the road may be completed within the time required by agreement with the government.' But this threat accomplished little. The provincial government had brought the matter of reversionary interest to court in British Columbia. Consequently, the department could not alienate the reserve while the case was *sub judice*.[17] Though GTP vice-president Wainwright lobbied minister Frank Oliver and Tate suggested that the matter be brought directly to Laurier, the DIA did not relent.[18]

The railway company again approached Oliver in the spring of 1909, but the minister continued to insist on the prior resolution of the reversionary interest dispute. In August, Tate complained that 'if the Minister's ruling is to prevail as to this Company, it may be many years before we have such right. From the Dominion,' the lawyer added, 'we have the right to expect genuine co-operation in carrying the line to the coast.' He suggested once more that the matter should be presented to Laurier. During the following two months, Tate hounded Wainwright to obtain a favourable decision from Oliver. The company lobbyist complained 'to have constantly before me Fort George.'[19] In early November, General Manager E.J. Chamberlin spoke to Oliver and convinced the minister to reopen the matter. The lobby was now having some effect. Yet another application by Wainwright in December prompted the deputy minister to suggest to Oliver that the company might acquire title to the reserve in two parts as it had in Metlakatla. The minister reversed his earlier decision and told Wainwright that if the railway company could obtain an assignment from the province, 'the Department would have clear title and would be able to deal with the Indians.'[20] Company lobbying had finally achieved a concession.

In January 1910, President Hays directed Tate to settle the acquisition of the province's reversionary interest in Fort George reserve. The solicitor informed the lands commissioner that the company expected to secure the reversionary interest on the same terms as Metlakatla. Though two other concerns had sought the province's title, the premier honoured his promise to Hays and undertook to transfer the province's title 'as soon as you have acquired title from the Dominion.'[21]

The railway company returned its attention to Ottawa. The DIA had wasted several months in a fruitless attempt to obtain directly the province's reversionary interest even though McBride had promised to cede it to the GTP.[22] By September 1910, the department had received another offer to purchase the reserve. Charles Millar, president of the B.C. Express Company, a thriving Fraser River steamboat concern, desired to acquire the eastern half of the reserve for docks and warehouses. The department turned down this application on the ground that the GTP should receive special consideration since it had filed its application two years earlier.[23]

With matters apparently settled in Ottawa and Victoria, the GTP now turned its efforts toward the negotiation of a surrender with the Fort George Band. The company had a low opinion of the Natives from the outset. GTP publicist Talbot dismissed them as 'some 200 Siwashes [who] drag out a miserable existence by some means or other, and live under conditions which an English dog would spurn.'[24] Unfortunately for the railway company, many whites had already made inquiries to the band concerning the sale of Reserve No. 1, and the Natives were well aware of the value of their land. The chief expressed the following view to a department official: 'For more [than] 200 years, perhaps 300 years, we live here, we die here, we bury here, we fish and hunt and trap here, by and by we make gardens here, we like this place. All our people no like sell this place.' To persuade them to surrender the tract, which was 'strategic in any line,' the official concluded the purchaser would require cash, land, and farm equipment, as well as 'tact, kindness and diplomacy.'[25]

In the fall of 1910, the railway company formulated a basic offer of

$68,300 ($50 per acre). The official's report on the attachment of Natives to their reserve induced the company to add a bonus of $10,000. The GTP also undertook to acquire extra land for the band adjacent to Reserve No. 2, fifteen miles north on the west bank of the Fraser River. Finally, the company also guaranteed to preserve the Native cemetery next to the village.[26]

The chief had indicated a willingness to consider the surrender of the western portion of the reserve. But under no conditions was he willing to sell the village and graveyard near the river. When the Indian agent made the GTP offer to the assembled band in December, the members initially voted 12-11 to accept. The chief was against it, however, and at a second meeting additional members rejected the proposal. A local newspaper illuminated the rejection. 'One of the Indians who has a penchant for the subdivision business reasoned it out in this wise: white man ketchum fifty dolla acre; sellum lot five hundred dolla; Indian dam fool sellum.'[27]

But two other factors played a role in the band's rejection of the offer. The band's adviser, Father Nicolas Coccola, head of the Oblate mission at Stuart Lake, did not attend the negotiations though the chief had insisted on his presence. The priest later informed his superior that he had wired the band not to sell for less than $100,000. The other factor was the Natural Resources Security Company (NRS), which marketed the townsite immediately west of the reserve and subsequently fought the GTP over the location of the district railway station. A newspaper of a rival townsite charged that this company gave a 'tea' for the Native people a few days before the Indian agent's arrival in the district and encouraged them to hold on to their land.[28]

The disappointing outcome of the bargaining was evidently distasteful to the DIA officials in Ottawa. After receiving the agent's report, the deputy minister informed the GTP that the Native people had expressed a willingness to sell. When Father E.C. Bellot, Coccola's assistant, claimed that he alone was the authorized spokesperson for the band and offered to come to Ottawa to settle if the department would pay his expenses, the deputy minister accepted with alacrity.[29]

After the priest's arrival in Ottawa, negotiations proceeded smoothly. Informed that no vacant land was available adjacent to the reserve to which the band would remove, Vice-President Wainwright agreed to add $5,000 in lieu of purchasing 1,000 acres for the band. On 22 February 1911, Bellot and Wainwright signed a memorandum of agreement calling for the surrender of the reserve for a total of $83,300 and for the removal of the band by the end of the year.[30]

Circumstantial evidence suggests that the interests of Natives did not prompt Bellot to sign the memorandum. Wainwright noted approvingly the priest's actions meant that the company would now pay only $65 per acre, 'a big come down from the $1,000 per acre he [Bellot] started with.' By holding out the prospect of an imminent arrangement on the station location, the GTP had also countenanced the payment of $10,000 by the Natural Resources Security Company to get the priest 'in the proper frame of mind to recommend the transaction.'[31] Shortly after signing the agreement, the priest submitted a bill of expenses totalling $1,711.25. Included were such items as $3.50 per day for residence in the Ottawa juniorate (the finest room in the Chateau Laurier cost $3.00 in 1912), and $47.00 for meals on the train between Vancouver and Ottawa. Over the objections of the department accountant, the deputy minister decided to pay the bill.[32]

In early April, the GTP received word that the deal could not be closed. Claiming that the band had set a price of $1,000 per acre at the time of the Indian agent's visit in December 1910, the band members unanimously rejected the proposed surrender agreement.[33] The Natural Resources Security Company, now disappointed in its station agreement with the GTP, held another banquet for the band and opposed the sale.

Unfortunately, few documents survive that describe the reaction of the railway company officers to the failure of the second GTP attempt to purchase the reserve. Not only had the company increased its offer by $5,000, it had probably also paid Father Bellot's expenses. While a local newspaper contented itself with the remark that Bellot was a financial innocent, the judgment of company officers was more severe. In 1915, Tate complained that the National Resources Security Company had bought the cooperation of the 'rogue priest' for its own plans rather than those of the GTP.[34] But the GTP officers realized that Bellot's signature did not guarantee surrender. In their desire to obtain the reserve at a low price, they chose to believe the priest's claims.

During the following months the GTP did not increase its offer. GTP officers apparently believed that the company's arrangement for the provincial government's reversionary interest prevented another party from acquiring the reserve. After two failed attempts to persuade the Natives to sell, the GTP disinclination to bargain actively and clarify publicly its intentions would not only discomfit the Natural Resources Security Company but also reduce the leverage of the band. During the summer the company lobbied Oliver, and the minister wrote to Coccola several times asking the priest to use his good influence. Company publicist Talbot expressed most bluntly GTP frustration and impatience.

> Fort George [Indian Reserve] will become the railway clearing centre of the interior; that is, if the Indians can be persuaded to assist in the march of civilization and progress ... But the Indians ... defied removal. The authorities coaxed and cajoled with the chiefs for more than two years, offering tempting sums of money and the allocation of other land as compensation. But in negotiations of this character the cunning of the red man is inscrutable, and masterly skill and tact is demanded to prevent him obtaining a bargain too overwhelmingly in his favour. Two or three times the subject was on the verge of settlement to mutual satisfaction, when just as everything was ready for the attestation of the documents, an obscure issue was thrust to the front and brought matters to a standstill.[35]

In late July, Wainwright again submitted the GTP offer of February.[36]

Coccola did not receive the offer until mid-September, and by this time he had presided over the sale of the reserve to F.G.C. Durnford of Ottawa to which he claimed all the Natives assented. The terms of 28 August called for $100,000 for the land, $25,000 to cover the cost of building houses on Reserves Nos. 2 or 3 for each family in the band, and $1,000 to cover the cost of removing the dead from the cemetery. This agreement satisfied the chief's desire for the band to escape the debilitating influence of the GTP construction labourers. But Coccola also received a separate undertaking from Durnford for a grant to the church of five acres in Reserve No. 1 and a total of $16,800 for the erection of Catholic churches, residences, hospitals, and schools in the future white community on the purchased land as well as in the transplanted Native one.[37]

Durnford was not an agent for the GTP as local observers first believed. Rather, he represented a syndicate that included Charles Millar, the frustrated applicant for the reserve in 1910, and James Carruthers, a Montreal businessman whom the GTP had treated badly in the early development of Prince Rupert.[38] There were irregularities in the arrangement, however. Durnford apparently only secured an option to purchase the reserve for one dollar. More important, there was no representative of the DIA present, and the department had not been informed. Coccola's celebrated later claim that Durnford had secured a telegram of authorization from the DIA is gainsaid by his disingenuous conclusion in a brief report to the department: 'Hoping that this arrangement will meet with approval of your Department.'[39]

Although a local newspaper later speculated on a sinister connection between the syndicate and the Natural Resources Security Company, the rival development company apparently alerted the GTP to the purchase.[40] Once the railway company realized that the reserve might be lost even though it had reached an agreement for the reversionary interest, it acted quickly. On 23 September, Wainwright telegraphed the DIA that the company refused to deal with outside parties for the reserve and suggested that a railway agent enter the negotiations directly. A company solicitor and J.T. Ramsden, chief superintendent for the DIA, left immediately and arrived in the Fort George district on 28 October. The company also protected its other concession. In early October, the GTP convinced Premier McBride to put through cabinet a formal undertaking to convey the reversionary interest after the GTP had acquired Indian title.[41]

When the deputy minister informed Coccola that the August surrender was invalid because Durnford had no authority from the department to act in the purchase, Coccola offered a fanciful explanation of the company's 'pull': '[I] considered bargain concluded and informed Ottawa of that. But Oh politics! The Federal elections were approaching and the Government was looking for votes, the G.T.R. with the votes of all their employees offered to buy for the amount stipulated and having a strong pull had the government, write me: saying that [Durnford] had no authority to buy, though I had seen a telegram giving him the authority.'[42]

In fact, Millar and Carruthers initially had some luck with the new Conservative minister of Indian affairs, Robert Rogers. Allowing that the purchase was 'badly mixed,' the minister decided to let the matter stand in favour of Millar pending a review and ordered Ramsden's recall. The GTP responded by threatening to relocate its divisional point if the minister terminated the negotiations for a new surrender. The local board of trade and the Conservative Association immediately petitioned the new minister of agriculture, Martin Burrell, who sat for Cariboo, to facilitate a surrender to the railway.[43] The threat and petitions probably convinced Rogers to relent. If the company moved its divisional point and the land lost its value, would Millar and Carruthers complete the purchase? And even if the minister accepted the Durnford purchase, he would still have to deal with the reversionary interest that the province had promised the GTP. On 7 November, the GTP informed its agent at Fort George that matters had been arranged although the department granted Ramsden authority to take a surrender only on 17 November. On 18 November, the assembled band agreed to a surrender that called for a payment of $125,000, including costs for new houses, the removal of Native people by 1 June 1912, and the preservation of the cemetery.[44] The GTP now paid a real price of $91.51 per acre, almost twice the basic price formulated in the fall of 1910.

Defeated in the field, Millar and Carruthers took legal action and achieved some success in advancing their prior claim.[45] In an out-of-court settlement, the GTP agreed to sell them 200 acres in the southern part of the reserve for $59,296 ($300 per acre). To make clear the punitive nature of the settlement, Wainwright petulantly concluded that 'had our Agents been subjected to the higher price of $140,000 agreed to by Mr. Durnford and his associates, the cost to you would have been even more, reaching $370 per acre. You are thus getting the benefit of the saving of $15,000 through our own personal negotiations, and at our own expense.'[46]

There is unfortunately no direct account of the role of Father Coccola in this final purchase. Though Ramsden had requested his presence, Coccola declined to come. The priest later claimed that he had advised the Natives, who did not want to sell the reserve again to the GTP agent, to settle for 'the figure given [in Coccola's version of the Durnford purchase], $150,000, not for less.' Yet the band settled for $125,000. In requests to the GTP and the provincial government for three lots each in the railway townsite for a church, Coccola claimed that 'it was through our efforts and influence that the Indians consented to abandon the place of their birth.' The GTP land commissioner would only agree to sell lots to the priest at half price, however, a privilege accorded all churches.[47] Two years later another Oblate priest contended that an arrangement with the GTP provided for the transfer of two townsite lots and $5,000 to the church on the successful surrender of the reserve. Neither the GTP nor the Oblate records contain evidence to support this claim, however. A GTP solicitor later offered a possible explanation for the absence of relevant documents: 'If there was such an understanding, it was obviously kept under cover owing to the nature of the arrangement.'[48]

Ramsden distributed the first payment of $25,000 immediately. When Coccola returned to the reserve in January 1912, he found many band members still feasting on the proceeds. Although they were supposed to

Local celebration after GTP purchase of Fort George Reserve

remove in June 1912, delays in conveyancing the parcel and the construction of replacement houses on other reserves, as well as the leisurely pace of railway townsite development, permitted the Native people to remain on the reserve until August 1913.[49] With the sale of lots expected in the fall, the GTP demanded that the department force the Natives to vacate. When some members of the band declared that they no longer wanted to move, an Indian agent arranged to have GTP railway labourers burn down some already vacant houses to demonstrate that the railway company now controlled the land and everything on it. The band vacated on the following two days.[50]

A photograph taken on the day of the surrender of the reserve showing the local Indian agent, the superintendent, and the GTP representative perched unsteadily on the shoulders of a number of smiling local inhabitants surrounded by dozens of empty liquor bottles suggests the significance of the purchase. After three and one half years of negotiations with two governments, the band, and its spokespeople, the railway company had finally acquired its chosen parcel of land in the district. The purchase allowed it to market a second townsite in the province, which promised to outstrip the returns from Prince Rupert.

THE CASE PRESENTED above sets out GTP actions to acquire townsite land that governments and rival development concerns considered valuable. It is only in the construction of its line along the Skeena River valley, however, that the surviving documents capture a part of the Native opposition to GTP acquisition of Indian land, if only because no other white institution or concern desired the strips of right-of-way the company expropriated through a series of Indian reserves. Here the federal Department of Indian Affairs also hindered the company's plans. Though opposition to GTP encroachment probably occurred on most reserves, the documents most clearly illuminate the company actions to overcome the resistance of the Kitsumkalum people.

The railway company had obtained federal government sanction for its general location along the north bank of the Skeena River in November 1906. When the GTP established its west end headquarters in Prince Rupert in the spring of 1908, company engineers still had little idea of the cultural, as opposed to physical, obstacles that would slow construction in the valley. It remained for the local Indian agent to inform the company of the reserves the GTP line would traverse.[51]

To expropriate right-of-way through each reserve, the company required the formal sanction of the DIA in the form of an order-in-council. In addition, it had to pay compensation for the land it took. But it was understood by both parties that regulation would not hold up construction. The company would submit a plan of the line's location through the reserve to the federal Department of Railways for certification. This plan received automatic endorsement by the department since it had already certified the location of the line through the district in which the reserve was located. When presented with the endorsed plan and a certificate stating that the land in question was required for railway purposes, the DIA would put the necessary order through cabinet. A company deposit to the DIA covering the 'reasonable valuation which [the GTP] right-of-way agent may place on the land required' would allow construction to go forward.[52]

The company approached both requirements with insouciance in the Skeena Valley. Although crews began to grade the prospective right-of-way in the summer of 1908, the GTP submitted its plans for the first group of reserves only in early 1909. The company officers ignored the request for a deposit until the following May.[53]

Included in the properties through which the company now admitted it would have to secure right-of-way were two reserves of the Kitsumkalum Band, part of the Tsimshian nation, located on the north bank of the Skeena, ninety miles east of Prince Rupert along the GTP line. Band members had probably listened in late spring 1908 to a chief from a neighbouring village urging them to 'stand up for their rights' in getting a settlement with the GTP for right-of-way. During the summer, the company located both a grading and an engineer's camp on the main reserve, Kitsumkalum No. 1, and the band entered into extended disputes with the GTP to secure rent and compensation for the use of timber and gravel.[54]

But the most important obstacle the Kitsumkalum people created for the company concerned the line's traverse of a Native graveyard on the western end of its main reserve. By the fall of 1908, the company had realized that its line would cross Native graveyards on several reserves. GTP right-of-way agent George Pope first decided to solve the delicate issue by obtaining a blanket permit from the provincial government for removal of all Native remains interred along the banks of the Skeena. Suspecting that exhumation under the provincial Graveyard Act might not soothe all Native concerns, however, the GTP agent offered Natives

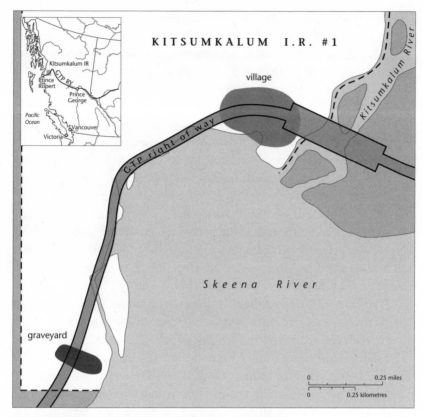

Figure 6.2 **GTP acquisition of Kitsumkalum Reserve right-of-way**

$15 to cover the cost of labour in removing each body.[55]

Such an arrangement ignored Tsimshian sensibilities, which recognized both the act of disturbing the grave and the feelings of family survivors. A supporter of the Native people later illuminated this outlook.

> To the White man it seems merely an affair of shovelling earth for the Grand Trunk Railway line to run through and disturb the interments of an Indian cemetery. To the Indian, such exhumation and reinterment are a very serious business ... It cannot be done privately as we would do it. There must be a public speech, and the rank and social standing of everyone present recognized by a suitable gift. Not only so, but the social status of the deceased determined the extent to which money and goods shall be distributed. From $300.00 to $1,500.00 is the usual outlay connected with the interment of a person of quality.[56]

Thus, Natives demanded compensation beyond Pope's offer of wages for mere labour. That the band made its dissatisfaction with the original GTP offer plain is suggested by reports of the local Indian agent to the department in January 1909 and an outright rejection of the GTP offer in April.[57]

The railway company chose not to heed the warnings of the Indian agent, however, and contractors sought to grade through the graveyard on the main reserve, as well as two other grave sites. Members of the band forced the contractors to desist. Indian agent E. Lorenz requested that the matter be settled in arbitration, but that the company be granted permission to remove the remains in the interval and continue working. The company went one better. Ignoring the Native demand for an additional compensation for disturbing graves, the company finally made its deposit to cover the eventual settlement for right-of-way. It then charged that Natives were illegally stopping construction. Tate requested the DIA to see to it that they offered no further opposition.[58]

The department asked the GTP to make an offer that would ensure that Natives were 'fairly compensated' and that 'no apparent violence is done to their feelings in this matter.' But Pope replied that he had already increased the price for removal beyond the standard of $10.00. 'I really cannot understand, if the Indians are paid for the expense and trouble of removing their graves, and I am sure the amount named is handsome compensation, why they should expect a big bonus for disturbing the graves.' In the meantime, in view of the company's record to 'pay reasonably for its right of way,' the DIA authorized the company to proceed with its construction.[59]

Perhaps because one of the graves was that of his grandfather, Chief Solomon Johnson demanded that the department, and thereby the company, 'be good and kind to us' about this matter. For right-of-way through the band's two reserves, which included the 'only place for homestead of our grandfather,' he asked $150,000. At the same time, for the removal of the cemetery that contained the remains of eighteen Natives in thirteen graves, the band, with the chief's apparent agreement, demanded $300 for disturbing each grave beyond $15 for removal of each body.[60]

While promising to deal fairly, the department refused to consider the chief's first demand. It turned to the local Indian agent for an appraisal. For the right-of-way proper, he made a valuation of $1,596

(35.53 acres at $50 per acre). For damage to improvements, $194.30. To settle the graveyard matter, the local agent also advised that the company should 'pay equivalent amount as in such cases is paid to white people,' and suggested it be established by arbitration. The department, however, insisted on a valuation of the graveyard dispute to which the company would agree. 'It does not appear to be just to claim any sentimental sum for the Indians in view of the company's disposition to pay liberally.'[61]

The company received a very different valuation from W.H. Dempster, the right-of-way assistant for British Columbia. For right-of-way, he suggested only $470; for improvements, $140. He was emphatic in his valuation of the graves:

> Land worthless, the track runs along a rocky bluff where there is neither land nor timber ... Although the graves are on the right of way, the graves are undisturbed, being about eight feet outside of the [railway grade] slope. If the paling around the graves was removed to place of safety during blasting, they [sic] could be replaced and graves undisturbed. The Indians have a fence across the track and refuse to allow the engineers to go on with their work. It is a hold-up business.[62]

Although the DIA had asked the company not to disturb the graves before settlement, the local engineer followed this instruction for only a week before he once more ordered construction crews onto the graveyard. The Natives again blocked the crews and this time erected a fence across the line to demarcate, and defend, the cemetery. General Manager E.J. Chamberlin demanded prompt action from the department; 'otherwise we will be seriously delayed.' Tate called for the DIA to enforce the removal of the graves from the right-of-way immediately. He secured a reply that apparently offered two ways to achieve the removal. First, the company was requested to send a special representative to the Natives to settle the matter directly. They would be more amenable because the secretary also sent an explicit notice to both the chief and the Indian agent authorizing immediate removal.[63]

But though Chamberlin wanted the 'hold-up out of the way,' he would not let the right-of-way agent in Winnipeg travel to the region and negotiate, and the delicate matter was left to his local assistant, Dempster. Dempster offered $15 to remove and $200 for a new cemetery, or alternatively, $20 for each body to remain in the location with the company preserving gravestones and paling. He could persuade neither the chief nor members of his band to budge from their May demands, however. He suspected that they must have a solicitor advising them, but then despaired that it was 'not possible to make any reasonable settlement with those people.' Dempster managed to persuade the chief to allow the company to construct temporary tracks around the fenced area but only by promising not to disturb the graves. Lorenz tried once more to interest the Natives in a settlement, but they passed a formal motion that the railway construct its permanent line around the graveyard as no settlement has been reached.[64]

Dempster's inability to reach a solution led the company to return to the department and suggest that it had not acted on its authorization of early July 1909. Tate's complaints convinced A.W. Vowell, the department's BC superintendent, to rebuke Lorenz for not solving the problem even though the DIA had earlier entrusted the resolution to the company. But the agent replied that his instructions did not allow him to discount the wishes of the chief. Even the GTP solicitor recognized that the 'removal of these bodies in a too arbitrary manner would intensify ... the considerable unquiet feeling among the [Kitsumkalum] Indians.'[65]

But the company required just such an arbitrary action from the minister, and Tate sought a meeting in the middle of August. Tate could not persuade the minister that the company had made a reasonable attempt at settlement because the GTP had 'refused to pay something for sentimental damage.' With disgust the lawyer reported the minister's proposed compromise of $50 per body. In the following days, the company altered the department's proposal to $1,000 damages for interference with the existing cemetery, beyond its already offered compensation of $15 for removing each body and $200 for a new cemetery. The key condition was that in the event of a refusal, construction was to proceed without reference to the chief.[66] The department accepted this offer and instructed Vowell to travel to Kitsumkalum. He would inform the Natives that the best offer had been made, and that construction must be allowed to proceed. If they did not accept the offer, Vowell would select a new cemetery and instruct the GTP to remove the bodies. If they held out, Tate declared, 'it is clear that they are bent on obstruction,' and the company would invoke the assistance of the provincial police.[67]

In late September, the superintendent arrived at Kitsumkalum and declared that the indulgence of the DIA rather than the Native blockade had caused the railway to halt construction so that the band might be afforded ample compensation. If they did not accept this offer, Vowell authorized the local company engineer to take necessary steps, implying that the company would desecrate the graves. Along with the company's acquisition of the required order-in-council for right-of-way through Kitsumkalum and five other reserves in early October, this threat apparently caused the band to comply. By the end of October, the division engineer reported that all the bodies had been removed.[68]

For damages to the existing cemetery, the creation of a new one, and the disinterment of eighteen bodies from thirteen graves, the company paid the department $1,470 in November. This rate, altered slightly to $110 per grave, became the standard of payment for the settlement of graveyard disputes at several other reserves located along the GTP right-of-way between Kitsumkalum and Hazelton. The compensation for the Kitsumkalum graveyard was distributed the following summer, but the monies for right-of-way were retained by the department. In 1915, the band complained to the McKenna-McBride royal commission that it had not seen a dollar from the GTP.[69]

At the conclusion of the company's actions concerning the two reserves, the GTP had secured the Indian land it sought. If one looks at these cases in terms of this outcome alone, then the company succeeded. But this most obvious conclusion is deceiving. Two elements in the acquisition process, cost increase and delay, can also be expressed in terms of outcome. The first is set out in Table 6.1 according to the chronological order of the acquisition. Though the company reduced the size (percentage) of its overruns, even the doubling of costs in the final case suggests a general inability to limit costs. The table does not include the additional cost of west end construction that the Metlakatla settlement required. Improvement is not evident in terms of delay.

But a narrow focus on outcome obscures the company's difficulties in overcoming the different combination of obstacles in each episode. In the case that offered the prospect of lucrative townsite sales, the greatest obstacle the company faced was not Native opposition. Although it did occur in Fort George, the company spent most of its time dealing with the federal Department of Indian Affairs and much of its money dealing with a rival development concern. Only in the case of Kitsumkalum did the company devote most of its energies to overcoming Native resistance. In their attempts to eliminate these different obstacles, company managers in every case committed a series of errors that increased expenditures and delayed acquisition and construction.

Table 6.1

GTP cost increase in acquisition of reserves

	Metlakatla (13,567 acres[a])	Kitsumkalum R/W (32.94 acres[a])	Fort George (1,366 acres)
Initial			
GTP offer or valuation	$1.00/acre	$610 (total)[b]	$68,300 (total)
Reversionary	–	–	$2.50/acre
Graves	–	$270 (total)	–
Total	$13,567	$880	$71,715
Final			
GTP offer or valuation	$7.50/acre	$1,981.60 (total)[b]	$125,000 (total)
Reversionary	$2.50/acre	–	$2.50/acre
Graves	–	$1,470.00 (total)	–
Total	$135,670[c]	$3,451.60[c]	$128,415[c]
Increase (final/initial)	10.00	3.92	1.79

a Acreage changes following surveys or revised location of right-of-way
b Includes compensation for damage to improvements on right-of-way
c Does not include survey and conveyancing fees

Table 6.2

GTP delays in acquisition of reserves

	Metlakatla	Kitsumkalum R/W	Fort George
Initial offer	Jan. 1905	Jan. 1909	May 1908
Settlement*	Feb. 1908	Sept. 1909	Nov. 1911
Interval	37 months	8 months	42 months

* Elimination of the final impediment preventing control and/or construction

Since the DIA and, in the case of Fort George, the missionaries did not clearly block or oppose the company's acquisitions, there are grounds here for another version of Harold Cardinal's 'great swindle,' the collusion of the railway company with other white interests and institutions to alienate the land from Natives.[70] Indeed, a Native community upriver from Kitsumkalum alleged that the GTP bribed the local Indian agent to set an inadequate valuation on its right-of-way through the reserve.[71] Such an interpretation, however, ignores the company reverses in the two cases outlined above. Though the Native bands along the GTP line undoubtedly regarded the company as a leviathan that could cripple and break the communities in its path, this parochial view mistakes the significance of the company's actions.[72] What company opponents perceived as the successful, if immoral, employment of GTP power was as much a demonstration of halting corporate weakness.

SEVEN

'IN THE HOLLOW OF THE CORPORATION'S HAND': PRINCE GEORGE

COMPANY ACTIONS in the new city of Prince George, the largest divisional point on the railway between Edmonton and the coast, suggest that GTP managers learned from their sometimes chastening experience in Prince Rupert. Certainly the GTP policy of disguising its actions or the motives behind actions that were necessarily public was successful since it led most early historians to overlook or diminish the company's role in the development of the second GTP city in British Columbia.[1] More recently, the use of A.F.J. Artibise's elaboration of boosterism to explain the early municipal development of Prince George has obscured the significance of the company's book returns from lot sales that clearly surpassed those of the Pacific terminus.[2] The increase implies that in this community the GTP dealt more effectively with threats to its returns. Indeed, the apparent success of company activity led a local ally to declare that 'the future of this young town lies in the hollow of the corporation's hand.'[3] This chapter confirms that the GTP could disrupt or destroy other economic concerns in the region and enlist the support of the provincial government in this activity. In doing so, however, company managers continued to overlook opportunities to maximize returns.

DURING THE PERIOD of negotiations for Fort George Indian Reserve, the site of the future GTP townsite, other individuals and organizations entered the district and purchased the land surrounding the reserve, often at inflated values. These parties intended to 'boom' their property, i.e., to sell lots at greatly increased prices as the railway approached the district. GTP officers were aware of this practice and attempted to combat it through the manipulation of the company's most important asset, the right to decide the location of the railway station that would serve the district.

It is necessary to heed the warning of a weary railway commissioner and alert the reader at the outset to the confusing names of the two townsites that marketed lots in Fort George district before the establishment of the GTP townsite of Prince George in 1913. During the fall of 1909, a local concern created South Fort George Townsite on two district lots south of the Indian reserve. With a dock on the Fraser River, this compact community became the centre of steamboat traffic and the district's economic centre before 1914.[4]

More notorious was the development of Fort George Townsite on the west side of the reserve. Gathering more than 2,000 acres on seven district lots, the Natural Resources Security Company, Ltd. (hereafter NRS) marketed its property through an extensive advertising campaign in which its townsite was billed as the Chicago of western Canada to which ten railways had been chartered. By 1912, NRS had spent $170,000 on improvements in its townsite and $100,000 on advertising.[5] An investigation of the local land title records indicates that the company served as a well-publicized selling agency for a group of holding companies that actually owned the land. The ebullient NRS president, George J. Hammond, was an accomplished promoter.[6]

During the period 1910 to 1912, NRS brochures extolled its townsite's climate (suitable for all soft fruits except peaches), its citizenry (Presbyterian and teetotal, unlike the disorderly elements of South Fort George), and especially its location.[7] In the summer of 1910, NRS ran a series of advertisements in Vancouver newspapers claiming that the GTP had decided to locate the district station adjacent to the eastern boundary of Fort George Townsite (Lot 937-938). Such advertising prompted the Hudson's Bay Company land commissioner to remark that the concern 'may be classed as one of a highly speculative character and statements issued under its auspices are not to be regarded as reliable.'[8] It also induced *Saturday Night* to run a series of articles on the questionable advertising techniques of NRS. At that time, the GTP had made no decision concerning a station; the railway company was still pressing Oliver for permission to begin negotiations with the Natives. NRS launched an injunction and libel action against the Toronto journal in August 1910 but saw its suit dismissed, the presiding judge exclaiming that a series of NRS maps featuring a peripatetic station had no basis in fact.[9]

This judgment seriously damaged the credibility of a company whose financial health depended on interested queries from distant potential lot purchasers. Accordingly, Hammond opened negotiations with the railway company concerning the location of the GTP station in the district. The promoter sought to secure a public statement from the GTP that fixed the station on or near NRS property. The lack of such a commitment threatened to overwhelm the townsite company because it had sold a number of lots with the guarantee that the purchase price would be refunded if the station were not built a certain distance from the lot.[10]

Hammond's primary lever was money. During the winter of 1910-11, NRS offered a series of increasing bonuses to entice the GTP to locate the station adjacent to Fort George Townsite. Having reached a tentative agreement with GTP general manager E.J. Chamberlin, Hammond boldly issued a circular in January 1911 that began: 'Confidential advance notice: to Lot Holders. The Grand Trunk Pacific Railway have selected a site for their passenger station at Fort George four blocks – less than 1320 [ft.] – east of Fraser Avenue, Fort George townsite [eastern boundary]. The railway company will make official public announcement within two weeks.' The circular concluded with the reckless statement, 'We guarantee everything stated above.'[11]

It appeared that the railway company might well come to terms with NRS. In February 1911, Chamberlin declared that NRS had offered the GTP $200,000 and free right-of-way through all its property in return for the location of a station within twenty chains (1,320 feet) of the eastern boundary of NRS property. Although the general manager had not visited the district, he believed Hammond's declaration that only the western portion of the Indian reserve, the portion closest to NRS property, was suitable for railway purposes. Citing NRS help in the negotiations leading up to the February 1911 agreement to acquire the reserve, the GTP officer concluded enthusiastically that the NRS officials had acted squarely.[12]

GTP president Hays's response deserves lengthy quotation. He intended to make as handsome a profit in the railway townsite in Fort George district as he claimed the company had done in Prince Rupert. Hays continued: 'I had not supposed that what had been done by the Natural Resources Security Company or any other townsite companies attempting to boom lots in that vicinity could amount to very much without having our cooperation and assistance in the way of the location of our station and terminals. This would seem to be recognized by them as the case if they are willing to pay us $200,000 to locate the station within twenty chains of their property.' Hays recognized that Hammond's advertising probably made NRS liable for selling lots under false representation, and the GTP president did not wish to help NRS escape from this dilemma by accepting the promoter's offers. If the railway company chose a station site to serve its own interest, Hays believed that it could eliminate competition in the district. 'We had ... better let them "stew in their own juice," taking our own time in laying out our property and await the return we are sure to have by reason of the advantage proposed by controlling the location of the station and other terminal facilities.'[13] This strategy informed GTP actions in the district over the next four years and ultimately led to the elimination of Fort George Townsite as a serious economic rival.

Upon receipt of Hays's instructions, Chamberlin used an NRS offer of deferred payment to break off negotiations claiming that the 'company cannot accept the terms of payment offered by NRS.'[14] Although Hammond was able to secure an interview with Hays in early June to request a relaxation of the railway company's conditions, the GTP president continued to insist on payment in cash. The NRS president protested that it was impossible to raise that sum of money from the banks using speculative real estate as collateral; Hays helpfully suggested trust companies.[15] When Hammond came to Montreal in early July with an offer of $175,000 in cash, notes, and Fort George Townsite lots, the GTP president made arrangements not to see him. The NRS president then offered to pay the GTP $1 million for the right to market lots on the reserve and retain the revenue above that figure. The GTP apparently did not respond to this offer, but it may well have alerted Hays to the danger of not closing with the Natives.[16]

By August 1911, Hammond was prepared to pay for a simple announcement that the railway would locate its line through Fort George Townsite and place its station between two points a mile and a half apart, presumably bracketing the NRS townsite. Such an arrangement was even less attractive to the GTP than the original NRS proposition. Nevertheless, in early September Hammond published a circular in which he claimed that an agreement had been reached with the railway company to place a station within 2,000 feet of the eastern boundary of Fort George Townsite, 'subject to confirmation in writing at a later date.'[17] Not surprisingly, the GTP provided no such confirmation.

In desperation, Hammond broke off negotiations and filed a petition with the Board of Railway Commissioners (BRC) in January 1912 to compel the railway to build a station at or near Fort George Townsite.[18] In February, Hays responded to this new stratagem with a letter obviously meant for publication to J.B. Daniell, the editor of the *Fort George Herald*. After praising Daniell's libellous allegation that Hammond was a 'former bucketshop operator' and a 'get-rich-quick artist' as a 'commendable effort to prevent misrepresentation,' the GTP president declared that 'any statements that have been made in the past [concerning the station location] have been absolutely without any foundation of authority from any of the officers of the Co. Neither have any arrangements been made with or any sums of money received from anyone whatsoever with respect to the location of our station at Fort George.'[19]

In March 1912, the first BRC hearing on the station site took place in Ottawa. Representing NRS, R.A. Pringle argued that the board should simply satisfy Hammond's objective of August 1911 – locate the station on or near the NRS townsite. Building his case on quotations from documents exchanged between the GTP and NRS during 1911, the Ottawa lawyer argued that the two companies had reached an understanding concerning the station location. GTP general counsel W.H. Biggar replied that the railway company had made no commitments and that it could make no decisions concerning the station location or any other aspect of the Indian reserve until it had received a formal patent and made a detailed survey. In the meantime, the GTP should not be compelled to fulfil the rash promises of a reckless promoter. Although the lawyers of all parties devoted much time to a comparison of the various geographical features of alternative locations along the located line such as the gradient to possible roads and the height above the river flood line, these observations played a secondary role in the outcome of the proceedings. At a later hearing, a GTP engineer admitted that any location on the line could be made into a suitable station site for an adequate amount of money.[20]

BRC chief commissioner J.P. Mabee responded to counsel's arguments by reading into the record assurances from the GTP that it would not build the station on the eastern 3,500 feet of the railway's traverse of its property, closest to the bank of the Fraser River (location 1 in Figure 6.1, p. 168). Accordingly, the commissioner did not issue a formal order fixing a precise depot location. He declared that when the end of steel reached the district, further representation could be made if any of the parties was not satisfied.[21]

Hoping that Mabee's ruling would discourage the GTP from establishing a competing townsite on the reserve, Hammond exclaimed that the statement represented 'a direct vindication ... that the railway company would be obliged to locate on the western part of the reservation ... The railway is pinned down, within a definite limit, effectually putting other townsites out of the contest.'[22] GTP secretary Henry Philips expressed a different interpretation of the ruling, however. 'The company has [the] opportunity to make proper surveys and present plans as to the best location when they will be approved in the customary manner.'[23]

In the latter part of 1912, the company surveyed and laid out its townsite on the Indian reserve. As Figure 6.1 reveals, the station location at George Street on the plan was 6,715 feet from the eastern boundary of Fort George Townsite and only 331 feet within the boundary set by the BRC ruling of 5 March 1912.[24] Although planners Brett, Hall & Co. later declared that the railway company did not dictate the station site, it is probable that they received and implemented Hays's views on the importance of station location in the growing dispute with NRS.[25] One of the firm's senior partners, it will be remembered, was Hays's son-in-law.

An examination of the architects' plan for Prince George Townsite reveals two outstanding features: the greenbelt in the south and the crescent streets in the west, as illustrated in Figure 7.1. As in Prince Rupert, these features stem in part from the architects' application of the principles of the City Beautiful movement.[26] The crescent streets, however, also served the railway company's interest in the NRS dispute. During the 1913 BRC hearing, a lawyer noted that the curved streets were designed to increase the distance between the station and the centre of Fort George Townsite. They represented 'a proposition the object of which is absolutely to kill the present population [of the NRS townsite].' In one of his many letters to the BRC, A.S. Norton, a New York investor in Fort George Townsite, supported this interpretation: 'It was a monstrous thing to do, to throw artificial obstacles in the way of the growth of the town in the one direction left open by nature. But this is precisely what these experts did do by creating the artificial barrier known as the crescent to the west ... Any man who knows anything about cities can see by a glance at the plan that a vicious angle was interposed to block traffic ... going west.'[27] Such thoughts must have informed the instructions of the company to the architects.

On 24 January 1913, GTP solicitor Hugh H. Hansard entered an

GTP railway yard on western part of its property at Prince George, facing Fort George Townsite, 1914

Figure 7.1 Brett, Hall & Co. plan of Prince George Townsite, 1913

application with the BRC for approval of the station site described above for the townsite of 'Prince George.' Under the signature of H.L. Drayton, Mabee's successor as chief commissioner, the BRC issued an order of approval on 31 March.[28] The railway company clearly disobeyed Mabee's instructions concerning future consultation between interested parties before settling on a particular site. There had apparently been some haste in the exchange. Both the application and the order were technically incorrect as the listed mileage of the station, 467.3 east of Prince Rupert instead of 466.3, placed the station on an island in the Fraser River.[29]

In April, NRS lodged a formal complaint, and the BRC had no choice but to rescind the order and schedule another hearing for 6 May. At the opening of the proceedings, one of the commissioners explained that the board had approved the GTP application because no one had checked the location of 'Prince George' against that of 'Fort George.' He concluded with the lame excuse that 'there were so many Georges out there that we got tangled.'[30]

At this second hearing the lawyers repeated many of the arguments presented the year before. Again representing NRS, Pringle contended that the GTP actions in the district during the past year demonstrated that the railway company intended to exploit the townsite development potential of the reserve just as aggressively as any other speculative real estate developer. The lawyer representing the property owners of South Fort George Townsite, now hostile to Hammond's efforts to locate the station in his townsite, replied that the NRS development was 'forced' and predicted that 'the people there [in Fort George Townsite] will move of their own accord to the Grand Trunk townsite and there will be no town there at all. Everyone knows that that will happen as soon as this station is located where it ought to be.'[31] This statement accurately described the demise of the NRS townsite two years later.

Displaying a judicious spirit of disinterest, the majority of the sitting commissioners ignored the economic implications of the arguments presented by the opposing parties and relied instead on the judgment of BRC chief engineer J.A. Mountain. During the 1912 hearing, the engineer had suggested a compromise location 3,000 feet east of the Fort George Townsite eastern boundary based on a misapprehension that NRS desired a location 2,000 feet east while the GTP sought a location 4,000 feet east. In fact, the railway company stated that only a location *more* than 4,000 feet east would be suitable. The engineer now restated this position, and the board gave the suggestion force of law in a formal order on 14 May (designated as location 2 in Figure 6.1, p. 168).[32]

This decision was clearly unacceptable to the GTP. A station located anywhere other than at the foot of George Street made the expensive townsite plan of the proposed townsite ridiculous. Thousands of dollars in architects' fees would be wasted, and the preparations to advertise the plan extensively would be ruined. Perhaps more important, the judgment also increased the value of property in the NRS townsite and the ability of merchants who had located there to carry on their business.[33]

Since an appeal to the BRC chief commissioner to reopen the case would probably result in little more than a repetition of the engineer's recommendation from which no further appeal would then be possible, the GTP legal department decided in late May to appeal the case to the federal cabinet as the Railway Act allowed.[34]

In early June, Chamberlin, now president of the railway company, issued the following statement. 'Moving the position [of the station] to the point designated by the Railway Commission will destroy the terminal so far as a divisional point is concerned and, if the order is sustained, will necessitate our abandoning Prince George as divisional point and moving east or west of that location.'[35] Such a statement was intended to damage the value of the May BRC decision in the NRS full-page advertisements of judicial victory currently appearing in several Vancouver newspapers. The declaration was also a bluff. McBride or Endako, the divisional points east and west of Prince George respectively, might be expanded at enormous expense, but such an action would violate the GTP agreement with the Pacific Great Eastern Railway for a union terminal in the Fort George district.[36]

While the GTP legal department in Winnipeg and Montreal prepared a case to present to the cabinet, the company also made preparations to market lots on the townsite. The chief engineer let a contract for clearing and grubbing the reserve for $101,000. The company had expected cabinet to hear the appeal within six weeks. Faced with a delay in the appeal in June, Chamberlin decided on an immediate lot sale similar to those held for Prince Rupert. The GTP president also instructed surveyors to adhere to the original Brett, Hall & Co. layout, including the station site.[37]

The GTP marketing campaign for Prince George revealed the company's haste. Though the GTP had acquired the reserve in late 1911, only a few references to Fort George district appeared in the company pamphlet

Grand Trunk Pacific Railway, Plateau and Valley Lands in British Columbia: General Information for the Intending Settler. In his two books, GTP publicist Frederick Talbot had touted Fort George district rather than Prince George Townsite. Yet when GTP land commissioner G.U. Ryley asked for funds to boost Prince George, he was told that the 'vicinity had already received very considerable advertising in the company's literature.' Ads in newspapers outside Vancouver and Edmonton were placed only a few days before the sale and consequently did not give customers time to obtain plans and bid on lots. Ten thousand lithographed copies of the townsite plan were badly coloured and did not contain the date and locations of sales. Ryley concluded that the campaign was 'badly managed.'[38]

Company managers were evidently more concerned with the auction's role in the NRS dispute than with maximizing returns. The legal department recognized the danger of marketing the lots under false representation while the station site case was under appeal to cabinet. Ryley instructed the auctioneers to read the following memorandum before the sale.

> The Railway Station will be called PRINCE GEORGE ... The Board of Railway Commissioners gave the Railway Company a station at the foot of George Street; but subsequently decided that the station should be placed 3000 ft. east of Fort George Townsite ... The Railway Company has appealed to the Privy Council of Canada for a rehearing and has asked that the station be placed at the foot of George Street. It is confidently expected that the petition will be granted as every unbiased person who has been on the ground has expressed an opinion that the present site is entirely unfit for a station.[39]

The last legal condition was satisfied in early September when Ryley presented the British Columbia Department of Lands with a plan for registration bearing the title 'Lot 343,' the department's district lot number for the Indian reserve.[40]

The result of the sales held at Vancouver, Victoria, and Edmonton in September 1913 suggest at first glance that the company required no coordinated campaign. Receipts for lots purchased at the Vancouver auction totalled $1,293,000; the grand total exceeded $2 million. A pair of lots on George Street sold for $14,500. These figures appear to support a GTP land agent's claim that the auction of Prince George lots 'met with almost sensational success.'[41]

The cabinet did not hear the company's appeal until January 1914.

The legal department made good use of the extra time, however. Hansard investigated Hammond's rather lurid early business career in Chicago. 'I think we should establish his [Hammond's] record before the ministers in some way ... a few affidavits from the people he swindled in the States would not hurt any.' The company also printed Biggar's appeal with an appendix of selected documents in a handsome book of 130 pages.[42]

In August, Hansard requested another promoter to call in some loans to NRS to stop Hammond from interfering with railway right-of-way work through Fort George Townsite. When Hammond submitted a bill to the GTP for lots through which the right-of-way passed, the GTP solicitor wrote: 'Our friend [Hammond] no doubt needs some of our money to fight us in connection with the Fort George station site ... He must think we are easy if he thinks he will get any money before the matter is finally settled. He is not deserving of any consideration.'[43]

In November, the railway company cooperated with a district real estate broker who had purchased many lots on George Street in the September sale to circulate a petition among the railway townsite lot purchasers and South Fort George Townsite businessmen supporting the George Street location. A petition with 659 signatures was sent to the cabinet.[44] The railway company engaged H.P. Hill, a lawyer close to Prime Minister Borden, to represent Prince George property owners other than the GTP. Hansard also asked James Carruthers, who had finally acquired one-fifth of the townsite through the out-of-court settlement of his prior claim to the Indian reserve, to speak to the minister of public works.[45]

Biggar's presentation to the cabinet was not impressive. He argued simply that the railway commissioners had given too much weight to the NRS claims and ignored the reasonable demands of the inhabitants of South Fort George Townsite, then the largest settlement in the district. Responding to Borden's request for new evidence, the GTP lawyer noted smugly that 'we have had two or three hearings and we now rest our case entirely on the record.'[46]

Although presented in a modest four-page booklet, Pringle's case for NRS was much stronger. While agreeing that all relevant evidence had been presented at the two previous BRC hearings, the NRS lawyer maintained that the BRC judgment of July 1913 was legally in order. To overturn that decision would therefore violate the Railway Act of 1903 and the purpose for which the board was established.[47]

Borden expressed the will of his colleagues when he stated that 'I should greatly doubt if we have very much to do with the real estate interests [of the GTP or NRS] in this matter.'[48] On the ground that the GTP appeal rested on the weighing of contradictory evidence that the cabinet could not do, the cabinet issued a unanimous decision against the railway company on 9 February 1914.[49]

This verdict seemed to end the matter. Indeed, NRS described the dispute as 'a fight for right against the rapacity of a great corporation whose officials did not hesitate to spread abroad false and malicious rumours.' Trumpeting the victory in broadsheets and special editions of the Fort George Townsite newspaper, which reproduced the order-in-council, Hammond enthused: 'Every prediction made by me in regard to Fort George is being fulfilled – this will be a great railway centre.'[50]

The railway company had no more intention of accepting this decision than it had done that of the BRC, however. In the middle of February, Vice-President Wainwright approached Minister of Railways Frank Cochrane, and the latter agreed to arrange matters with Drayton so that the board would accept an application to rehear the case once more. This time Biggar, Hansard, and H.P. Hill decided to keep the railway company in the background. They chose two of the largest lot purchasers in the September sale to make the application on behalf of the independent property owners of Prince George Townsite. In consultation with the GTP lawyers, Hill drafted the appeal and submitted it to the board on 2 April and served it on the railway company.[51]

The appeal claimed that the two petitioners had purchased lots in September 1913 on the basis of the GTP lithographed plan showing station grounds (but not the station) at the foot of George Street and the statement of the auctioneer. Another hearing was necessary to consider the interest of a new party, the railway townsite property owners. When they received the appeal, both NRS and the Fort George Townsite Board of Trade protested. NRS claimed that the application simply repeated GTP arguments that the BRC had already heard. The Board of Trade remarked that many people were about to make investments in the British Columbia government sale of its portion of lots on the basis of a published government map showing the station at the foot of Maple Street as ordered by the BRC and sustained by the federal cabinet.[52]

These protests convinced D'Arcy Scott, the railway commissioner who had presided at the 1913 hearing. He dismissed the application on the ground that it presented no new evidence. Chief Commissioner Drayton had other intentions, however. At the end of May, he made a flying visit to the district and instructed an accompanying BRC engineer to make a technical report on the various sites. The engineer reported that the exact location specified in the 1913 BRC order was unsuitable because it was a small depression, a point that the GTP lawyers had made at both previous hearings. On the strength of this report, the BRC issued an order for another hearing, in the Fort George district this time.[53]

Once more the railway company marshalled support for the George Street location, notifying the lawyers of interested friendly parties. Shortly before the hearing, Hansard informed the chairman of the Joint Incorporation Committee representing the three townsites in the district that construction of a permanent station depended on the BRC decision for George Street. Displaying some want of discretion, the GTP solicitor asked H.G. Perry, who was also president of the Fort George Townsite Board of Trade, to intervene personally for George Street.[54] Convinced also that strong local representation at the hearing was essential, Hansard hired J.T. Armstrong, a real estate broker and 'outside-right-hand man of the [British Columbia] Minister of Lands,' to travel to the district and 'stir up the situation.'[55]

In the early morning of 12 November an entire block of Fort George Townsite burned to the ground. Local historian F.E. Runnalls comments that the NRS townsite never recovered from this blow. Both the *Fort George Herald* and the *Fort George Tribune* speculated that an exploding boiler might have caused it. They also agreed that the fire was an act of God. The railway company evidently was not so sure, however. On 16 November, the GTP agent who sometimes acted as a messenger for Hansard, telegraphed the railway's Edson, Alberta, office in code requesting that it obtain details of the fire, its cause, and its expected role in the upcoming hearing. The sender of the telegram must have expected a reply connecting the fire in some manner to the company.[56] No reply remains in the file.

At the third BRC hearing in November 1914, the cases of both the GTP and NRS offered little that was new. More significant was the testimony of many of the inhabitants of the district who crowded into a large hall on George Street to hear the proceedings. Fort George Townsite clothing merchant H.G. Perry admitted that if the temporary shed that the GTP had placed at the foot of George Street after the arrival of steel continued to serve as the district station, the railway townsite would soon dominate the district. A member of the newly formed Prince George Townsite Chamber of Commerce remarked with satisfaction that business in the district was centralizing on George Street. Other merchants from both townsites agreed that the station location would determine the business centre of the district. A GTP agent also revealed that the Fort George Townsite merchants, the most visible supporters of a station location west of George Street, now received only 25 per cent of the freight that the railway delivered to the district.[57]

This evidence did not impress the two sitting commissioners, however. Scott's opening remark that the district's citizens could better spend their time making money outside than by wasting his time inside indicated his lack of interest. Mountain had already proposed an alternative location between Oak and Ash streets, 1,000 feet east of the 1913 location but more than 2,000 feet west of George Street (as shown in location 3 in Figure 6.1, p. 168). Scott accepted this location in his decision and ordered the railway to file plans for the new station by 15 January 1915 and complete the building by 1 June. He also ordered the GTP to grade a new road to the new site. The *Herald* fumed that Scott had arrived in the district with his mind made up.[58]

The railway company was evidently prepared for an unfavourable decision because it quickly took a number of complementary actions. When Hansard received the decision, he immediately instructed a GTP engineer to prepare a technical report critical of the BRC findings. After the company rejected a plan to build a toy 'official' station at the BRC location and a real passenger and freight station at George Street, the legal department initiated two actions, an intervention by another railway company and a citizens' petition to the governor-in-council, to foil the board.[59]

The Pacific Great Eastern Railway (PGE) had entered into an agreement with the GTP for joint use of the terminal in the Fort George district in 1912. D'Arcy Tate was now vice-president of that company and still on friendly terms with his former employer. On 30 November 1914, the PGE's Ottawa lawyers submitted a draft of a notice of intervention to the GTP legal department for vetting. The following month, Biggar and the PGE lawyer agreed to proceed with the intervention while holding the citizens' petition in reserve. The lawyers for both companies decided to concentrate on the engineering aspects of the case to eliminate grounds for a protest from Hammond in terms of interest. In January 1915, the PGE served notice of intervention on the GTP.[60]

When the secretary of the BRC sent Hansard a series of increasingly irate notes after demanding the plans for the station at the BRC location, the PGE lawyer advised Hansard not to file plans as it might imply that the GTP acknowledged the BRC order of November 1914. Instead, Hansard replied that the railway company could not file plans while the PGE intervention was under consideration.[61] Though PGE withdrew its intervention in April 1915 because its lawyers had determined that the BRC would not accept its application, the action allowed the GTP to ignore the BRC order for four months. Biggar immediately instructed Hansard to proceed with the citizens' petition.[62]

When P.E. Wilson and N.E. Montgomery, the local lawyers who represented the property owners of Prince George and South Fort George respectively, heard Scott's decision in November, they turned to Hansard for instructions. The GTP solicitor drafted a petition of 'property owners and residents' of both townsites and provided detailed instructions to serve notice on the railway company to prevent it from being found in default of the board's order. He underlined the importance of the facade of independence. 'You understand of course that my name and the Railway Company must be kept out entirely of this matter. Any evidence of collusion will defeat our object.'[63]

Two weeks later, Wilson informed Hansard that notices of the appeal by the 'Citizens' Committee' had been sent to the parties that Hansard requested. At this time Hansard informed the GTP general manager that the company could stay in the background while the PGE and the 'citizens' led the fight. 'The matter was well in hand.' One day after the PGE withdrew its intervention, Hansard's petition from 'citizens' to the governor-in-council was circulated in the district.[64] Since the forthcoming election on 20 May for the first council of the new City of Prince George would keep the municipality and its citizens as a new legal party out of court until that date, Hansard instructed Wilson to wire Drayton on behalf of the residents requesting a delay in the station proceedings until the election. In the face of this endless series of delays, the Fort George Townsite Board of Trade called in desperation for a royal commission to investigate the operations of the GTP.[65]

In the station site dispute up to the summer of 1915, one can interpret the GTP actions in two different ways. From a strictly judicial perspective, the rejection of the GTP case in three BRC hearings and its confirmation by cabinet indicates a weakness in the GTP legal department. If, however, one views the dispute as a struggle between two development organizations for dominance in the district, the significance of the legal decisions is much diminished.

For four years the actions of the railway company in the district were generally consistent with Hays's instructions to Chamberlin in 1911. The GTP exploited its ability to locate the district station. The precise legal status of the building had little effect on the role of the station in the economic life of the district. As soon as the end of steel reached the district in January 1914, the GTP established a freight shed and temporary station at the foot of George Street. During the fall of 1914, the railway company demonstrated its determination to maintain the station at that location by fitting the shed with steam heat and electric light. When the NRS lawyer complained about the unofficial station during the November 1914 hearing, Hansard explained that the building housed only ticket, telegraph, and freight offices necessary for the construction of the railway. The railway company had to give the public some place in which to conduct business. The NRS lawyer observed, 'That is just what stations are for.'[66]

It is difficult to assess the exact effect of the George Street station on the economic activity of the district. In May 1914, Hansard boasted that the combined traffic of Prince George and South Fort George accounted for 90 per cent of the railway's freight to the district. During the November 1914 hearing, a GTP freight agent reduced this figure to 75 per cent. A census made for the 1914 hearing showed the population of Prince George Townsite as 1,731, more than twice the combined population of the other two townsites, when the railway townsite was just a year old.[67]

James Thomson, the HBC land commissioner, offered a graphic description of the railway company's apparent success. Writing to the London secretary in 1915, Thomson declared that 'during the 12 months which have elapsed since the [Prince George] lots were placed on the market, the town of "Prince George" has risen phoenix-like from the ground. Probably no other new centre in the West can boast such rapid growth. In the matter of hotels, stores, and banks, Prince George has facilities which older cities with double the population do not possess.' He added that 'business premises had so far been concentrated almost wholly on George Street.'[68] The listing of the opening of numerous firms on or near George Street in the district newspapers of 1914-15 supports Thomson's description.[69]

Also suggestive are a number of observations concerning the migration of both people and buildings from Fort George Townsite to Prince George. After the May 1914 government lot sale, in which the auctioneer boosted property around George Street, property values in the NRS townsite declined. In July 1915, the chairman of the Fort George Townsite School Board wrote to the BRC that people were disheartened and abandoning their homes. This period also witnessed the removal or demise of the district's first two newspapers; the *Fort George Herald* moved to the railway townsite in 1915, and the *Fort George Tribune* closed in 1916.[70]

Even the *Tribune*, the organ of NRS, admitted indirectly the migration out of Fort George Townsite. In November 1914, it ran the following NRS advertisement: 'Due to War Conditions. We are authorized to offer for the winter some very low rentals to reliable parties by our clients who own residences, bungalows, storerooms.' The defiant conclusion, 'Times are as good here as in most places,' was evidently not convincing.[71]

But the most perceptive description of the migration of economic activity to Prince George came from A.S. Norton, one of the hundreds of investors who protested the railway company's failure to follow the orders of the BRC. During the winter of 1914-15, this New York entrepreneur, who had invested $20,000 in lots close to the BRC station location, wrote a series of angry letters charging that the GTP instigated a small group to develop George Street in blatant disobedience of the orders of the board. He warned that if the Canadian government permitted the open defiance of its agency, American investors might well place their capital in South America or Mexico, places where risks were openly acknowledged, rather than in Canada.

By June 1915, Norton's analysis of the development of Prince George had become more nuanced. Although he still inveighed against the railway company's de facto station on George Street, he no longer regarded its supporters as a small, conspiratorial group:

> It goes without saying that the people who move into new towns either for business or residence, or any other purpose, locate as near as practicable to the station. Hence the development at George Street ... In a new town the first development clusters about the station ... [It is] difficult, if not impossible ... after a community has grown up in one spot to shift it

to another spot, even though only a short distance away ... If the enforce-
ment of your order is much longer delayed, the community of Prince
George will get past the fluid stage which would permit it to flow toward
the point designated by you as the station site ... It is doubtful whether
the unfair advantage that George Street has had already can be overcome. Those people now settling in Prince George have naturally located
near the station and naturally are in favour of George Street.

Norton concluded with the following evaluation of the opposing sides in
the station site dispute. 'We [outside investors] acknowledge that they
[local people] have outgeneralled us. The law and its administration have
permitted the decisions of your board to serve as a delusion and a snare
to us.'[72]

The eighteen-month 'delay' in complying with the BRC and cabinet
orders saw Prince George Townsite pass through the 'fluid stage.' The
GTP's ability to locate and maintain a 'temporary' station at the foot of
George Street during that period established George Street as the business centre of both the new city and the district and eliminated Fort
George Townsite and the development company behind it as a significant
economic rival. At the conclusion of the November 1914 hearing,
Hansard exclaimed: 'I do not think that the delay in fixing this station site
has hurt anybody.'[73] The remark suggests a note of irony. Norton's conclusion was incorrect in one aspect, however. The generals who defeated
him resided in the Montreal and Winnipeg offices of the GTP, not the
city of Prince George.

The capitulation of the BRC to the wishes of the GTP did not occur
until 1921. The BRC then issued an order on yet another compromise
location – one and one-half blocks west of George Street.[74] During the
intervening six years, the company had compelled the new city council of
Prince George to support the George Street location.[75] But questions of
legal precedent and procedure rather than conflicting economic interests
informed most of the debate. The legal department files indicate that the
company paid less attention to the progress of the dispute after 1915; it
had effectively eliminated its opponent. By 1919, Fort George Townsite
received less than one per cent of the total freight unloaded at Prince
George station. In the same year a BRC engineer reported that the NRS
townsite was almost deserted; only one of the remaining forty commercial buildings was open for business. Hammond was reduced to the role
of an insignificant supplicant. In 1919-20, the once-influential president

of NRS wrote a series of plaintive letters to several federal politicians drawing attention to the railway's continued defiance of the law. Both the politicians and the BRC ignored his charges.[76]

The company's city building also revealed a surer hand in dealing with the provincial government. The railway company exerted a decisive influence in Victoria to secure its desired civic name and municipal incorporation boundaries to hasten the demise of NRS.

That the railway company had the power to choose the name of its townsite is not surprising. But its choice provoked controversy and requires explanation. The district of Fort George, which derived its name from the Hudson's Bay Company trading post, embraced the two town-sites beyond the Indian reserve as well as the GTP parcel. After having popularized 'Fort George' in its advertisements in 1910, NRS obtained a legal claim on the name in 1911 when it registered one of its district lots as Fort George Townsite.[77]

At first glance the railway company's name for its townsite, 'Prince George,' seems as foolish and inappropriate as the GTP name for the Pacific terminus. Accepting a judge's advice that a distinctive, original townsite name would benefit residents and tourists alike, the GTP had adopted a policy in 1910 of selecting Native names for some of its British Columbia townsites. Yet the euphonious Carrier name for Fort George district, *Lheitli* ('where the two rivers join'), was apparently not considered.[78]

In 1914, the company advanced two public explanations for its choice. General Manager Morley Donaldson argued that the GTP had named the townsite after the king. But the choice of 'Prince' makes this claim ridiculous. Somewhat more probable was the claim that the intent of the name was to connect the townsite to the larger GTP venture in Prince Rupert for advertising purposes. The most convincing explanation, however, comes from an internal company note from President Hays, the individual who probably made the decision. Hays claimed that 'Prince George' would give the company a townsite 'permanently distinguished from the numerous towns now called Fort George, South Fort George, etc., which are in the vicinity' and make it clear that none of the others carried the company's endorsement.[79] In a private note to British Columbia attorney general W.J. Bowser, however, GTP solicitor Hugh H. Hansard expressed his distaste for both 'Prince George' and 'Fort George' and asked Bowser to suggest 'something more musical.' Bowser's less than lyrical compromise of 'George' prompted the railway company to insist upon the original choice. Donaldson argued that '"George" was insufficient for a townsite, why should an outside American [Hammond] have the power to rob the company of a vast expenditure ...? We are entitled to first consideration.'[80]

When GTP president Chamberlin announced 'Prince George' as the official name of the railway townsite in the spring of 1913, those interested in Fort George Townsite protested in Victoria. Businessmen located on the NRS townsite persuaded provincial archivist R.E. Gosnell to attack the GTP name as a demonstration of the callous disregard of the railway company for the heritage of the district. 'Fort George is one of the most historic points of the northern interior; Prince George means nothing to anybody.' More important was the threat from GTP advertising of the new name to the value of investments in Fort George Townsite. 'If there is one thing B.C. has stood for in the past,' a district petition declared, 'it is that the works of those who have rough graded the paths of progress ... shall not ruthlessly and unreasonably be torn from under them.' The NRS protest was more succinct. 'The change [in name] produced injuries by creating confusion and uncertainty in the minds of the investing public.'[81]

The response of the attorney general to these complaints was equivocal. Trumpeting a policy of even-handedness in the treatment of competing names, Bowser soothed the worried investors with the assurance that his department would not allow the GTP to register a townsite plan under the name 'Prince George.' Yet the attorney general had directed the provincial inspector of legal offices to reserve the name for the exclusive use of the railway company in 1912.[82] The provincial lands department policy was just as unresponsive. During the spring of 1913, the lands minister informally approved the GTP townsite plan, including the station site. In September, the department registered the GTP townsite plan under the title 'District Lot 343.' In private correspondence, officials acknowledged the name of 'Prince George' and finally published it in conjunction with the lot number to advertise the sale of government lots in the spring of 1914.[83]

Initially the post office sided with the traditionalists and rejected the GTP application 'as "Fort George" Post Office and townsite is within close proximity, being not more than half a mile away.' In April 1914, Donaldson elaborated the company's reasons for another post office. 'Present P.O. [at Fort George Townsite] 1.72 miles to our station [direct]

... Very heavy climb without road. From our works George Street, P.O. must by [sic] 2 1/4 miles and very indifferent road 7/8 of distance.' Perhaps more important, the general manager noted that the majority of the district's white population was now located on the GTP townsite. In August 1914, the railway townsite received a post office.[84] 'Prince George' had acquired legal status.

The acceptance of the GTP name for the railway townsite in 1914 did not improve the company's legal position before the Board of Railway Commissioners in the station site dispute, however. The BRC shift of the station location in November 1914 still left it 2,700 feet west of George Street. If corporate pressure would not suffice, the company encouraged 'spontaneous' civic action. Railway company officers had long realized that only a new legal party in the dispute had a chance of overturning the BRC order. This view informed all railway company activity concerning incorporation of Prince George.

The first request for incorporation did not come from the GTP, however. Arguing that the district required the extensive taxing powers of a municipality to deal with the growing problems of water supply, fire prevention, and sewage disposal, the residents of South Fort George Townsite made application for incorporation to the provincial government in August 1913. When the residents of the NRS townsite protested, the government rejected the application but suggested that interested parties in the two townsites might combine with residents of the new railway townsite to establish a common incorporation movement. The Fort George Townsite Board of Trade arranged a truce and established a Joint Incorporation Committee with representatives from all three townsites. The committee quickly agreed on an area for incorporation made up of sections of all three townsites, a parcel of 1,926.4 acres. Although it did not discuss the station site issue, the committee implicitly acknowledged that Prince George Townsite would be the centre of the proposed city by according it the largest acreage, 1,204.[85] To facilitate the preparation of the joint application, Bowser agreed to visit the district in July 1914.

Realizing the significance of incorporation in the emerging struggle with NRS in 1911, Hays had called for the incorporation of the railway townsite as soon as the company had acquired the Indian reserve. When Hansard learned that the provincial government intended to incorporate some area within the district, the GTP acted to have its townsite alone included. In an offer to accompany Bowser to the district and provide a

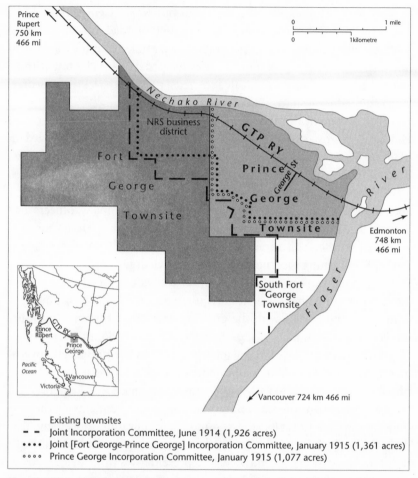

Figure 7.2 **Incorporation boundaries for proposed municipalities, Fort George District,** 1914-15

special train, the GTP solicitor stated bluntly: 'Our Company's position is that our townsite of Prince George will be the centre of the future city. Under such circumstances we would not of course want city improvements outside of Prince George at the expense of Prince George property.'[86]

At the July meeting with Bowser and the Joint Incorporation Committee, Hansard expressed the company view that the future city would prosper whatever its name. Drawing on the company's experience in Prince Rupert, he stated the company's major condition for support of incorporation: the exemption from taxation until 1921 of all GTP land within the city boundaries used for railway purposes. In response to a question concerning the delay in the construction of major shop facilities in Prince George, the GTP solicitor blandly assured the residents that the railway company would fulfil its promises.[87]

In a formal offer of support to the incorporation committee in August, however, Hansard added conditions. More important now was the requirement that the station be located at the foot of George Street. The draft of this letter makes the condition absolute; the final version adds the qualification 'subject to the approval of the Railway Commission.' For this provision Hansard offered to pay $14,000 in taxes before 1922 but then demanded that the city limit taxes for the subsequent fifteen years to $54,000 (an average of $3,700 per annum).[88] In a letter to committee chairman H.G. Perry two weeks before the BRC hearing in November, Hansard emphasized the importance of civic support for the railway company's case: 'Much will depend, I take it, on the decision of the Railway Commission on the location of the station site as to what kind of a permanent station, roundhouse, engine works, machineshops, and other structures and accessories will lie erected on the railway premises. If ... your people will show a disposition to work more closely with the Railway Company in the development of the future city, which is of the utmost importance to both of us, something might be accomplished.' One of the committee members described this suggestion as open coercion. Perry, also president of the Fort George Townsite Board of Trade, did not succumb to this pressure. The joint committee passed a resolution saying that it did not have competence to intervene in the station dispute.[89]

The British Columbia government had its own ideas about the area in the district more suitable for incorporation. While Bowser did not reject the proposed area of the Joint Incorporation Committee, he commissioned a detailed study of the reservoir potential and drainage problems of the three townsites. In August 1914, government engineer R.H. Thompson arrived in the district and publicly expressed a view to a meeting of residents that a restricted area – an area considerably smaller than the 1,926 acres the incorporation committee had proposed – would impose a more manageable tax burden on the residents of the future city.[90]

When the attorney general informed Hansard that he was considering the removal of South Fort George from the incorporation area for reasons of economy, the GTP solicitor revealed his president's instructions that only Prince George Townsite be included within the city limits. Hansard then argued that the residents of the southern townsite should receive some compensation: the George Street station. During November and December 1914, the *Fort George Herald* ran a series of articles concerning the expense of a common reservoir and sewer system with the other two townsites. On 29 December, the representatives of South Fort George withdrew from the joint Incorporation Committee.[91]

The representatives of Fort George Townsite were determined to continue with the joint incorporation. To restrict incorporation to Prince George Townsite, the railway company had to wreck the work of the Joint Incorporation Committee. In a later letter, the publisher of the *Fort George Tribune* noted that Hansard spent the evening of the BRC hearing (23 November) in the district in private discussion with GTP local agent J.T. Armstrong, real estate broker F.M. Ruggles, and J.B. Daniell, the former editor of the *Herald* who now published the *Prince George Post*, a newspaper supported by a secret GTP advertising contract. When the remaining members of the incorporation committee held a mass meeting on 12 January 1915 to obtain support for a revised incorporation area, these three individuals and Frank Ellis, the auctioneer for the GTP lot sale of 1913, broke up the meeting with vitriolic attacks on the Fort George Townsite representatives. The next day a Prince George Incorporation Committee was formed and a separate application for incorporation of the railway townsite was submitted to the provincial government.[92]

The Fort George Townsite residents, aware of the GTP's hostility, persevered and filed an application for incorporation of sections of both townsites, a parcel of 1,361 acres.[93] Both groups immediately circulated petitions and sent them to Victoria. Bowser requested Thompson, who had submitted a detailed technical report on the district in December, to examine the competing applications. Thompson decided that the Fort George proposal made more sense from a geographical point of view and concluded his findings with the declaration: 'I am inclined to favour the larger area.' But the provincial cabinet decided to incorporate only 1,077 acres within Prince George Townsite. Bowser may have wanted to put the lie to the 'common rumour' that 'Hammond has got a stranglehold on the Legislature which is of course composed of one man, the Attorney General.' It is more probable that the number of voters within the competing areas may have influenced the decision. The chairman of the

Prince George Incorporation Committee informed the attorney general that the railway townsite currently had a population of 2,100, South Fort George 700, and Fort George Townsite only 326. The Fort George Townsite Conservative Association's warning of certain defeat for the local government candidate in the next election was not taken seriously.[94]

Other opponents of restricted incorporation argued that the railway company determined government policy. A local businessman begged the premier not to sell Fort George to the railway company. The *Tribune* publisher charged that the weight of the railway was greater than that of the people. The individual who stood to lose most, George Hammond, offered the following interpretation in a letter to McBride. 'The incorporation movement, backed by interests which are plainly in sight, is for the sole purpose of injecting a new situation into the station matter. The company is bending every energy to secure the incorporation of the municipality for the sole purpose of influencing adversely the two cases still pending.' These were an earlier PGE intervention and the citizens' notice of appeal to prevent the BRC from declaring the GTP in default of its decision.[95]

Hansard had arranged with Bowser to come to Victoria before the cabinet made its decision. The GTP solicitor's only description of his activities there follows in a telegram to Armstrong on 17 February. 'After long fight against full Hammond forces succeeded in getting Government decision for incorporated area within Prince George Limits.' In early March, Bowser introduced an incorporation bill vetted by P.E. Wilson, the marshal of the Citizens' Committee, as one that conformed to Thompson's report. The people in the residential districts (i.e., Fort George Townsite) would, he predicted, in time thank the government for having left them out. Two Liberal members alleged that the government was simply favouring one group of real estate sharks over another, but there was never any doubt about the outcome of the debate. Although Bowser preferred the old, historic name for the new city, he added an amendment providing a plebiscite that would determine the civic name.[96] Hansard's explanation of his role in the passing of the bill was also slight. 'We got in a little ahead of Hammond and his crowd with Attorney General Bowser, and got him more or less to commit himself so that he forced the measure through.'[97] To finish off NRS, the GTP had conspired with the provincial government to fix the boundaries of the new city.

The GTP defeat of Hammond represented the company's major victory in the area, but the company settled another score. Though it had sold one-fifth of the townsite to Carruthers and Millar in settlement of their prior claim to the Indian reserve, it struck back at them indirectly for wresting part of Prince George from its grasp. The GTP took advantage of an oversight in the federal regulatory process to strangle the traffic of the B.C. Express Company (hereafter BC Express), one of Millar's concerns. Expecting the lively river traffic on the Upper Fraser to increase during construction of the railway, a federal public works engineer declared early in 1912 that the railway crossing of the Fraser into Fort George district must contain a draw for steamboats. He recommended permission be granted to build across the Fraser above Fort George two other GTP bridges without draws, only 'with the understanding that if at any time in the future it is found that passage ways are required in these bridges they shall be provided by the GTP R. C. on being directed to do so by this Department.'[98]

When the company received an order-in-council sanctioning construction of the bridges, GTP chief engineer B.B. Kelliher chose to regard the proviso as a meaningless formality, similar to those that had earlier been disregarded without incident in bridge construction across the Assiniboine and Saskatchewan rivers. The company ordered steel structures for low-level crossings and used the minimal reporting requirements of the Railway Act to hide its intentions.[99]

Only in the spring of 1913 did the steamboat operators become aware of the company's plans, perhaps because the steel for the low-level structures had been hauled to Tête Jaune Cache. Millar protested to the railways minister that obstruction of the Fraser represented a 'serious loss to the public and to ... transportation companies.' Others also began to apply pressure. Letters from the Quesnel Board of Trade, the provincial public works department, and the local MLA and MP expressed concern about the GTP actions. Kelliher responded by lauding the original report of the public works inspector and ignoring the proviso for passageways. He also stated that alteration in construction at this date after the low-level steel superstructures had already been fabricated would result in a year's delay in completion of the road. More to the point, Hansard declared that the company had already secured government sanction for the plans under the Railways Act. The company could therefore not be expected to make changes.[100]

Although the federal public works department conceded that a change in construction would damage the GTP, it decided that its engineer's proviso must be adhered to 'before the evil has arrived.' The department secretary requested that the company submit new plans for the upper crossings. A GTP engineer later testified that Kelliher facilely 'concluded that there was no possibility of making any provision for navigation that year, and he didn't think there would be any thereafter.' To eliminate the reason for navigation, the GTP placed an embargo on all freight to be handled by the steamboat firm without informing it. Late in August a steel cable was inserted across the Fraser at Mile 142 (Alberta border westerly), the site of the second Fraser Crossing. This effectively prevented the steamer *BC Express*, which had been designed for navigation on the Upper Fraser, from reaching Tête Jaune Cache at the headwaters (Mile 53).[101]

Demands for compliance with the public works requirement for new plans were ignored by GTP vice-president Wainwright. In the spring of 1914, the GTP officer explained that his ill health was reason enough to let the matter 'remain in abeyance.' This transparent, unconvincing delay permitted the erection of two low-level bridges that effectively barred steamboats from navigation above Fort George district. Millar sought an injunction in May 1914 to prevent obstruction, but the action was dismissed with a counsel to seek damages instead.[102]

The GTP was able to strike at both Millar and NRS in 1914. After the 1913 navigation of the lower Fraser had concluded, the *BC Express* was pulled out of the water for the winter on the banks of the Nechako, i.e., above the projected GTP crossing to Prince George. A temporary railway bridge was laid in January 1914 and not removed until June. Only the similar plight of the steamboats owned by the railway's principal contractor, FWS, persuaded bridge workers to remove part of the temporary bridge and false works for the permanent structure to allow all steamboats caught upriver to escape. Though the permanent bridge at Prince George was completed in June, its lift span was not put into operation until October, preventing all southern traffic from reaching the Fort George Townsite wharf on the banks of the Nechako above the bridge during the 1914 season.[103]

BC Express returned to the courts to secure damages for obstruction of navigation for both seasons. A steamboat employee alleged that a GTP solicitor had admitted that he was at a loss to offer a plausible defence of the company's actions. At the trial, the GTP plea certainly fell far short of

GTP Prince George Bridge lifting for FWS steamboat

Lincoln's renowned defence of the Rock Island railroad bridge across the Mississippi. Counsel for the company maintained that the river was not navigable, and in the face of documents and testimony to the contrary, declared that the need for navigation had ceased by virtue of the railway's arrival. An inappropriately worded claim allowed the GTP to escape damages for its actions in 1914, however. The plaintiff's inexperienced lawyer apparently led the judge to dismiss damages for 1913.[104]

A reference to the provincial Court of Appeal led to an award for damages for obstruction during the 1913 season. The railway company then appealed to the Supreme Court of Canada maintaining that evidence revealed 'several marked acts of [GTP] friendliness shown to the plaintiff.' The BC Express claim that the GTP embargo represented 'an open declaration of war' was more accurate, but both sides declined to inform the court of earlier relations between the principals. The GTP declared that the public works order to submit new plans did not necessarily mean that it should halt construction according to the earlier plans. The Supreme Court accepted the GTP appeal on a split decision. BC Express made a final, foolish recourse to the Judicial Committee of the Privy Council, but their lordships confirmed the GTP position.[105]

Though the company drove both NRS and BC Express from the district, the GTP did not achieve in Prince George Hays's objective for townsite development, the maximization of returns. The actual return the company extracted from the townsite was much less spectacular than the newspaper claims. Detailed sales records have not survived, but the GTP Development Co. Minute Books provide an annual summary of expected and actual returns. Table 7.1 provides data from the year 1913-14, in which the auction occurred, to 1918-19. When one considers the terms of sale for lot purchasers – one-quarter cash down payment, balance in three annual payments – the GTP received little beyond the down payments. By the summer of 1918, the company was owed more than $1.5 million in arrears. The cumulative development costs – acquisition of the reserve, survey, layout (townsite design), clearing, and taxes – amounted to $297,520.80 in 1918. The actual return in the cumulative balance of the GTP Development Company for Prince George Townsite for years 1911 through 30 June 1918 was $541,633.

Of course, the shortfall in returns stemmed in large part from the general collapse of the real estate market during the First World War, a factor the company did not create and probably could not anticipate.

Table 7.1

GTP annual reports, Prince George Townsite

Year end 30 June	Lands purchased (acres)	Surveyed (acres)	Surveyed (lots)	Lands sold (lots)	Lands unsold (acres)	Lands unsold (lots)	Cost of lands purchased ($)	Lands and lot sales ($)	Balance ($)	Cash received ($)	Cash less cost of land ($)	Deferred delinquent payments ($)
1914	1,366	762	5,263	3,575	604	1,688	128,415	2,914,480	2,786,065	709,735	581,320	2,204,744
1915	1,198*	762	5,463	4,756	535	707	128,415	3,001,021	2,872,606	775,162	646,747	2,159,762
1916	1,198	762	5,463	4,752	436	711	128,415	2,987,601	2,859,186	807,768	679,354	2,114,128
1917	1,198	762	5,463	4,582	436	881	128,415	2,747,891	2,619,476	835,665	707,249	1,857,658
1918	1,198	762	5,463	4,602	436	861	128,415	2,748,077	2,619,662	839,154	710,739	1,853,427
1919	1,111*	1,094	5,463	4,602		861	128,415	2,278,195	2,599,760	849,828	721,413	1,823,001

* Minus right-of-way

Source: NAC, RG 30, vol. 1074, 1075

Given Hays's requirement for immediate returns to offset construction, however, one wonders whether the company should have accepted the NRS 1911 offer of $100,000 – $200,000 (depending on the value of NRS notes and lots) for division of the real estate returns in the district. While the percentage of district lot sales in the GTP townsite would have undoubtedly decreased, the value of GTP lot sales might well have increased with the support of Hammond's imaginative promotion schemes for a station, and therefore city centre, which would still have been on GTP land. Had the company also invited Carruthers and Millar to enter the development in 1911 as the owners of a 'suburb,' the company could probably have extracted a much higher price for the 200 acres than it obtained to stop their legal challenge. As in Prince Rupert, however, the territoriality of GTP officers, though more successful in disrupting opponents, prevented the company from maximizing returns.

EIGHT

'FOR PURE SPITE':
HAZELTON DISTRICT

THE PRECEDING CHAPTERS have contended that GTP actions in town-site disputes sometimes reduced potential traffic by placing obstacles in the way of local initiative. The absence of detailed freight records or sta-tion receipts for Prince Rupert or Prince George has prevented estimates of the traffic loss that stemmed from the company's struggle with groups or concerns such as the Prince Rupert city council and the Natural Resources Security Company. Only for the Hazelton district do records survive that suggest how the GTP actually damaged concerns that could have provided valuable traffic for the line.[1] Material in the company files, when supplemented by the relevant records of provincial and federal government departments and agencies and the local newspapers, illumi-nates the activities of several company officers during an extended town-site dispute during the period 1910-18.[2] The territoriality that these managers had imbibed from President Hays resulted in the company promoting a townsite whose insignificant lot sales would not cover large engineering and legal expenditures. Because district mine owners would not accept the uneconomic location of the company townsite, the GTP then discouraged the development of mines that could have provided desperately needed local traffic. An examination of the company's activi-ties in the Hazelton district suggests that the GTP did not lay 'Rails of Steal [sic]' as Martin Robin charges.[3]

Established during the 1870s at the head of navigation on the Skeena River, 180 miles inland, the white community of Hazelton had served as a staging centre for treks to the Omineca gold fields, a fur trade post, and a missionary centre. It was news in 1903 of the construction of the Grand Trunk Pacific through northern British Columbia that provided the cat-alyst for development in the district. The increase in prospecting during the current season, the provincial gold commissioner of Omineca (Hazelton) district reported, was bound to spread over the entire region now that the building of the GTP was assured.

> Whatever Pass is chosen through the Rockies, the road will run through the district from east to west and open up to the prospector and capitalist hundreds of square miles of new country which up to the present time has been forced to lie idle and unexplored, owing to its isolation and the prohibitive cost of getting in provisions and supplies. Once the difficulties and cost of transport are removed by the completion of this transcontinental road, large tracts of ground that today are known to contain gold, but which under the existing conditions cannot be worked with profit, will be taken up and developed and will add to the prosperity of the district.[4]

With the announcement in 1906 that the GTP would build its line through northern British Columbia to the new port of Prince Rupert on Kaien Island, both prospectors and prospective farmers streamed into the district that the railway would probably traverse. Now, rejoiced the *Omineca Herald*, the district newspaper that had begun publication in Hazelton in June 1908, development could begin in earnest.[5]

In 1910, prospectors sold two claims on Glen Mountain, northeast of Hazelton, for $86,000 to a syndicate of railway contractors that included John W. Stewart, one of the partners of Foley Brothers, Welch, and Stewart Company (FWS), the principal contractor for the GTP line. The following year a strike of a six-foot vein of silver-lead ore was reported on the property, now named the Silver Standard Mine. Purchasing adjacent claims, the syndicate then embarked on a ten-year development program costing $280,000, which made the mine the most important development east of the town.[6]

In the Rocher Déboulé Mountain Range, south of Hazelton across the Bulkley River, prospectors discovered massive veins of copper ore in 1910. The following year, local promoters sold claims bonded at $65,000 to a Salt Lake City broker who formed the 'Rocher de Boule [*sic*] Copper Company.' Incorporated in 1912 with an authorized capital of $1 million, the company leased its property in August 1913 for a period of three and a half years. The lessee embarked on an ambitious plan of development that included the construction of an electric compressor and hydroelectric plant on the mountain for mechanized drilling, and most spectacularly, an aerial tramway three miles long that would transport

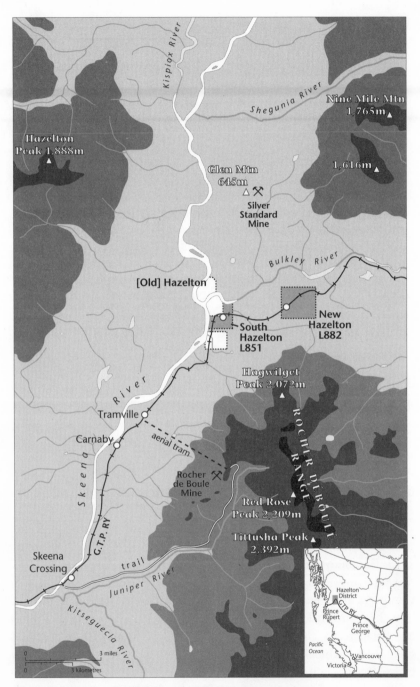

Figure 8.1 **Townsites, district lots, and mines in Hazelton district**

ore to the railway. It continued development even after the outbreak of the war and expected to ship 100 tons of ore a day once production started.[7]

Promoters viewed the approaching rail connection as the key to mining prosperity. In his report for 1911, the gold commissioner noted that by providing transportation for the district's minerals, the GTP would effect a remarkable change in the area. Amidst a steady stream of editorials complaining about poor mail service, the local newspaper acknowledged that the greatest handicap to development was the lack of rail transportation. The arrival of the end of steel would not only produce a steady mail service and greatly reduce the cost of freighting in goods, it would be the conduit for the district's ore. Indeed, one promoter viewed the GTP as a northern CPR cutting a wide swath through a mineral district whose production, he predicted, would soon equal that of the Kootenay region.[8]

An examination of district newspapers and the Department of Mines annual reports indicates that while the actions of the GTP sometimes provoked complaints from the miners, the railway company initially fulfilled the expectations of local boosters by providing the incentive for commercial production as well as the means of export of copper and silver-lead ore. Because of its large-scale site preparation, the Rocher de Boule Mine entered production only in 1915, two years after the end of steel reached the district. During the period 1915-18, the mine shipped almost 40,000 tons of ore to Prince Rupert for forwarding to smelters at Tacoma or Granby Bay where 4,214 ounces of gold, 62,865 ounces of silver, and 5,746,306 pounds of copper was extracted. Such a volume probably made ore from the mine the largest single commodity (by weight) hauled west on the British Columbia line during the war. Charging a rate of approximately $3 per ton, the GTP obtained a revenue of almost $120,000 from the traffic for the Hazelton-Prince Rupert leg alone. Even without a share in the forwarding charges to smelters on the west coast, this sum made the mine one of the railway's most important sources of revenue in British Columbia.[9] More data are available concerning the railway's role in the operation of the Silver Standard. Between 1913 and 1918, this mine forwarded 3,500 tons of crude and concentrated ore with an approximate assay value of $382,000 to smelters in Trail and Oklahoma. This traffic provided the GTP with a gross revenue of $51,396 and made the Silver Standard the company's second most important customer in the district.[10]

But though the newspapers and Department of Mines reports give some attention to the GTP's role in opening the mines, they virtually ignore its part in their closure. In late 1918, both mines suspended operation, but the Mines reports offer as explanations only abnormal conditions and a poor copper market for Rocher de Boule and 'an inability to market satisfactorily the silver-lead and silver-zinc concentrates' for the Silver Standard.[11]

To understand the railway company's motive for discouraging the operation of the mines in the Hazelton district after the end of steel reached there in late 1912, the company's actions and the miners' opposition in a townsite dispute must be considered at some length. For the GTP, the struggle to establish a railway townsite in the district became the overriding objective. But the company promoted a townsite at an inferior location because it could not extract an agreement for half the returns from a series of owners of District Lot 882 on the south bank of the Bulkley, the most appropriate station location on the railway's route through the district. Indeed, GTP land commissioner George U. Ryley could only secure right-of-way through the property by undertaking to install a siding at the prospective station site. This commitment led Vancouver provisioner Robert Kelly to purchase the property in 1911 and market it as New Hazelton Townsite, the inevitable centre of Hazelton district once the railway arrived. After failing to obtain company approval for an alternative site that no one accepted, Ryley, now desperate to 'save his own skin,' committed the company in October 1911 to erect a station and share the promotion of a townsite at South Hazelton on Lot 851, three miles west of New Hazelton. For a station that would load ore, the location was absurd since the railway line held to a steep gradient of .32 per cent and a sharp curve of more than 5° around a bench thirty feet below the crest and 200 feet above the level of land below.[12]

The GTP announcement prompted Kelly to apply to the Board of Railway Commissioners (BRC) to compel the GTP to erect a station on his property and restrain the GTP from locating a station at South Hazelton. A hearing was scheduled in December. District miners also expressed their concern about the GTP location of the station yards, as it meant large sums of money in getting their ore to the railway. They were, 'to a man,' opposed to South Hazelton because of its steep approach and its greater distance from the mines.[13]

In their haste to repeat the success of the 1909 Prince Rupert lot sale, company officers not only ignored the earlier GTP undertaking to build a siding on Lot 882 but also arranged with the provincial government to hold a joint auction of South Hazelton lots before the BRC hearing. The South Hazelton lot sales held in Vancouver on 14 December and in Victoria on 19 December certainly did not resemble the wild stampedes for lots in Prince Rupert and Prince George, however. By January 1912, the GTP had sold only eighty-two of its lots for a total of $48,830.[14]

Insouciance characterized the railway company's preparations for the hearing. Only on 28 November, after the sale of South Hazelton lots had been set in motion, did Ryley inform the legal department that the GTP should immediately obtain BRC sanction for the station location on Lot 851, because the owners of the next siding to the east might apply for a station. GTP solicitor D'Arcy Tate did not make the application until 7 December, however. Although he considered Ryley's presence at the hearing indispensable, General Manager Chamberlin, apparently assured that the GTP would win, rejected his solicitor's advice. 'The Railway Commission will feel it is time enough to say if Kelly should have a station after the railway has reached that point and whether sufficient business warrants it.'[15]

The hearing took place in Ottawa with lawyers appearing for Kelly, the GTP, and the merchants of the district. Ottawa solicitor Clive Pringle, claiming that he represented nine-tenths of the business firms of [Old] Hazelton, presented a forceful case. After observing that 'mining is the industry of that vicinity and ought to be considered more than anything else,' he read a telegram from local mine owners and promoters of camps east of [Old] Hazelton, which stated that the increased distance and adverse wagon grades to South Hazelton would increase the cost of hauling ore to the railway line by $4 per ton. He concluded that 'the natural inclination is for settlement to spring up where a station exists, and the mere fact that there are two stations close together where trade does not demand it is going to bring about nothing but trouble and difficulty.'[16]

BRC chief commissioner J.P. Mabee was probably inclined to reject the company's defence that it was obligated only to build a siding. Such a disposition afforded the commissioner another opportunity to harass GTP solicitor Tate with whom he had clashed during an earlier hearing concerning Cameron Bay in Prince Rupert. An acrimonious exchange with Tate as well as the force of Pringle's argument led Mabee to deliver an emotional judgment directly after the lawyers had completed their cases. He cited the advertisements for the lot sale of South Hazelton as strong evidence that the GTP had succeeded in extracting from the owner of Lot 851 what the owner of Lot 882 had refused: one-half interest in a townsite. Maintaining that the company had repudiated an agreement made with the owner of Lot 882, Mabee then declared: 'It is a public scandal that a railway corporation should go about the country and obtain conveyances of this kind under false pretences. If a private individual had done what this company through its officials have done ... he ought to be landed in the Penitentiary. The land was obtained through the grossest deceit on the part of the representatives of this company.' Describing the activities of the GTP as a 'violation of the solemn contract with the predecessor of Kelly in title,' the commissioner ordered the company to build a station on Lot 882 by the time the end of steel reached the district and forbade the establishment of a station on Lot 851.[17]

The extensive coverage that the press accorded the provocative judgment was galling for the railway company. The Vancouver *Saturday Sunset* claimed that the GTP had 'stooped to deals unworthy of a two-spot real estate shark,' and that its land department had 'worked its way across the country spreading desolation in the shape of broken agreements and sore land owners behind them [*sic*].' But the commissioner did 'not respect the divine right of railway corporations to treat all law and ethics with unconcern.' In several papers, a paraphrased version of the judgment that was even more damning of the GTP appeared as part of an advertisement touting New Hazelton. The ads apparently had the desired effect. By the end of December, Kelly's Vancouver agent had sold $200,000 worth of lots while a local broker sold Hazelton district residents fifty lots in two days. Even Aldous & Murray, the local real estate firm that had boosted South Hazelton, admitted that New Hazelton would be the future city of the district.[18]

The *Omineca Herald* described the BRC decision as a handsome Christmas present that had effectively ended the dispute. It also trumpeted the fact that the judgment guaranteed the railway company would not 'establish a rival townsite for pure spite.' But the continuing opposition of the GTP to New Hazelton over the next six years suggests that spite rather than the long-term interests of the railway company now directed the actions of company officers.

Stung by the sensational headlines, Hays personally reviewed the files from all departments concerning the case. Responding to the president's censure, Ryley admitted that he had been too hasty in putting South Hazelton lots on the market before the company had obtained BRC approval for a station location. While he accepted responsibility for the mistake, the land commissioner continued to maintain that South Hazelton was the proper location for the district station. After issuing an order that no further townsites were to be placed on the market without BRC station approval, Hays complained that if the president had to handle this type of detail work, he might as well abolish the departments.[19]

But the president did more than censure his subordinates. Although he twice requested Mabee to grant a rehearing for an undertaking to locate stations at both points 'for the purpose of so far as possible putting an end to the difficulties,' Hays also instructed company officers to seek alternative solutions as soon as the decision was rendered. When Mabee rejected his request by citing the miners' telegram opposing the railway townsite, Hays determined to go around the BRC by appealing directly to the federal cabinet. He would then be able to deal with opposition in the district.[20]

On 28 February 1912, GTP general counsel W.H. Biggar completed the company's brief to the cabinet. The BRC order was unfair to the railway company, Biggar claimed, since the GTP had made no undertaking to locate a station on Lot 882, and the board had approved no application for a station there. In contrast, Lot 851 was 'admirably suited as a site for a town,' and the company's proposed station site was 'the best adapted and most suitable for the purpose, regard being had to the future operation of your petitioners' railway, and to the convenience of the residents of the present Town of [Old] Hazelton.' Adding that the British Columbia government was also very desirous of locating a station on Lot 851, he asked the cabinet to rescind the order.[21]

Even before Biggar had completed the petition, GTP officers expressed confidence in the company's ability to overturn the BRC judgment. Just four days after the hearing, Chamberlin predicted that in spite of present difficulties, the 'Railway Commission will have no jurisdiction over South Hazelton if we desire to develop the point.'[22] By early January, he was so confident that the company would 'secure [a] decision which will not interfere with South Hazelton townsite' that he destroyed an opportunity for reconciliation by rejecting out of hand an offer from Kelly's agent to place all South Hazelton lot purchasers in New Hazelton without remuneration.[23]

To strengthen its case for the appeal, the GTP had to alter the impression made at the BRC hearing that the majority of residents and mine owners of the district favoured New Hazelton. Consequently, Tate wrote and circulated a 'Petition to the Premier' favouring South Hazelton, which 55 people or firms in the district signed. The company also paid W.P. Murray, the local broker who marketed South Hazelton, to spread rumours concerning the importance of South Hazelton in GTP development plans to sway the Hazelton Board of Trade. Although patently untrue, his arguments had some effect on the community since the Board of Trade resolved in March to support the location of the railway station for the district at South Hazelton because it offered a commanding view, could be easily drained, and was closer to [Old] Hazelton. The resolution did admit that because of South Hazelton's 'slight grade,' heavy ore might have to be loaded at New Hazelton. The *Herald* complained that the board had been 'railroaded.'[24]

The appeal before the cabinet was heard on 3 May. While the evidence presented convinced one minister that 'the GTP people played it down low on Kelly,' the cabinet apparently heeded the opinion of counsel for the British Columbia government and referred the case back to the BRC on the ground that the last hearing overlooked the public interest by concentrating on the GTP's breach of contract.[25] An order was so issued on 10 May.

The unusual cabinet decision attracted attention from the national press.[26] The *Monetary Times* declared the decision a bad omen after the untimely death of Commissioner Mabee. Only if the BRC adhered to the late chairman's views could it retain the people's faith. Not surprisingly, the *Herald* viewed the outcome of the appeal as an example of the 'avaricious and crushing policy of the defeated,' and lamented wasting the railway commission's time again.[27]

Both sides acted quickly to marshal more evidence for the forthcoming rehearing before the BRC, however. Most interesting were affidavits of local residents supporting the competing townsites. V.W. Smith, local manager of FWS and director of a small district mine, submitted 149 affidavits from 'residents of New Hazelton' supporting their town. Although the mimeographed forms contain only the general address of 'New Hazelton,' the individual names and occupations suggest that during the summer of 1912, New Hazelton housed both a service community (53 merchants and various shop owners or workers) and a significant number of miners (38 prospectors, miners, mine owners, mine brokers, mine secretaries, and cooks). In response, the supporters of South Hazelton could muster affidavits from only 23 residents of [Old] Hazelton, which included no miners and revealed that no one was living on the railway townsite.[28]

Probably more important at the time were affidavits from owners or managers of nine mines located on Four-Mile, Nine-Mile, and Glen mountains, east of [Old] Hazelton. With two exceptions, the ranking of their estimates of the cost of hauling ore from the mine head to New Hazelton accords with their respective distance from the townsite. The owners claimed that the removal of the station from New Hazelton to South Hazelton would increase the average cost of hauling ore to the line from $2.50 to $4.50 per ton.[29] Surprisingly, the railway company sought no affidavits from the owners of the camps on the Rocher Déboulé Range, which was closer to South Hazelton.

The rehearing in Ottawa dragged on for three days in early June. If nothing else, it represented a feast for lawyers, with counsel representing ten supposedly separate parties. While most of the testimony simply elaborated or repeated arguments made during the first hearing, engineering appraisals of both sites were far more detailed. Smith claimed that the wagon road from the river to South Hazelton was so steep that steamboats had delivered FWS supplies for work to a small bridge at Sealey, three miles 'west' of South Hazelton on the grade. A bridge engineer testified that a Bulkley River crossing from the mining camps to New Hazelton would cost only $60,000 while a bridge closer to lot 851 would cost more than $225,000. Finally, a GTP engineer who had left the company's service in April 1912 testified that Lot 882 had the best gradient and curvature of any site in the district.[30]

The arguments offered by the GTP and its allies in support of South Hazelton seemed relatively weak, by comparison. The company produced an engineer from the Ottawa section of the parent Grand Trunk Railway who estimated that the cost of improving the South Hazelton site would amount to only $20,000. Most important, however, was Ryley's admission that the gradient from the river below the townsite to South Hazelton on the bench required a steep zigzag road, which would create difficulties for wagons with a heavy load of ore. This was supported by a murky panoramic photograph that suggested the height of the bench on which the South Hazelton station would perch.[31]

To counter the impression that close to 200 people already lived at New Hazelton, Biggar argued that half its business came from the temporary location of FWS headquarters there. The GTP lawyer also charged that supporters of New Hazelton were interested in the establishment of that station only as a means to sell townsite lots. When Commissioner McLean ventured that this might also explain the GTP interest in South Hazelton, Biggar responded that the 'GTP interest depends on a place being built up.' In summing up the case for South Hazelton, Biggar brazenly claimed that the late BRC chief commissioner had informed him that he would be happy with stations at both points. There is no indication in the surviving files of the BRC or the GTP, however, that Mabee had changed his mind since rejecting Hays's proposals out of hand in January 1912.[32]

These professions of the engineering advantages of the competing locations as well as several others in the district led McLean to observe dryly that only a continuous station and station ground from New Hazelton to South Hazelton would meet the situation. But when Ryley came to the stand, the commissioner's resentment at the company's success in forcing the BRC to hear the case again led him to take up where Mabee had left off, for he condemned the railway company's location as a 'corkscrew curve with maximum grade.' When Biggar protested, McLean stated angrily that 'the GTP finds no difficulty in locating a station which is unsatisfactory to us while under similar conditions it can find all sort of difficulties.' Yet when the hearing ended, McLean reserved judgment.[33]

Four days later McLean wrote a surprising judgment. He observed that much of the evidence submitted at the rehearing could be little other than speculative and reaffirmed the board's determination to compel the railway company to establish a station on Lot 882. 'For the Board to assent to the modification of this term of the Order would make it an assenting party to a vital injustice.' But giving 'due weight to the mass of material presented ... much of it contradictory, much of it conjectural,' he decided that the representatives of the town of [Old] Hazelton had made a case for a station location nearer to them than that on Lot 882. The learned commissioner therefore rescinded the restraint on the GTP and invited the company to submit an application for a station site that would give adequate facilities to the people of Hazelton. Noting that the original plan for a station location on Lot 851 departed from practically every GTP engineering and operating standard, McLean insisted that the company conform to its standards at this location. And if the GTP were to flout Mabee's decision concerning New Hazelton, the commissioner warned that the company would pay for it. On 25 June an order was so issued.[34]

It is not surprising that the *Omineca Miner*, which had begun publication in [Old] Hazelton in 1911 and as the recipient of GTP advertising supported South Hazelton, viewed the decision as a victory for the GTP. On his return from Ottawa, Murray informed the *Miner* that the BRC had practically recommended that the GTP file plans for South Hazelton, and claimed that Lot 882 would be worthless if Lot 851 went ahead.[35]

The supporters of New Hazelton took what comfort they could from the decision. Claiming that the railway company would have to spend half a million dollars to bring the South Hazelton site up to standard, the *Herald* maintained that 'no sane corporation would attempt it unless it would serve a great city.' While an agent for New Hazelton maintained that 'anything the GTP might say in the matter should not be taken seriously,' the report that Chamberlin, now president of the GTP, would still not compromise with New Hazelton interests must have caused the readers concern.[36]

Accordingly, the directors of Kelly's land company approached the GTP about pooling their respective interests in one townsite. One of the partners in South Hazelton was ready to accept Kelly's offer for half the proceeds of New Hazelton. But when a realtor repeated Kelly's 'very liberal offer,' to Chamberlin in August, the GTP president refused the proposition and shortly afterwards publicly expressed his support for the development of South Hazelton.[37]

The railway company obtained no economic advantages from the BRC order, however. By July 1912, for compensating track in South Hazelton 'so as to bring it down to as nearly as possible our standard conditions,' the railway company had expended $40,000. Although the general manager claimed that the country did not offer many possibilities for better or more satisfactory accommodation, he admitted that the main reason for utilizing the station privileges that the GTP had secured was that the company could not now afford to give them up.[38]

BRC approval for the site now became urgent. In spite of the new BRC order, the British Columbia government demanded that lot purchasers at South Hazelton receive the option of withdrawing from their agreements. When Chamberlin rejected this request on the grounds that the railway had made no collections on payments for the lots since the matter had gone to the BRC, the deputy minister recommended that the government act on its own, and the lands minister circulated an option to withdraw in thirty days in November 1912. Of the seventy-eight lots on GTP property purchased at the auction, only twenty agreements remained in force by May 1913.[39]

The company officers ignored the deteriorating economic position on Lot 851, however, and sought the advantage that they believed the BRC order conferred. Following the advice of a sympathetic commissioner, Biggar submitted a revised plan for the site that the company's engineers had completed at the end of August and formally requested the board's sanction to erect a station. While a BRC inspector complained that the GTP location was 'not a desirable one for a station either from a railway engineering or an operating standpoint,' the board apparently gave more weight to a series of identical telegrams from 'Hazelton' urging immediate acceptance of the South Hazelton application. On 2 October, Commissioner McLean claimed that since the people of [Old] Hazelton were apparently willing to accept these 'limited and inadequate' facilities, the board would sanction the plan.[40]

When McLean agreed to hold back the issue of the order to allow the protesters to present new evidence, Biggar demanded that the order should be issued at once. A promoter of Lot 851 complained to another commissioner that the delay of the order caused an economic loss to Hazelton. Additional pressure came from a resolution of the Hazelton Board of Trade calling for the immediate authorization of South Hazelton. Only two days after the resolution had been wired did the secretary of the Board of Trade inform the BRC that the board was far from unanimous on this question. The local merchant complained that no notice for the vote was given and argued that the 'actual' majority still favoured New Hazelton.[41]

Although the opponents of South Hazelton maintained that the intent of the GTP application was to 'destroy forever the [original] order of the Board,' McLean waited no longer and stated that the BRC was not going to

> mingle in townsite matters *qua* townsite ... It [BRC] is not concerned with whether two townsites grow where one grew before. There may be abuses in the matter of location of townsites; there may be too many of them; some of them may be simply the capitalization of an iridescent

optimism. But be that as it may, there is not within the four corners of the Railway Act any statement that the Board is the official Guardian of townsites, and the Railway Act nowhere overrules the necessity of investors exercising common sense.

Over the protests of the representatives of New Hazelton, McLean finally issued the order.[42]

But though the railway company had now won a notable legal victory by securing sanction to establish a station at its townsite in the face of protest from the district, its economic position did not improve. In December, Ryley declared to the *Miner* that the 'GTP will carry out its proposals at South Hazelton.' These presumably included making South Hazelton the district trade centre. The local townsite partner celebrated the company's commitment in a lavish pamphlet entitled *GTP South Hazelton: Northern Interior Metropolis*. It contained declarations of the railway townsite's potential by persons of 'character and integrity' whose opinions 'could be taken at least at face value.' It also offered a misleading map showing an aggrandized South Hazelton on virtually flat land and a track traversing an unbroken wilderness in Lot 882.[43]

But despite declarations that South Hazelton was receiving a large amount of freight and passengers and that clearing was going on apace for the construction of a large freight shed, the company only shunted two boxcars onto the siding to increase the 'buildings' in the townsite from one tent and two restaurants. Small wonder that a school inspector dismissed the GTP townsite as 'little more than a name on the railroad timetable' whose lots would eventually be offered as dubious premiums for a subscription to an eastern Canadian magazine. At the same time, New Hazelton claimed a population of 350 people and 121 permanent buildings.[44] By the following summer, even the GTP's original partner in South Hazelton deserted. In July 1913, W.J. Sanders agreed to abandon South Hazelton for Kelly's offer of three-sevenths of the shares of New Hazelton, payment of Sanders's debts for Lot 851, which amounted to $9,800, and the transfer of lot purchasers to the Kelly townsite. One of the conditions of the agreement was that both parties would 'use their utmost endeavours to induce the Grand Trunk Pacific Railway Company to recognize the said Lot [882] as the official Townsite' and that they would compensate the company to accomplish that object.[45] This move led an Anglican bishop who had bought two lots for churches in 1911 to complain that South Hazelton was now 'practically worthless except for

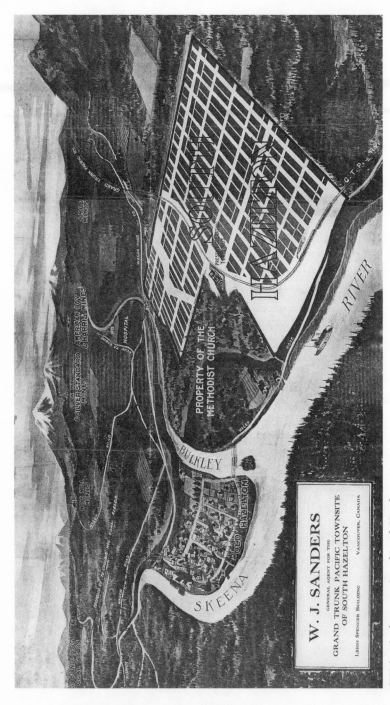

GTP-inspired perspective of South Hazelton, 1913

farm purposes.' The agreement also prompted the British Columbia government to allow those who had purchased lots on government property in 1911 another opportunity to withdraw in view of the 'intention to abandon the townsite.' But the company determined to hang on and would not allow its lot purchasers to withdraw or transfer to New Hazelton.[46] By March 1913, the *Herald* charged that the GTP had spent $60,000 on its townsite, more than it obtained in the auction sale in 1911. Thus, in its attempt to establish and maintain a station at an economically unsuitable location, the GTP not only incurred a substantial financial loss but also antagonized many residents and investors in the district's major town on the line before it had hauled out a single carload of freight from the district.[47]

ONLY IN THE CONTEXT of this townsite dispute does the series of GTP actions after 1912 that hindered development and eventually closed local mines become comprehensible. Prominent among the district residents who, in Hays's words, wanted only to hold up the GTP were the miners, who had opposed the company's project at every turn. This perception led company officers to retaliate in ways that discouraged the mines from increasing their production and, consequently, increasing the amount of ore the railway would forward.

While the GTP had obtained BRC authorization to run trains over its line to South Hazelton (Mile 177) in October 1912, it 'neglected' to apply for running rights to New Hazelton (Mile 180) at that time. When the end of steel neared the district at the end of November, Commissioner McLean reminded the company that a station must be completed at New Hazelton before traffic could be carried beyond that point. On 22 November, the New Hazelton Citizens' Association was formed for the task of getting freight and passenger service to the town. Later that week it sent a petition to the BRC to request service.[48] Chamberlin replied to the petition that the GTP had not yet built a station at New Hazelton owing to 'severe winter conditions' but promised that the company would eventually carry out the order. During the month of December, however, all traffic for New Hazelton was stopped and unloaded at South Hazelton and then shipped by wagon to the larger town. The trains then proceeded to New Hazelton empty to turn around on a wye before returning to South Hazelton and loading. This economically foolish action provoked the *Herald* to charge that the company was criminally dumping freight and passengers 'miles from anywhere.' Commissioner Scott's comment that 'the GTP is attempting to get square with those people interested in New Hazelton' was probably not far from the mark.[49]

But the company persisted in its attempts to boost South Hazelton in spite of its unpromising economic prospects and the hostility of many district residents. In February 1913, GTP general manager Morley Donaldson decided that confusion resulting from the similar names of adjacent stations must be ended. By March the railway company had designated South Hazelton as 'Hazelton' on its timetables and maps over the objections of the residents of New Hazelton.[50] When the company held up four carloads of timber that were necessary to continue work on the bridge across the Bulkley River from New Hazelton to the mines, BRC chief commissioner H.L. Drayton demanded that the delay end and that the company justify its actions or face the imposition of a stiff penalty for failure to comply with an order of the board. Donaldson quickly instructed the legal department to apply for authorization to run trains to New Hazelton, but service did not begin until the middle of January. GTP solicitor H.H. Hansard's ingenuous explanation that the delay stemmed from the absence of company officers at the office during the Christmas season was not convincing. The long delay prompted the *Herald* to charge that transportation was better in the days before the advent of the railway when the residents of the district mushed to Prince Rupert and brought all their supplies in by canoe in the summer. 'At least no corporation in those days tried to club them into submission.'[51]

When trains finally entered New Hazelton with goods, the newspaper proclaimed the event as a great victory for the people over the railway company, which wanted to sidetrack the town for the winter.

> It is a fact known to everyone that has ever been mixed up in a GTP townsite, that the 'backing' of the railway company does not amount to a row of pins. The GTP has never been known to make a move for the benefit of a town. In every instance the town had to fight to the last ditch ... Ryley would naturally favour South Hazelton. That townsite was his last hope from an utter route [*sic*] in the townsite game ... But Ryley is so thoroughly discredited in the North and along the GTP Railway [line], that any statement from him is a huge joke.[52]

A few days after the BRC had authorized trains to run to New Hazelton, the first carload of ore destined for the Trail smelter left New Hazelton for Prince Rupert. If the GTP could put the townsite dispute aside, the

Herald predicted that it could obtain from the district 'a line of down freight [to Prince Rupert] that will give them profit.'[53]

But the company did not separate the potential traffic in ore from the townsite dispute. And so it instituted a rate that effectively discouraged the Silver Standard and other mines from hauling their ore to New Hazelton for forwarding on the railway. For carloads of ore hauled to Prince Rupert from New Hazelton, the GTP charged a rate of $6.40 per ton, almost as much as the CPR rate for the much longer journey from Prince Rupert to Trail via Vancouver. The *Herald* complained that the GTP rate was 'nothing short of robbery – the people of the district are entitled to a freight rate which will enable them to get ore to market and make a profit.' It contrasted this exorbitant rate with the much lower rates on American railways and observed sarcastically that $6.40 looked 'nice on top' of total costs of the development of mines, the products of which must be shipped from the district. To compel the company to reduce its rate, the miners threatened to send their ore to Prince Rupert by river steamer.[54]

In June, it appeared that the GTP local agent had been instructed to work out a rate more satisfactory to the miners, and the company lowered its rate to Prince Rupert from $6.40 to $4.00 per ton, reducing the total cost of shipment to Trail from $13.20 to $11.00 per ton. But the reduced New Hazelton-Prince Rupert rate was still 60 per cent higher than the rates on twelve American lines that hauled ore a similar distance over less favourable grades. At the start of the war, miners protested that the rate forced them to ship at a loss and threatened once more to take their case to the BRC. But their disillusionment with the regulatory agency's failure to curb GTP harassment of New Hazelton and the prospect of a further reduction apparently dissuaded them from pressing the action. By the end of 1915, the rate for the New Hazelton-Prince Rupert leg was lowered to $3.00 per ton though the total rate apparently did not change. With this rate, the *Herald* predicted the district's mining industry would revive.[55]

By the end of 1913, four mines in the district had shipped almost 400 tons of ore of which the Silver Standard's shipment of 282 tons was by far the largest. Such production brought the owners approximately $38,000, from which the railway company charged at least $1,600 on the Prince Rupert leg of the journey, as well as an indeterminate sum for transporting some of the ore in its steamers from Prince Rupert to

Table 8.1

GTP freight and freight charges from Silver Standard Mine, 1913-18

	Smelter destination	Ore hauled (tons)	Rate to smelter ($ per ton)	Freight charge ($)	Ore value ($)	Freight charge / Ore value (%)
Crude ore						
1913	Trail[a]	282	11.00	3,102	28,600	10.9
1914	Trail	736	11.00	8,096	80,600	10.1
1915	Trail	154	11.00	1,694	15,700	10.8
1916	Trail	651	11.00	7,161		
	Dewar, OK[b]	109	14.10	1,537		
Total 1916		760		8,698	81,700	10.7
1917	Trail	866	11.00	9,526		
	Dewar, OK	210	14.10	2,961		
Total 1917		1,076		12,487	87,100	14.3
Concentrates						
1918	Trail	266[c]	26.65	7,089		
	Silver Sands, OK	300	34.10	10,230		
Total 1918		566		17,319	88,100	19.7
Hypothetical freight charge without GTP waybill advance				(8,937)	88,100	(10.2)

a Ore hauled to Trail via Prince Rupert and Vancouver
b Ore hauled to Oklahoma smelters via Winnipeg
c Estimated on ratio of concentrates to crude ore for 1919: 16 per cent

Sources: BC Department of Mines, *Annual Reports*, 1913-19; *Omineca Herald*, 1913-19

Vancouver. An agent of the mine owners observed that although the railway company had 'scorned and hampered' the district, the current ore on dumps waiting for shipment was 'probably the forerunner of more revenue earning traffic on ore, machinery and mining supplies than will be offered the GTP in the future at any point on its new transcontinental line.'[56]

For the Silver Standard Mine, the GTP's reduction of the rate to Prince Rupert in June 1913 lowered the proportion of freight charges to estimated ore value to less than 12 per cent. And according to the calculations of Smithers mine owner James Cronin, this was the freight charge ceiling necessary for the profitable operation of a silver-lead mine along the GTP route.[57] The mine owners thereupon shipped out ten cars of ore on which the GTP placed banners and photographed for advertising purposes. The resulting assay of $106.42 per ton gave the Silver Standard a reputation as the richest mining camp in the North, and its ore probably represented the most lucrative freight (total value) that the GTP hauled west to Prince Rupert before the Rocher de Boule Mine entered production.[58]

The figures in Table 8.1 calculated from data in the Department of Mines annual reports and the *Herald* indicate the weight and value of freight the Silver Standard, the most important mine loading at New Hazelton, brought to the railway. Although the government and newspaper reports do not usually state explicitly the weight of ore hauled, accompanying data on the value of metal extracted from the ore after smelting suggest that all ore produced was shipped before the installation of an ore concentrator in late 1917. If one includes the waybill advance of 1918, the railway obtained $51,000 from the mine for transporting ore.[59]

The actual operation of the mine was more erratic than these figures indicate, however. During the years 1913-19, the Silver Standard closed for three extended periods: August 1914-June 1915, because of market disruption when the Trail smelter refused to accept silver-lead ore; October 1917-May 1918, for the installation of an ore concentrator; and December 1918-April 1919, because of 'an inability to market satisfactorily the silver-lead and silver-zinc concentrates.'[60] These data suggest that operation of the mine and its continued supply of freight to the GTP was precarious in the years before 1919. But instead of encouraging production at the Silver Standard and other mines east of [Old] Hazelton by improving facilities at, and roads to, New Hazelton, the railway company attempted to stop the hauling of ore to New Hazelton by removing its station agent.

The first closure of the Silver Standard in fall 1914 and the accompanying decrease in ore shipments from New Hazelton suggested to some company officers that the GTP could cut its expenses in the district by removing its agent from the Kelly townsite station. In June 1915, GTP general superintendent W.C. Mehan in Prince Rupert claimed that with the removal of FWS from New Hazelton after the completion of the railroad, few people and little business for the railway remained. Hansard immediately had the local auditor draw up tables of traffic for both New Hazelton and South Hazelton for the period January 1914-April 1915. In 1914, freight hauled in and out of the two stations was roughly equal in value, but New Hazelton had twice as many passengers. In the period May 1914-April 1915, the value of freight at New Hazelton declined by almost 50 per cent, and the value of passenger traffic decreased by more than one-third. But total receipts for both New Hazelton and South Hazelton exceeded $15,000 per annum, and the BRC would have prevented the company from closing New Hazelton.[61]

That some company officers were disposed to close New Hazelton is indicated by Mehan's presentation of the falling receipts of New Hazelton station as 'an opportunity to settle matters' and Hansard's response that the figures are 'still not enough to justify discontinuance.' In July 1915, General Manager Donaldson instructed Hansard to start procedures for cancelling the New Hazelton agency if the receipts continued to fall.[62] Internal correspondence leading up to the formal application permits a rare view of local traffic patterns on the GTP. Only after he had examined the receipts for the first nine months of 1915 did the GTP solicitor feel confident enough to apply to the BRC for the discontinuance of an agent at New Hazelton. To support his case to the GTP general manager, Hansard enclosed the auditor's calculations for both stations from January 1914 through September 1915. A summary of the data is found in Table 8.2.[63] The receipts are not complete since they omit passengers inward and express revenue. But they indicate that New Hazelton, in spite of the closure of the Silver Standard from August 1914 to June 1915, continued to ship more ore out of the district than did South Hazelton, which had practically no freight outward. A large shipment of construction material to repair or ballast a part of the line in the district probably accounted for the increase in 1915 of freight inward for South Hazelton, which the railway company would of course have credited to the station it promoted. Hansard decided to send the BRC figures

Table 8.2

GTP freight and revenue from New Hazelton and South Hazelton stations, 1914-15

	1914		January to September 1915	
	New Hazelton	South Hazelton	New Hazelton	South Hazelton
Freight in (tons)	830	1,002	211	652
Freight out (tons)	1,025	211	288	85
Freight total (tons)	1,855	1,213	499	737
Number of passengers	3,642	1,805	1,571	1,243
Value (total)	$24,674	$18,035	$7,180	$10,777

Source: NAC, RG 30, vol. 3453, file 3115

only for the period October 1914 to September 1915, which encompassed the closure of the Silver Standard.

The application immediately led to protests from the district. On 7 December, H.S. Clements, the former broker for New Hazelton and now local MP, intervened in the matter. Declaring that he no longer had any personal interest in the townsite, he argued that the completion of a $40,000 bridge across the Bulkley to the recently reopened Silver Standard would soon increase New Hazelton's freight receipts.[64] More telling was a protest of the New Hazelton Citizens' Association. It claimed that the figures the GTP had submitted covered only the period during which the Trail smelter refused to accept ore. 'The closing of our principal revenue producers naturally crippled all other branches of our business.' Since the Silver Standard and other mines had begun to ship ore again, the citizens believed that they would soon exceed their shipments for 1913 and 1914.[65]

The association's contention that the company had unfairly deprived New Hazelton of receipts on the Prince Rupert-Vancouver leg, which would effectively double its receipts for its shipments, won the support of the BRC. When an inspector examined Hansard's figures, he concluded that the receipts also ignored incoming passengers, which would put New Hazelton over the $15,000 mark. Observing that an average of 55 pieces of less than carload freight had been received or forwarded every day at the station for the past three months, the BRC chief operating officer recommended that revised calculations be made with the inclusion of these items. After receiving this report, Commissioner Drayton ruled that the railway must include returns on freight forwarded from New Hazelton to Vancouver in its calculation of New Hazelton's station receipts, which, even with the small amount of ore shipped in

1915, would push it over the $15,000 mark. He also stated that it would be impractical to take material from New Hazelton to South Hazelton by wagon road, admitting what the mine owners had argued for years, that the GTP station site was completely unsuitable for forwarding the district's most important freight, ore.[66]

In explanation of the GTP's defeat at the hearing, Mehan could only speculate that the editor of the *Herald* had given the BRC inspector a 'spiel of air castles,' purposely misrepresenting existing conditions to carry a point against the railway company. He rejected the decision to include the sea leg in the returns since shippers could use CPR vessels rather than the GTP steamers if they so chose. He did show that ore in 1915 shipped to Trail totalled 209 tons, which produced a revenue of $605 to Prince Rupert and an additional $605 to Vancouver. By itself this revenue would not have pulled New Hazelton over the $15,000 mark, but the company did not pursue the matter.[67]

The company eventually did have its way. When the railway companies obtained sanction from the federal government in the so-called '15 per cent' and '25 per cent' cases to advance freight rates twice in 1918, the GTP greatly exceeded the limits in its application of the rate to ore shipped from New Hazelton to Trail and to the United States via Winnipeg.[68] Although the government allowed a total increase of 25 per cent on rates for hauling concentrated (ground) ore in British Columbia, the GTP compelled the Silver Standard after June 1918 to pay an additional tariff of 94 per cent on all ore hauled that assayed at more than $50 per ton at the smelters. It obtained this additional revenue by issuing waybills that, the BRC later ruled, required the railway company, not the shipper, to pay the additional tariff. Although the GTP refunded this additional tariff in part voluntarily, in part under duress, it did so only in late 1920. During the long interval, the sudden increase in transportation costs to over 19 per cent of ore value caused the Silver Standard and the other mines to suspend production in December 1918 for six months.[69] Thus, the railway company ensured that New Hazelton, the natural site for forwarding freight to the railway, declined as did its own uneconomic townsite, only by eliminating one of the major sources of freight in the district at a time when the GTP desperately required traffic.

Although the GTP legal files provide little information on the company's relations with the Rocher de Boule Mine, newspaper reports suggest that it fared no better than the Silver Standard. Above South

Hazelton on the same side of the river as the railway, the largest mine in the district promised to make up the shortfall caused by the company's reluctance to serve the mines at New Hazelton. But though company officers must have realized that the development of such an important provider of freight close to South Hazelton might have supported the GTP's case for location of the district station there, the railway company encouraged its development no more than it did the mines that supported New Hazelton. West of South Hazelton along the railway line, the GTP constructed a siding at Tramville, the site of Rocher de Boule's ore dumps and the lower station of the mine's tramway, for a 6 per cent annual rental. The railway company refused, however, to establish a regular station there and insisted that the mine use the station located almost a mile further west at Carnaby. The difficulties in picking up ore and setting down supplies at a site without a regular station and station signal caused delay and expense for both the railway company and the mine.

In the summer of 1916, representatives of the mine complained that inadequate train service had filled up all available space in its Prince Rupert ore bunker, its dump at Tramville, and even its stopes at the minehead. During that summer, 3,000 tons of ore were waiting for shipment. If the service were improved, the mine could ship 100 tons of ore a day. In June, the mine manager took his complaint about inadequate service to the BRC and apparently secured promises of improvement from the company.[70] This promise turned out to be one special freight train a week, which could not remove 100 tons of ore a day. Even this service did not always occur as it was often difficult to obtain cars. In September, a mining promoter noted that the output of Rocher de Boule was still piling up and the railway simply could not take care of production. The editor of the Prince Rupert *Empire* charged that 'Rocher de Boule was forced to slacken its production to suit the haulage of this sluggish and unprogressive outfit.' By December, the transportation difficulties had not been overcome.[71]

The development of this mine and other claims on Rocher Déboulé Mountain Range led the provincial government to construct a winding eleven-mile tote road from a point near the summit to the railway line on the east side of Skeena Crossing (Mile 164). Although the GTP admitted that way-freights stopped on the main line at that point to set down passengers, supplies, and mine machinery, it again refused to construct a station and siding there and insisted that miners make use of Nash station, one mile west of Skeena Crossing. This demand prompted the Prince

Tramville, loading ore from Rocher de Boule Mine onto GTP cars, 1915

Rupert editor to observe that miners would require an airship to reach this station since it was located on the other side of the Skeena River.[72]

When B.R. Jones, one of the principal promoters of the Delta Group of claims on Rocher Déboulé Range, which was capitalized at $1 million, sent a petition to the BRC signed by 104 miners and other residents for a station at Skeena Crossing, the GTP general superintendent dismissed him as a convicted gambler and bootlegger without capital and claimed that no one took his partners seriously. While the GTP general manager recognized that the company had set a precedent by stopping all its trains at Skeena Crossing, he maintained that the precedent could only apply to the railway's construction phase, which ended in 1915. He admitted that increased mining activity on the mountain would make a siding and station necessary but claimed that the company's large losses on the British

Columbia line prevented it from making what he regarded as a needless expense. He suggested that the provincial government should construct a bridge across the Skeena beside the railway bridge so that the miners could use Nash.[73]

Hansard repeated this argument to the BRC, but the commissioners did not find it convincing and ordered that the GTP construct a siding and small station within thirty days. Such actions led a British Columbia mining journal to describe the GTP's treatment of the largest shipper of ores over its line as disgraceful.[74] Hindered by the railway in recovering its investment by exporting ore when copper prices were high, the Rocher de Boule Mine could not survive the decline of copper prices in 1917 and suspended production the following year.

Thus, the activities of the GTP in the Hazelton district confirm in part G.R. Stevens's contention that the actions of the railway company's land department alienated residents and harmed the long-term interests of the company.[75] But the GTP determination to support its townsite in the face of opposition from both local residents and outside interests was not limited to the land department, although George Ryley was probably responsible for the initial decision to support South Hazelton. Even though several company officers recognized that the land commissioner had made a serious error, the fact that two presidents and a general manager as well as the entire legal department supported Ryley suggests that this harmful obsession with territoriality permeated the entire company. By continually attempting to damage or dispose of what it regarded as wildcat townsites, the company in fact attacked a prerequisite for the profitable operation of mines on which it depended for traffic. The railway company's patent lack of interest in generating and increasing traffic in ore suggests that GTP officers practically disregarded not only development requirements in the region, but also the railway axiom for financial survival of a new line.[76]

Of course, the elimination of ore shipments from the Hazelton district by 1918 did not by itself force the GTP into receivership in 1919. But the case presented here indicates that Innis's argument concerning the importance of local traffic for the survival of a transcontinental railway system in British Columbia can be applied to another line in a different region.[77] As well, it suggests another meaning for Innis's contention that railways were at once the cause and effect of the sudden economic disturbances peculiar to mining regions.[78]

NINE

'GRAND TRAFFICKER OF PROMISES':
OPERATIONS, 1914-19

WE KNOW a good deal about the impact the brief operation of the GTP had on the fortunes of the parent Grand Trunk Railway Company of Canada and the evolution of federal government railway policy. After little more than a year of GTP operation as a through line, the Grand Trunk asked the government for relief from its obligations to the GTP. Only a series of government loans and a *de facto* dispensation from assuming the operation (and the charges) of the National Transcontinental persuaded the Grand Trunk management to continue running the GTP for three more years. Like other lines, the GTP's operating problems during the war resulted in part from the disinclination of the government to raise freight rates to match increased costs. The government's major response to problems that the GTP and other lines encountered, the Royal Commission on Railways and Transportation, instead investigated the cost of construction of the GTP. Accepting in large part the majority report of the commission, the government began negotiations early in 1918 to take over not only the GTP but also the Grand Trunk. In response to a Grand Trunk declaration in March 1919 that it could no longer afford to operate the transcontinental, the government used the War Measures Act to put the GTP into receivership.[1]

Resting for the most part on sources concerning the deteriorating financial position of the Grand Trunk and the attempts of the London board to defend the parent company, these studies say little about the operation of the GTP in general or its activities in British Columbia in particular from completion until receivership. Describing the GTP as 'traffic-starved,' T.D. Regehr implies that the British Columbia line, like that of the Canadian Northern, was the major source of the company's operating deficits because it could not generate local traffic. Asserting rather than demonstrating that the operation of the GTP Mountain Section represented a failure, historians of the GTP point to the extra length of the main line, the location of Prince Rupert, and small population as causes. None presents data to support these claims.[2]

After a review of traffic predictions for the Mountain Section, this chapter analyzes scattered quantitative data to confirm that traffic on the British Columbia line and overseas trade at Prince Rupert fell far short of company expectations. It then examines the company operation of the largest industrial enterprise outside the line itself in British Columbia, the Prince Rupert drydock. Finally, it reviews some influential general evaluations of the line's shortcomings.

Chapter 3 outlined how the wildly optimistic predictions of traffic made by the GTP engineers during the planning and building of the Mountain Section justified the selection of the expensive Montreal-Toronto standard. During construction, the company maintained that both natural resources and strategic location for trans-Pacific trade assured the profitability of the British Columbia line. Between 1911 and 1919, the GTP published eight editions of a pamphlet concerning the agricultural potential of north-central British Columbia. By claiming that the construction of the railway would now allow the arable lands along the line to support a population of 350,000, the company implied that traffic produced by this population would soon be generated.[3]

In an interview for an American newspaper in September 1911, GTP president Hays made his most grandiose claim for the company's British Columbia line. While admitting that the Mountain Section would not pay at once, the president predicted glorious things for 'the most interesting place on the line,' Prince Rupert. After rehearsing the advantages of location and climate, Hays suggested that its rapid growth and development had so far followed that of Winnipeg. Within a few years, Prince Rupert would become 'a duplicate of Vancouver for north British Columbia.'

The president based this claim not only on the terminus's entrepôt and fishing potential but also on an astounding prediction concerning the GTP export of wheat.

> We will ship 100,000,000 bushels of wheat annually from Prince Rupert to Europe when the Panama Canal is open for business ... We will be able to deliver wheat in Liverpool by way of the Panama Canal from Prince Rupert at the same cost and almost in the same time that it now takes to carry by way of the Great Lakes and the Atlantic ports ... I venture to

Table 9.1

Smithers's estimates of GTP earnings, 1912 and 1914, and actual GTP system earnings, 1913-19

	1912 estimate (1913-14: Prairie Section only; 1915- : add Mountain Section)			1914 estimate (Prairie and Mountain Sections)			Actual (main and branch lines)	
	Gross earnings ($ millions)	Net earnings (OR = 70) ($ millions)	Balance after charges ($ millions)	Gross earnings ($ millions)	Net earnings (OR = 70) ($ millions)	Balance after charges ($ millions)	Gross earnings ($ millions)	Operating ratio (OR) (%)
1913	10.0	3.0	-.03				8.3	92
1914	12.0	3.6	+.47				6.7	110
1915	14.0	4.2	+.36				7.0	84
1916	16.0	4.8	+.86	10.0	3.0	-2.11	8.3	105
1917	18.0	5.4	+1.38	12.5	3.75	-1.44	9.7	111
1918	20.0	6.0	+1.90	15.0	4.5	-.77	9.6	156
1919	22.0	6.6	+2.42	16.5	4.95	-.40	11.3	132
1920	24.0	7.2	+2.94	18.0	5.4	-.03		
1921	26.0	7.8	+3.46	19.5	5.85	+.35		
1922				21.0	6.3	+.60		
1923				22.5	6.75	+.97		

Note: The actual earnings are calculated for the company's fiscal year, 1 July to 30 June. Thus, the actual earning for 1913 embraces the period 1 July 1913 to 30 June 1914.
Source: NAC, RG 30, vol. 10,712

predict that within the next decade as much Canadian grain from Manitoba, Saskatchewan and Alberta will find its way to Europe by way of Prince Rupert as will get out by the Atlantic ports.

To handle this traffic, Hays claimed that the company was already building docks and elevators at the terminus and would shortly order a fleet of specially designed steamships. Of course, one can view Hays's claim as a clever attempt to justify the request for an additional subsidy to complete the Mountain Section, which the company would soon make to the government after the forthcoming election. But other officers repeated their chief's predictions long after the subsidy request.[4]

After Hays's death in April 1912, the company's predictions for traffic became even more sanguine. Two estimates that Grand Trunk chairman A.W. Smithers had prepared in 1912 and 1914 concerning earnings for the entire GTP main line over the next decade reveal the extent of, and flaws in, management expectations for traffic, illustrated in Table 9.1. While Smithers acknowledged that these estimates were speculative, President E.J. Chamberlin and the other GTP officers in Montreal did not regard them as excessive. In the estimate prepared in late 1912, Smithers tacitly admitted that the Mountain Section would generate little traffic since its inclusion in calculations of gross system earnings from 1914 onward does not change the rate of growth. More ominous was his failure to recognize that the heavy maintenance costs of the Mountain Section would significantly decrease net system earnings. The estimate's prediction of a steady increase in traffic would allow the railway to pay even the fixed charges of the Mountain Section from 1914.[5] By November 1914, Smithers realized that the outbreak of war and a bad harvest had kept traffic far below the levels set out in the 1912 estimate. What was remarkable in his second estimate was the steady progression of gross earnings, albeit from a lower base, and the rigid adherence to the calculation of net earnings at 30 per cent gross. While the system would now pay its fixed charges only after 1921, the chairman still believed that it would pay its operating expenses by 1916.[6]

Not everyone considered the Mountain Section as profitable as did Hays and Smithers. A consulting engineer regarded the British Columbia line primarily as a costly link between the prairies and the ocean. The resources of the region did not impress H.A. Parker, who inspected the Mountain Section route for Hays in 1909. He noted that little had been done to prove the agricultural worth of the region and that farmers sought land for speculation rather than development. With the phrase 'a country well-timbered but with poor timber,' he dismissed prospects for large-scale lumbering.[7] In reply, GTP chief engineer B.B. Kelliher admitted that 'the only present justification for constructing the line through the mountains is as a through line to the coast.'[8]

Occasionally even the GTP management would acknowledge the limited prospects for immediate returns from traffic on the British Columbia line. In support of the GTP request for a subsidy from the provincial government for a branch line from Fort George to Vancouver, the general manager explained that 'while the main line to Prince Rupert will be completed, greater traffic possibilities will be created with the extension of the line to Vancouver. At best, through traffic to Prince Rupert cannot be very large for years to come whereas a big tonnage can be secured by building to her southern rival on Burrard Inlet.'[9]

When McBride provided subsidies for the construction of this line as the Pacific Great Eastern Railway, the newspapers in Prince Rupert protested. The *Daily News* fumed that the new line 'would reduce by one-half the traffic this port had every reason to expect. If the PGE is completed first, all traffic from the Prairies will be switched at Fort George to Vancouver instead of coming here.' In its claim that Vancouver did not require a subsidized railway, the *Empire* implied that the GTP Pacific terminus did.[10]

But these doubts concerning traffic did not circulate widely in the press, or, apparently, among company managers. Shortly before completion of the railway in British Columbia, Smithers could still announce to shareholders:

> The railway will bring the fertile valleys of British Columbia (expected to be especially valuable for fruit growing), the large areas of timber, and the unexplored mineral resources of that Province within practicable distance of the world's markets. The line has a terminus at Prince Rupert ... splendidly situated to command the traffic which will arise from the development of Alaska and the Yukon territory ... It is to be remembered that the Grand Trunk Pacific Railway, in addition to its easy grades will be 500 miles nearer to many points in the Far East than any other route.[11]

The railway company's view of the British Columbia line had not evolved beyond its early predictions to obtain support and solicit funds.

The destruction of the records of the GTP freight department, the richest company source for traffic information, makes difficult an account of the operation of the GTP British Columbia line. The files of the company's Winnipeg legal department office, which illuminate much GTP activity in British Columbia, say little about the enterprise's operation after 1914. Though the legal department undoubtedly received and incorporated traffic data in company petitions for freight rate increases, the head office in Montreal dealt with this crucial matter, and its files have not survived. Unfortunately, the government institutions that received these petitions have not preserved them.

There is little specific information in the sources that do survive. Although the annual returns that the company submitted to the Department of Railways provide data on both the weight and value of traffic, they provide no breakdown for particular sections of the road. Newspapers from communities along the line contain innumerable stories about the arrival or departure of particular trains, but little else. And the authors of the annual reports published by the boards of trade for Prince Rupert and Prince George, while laboriously mining statistics from both federal and provincial government sessional papers, apparently did not take the trouble to walk to the local station to gather data on the GTP receipts for their own communities. Even in a 1919 report on economic activities in western Canada that generated traffic for the railway, the GTP's own industrial department did not provide traffic data. Concerning the Pacific terminus, for example, the department commissioner remarked broadly that 'commerce invaded the harbour of Prince Rupert and new wharves had to be constantly added.'[12] Such reticence reveals only the company's unwillingness to disclose the level of traffic on the Mountain Section.

The discussion of traffic below lacks the precision of information that could have been provided in a department accounting sheet or in the line of a company or board of trade annual report. Nevertheless, the calculations that follow lead to a plausible estimate range of the volume (weight) of traffic that the GTP hauled along its British Columbia line after completion in 1914. These estimates draw on data from company annual returns, federal customs statistics for the port of Prince Rupert, tariff schedules, railway timetables, and two traffic reports prepared in 1919 and 1921. Data from the first two sources are available for the entire period 1914-19; tariff and timetable information has been located for parts of the year 1914-15. To illustrate trends more clearly, some quantitative data have been presented as graphic figures rather than as tables.

The company's annual returns to the federal Department of Railways allow some preliminary observations.[13] Because the data in these returns are aggregated for the entire line, they contain no regional or directional breakdown of traffic. Yet the unusual practice of keeping separate books for traffic on the GTP branch lines means that these data refer to operation on the main line only between Prince Rupert and Winnipeg, a distance of 1748.2 miles.[14]

Like most roads in Canada, freight produced between 70 and 80 per cent of the company's revenue on its main line after completion. But the scale of operation was much smaller than the GTP's two Canadian transcontinental rivals. During the 1918-19 fiscal year, the GTP main line reported operating revenue less than 5 per cent that of the admittedly much larger CPR system; less than 15 per cent of the Canadian Northern. More revealing is the deteriorating operating ratio, the comparison of expense against revenue, which served as a common, if imperfect, indicator of a company's financial position. In an era when an operating ratio of seventy was considered the necessary benchmark of a sound concern, as its incorporation in Smithers's estimates confirms, the GTP carried a ratio of 110 at completion, which exploded to 155 during its final year. Only in one fiscal year after its completion, 1915-16, did the company show an operating profit. During the other years, the GTP could not pay its expenses, let alone meet the fixed charges on its enormous debt.

The annual returns also reveal some elements of the nature and composition of freight traffic. Completion of the main line did not increase the tonnage hauled. This suggests that most freight was hauled across the Prairie Section. Ton-miles, perhaps the most common indicator of volume of freight hauled, actually decreased during the three years following the outbreak of war. A good harvest and increased production of coal in Alberta caused in large part the increase in ton-miles for the 1917-18 fiscal year.

Grain represented the most significant commodity, accounting for 53 per cent of the total freight by weight originating on the GTP main line. Although some areas along the British Columbia line could grow grain, most of the grain hauled by the GTP came from the prairies. Coal, the second largest commodity by weight, was not mined extensively along the British Columbia line during this period. The GTP had incorporated

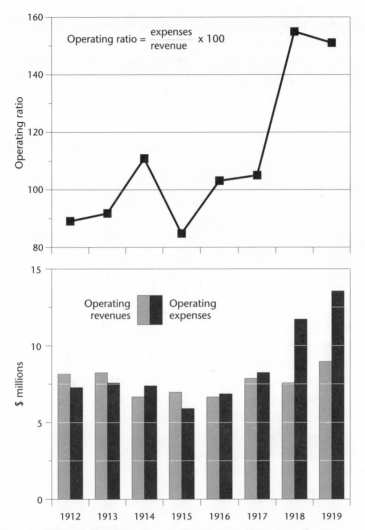

$$\text{Operating ratio} = \frac{\text{expenses}}{\text{revenue}} \times 100$$

Figure 9.1 **GTP main line, 1912-19, operating revenues, expenses, and ratios**

the Bulkley and Telkwa Coal Company in 1905, but the company was inactive by the time of completion. By 1917, the GTP president dismissed it as a 'myth.'[15]

During the GTP construction period in British Columbia (1908-14), dozens of small sawmills were established in the north-central corridor to provide ties for the railway and lumber for the expected towns. Twenty mills operated at various times between Prince Rupert and Smithers, although only one remained by 1922. Lumber production was more sustained on the 'East Line' between Prince George and the Alberta border. By 1917, ten mills in this section shipped lumber to the prairies and points east over the GTP. A decline in the housing market on the prairies reduced the demand for lumber during the first two years of the war. Only by 1918 did lumber traffic on the GTP main line reach the 1914 (pre-completion) level.[16] The GTP industrial department's 1919 report provides some cumulative data for this commodity alone. By the end of 1919, the GTP had hauled from mills in British Columbia 11,716 carloads of lumber and shingles and 168 carloads of pulp and paper. Since the average capacity of a GTP freight car was 33 tons, we can estimate that the company hauled approximately 390,000 tons of lumber products along all or part of the British Columbia line.[17]

The only commodity originating in British Columbia that experienced sustained growth during the period was fish. One must note, however, that the proportion of this commodity to total freight for the main line was minuscule though it increased eightfold from 1914-15 to 1919.

Although an official of the Northern Pacific was confident that the GTP would not compete for his company's other markets, he realized that the proximity of Prince Rupert to north Pacific fishing grounds would give the GTP a comparative advantage in hauling fresh fish to markets in eastern North America. And an American fisheries commissioner warned the Seattle Commercial Club that the GTP's ability to haul fish at much lower cost would allow Prince Rupert 'to grab American industry.'[18]

To capture the American as well as the Canadian market, the company had to haul a significant part of the Alaska catch. This traffic depended on an expansion of the intermittent bonding privileges that American fishermen had enjoyed in Canadian ports since 1897. At the end of 1914, the company officers apparently cooperated with the merchants of Prince Rupert to convince the federal government to extend this privilege to small American operators who could pool their catches into carloads. A Seattle newspaper regarded this extension as the product of a devious plan of the GTP, the merchants, and the Canadian government to strip the American port of its trade.[19]

In this single case, the company's ability to ship fish more quickly overcame the line's disadvantage of greater distance between the Pacific coast and Winnipeg. By 1919, it had replaced the CPR as the major supplier of fresh fish in Winnipeg. But the company did not exploit this advantage to build up more traffic. By charging the same rates as the

Table 9.2

Fish products hauled from Prince Rupert, 1914-19

	Express					Other methods
	Carloads (no.)	Carloads (tons)	LCL* (no.)	LCL (tons)	Total (tons)	Total** (tons)
1915	492 ·	5,263	6,732	682	5,945	3,600
1916	644	7,237	6,549	778	8,015	2,900
1917	548	6,294	8,878	888	7,182	4,200
1918	415	4,930	7,409	654	5,584	11,000
1919	488	6,330	5,738	583	6,913	22,000

* Less than carload
** Figures for 1915-19 are based on year ending 30 June.
Sources: Canada, *Sessional Papers*, Department of Naval Service, Annual Reports, 1914-20; NAC RG 23, vol. 1166, file 724-3-2; NAC, RG 30, vol. 1142

CPR, the GTP obtained a greater profit from each shipment but probably lost a share of the market that a lower rate would have provided.[20]

Of the methods to carry this commodity, the most profitable for the company was shipment of fresh fish in iced refrigerator cars. Both the local newspapers and GTP pamphlets extol the speed of the 'fish express' in 1915, a fast train that brought the products of the north Pacific to the tables of Montreal and New York.[21] The fish traffic appears in Table 9.2.

That the express traffic did not follow the increase of the fish traffic as a whole stems from the company's continual inability to provide an adequate number of refrigerator cars. Since they were frequently diverted or held up in the United States, these cars could not make a round trip from Prince Rupert in less than thirty-five days. Two months after service began, the Prince Rupert Board of Trade complained that the GTP would not provide enough cars. By 1917, the company's express subsidiary admitted that shortage of cars was holding back the growth of traffic. In 1919, there was a continual stream of complaints from Prince Rupert fishermen concerning the lack of refrigerator cars. And yet the company was unable to secure additional cars until after 1920.[22]

To carry traffic on the British Columbia line that would at least pay costs, the company had to attract a substantial overseas trade at Prince Rupert. Although not accurate, the customs statistics for the port of Prince Rupert suggest that this trade did not occur. Figure 9.2 illustrates the weight of goods shipped into and out of Prince Rupert.[23] A comparison of these figures with data concerning the weight of goods hauled on the GTP main line produces little correlation. Unlike the data that the

First GTP car of fresh fish shipped from Prince Rupert. This provided one of the few occasions to celebrate the opening of the GTP line in British Columbia.

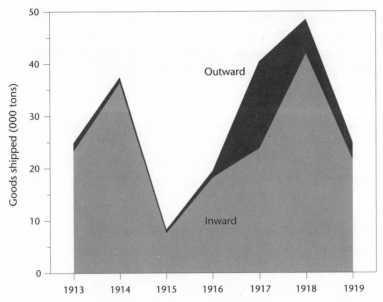

Figure 9.2 **Goods shipped through Prince Rupert, 1913-19**

company submitted to the Department of Railways, customs statistics included those commodities used in the construction of the railway. Thus, the completion of the railway in the summer of 1914 explains in part the significant decrease in imports during the 1915 fiscal year. After 1915, the trend in imports moves in the same direction as does that for manufactured goods hauled on the entire main line. It is possible that a significant part of the imports at Prince Rupert after 1915 represent manufactured goods consumed along the British Columbia line. The small tonnage exported from Prince Rupert suggests that westbound traffic along the British Columbia line for export was almost non-existent.

The customs data indicate that Prince Rupert failed to capture the overseas trade that the company had continually predicted for its north Pacific terminus since the inception of the railway project. A 1921 traffic report suggests that the location of the terminus, which the company had touted as a trade asset, actually inhibited the development of overseas trade. To Chicago, for example, the representative destination of 75 per cent of Vancouver's traffic from Asia, the distance from Yokohama was practically the same via Vancouver or Prince Rupert. Although the GTP route offered the shortest sailing distance between a North American railway terminus and Japan, the extra length of its line from Winnipeg to the coast, which entailed a larger operating cost, effectively eliminated this advantage. Since the southern and eastern industrial states provided the principal North American exports to Asiatic ports, the decision to carry these goods via Prince Rupert would actually entail a higher cost, which shippers were reluctant to accept.[24]

It is astounding that freight officials of the company did not apparently realize this important disadvantage before completion of the line. Only in October 1914, two months after the opening of commercial service, did the petitions and complaints of the Board of Trade and other local businessmen persuade company officials to create a Prince Rupert town tariff that matched tolls between Winnipeg and Vancouver. The special rate, of course, transferred the cost of operating a longer line from the shipper to the company. As the inspector noted, with rates equal to the CPR, the 'difference in service rendered [by carriage over longer distance] may at times represent the carriage of traffic at less than cost by the GTP line when the same traffic yields the CPR a profit for its shorter haul which fixes the rates.'[25]

The terminus's location on sea routes was no better than its isolated position on land. Clearly the distance from Prince Rupert to Europe via the Panama Canal was greater than from Vancouver or an American Pacific port. In the mid-1920s, the Canadian National Railways Company, the successor to the GTP system, canvassed steamship company agents for their views on Prince Rupert. At that time, companies in the European trade would direct ships to call at Prince Rupert only if the shipper paid an 'arbitrary' or rate differential one-sixth to one-third above the corresponding rate to Vancouver. Rather than the cost, companies that traded with the Orient complained that the delay caused by this problematic call would upset their extremely tight schedules to call at other ports.[26]

The GTP's failure to obtain a regular trans-Pacific steamship service for Prince Rupert suggests that the disadvantages of the port noted above also applied during the period before 1920. In a letter to an American steamship line official in February 1916, the GTP traffic manager noted: 'To make a definite charter of five to six thousand tons at Prince Rupert for a certain time would be too precarious and might very likely result in a sacrifice of more revenue than we would obtain in the entire movement of the business transcontinental.'[27]

By 1924, the GTP British Columbia line had been relegated to a branch line of the Canadian National. A comparison of exports from

Vancouver and Prince Rupert is nevertheless arresting. From the port of Vancouver during 1923 and 1924, the CNR exported 625,000 short tons; from the former GTP terminus for the same two years, the company shipped less than 5,000 short tons.[28]

The Standard Freight Mileage Tariff for the GTP, which went into effect on 1 September 1914, the beginning of regular commercial service on the British Columbia line, provides some insight into the company's difficulty in encouraging through traffic to the Pacific coast.[29] This tariff determined rates on the main line until the implementation of the 15 per cent increase in early 1918. A graph of the rates in Figure 9.3 for class 8 (grain) and class 10 (forest and mineral products) reveals that rates through the Mountain Section were significantly higher than those for the Prairie Section. A comparison of the grain rates for the Prairie and Mountain sections reveals that a farmer could forward grain to Fort William more cheaply than to Prince Rupert from any point five miles east of Wolf Creek, the western boundary of the Prairie Section. Although commodity rates (not located) probably reduced the cost of hauling bulk goods through the Mountain Section, the basic rate structure clearly inhibited the flow of most prairie grain to Prince Rupert.[30]

Thus, the structure of freight rates as well as the location of major markets and export ports in eastern North America discouraged shippers of commodities produced on the prairies from sending their goods westward over the GTP British Columbia line. And because the local market along the GTP line in the Pacific province was much smaller than those on the southern transcontinentals, the GTP carriage of westbound manufactures was insignificant west of the Rocky Mountains.[31]

Two construction timetables allow an estimate of the volume of freight hauled over the British Columbia line during a discrete period. Most published timetables give no indication of the frequency of freight trains. An employees' timetable for January 1915 indicated that four way-freight trains traversed the Prince Rupert-Prince George section of the line each week (two eastbound, two westbound) along with four passenger trains. Although freight trains are not listed on the corresponding timetable east of Prince George, the number of passenger trains remains constant.[32] There is no reason to think that the amount of freight traffic increased east of Prince George since the area had a smaller population. It is therefore probable that a maximum of four freight trains traversed the British Columbia line each week during the early part of 1915.

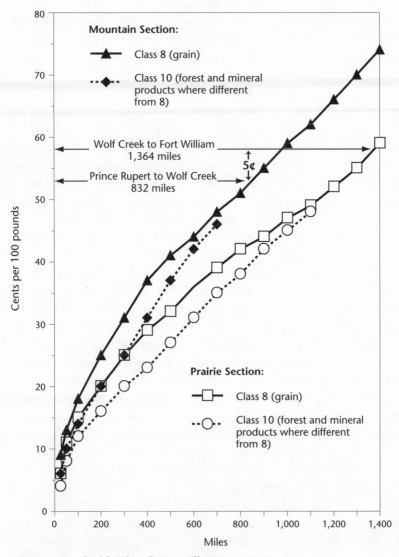

Figure 9.3 **Standard freight mileage tariff, 1914**

Let us now assume that this frequency held for the entire part of the fiscal year during which British Columbia enjoyed regular freight service (1 September 1914-30 June 1915; ten months). During this ten-month period, then, 172 freight trains traversed the British Columbia section (4 × 43 weeks). Let us also assume that the statistic for the 'average number of tons of freight per train-mile' applied equally to the Mountain and

Prairie sections of the main line. For the 1914 fiscal year, the figure was 351 tons. If the 172 freight trains each carried this load across British Columbia, they would generate 40.8 million ton-miles of freight (172 × 351 × 677). If we assume that all the fish for the 1914 fiscal year travelled east through British Columbia in special express trains not noted on the timetable, this freight produces 2.7 million ton-miles. Over the British Columbia line for ten months, then, the ton-miles total is 43.5 million. This figure represents only 7.6 per cent of five-sixths (ten months) of the total ton-miles (569.3 million) generated on the GTP main line during the 1914 fiscal year.

For the Grand Trunk arbitration proceedings, an investigator provided some rare figures concerning freight hauled east from Prince Rupert in 1919. This freight totalled 60,000 tons of which the largest components were wood products (29,000 tons) and fish (22,000 tons). Of this total, 12,000 tons were hauled to 'local GTP Ry points' while 48,000 tons were hauled to 'points beyond the GTP Ry.' Concerning return traffic, the report notes only that 'cars ... had to be hauled empty to Prince Rupert, the westbound loading being very light.'[33] If all the local freight as well as the through freight traversed British Columbia, 40.6 million ton-miles would be generated on the British Columbia line, less than 7 per cent (6.32) of the ton-miles generated on the GTP main line for the calendar year 1919.

These estimates of traffic during discrete periods can be compared to an estimate of the total volume of the three most important commodities that the GTP hauled along its British Columbia line from completion to receivership. Figures in several reports allow us to estimate for the British Columbia line the aggregate ton-miles generated by fish (43.9 million), lumber products (132.9 million), and ore from the Hazelton district (7.8 million) between 1914 and 1919. The total ton-miles of these three commodities along the British Columbia line (184.6 million) represents less than 6 per cent (5.4) of the ton-miles of all commodities generated on the entire GTP main line (3,421 million) during 1914-19.[34]

One other series throws light on the value of traffic that the GTP carried on the Mountain Section, i.e, the 677-mile British Columbia line and 129 miles east of Red Pass Junction in British Columbia and Alberta. From the summer of 1913 through 1918 the *Canadian Railway and Marine World* published monthly (gross) earnings of the GTP Prairie and Lake Superior sections. Since company reports to the Department of

Railways provide corresponding annual earnings for the entire main line, earnings for the Mountain Section can be calculated, and are illustrated in Table 9.3. With the onset of commercial through service in British Columbia in August 1914, the relative gross earnings of the Mountain Section rose considerably from 17 to 27 per cent of main line earnings. I have not discovered an explanation for the drop in earnings between 1915 and 1916. Over the five years the average percentage was 19.0. The significant difference between this estimate for the entire Mountain Section and the estimates presented above for the British Columbia line probably stems from a substantial traffic in coal that the company hauled from its branch line, the Alberta Coal Branch, to its main line east of Jasper, and thereafter hauled almost exclusively eastward.[35]

In all these estimates, one must allow for a considerable margin of error. With a 25 per cent margin, the estimates indicate that the total gross traffic earnings of the Mountain Section before 1919 were less than 24 per cent of the main line earnings. Along the British Columbia line, the company probably hauled less than 10 per cent of its main line freight traffic. Taken together, the estimates strongly suggest that the relative volume (weight) and value of freight traffic on the British Columbia line was much less than its relative distance (38.7 per cent) or relative first cost of construction (64.2 per cent).[36] The company sought to shift responsibility for this low traffic to others, of course, most often to the federal government for removing its track and compelling it in 1917 to share the inferior grade and rails of the Canadian Northern line for 170 miles east of Red Pass Junction. That the government decided to abandon the GTP grade for most of the joint line accords with passenger complaints that the GTP had not maintained its own roadbed.[37] But even when the line was 'intact,' the estimates above suggest that the company had found little freight to haul across it.

The GTP operation of its Prince Rupert drydock, on which it had expended more than $2.8 million, illustrates the company's inability to attract custom or labour force, deal with the city, and escape the bureaucratic federal subsidy requirements that paralysed the enterprise. With the outbreak of the war, the company had suggested that the government put more money into the dock to hasten completion, but Borden was uninterested in doing anything to expedite the work. Early in 1915, as the GTP used scarce funds to push the dock toward completion, the company's naval architect suggested that the GTP could put the machinery

Table 9.3

GTP Mountain Section earnings as percentage of main line earnings, 1913-18

	Mountain Section earnings ($ millions)	Main line earnings ($ millions)	Mountain Section earnings as % of main line earnings
1914*	1.33	8.11	16.4
1915	1.75	6.53	26.8
1916	1.61	6.62	24.3
1917	.94	6.35	14.8
1918	1.05	7.62	13.8
Total	6.68	35.23	19.0

* Figures are based on year ending 30 June.
Sources: Canadian Railway and Marine World, 1913-18; NAC, RG 46, vols. 927-8

into immediate use and generate much needed revenue by building wooden halibut boats. But the GTP president, relying on the architect's claim that the dock had the best set of machines on the Pacific coast, asked the government instead for a submarine contract. The British Admiralty, however, had decided that Prince Rupert lacked facilities to complete modern submarines, and Borden refused.[38]

Those who had regarded the dock as the visible guarantee that Prince Rupert would develop became indignant over the company's delay in commencing operations. Early in 1916, the *Empire* pointedly replaced the illustration of the dock holding the liner *Minnesota* with an empty box and the caption, 'Those who poured money into the plant were not fools. At least if they were, they must be more than the ordinary type.' In March, the Prince Rupert mayor lamented the decline of the city's population from 6,000 to 4,000 despite the availability of the dock. In the absence of ship refits, citizens petitioned the company and the government for a munitions contract for the plant.[39]

Since the company required immediate payment of the subsidy to cover its large expenditure, the GTP president supported the residents' call for operation of the dock. But Chamberlin claimed that the high cost of local labour had deterred several manufacturing and shipbuilding interests that the company had invited to make use of the plant. To the mayor, Chamberlin declared that the dock would commence operation when the company constructed its line of ocean steamers; to the government, he confided that there was little prospect of immediate business.[40]

The citizens' petition may well have had some effect, however. In

May 1916, an American syndicate represented by Vancouver engineer M.P. Cotton commenced negotiations with the company, the city, and the federal government for an arrangement to lease the dock and produce steel vessels. By June, the syndicate had obtained from the provincial government and the city respectively a subsidy and tax relief. GTP lawyer H.H. Hansard drew up an agreement in which the syndicate would commence operations as soon as possible, operate continuously, and accept a GTP traffic clause. Although the syndicate's offer of $265,000 over ten years was not large, he admitted that the expense of getting the plant into operation and the poor outlook for business entailed considerable risk. Not only would the arrangement get the 'tremendous plant' into operation; it would also allow the company to finally obtain the government subsidy.[41]

Laurier rightly charged that in this matter the government did little to forward the war effort. Even though a public works inspector recognized that the company's shortage of funds had prevented it from completing the dock for more than a year, the minister insisted that both parties must adhere to the contract. In the summer of 1916, Public Works Minister Robert Rogers discouraged the prospective lessee because the GTP had not completed every item of the contract. But the minister informed anxious residents that the company would make the final decision.[42]

The government tied Chamberlin's hands when it informed him that it did not wish the dock to change hands during the investigation of the Royal Commission on Railways. But when the GTP president simply passed on this decision, he brought the community's resentment upon the company rather than upon the government. Railing against the expense of guarding a 'dead monstrosity,' the *Empire* editor claimed that the GTP was the real culprit in the dock 'holdup.' The company had apparently forsaken the opportunity to start up the dock.[43]

The company's parent had tried another track. Since the outbreak of the war, the Grand Trunk head office in London had passed along information on the progress of the dock to the Admiralty. In the fall of 1916, the Admiralty arranged to have the cruiser HMS *Orbita* overhauled on the GTP dock. When the 16,000-ton cruiser was docked successfully, the company's agent described the event as a remarkable illustration of the ability of the dock to handle large ships. Naval officers were less impressed, however. The chief engineer of the Naval Service complained

GTP dock lifting HMS *Orbita,* 1916

that there was no skilled labour of any kind available in the north. The captain of the *Orbita* reported that a mechanical flaw in the construction of the pontoons reduced the lift by 1,000 tons. To increase the navy's enthusiasm, Chamberlin waived charges on the docking, and a second cruiser was docked in December.[44]

Early in 1917, Smithers suggested that the company should try to convince the Admiralty to use the dock for the duration of the war. Accordingly, the general manager informed the Naval Service that unless the government assumed the expense of keeping the fires up in the plant, the GTP would close the dock entirely. The Admiralty agreed to pay a subsidy of $779 per month to keep the dock open.[45]

A more serious consideration than the price of dock maintenance for naval repairs was the availability and cost of skilled labour in Prince Rupert. For the first two refits, the Admiralty had to import some of the labour force from the Esquimalt dock. In February, an officer in the Naval Service complained that mechanics at Victoria were asking exorbitant rates for work in Prince Rupert and that it was impossible to obtain the services of skilled workers locally. The shortage of affordable labour eventually persuaded the Admiralty to switch its dock work from Prince Rupert to the large American naval yard at Bremerton, Washington, over the protests of the residents of Prince Rupert and the new Liberal premier of British Columbia.[46]

Even more damaging was the consequence of building the dock without machinery for heavy steel work. In June 1917, the Imperial Munitions Board received some queries concerning the construction of ships in Prince Rupert. When the board sent an official to inspect the facility, he reported bluntly that the shipbuilding plant was 'intended for wooden ships' and 'not equipped for steel shipbuilding.' But the inspector also reported that operation of the plant would be feasible for a program of wooden shipbuilding that would last two years or more, provided timber could be imported from Vancouver Island. This observation led a Prince Rupert lawyer to lament that upwards of 60,000 tons of wooden ships could have been built at the plant during the past three years.[47]

The announcement in December 1916 that the GTP would overhaul its steamship *Prince Rupert* in Esquimalt rather than at its own dock angered both the Board of Trade and the Merchants' Association. In January 1917, the association sent a letter to Chamberlin regretting that 'your magnificent drydock stands idle' while one of the GTP ships was refitting in the south. They requested the company to strengthen its bonds of goodwill with the city and implied that its 'neglect may result in the further development of traffic for competing [steamship] lines to Prince Rupert.' Chamberlin replied that the steamship had to go to Esquimalt as there was no stock of the necessary steel plates in Prince Rupert. He also indicated that the arrangements with the navy necessitated keeping the dock open for use by warships at any moment.[48]

When the merchants received this lame reply, they hurriedly called meetings and, in a storm of rhetoric, called for a boycott of the routing of goods over GTP lines because of the company's preference for purchasing elsewhere, its refusal to transfer the headquarters of the steamship line to Prince Rupert, and its failure to put the dock to use. To remedy the gaffe, an officer had to go to Winnipeg to obtain permission to purchase plates for the dock before the *Prince George* could be overhauled in Prince Rupert.[49] With this gesture, civic indignation subsided.

Mesmerized by the image of producing a steel giant like the *Minnesota*, the railway, the Munitions Board, and the government continued to search for prospective builders of steel ships. When a San Francisco firm inquired about leasing the works to construct twenty-five 12,000-ton freighters, the board eagerly sent the company to the GTP.

Although Chamberlin received it enthusiastically, the proposal stopped when the American company was unable to secure steel. Borden commiserated with Chamberlin that the president had made 'every reasonable effort to have the dock utilized for national purposes.' Yet when citizens questioned the delay, the board stated baldly that the property was vested in the company, and the citizens should direct their inquiries (and their disappointment) there.[50]

In March 1918, the Department of Public Works finally completed its audit of the GTP books for construction and pronounced the dock complete. According to the report of the inspecting engineer, the company had spent $2,680,348.10 in construction, but the chief engineer would allow a subsidy only for the amount in the 1911 agreement, $2,199,168.02. Although the department engineer pronounced himself satisfied with small discrepancies in office furniture, the assistant secretary insisted that the matter be referred to the Ministry of Justice. The railway company's lawyer persuaded the ministry that the delay over this trifling amount was a waste of money, but the new minister, Frank Carvell, insisted that every item in the estimates be accounted for before he would sanction the subsidy. Only in September 1918 did the government begin payments from the date of official completion, 11 March of that year, rather than the date of the first docking in September 1915, a decision that deprived the company of more than $260,000 at a time when it desperately required revenue.[51]

Still the company, the citizens, and the government endeavoured to find a steel shipbuilder to lease the dock. In July 1918, John L. Mullen, the president of a Pittsburgh firm, visited Prince Rupert and opened negotiations with the GTP for the lease of the dock and shipbuilding plant. He interviewed the new GTP general manager, W.P. Hinton, and entered into a lease with the company for a period of ten years. After a deal to build American ships was disallowed, the GTP arranged for Mullen to come to Ottawa where he met provincial and federal ministers. Once Hansard obtained assurance that a lease would not hinder the payment of the subsidy, the company supported the award of a contract to Mullen for the construction of two ships at a cost $1,693,000 each. Mullen assigned both his lease and the contract to the newly incorporated Prince Rupert Drydock and Engineering Company, but work was seriously hampered when a New York banker failed to provide the necessary funds, and, after a strike in May, the operations of the company were suspended in July 1919. A protracted legal battle for control of the assets and the lease ensued. There is no evidence that the GTP or its successors obtained any funds from the enterprise after July 1919.[52]

For two years, the company had delayed the construction of its most important industrial venture in British Columbia; for more than three years, the government delayed the payment of the subsidy. The company overspent during its construction; its financial woes during the war delayed its official completion and the recoup of at least part of its investment. Even the operation of the dock was not satisfactory. In 1916-17 the dock ran a loss of $3,000 and saw only a small improvement ($26,000 profit) during the following year. Such a small return scarcely dented the fixed charges on its investment. The monster dock had become a dead monstrosity, a visible symbol of the railway company's inability to initiate sustained industrial activity in Prince Rupert and a painful reminder of the dreams that had brought its citizens there.

UNLIKE THE CANADIAN NORTHERN, no detailed study of the operating potential or problems of the GTP before 1920 survives.[53] But the reports discussed below at least had some specific data on which to base their evaluations of the British Columbia line.

Chapter 3 has mentioned the appraisal of Thomas Macnabb, a CPR engineer who inspected the GTP line in the summer of 1914. His photographs of the line led the CPR chief engineer to conclude that the design was too good for the traffic that the line would attract. Macnabb also predicted that the line would not attract the necessary traffic to pay for the high standard.[54] Several years later, T.G. Shaughnessy may have perused Macnabb's report to support his argument that the GTP line to Prince Rupert had been 'extravagantly constructed.' What made the GTP a 'most disappointing enterprise,' the former CPR president argued in 1921, was the inability of the line to attract traffic over most of its route.[55]

In late 1915, Smithers had predicted that the GTP would overcome its liabilities within a few years. Only the necessity of avoiding an immediate deficit compelled the parent company to ask the government to take over its obligations. Appearing as a witness before the Royal Commission on Railways and Transportation a year later, Chamberlin complained that the position and manner in which the GTP had been built made the subsidiary's connection with the Grand Trunk 'not ... natural.'[56]

Although the commission's investigation concentrated on the cost of construction of the GTP and the Canadian Northern, the commissioners made some observations on the traffic potential of the GTP. Even the commissioner sympathetic to the continued existence of the Grand Trunk and its subsidiary acknowledged that the GTP's immediate prospects were bleak. The GTP, W.H. Smith concluded, 'was located on a scale that would do credit to any single track line. There is not enough business to justify such an outlay, and the prospect for business which will warrant cost seems quite remote.' Although he claimed that the resources along the British Columbia section were abundant, he admitted that the ocean traffic of Prince Rupert had been non-existent.[57]

In their majority report, Commissioners H.L. Drayton and W.M. Acworth made no direct comments on GTP traffic. But a table of financial data showed that the current Grand Trunk liability for the charges on the GTP was more than $5 million per annum while the transcontinental's net income had never exceeded $1 million. The difference between charges and earnings made the GTP a 'mistaken investment.'[58]

While the commissioners of the Grand Trunk Arbitration Board, which the government established to determine compensation for its takeover of the Grand Trunk, split on the award to the British investors, they all noted the weakness of the British Columbia line of the GTP. W.H. Taft, the commissioner nominated by the Grand Trunk to defend its interests, offered the following sketch of GTP fortunes in British Columbia. 'Hays' evident object in carrying the line to Prince Rupert where there is a good harbour, was to make the system one for oriental business by steamship lines organized to run from Prince Rupert to Yokohama, but in view of the current financial straits, no such lines have been organized.' Although he noted the potential of natural resource development along the line in British Columbia, Taft concluded 'that it will need ... a good many years' development to create a business that will make it [the British Columbia line] profitable.'[59]

The judgment of W.T. White, former finance minister and a key figure in the nationalization of the Grand Trunk, was much harsher. He argued that the construction of the GTP was a misconceived project: 'For the remaining [most westerly] thousand miles to Prince Rupert, the main line traverses for the most part a difficult country, largely mountainous, whose development for the purpose of furnishing local traffic must await settlement and business enterprise and terminals at Prince Rupert, a port as yet without any considerable trans-Pacific or other external trade.'[60] White's conclusion was blunt. 'When it is considered that the Grand Trunk Pacific was built from Winnipeg to Prince Rupert at a very high standard of construction and at enormous cost, particularly the Mountain Section, the magnitude of the mistake of going forward with the enterprise is apparent.'[61]

The estimates drawn from the quantitative data above support the commissioner's judgment. The GTP had constructed an expensive infrastructure to carry traffic that did not materialize. The returns from through traffic from and to Prince Rupert and local main line traffic probably did not pay the operating expenses of the Mountain Section, let alone its fixed charges. In its operation of the British Columbia line after 1914 as well as in its bumbling attempts to work the drydock, the railway company well deserved the *Empire* editor's derisory label: 'Grand Trafficker of Promises.'

TEN

CONCLUSION: 'THE TENDERLOIN
AND THE HOOK'

IT HAS LONG BEEN ARGUED that the inability of the Grand Trunk
Pacific Railway Company to pay its way after 1914 demonstrates that the
GTP management failed in the planning, construction, and operation of
its line. But to blame President Hays and other GTP managers, without
qualification or explanation, as the authors of the GTP failure, isolates
the performance of the GTP from the record of those systems with which
it should be compared.[1] As Julius Grodinsky points out in his important
study of American transcontinentals, failure, in the form of receivership,
reorganization, or sale at ruinous prices, was the normal outcome of the
first and sometimes second attempts to build and operate lines across
long distances that produced little immediate traffic during the later
nineteenth century. The effects of low traffic density could be postponed,
if not eliminated, on the prairies by lower construction costs.[2] For all
these systems, however, traversing the Pacific slope required the construction and maintenance of a land bridge, an expensive edifice across
largely empty and unproductive territory connecting the prairies and the
ocean. None of the land bridges paid their way initially; all represented a
burden on the treasuries of the respective systems, which only rapidly
increasing traffic would control or remove.

Thus, it is not surprising that the Grand Trunk Pacific, along with
the three other transcontinentals built to the Pacific coast during the
early years of the twentieth century, the Chicago, Milwaukee & St. Paul,
the Western Pacific, and the Canadian Northern, failed.[3] Success, not failure, would have been aberrant. Given the dismal record of transcontinentals, the only sure strategy to avoid failure was to decline to embark.[4]
Hays and the other company managers did not destroy the GTP as an
economic venture because, like the other systems, this transcontinental
was probably never economic.

This study has responded to the teleological dilemma by employing a more modest, functional standard of failure, i.e., those acts or omissions that increased the company's net deficit or reduced the company's net gain, against which to measure GTP actions. With this standard, a more practicable strategy for company managers suggests itself: to postpone, if not avoid, failure, managers should limit or reduce losses at both a system and a local level.

The preceding examination of company actions on the western span of the GTP land bridge, the 677-mile British Columbia line from Prince Rupert to Red Pass Junction, demonstrates that the company managers generally did not follow this strategy. Indeed, what makes the Grand Trunk Pacific experience singular is not that the actions of its managers contributed to the company's failure, but that both senior and junior managers so frequently ignored or opposed the 'business' principle suggested above.[5]

The study first provided several examples of departure from this principle at the senior management level by investigating the actions and decisions of the instigator and first president of the GTP, Charles Melville Hays. At the turn of the century, the major incentive for building a line west from central Canada was the prospect of capturing a share of income from hauling grain eastward from the prairies.[6] Across the long, unremunerative territory bracketing 55° latitude west of the Rockies, even the most primitive pioneer road would probably have not paid its way. But Hays persuaded the Grand Trunk board to transform a relatively modest project for a granger line to compete with the CPR into a transcontinental to the Pacific coast to capture traffic that did not exist.

Construction eastward from the Pacific coast represented a burden for most transcontinentals because the west end line carried almost no traffic and therefore did nothing to cover expenditure until connection with the east end.[7] By adhering to its original plan to build only on the east end, the GTP would have at least delayed the heavy expenditure in British Columbia until the Prairie Section was producing returns. This plan also preserved for the company an opportunity to escape the outlay on the Mountain Section, if only by default. Most damaging, then, was Hays's commitment in 1907 to build the Mountain Section concurrently with the Prairie Section by starting construction on the west end.

Recent studies have contended that the Great Northern and the CPR, at least after construction of their main lines, adhered to the axiom of railroad construction that extension and improvement must be tied to realistic estimates of the resulting income from increased traffic. Before the construction of branches and main line improvements, both systems made detailed investigations of traffic potential.[8] The GTP president, on the other hand, inspired, if he did not create, offhand, arbitrary estimates of traffic on the Mountain Section. He accepted an inappropriate standard of construction for the road and the unwarranted expenditure it entailed. While the government may have proposed the standard, Hays justified the huge outlay by encouraging the engineering department to continue making unrealistic predictions of traffic. Presaging the recent North East Coal Project, which included the expensive upgrading of what had been the GTP British Columbia line, the first megaproject of the north-central corridor also deserves the label of a 'great planning disaster' in which 'enormous public resources [were] committed to a project which [did] not achieve its objectives.'[9]

While economies in transport of material made some construction from the west end desirable for all transcontinentals, only after connection with the east end would this expenditure begin to produce returns. Thus, it was essential to minimize construction time on the west end. The Great Northern, for example, built from the coast to connection at the summit of the Cascade Mountains in fourteen months. The GTP management's inadequate response to the labour shortage on the construction of the Mountain Section slowed progress on its west end and probably delayed completion for two years. This delay in completion not only increased fixed charges for the system, it also pushed back the *opportunity* to generate income by hauling traffic to cover at least part of the great expenditure on the west end. Finally, it eliminated the interval for the port of Prince Rupert to attract shipping business for the transcontinental during peacetime.

All of the president's actions set out above indicate Hays's failure to control or reduce expenditure. Hays's one positive strategy to increase income, his scheme for railway townsites, was even more damaging for the company because it overrode the cautions of sound railway management toward allowing large expenditures with no secure, 'conservative' prospect of income. As a predilection for quick returns from townsite lot sales, the scheme led Hays to commit the company to Pacific construction. For the president and other company officers, it soon became a desire to assert an impossible corporate hegemony, the acquisition and domination of territory in the face of opposition from individuals, rival businesses, and governments.

Perhaps the most vivid expression of this obsession with territoriality, because it served no economic purpose, came from GTP publicist Cy Warman in a speech to a Vancouver business club in 1913. After explaining that the company required returns from townsites to cover construction costs, Warman attacked those who would share them: 'The railroad is the pioneer. It precedes all other development, building into unprofitable territory, taking all the risk ... It is not fair that men, irresponsible, coming from the four corners of the earth, as vultures follow a fighting army, should swoop down in the wake of the builders and feed upon the fat of the land.' Not content with one jab, Warman poured out the company bile in a confused metaphor.

> The railway ought to be protected from advertisers, camp followers, snap hunters, who are called to the front with a hope of getting something for nothing. The railway builders are the braves, the mighty hunters who round up the buffalo; the floating land sharks are the wolves who rush in to tear out the tenderloin and feast upon the fat steaks of the kill. With amazing affrontry [*sic*] one of these camp followers will stake a claim and say to the public 'here there should be a town.' If one or two of the 'people' get together, employ a shrewd lawyer and put up their fight in the name of the people, they usually get the tenderloin and the railway the hook.[10]

Though the language was intemperate, the resentment, and the illogic, reflected those of the GTP president. Hays himself had ignored the strategic townsite concerns of the company in his lengthy dispute with the Prince Rupert City Council in 1910-11. Like other disappointed parties in western North America, Warman's sense of victimization obscured his employer's complicity in its situation.[11]

One may object that this harsh judgment of Hays's actions depends largely on hindsight. But with the exception of the impact of labour relations on completion time, all these observations stem from evaluations of data that were available to the president when he made decisions. In the cases of standard and west end construction, Hays's decisions rested in part on explicit, patently illogical, *ex ante* calculations. While the strategies of other systems probably would not have saved the GTP, they could have reduced net losses and thereby delayed the company's collapse. Because Hays was 'in too much of a hurry,' even Grand Trunk president Sir Charles Rivers Wilson came to believe that the decisions of the GTP president 'constitute[d] a danger for the Company ... He [Hays] must be stopped from entangling us in new engagements likely to involve early financial demands.'[12] Hays's sorry record on the GTP invites a closer investigation of his alleged successes in the management of American roads and the Grand Trunk proper.

For the British shareholder in the Grand Trunk, the Canadian finance minister, and most historians of the company, the actions of Hays and other senior officers in British Columbia set out above are most important because they comprised company strategy, the general policies that the GTP followed in its quest for returns. This study has moved beyond the confines of head office, however, to examine GTP activity in several communities. With an eye to Hays's decisions as well as his demise, one might dismiss company activities in the townsites and Indian reserves as peripheral, little more than rearranging deck chairs on the *Titanic*. But such a view circumscribes a crucial impact of the GTP on the north-central corridor. Within the communities, decisions were usually made and actions carried out not by the president, but by the junior officers. While the GTP legal department, for example, could not overcome the fixed charges that the construction standard entailed, it could secure and enhance numerous returns for the company. And in each community, choices did present themselves to junior as well as senior officers. However, the preceding examination of the files of the legal department branch office, which comprise the greatest part of the surviving company records, suggests that many activities of the junior officers at the community level represented tactical errors that exacerbated the consequences of the decisions taken by the president and general manager. Rather than 'independent intermediaries' who elaborated the corporate culture of a successful American road, GTP junior officers more often resembled 'Napoleonic understudies' whose quarrels and extravagance, a Laurier partisan charged, aggravated the entire project.[13]

The functional standard of failure, set out above, applies to tactics as well as strategy. Studies of the Burlington, Santa Fe, and Great Northern suggest that these systems usually declined to maximize immediate returns from townsite lot sales in order to encourage the growth of prosperous communities, which in turn would generate more traffic for their respective lines. Although the CPR and the Canadian Northern certainly benefitted from townsite speculation, they also shared townsite profits with local communities in an effort to build up a regional economy.[14]

Like the contemporary Trans-Siberian Railway, whose management was rigidly centralized, the GTP was 'a monument to official ... bungling and laxity of administration.'[15] In theory, the departmental organization of the GTP both reflected and strengthened metropolitanism. In 1909, Rivers Wilson attested to Hays's power within the company by complaining that the GTP had become 'a "one-man" management, undivided and practically uncontrolled.'[16] Junior officers apparently learned, if they did not share, the president's territoriality. Many GTP junior officers viewed railway townsites in British Columbia as fortresses into which only those who acknowledged company dominance would be admitted.

At the community level, then, the activities of the junior officers, particularly those in the legal and land department offices in Winnipeg, frequently did not forward the economic interests of the company. In Prince Rupert, the company explicitly indicated its preference for a fortress rather than an entrepôt by implementing a townsite design that inhibited commerce. Instead of boosting the port energetically, the GTP sought immediate returns from townsite lot sales. It scrabbled with the provincial government to regain control of the waterfront, but then hung back in developing it. Only the prospect of a federal government subsidy prompted the company to build a drydock that had little economic justification. Challenges to GTP activity in the Pacific terminus and other townsites came from 'land jumpers' or 'small-minded pedlars of alleged harbours that will not float a Siwash canoe,' according to Warman. Instead of searching for compromise, the GTP legal department not only turned back the court challenges but also sought to cut out the economic support of those who opposed the company.[17] But the department proved singularly unable to neutralize the unwelcome support of federal politicians and the Board of Railway Commissioners for its opponents.

Though the GTP finally secured right-of-way and townsites from a series of Indian reserves along its route, company managers were no more adept at dealing with Natives, and the institutions that supposedly represented and protected them, than with whites. The acquisition of the Fort George and Kitsumkalum Reserves reveals managerial miscalculations that delayed completion of the road and endangered important returns.

GTP activities in Prince George provide a counterpoint to those in the Pacific terminus since townsite lot sales in the interior community provided a clear net return for the company. The company repeatedly failed, however, to maximize possible returns. It drove out the most imaginative promoter of the district in an extended struggle that discouraged investment. To settle an old score with the principals of a steamboat concern, it shut down a thriving river traffic on the Upper Fraser that might have increased its own freight. The legal department did secure a tactical victory with the establishment of a municipality that favoured the railway company. The department's voluminous files on these matters, however, suggest a complete disinterest in the effect of company action on economic activity and traffic for the region.

The Hazelton district, on the other hand, offers the clearest example of how the obsession with territoriality led junior officers to deliberately harm local concerns that could have provided valuable traffic for the line. In an effort to promote lot sales in a townsite whose station could not serve the local mines, the GTP attempted to destroy a rival townsite by shutting down the only station in the district that could effectively forward ore. When local mine owners declined to use the uneconomic station, which the company preferred, the GTP set high rates on ore that probably drove the Silver Standard Mine to cease production at a time when the railway desperately needed traffic.

An important common characteristic of the GTP's activities in these townsites was the lack of attention that the company officers gave to government intervention. While the superior resources of the company allowed junior officers to defeat individuals, disputes that drew in governments or their agencies frequently led to delays that damaged the company more than the original challenges. Yet only at the municipal level did the GTP move, however clumsily, to address the problem. Although the GTP employed from its inception the Grand Trunk lobbyist in Ottawa, it did not install a permanent officer in Victoria until 1917. Legal department files reveal that company officers frequently petitioned federal and provincial ministers without avail. They also suggest that the company misunderstood or underestimated the role of the Board of Railway Commissioners in the development of the enterprise. The GTP proved no more adept at finding its way through the range of government supervision and regulation than it had at locating its line through the mountains.

In 1913, a GTP vice-president boasted that his company's activities along the Mountain Section had placed it 'in the front ranks of development of British Columbia.' Instead of encouraging the development of concerns and communities that would generate traffic, however, the company's tactical actions in Prince Rupert, Prince George, and Hazelton district led an exasperated editor to lament that the 'GTP does not enjoy putting itself in a position to do business if it can get away from it.'[18]

GTP corporate territoriality among junior officers stemmed in part from a feeling of inferiority, in this case toward the CPR, and a desperate desire to match the established rival's achievements immediately. As the GTP completed its establishment of the City of Prince George, Solicitor Hansard lamented that the GTP 'suffer[ed] from the fact that the pace is being set in the West by the Canadian Pacific, and we have not the staff, facilities or the money to follow suit.'[19] The GTP's actions to catch up in the Pacific province produced caricatures that exaggerated the company's power. A cartoon in a Vancouver paper portrayed the GTP as a monstrous locomotive leviathan trampling on the communities of northern British Columbia while brandishing a sword of greed. What outsiders perceived as evil genius or a flagrant exercise of corporate power was, however, more often stumbling incompetence.[20]

Analysis of scattered data suggests that traffic after completion fell far short of company expectations. The GTP engineering department justified the route decision and construction with a calculation that fourteen trains per day would traverse the Mountain Section immediately after completion. Throughout its brief operation, the GTP British Columbia line was probably traversed by fewer than eight freight and passenger trains per week. During this period the company's inept management of the drydock also ensured that it would not recover its largest investment in British Columbia outside the railway line itself.

In 1919, the GTP British Columbia line, completed at enormous cost, lay almost empty with unused capacity. Humorist Stephen Leacock aptly described it as a road 'from nowhere to nowhere, passing nowhere.'[21] Because the provincial government did not aggregate assessment figures by region, a comparison of GTP investment with other economic activity in the north-central corridor is necessarily tentative. But while the surviving data do not allow a precise 'mapping of capital,' they indicate the predominance of GTP investment and the corresponding economic weakness of the narrow hinterland that the railway created.[22] In 1917, more than a decade after the company had begun work on its Pacific terminus, the ratio of total assessment of Prince Rupert to GTP expenditure on its British Columbia line was less than half that of

Caricature of the GTP as Leviathan in northern British Columbia

Vancouver assessment to CPR expenditure after a similar duration.[23] The 'road of a thousand wonders' had linked the adjacent communities in what might be called a corridor of corporate failure. Not only did the Grand Trunk Pacific Railway Company unite the towns with its grade and steel, it also attached them to its mistakes, the repeated errors of company officers in building and operating a line that was not economic. This study has regarded the railway company as a product of the aspirations and fears of its creators.[24]

NOTES

Abbreviations

BCARS	British Columbia Archives and Records Service
CN	Canadian National
CN Eng	CN Engineering, Edmonton
CN RE	CN Real Estate, Edmonton
FB	Foley Brothers Records
GR	Government Record Group
HBCA	Hudson's Bay Company Archives
NAC	National Archives of Canada
PC	Order in Privy Council
RG	Record Group

Chapter 1, Introduction: 'A Tragedy Rather than Otherwise'

1   See P.N. Limerick, *The Legacy of Conquest: The Unbroken Past of the American West* (New York 1987), 41-8. For discussion of another artistic celebration of Grand Trunk expansion in 1908, see C. Rolfe, 'A British Artist and the Romance of Canada's Railways,' *British Journal of Canadian Studies* 8, 1 (1993):42-52.

2   A recent article suggests that the parent Grand Trunk may still have been economically viable at the time of its takeover by the federal government. However, it makes no such revisionist claim for the Grand Trunk Pacific. See A. Perl, 'Public Enterprise as an Expression of Sovereignty: Reconsidering the Origin of Canadian National Railways,' *Canadian Journal of Political Science* 27, 1 (March 1994):23-52.

3   The term stems from the title of Frank Norris's celebrated anti-railroad novel, which excoriates and exaggerates the power of the Southern Pacific in California. See W. Deverell, *Railroad Crossing: Californians and the Railroad, 1850-1910* (Berkeley 1994), 172-4.

4   I have usually followed the nineteenth-century American practice of using 'transcontinental' to describe a railway line from the interior of North America to the Pacific coast that completed a coast-to-coast system, frequently of different companies.

5   National Archives of Canada (hereafter NAC), RG 36/35, Canada, Grand Trunk Arbitration, vol. 6, 2810-11, 4 March 1921.

6   For a recent example of this emphasis, see G. Murphy, 'Canada's Forgotten Railway Tycoon,' *Beaver* 73, 6 (December 93-January 94):29-36.

7   *Railway Age Gazette* 53 (19 April 1912):891. See, for example, Canadian Liberal Party, *The Railway Question in Canada* (Ottawa 1915), 18-56; and O.D. Skelton, *The Railway Builders: A Chronicle of Overland Highways* (Toronto 1916), 200-12.

8   H.A. Lovett, *Canada and the Grand Trunk 1829-1932* (Montreal 1924); L. Fournier, *Railway Nationalization in Canada* (Toronto 1935); and L.R. Thomson, *The Canadian Railway Problem: Some Aspects of Canadian Transportation and a Suggested Solution for the Railway Problem* (Toronto 1938).

9   J.A. Lower, 'The Grand Trunk Pacific Railway and British Columbia' (MA thesis, History, University of British Columbia, 1939), 131-2. See also Lower, 'The Construction of the Grand Trunk Pacific Railway in British Columbia,' *British Columbia Historical Quarterly* 4, 3 (July 1940):163-81.

10 A.W. Currie, *The Grand Trunk Railway of Canada* (Toronto 1957), 407, 431.

11 The authors of three studies have repeated Clifford Sifton's condemnation of Hays as the most 'cold-blooded ... raider of the treasury' that the minister had ever encountered. T.D. Regehr, *The Canadian Northern Railway: Pioneer Road of the Northern Prairies, 1895-1918* (Toronto 1976), 116, n. 45; D.J. Hall, *A Lonely Eminence, 1901-1929*, vol. 2 of *Clifford Sifton* (Vancouver 1985), 272; and J.A. Eagle, *The Canadian Pacific Railway and the Development of Western Canada, 1896-1914* (Montreal 1989), 89.

12 G.R. Stevens, *Towards the Inevitable, 1896-1922*, vol. 2 of *Canadian National Railways* (Toronto 1962), 249. The view of Hays as Prince of Darkness, an able, if unscrupulous, protagonist, has found support in an examination of the 1910 Grand Trunk strike. See Paul Craven, *'An Impartial Umpire': Industrial Relations and the Canadian State, 1900-1911* (Toronto 1980), 318-50.

13 W.K. Lamb, review of *Asian Dream: The Pacific Rim and Canada's National Railway*, by D. MacKay, *Canadian Historical Review* 61, 1 (March 1988):121-2; Stevens, *Towards the Inevitable*, 255; D. MacKay, *Asian Dream: The Pacific Rim and Canada's National Railway* (Vancouver 1986), 103-5, 118-21. MacKay also points to the defeat of the Laurier government in 1911 as a cause. J.A. Eagle, 'Sir Robert Borden and the Railway Problem in Canadian Politics, 1911-1920' (PhD diss., History, University of Toronto, 1972), demonstrates that the Conservative government continued to honour the GTP contract as long as the company carried out its obligations.

14 R. Overton, *Burlington West: A Colonization History of the Burlington Railroad* (Cambridge, MA 1941), 339.

15 W.K. Lamb, *The History of the Canadian Pacific Railway* (New York 1977), 219-21.

16 Max Foran, 'The CPR and the Urban West, 1880-1930,' *The CPR West: The Iron Road and the Making of a Nation*, ed. H. Dempsey (Vancouver 1984), 89-105.

17 Regehr, *Canadian Northern*, 225-33, 240-1.

18 H.S. Stromquist, *A Generation of Boomers: The Pattern of Railroad Labor Conflict in Nineteenth-Century America* (Urbana, IL 1987), 144.

19 Margaret Ormsby, *British Columbia: A History* (Toronto 1958), 345.

20 Martin Robin, *The Rush for Spoils: The Company Province, 1871-1933* (Toronto 1971), 103.

21 Jean Barman, *The West beyond the West: A History of British Columbia* (Toronto 1991), 179-80.

22 Stevens, *Towards the Inevitable*, 205-7, describes GTP townsite activity in British Columbia as a 'sorry and shabby business' that 'mortally damaged the reputation' of the GTP. Ignoring the cost to the railway company as a whole, however, he implies that returns from lot sales represented a net gain for the GTP.

23 See, for example, A.M. Wellington, *The Economic Theory of the Location of Railways* (New York 1887), 95; W.Z. Ripley, *Railroads: Finance and Organization* (New York 1915), 47; and W.T. Jackman, *Economics of Transportation* (Toronto 1926), 54. Both the CPR and the Canadian Northern generally adhered to this principle. G.C. Backler, 'The CPR's Capacity and Investment Strategy in Rogers Pass, B.C., 1882-1916' (MSc thesis, Business Administration, University of British Columbia, 1981), 109; Regehr, *Canadian Northern*, 159-60.

24 Harold Innis, *A History of the Canadian Pacific Railway* (Toronto 1923), 72, 96, 140-2.

25 Harold Innis, *Settlement and the Mining Frontier* (Toronto 1936), 313-15. Other factors in the CPR success in the Kootenay region included CPR control of the major local smelter, its ability in both Ottawa and Victoria to prevent or delay government sanction for the construction of competing branch lines from the Great Northern Railway south of the border, and, of course, the subsidies provided in the Crow's Nest Pass Agreement.

26 R.C. Harris, 'Moving amid the Mountains, 1870-1930,' *BC Studies* 58 (Summer 1983):3-39. In his study of Shaughnessy's direction of the CPR in western Canada, J.A. Eagle contends that the company secured revenue from many sources in British Columbia besides railway

operation. These included townsites, land grants attached to acquired lines, mines, a smelter, hotels, and oceanic and coastwise steamships. See Eagle, *Canadian Pacific Railway*, 108-47, 156-68, 213-16, 232-45, 252-7.

27   Innis, *History of the Canadian Pacific*, 294. Innis's elucidation of continent-wide systems of communication, including the railway network, has recently been mooted as 'the essence of metropolitanism.' His research during the 1920s and 30s provided evidence of the power of the centre over the development of the periphery for the metropolitan school. D.F. Davis, 'The "Metropolitan Thesis" and the Writing of Canadian Urban History,' *Urban History Review* 14, 2 (October 1985):95-114. Davis offers both a taxonomy of metropolitanism and a critique of its efficacy as an analytical tool.

28   Regehr, *Canadian Northern*, 301-2. The most important management decisions of the Canadian Northern were made by its owners, who were also accomplished entrepreneurs in other concerns. See R.B. Fleming, *The Railway King of Canada: Sir William Mackenzie, 1849-1923* (Vancouver 1991).

29   Alfred D. Chandler, Jr., *Strategy and Structure: Chapters in the History of the American Industrial Enterprise* (Cambridge, MA 1962), 11-12. Chandler contends that the tasks of senior managers are in large part strategic, those of junior managers tactical. 'Wherever [senior managers] concentrate on short-term activities to the exclusion of or to the detriment of long-range planning, appraisal, and co-ordination, they have failed to carry out effectively their role.' He concludes that this standard 'should provide a useful criterion for evaluating the performance of an executive in American industry.'

30   These include 'The Railroads: Pioneers in Corporate Management,' *Business History Review* 39 (Spring 1965):16-40; *The Railroads: The Nation's First Big Business* (New York 1965); *The Visible Hand: The Managerial Revolution in American Business* (Cambridge, MA 1977), 81-187; and, with S. Salsbury, 'The Railroads: Innovators in Modern Business Administration,' *Railroads and the Space Program: An Exploration in Historical Analogy*, ed. B. Mazlish (Cambridge, MA 1965), 127-62.

31   Chandler's most explicit statement of the problems of the departmental organization appears in 'The Railroads: Innovators,' 141-2. For a detailed comparison of the British departmental organization with the American divisional one, see R. Morris, *Railroad Administration* (New York 1915), 123-50.

32   Currie, *Grand Trunk*, 395-6.

33   Neither the GTP nor the parent Grand Trunk produced an organization manual comparable to those that played such an important role in shaping the managerial structure of many American roads. The parent company's only formal statement of organization during this period, *The Synoptical History of the Grand Trunk System of Railways* (Montreal 1912), says nothing about the different managerial structure of its transcontinental subsidiary. The president and general manager of the GTP also held titles and some of the functions of officers of the parent company.

34   NAC, RG 30, Canadian National Railways Records, Grand Trunk Pacific Railway System, vol. 3291, file 826, pt. 1, Hays to Chamberlin, 4 October 1909; vol. 3284, file 698, D'Arcy Tate (solicitor) to W.H. Biggar (general counsel), 11 May 1909.

35   NAC, MG 30 A 93, A.W. Smithers Papers, file 4, C. Rivers Wilson, 1909, Visit to Canada, 29 September 1909.

36   J. Yates, *Control through Communication: The Rise of System in American Management*. (Baltimore, 1989), 56-63.

37   Chandler, *Visible Hand*, 3.

38   Regehr, *Canadian Northern*, 456. Comparing the GTP and CPR with the Canadian Northern, Regehr uses the more pejorative term, metropolitan imperialism. Drawing in part on the work of Canadian historians, William Cronon offers a provocative discussion of the role of railways in the advancement of metropolitan interests. *Nature's Metropolis: Chicago*

and the Great West (New York 1991), 63-93, 400-1, n. 110.

39 See, for example, A.F.J. Artibise, 'In Pursuit of Growth: Municipal Boosterism and Urban Development in the Canadian Prairie West,' *Shaping the Urban Landscape: Aspects of the Canadian City Building Process,* eds. G.A. Stelter and A.F.J. Artibise (Ottawa 1982), 116-47. On the shortcomings of boosterism, see Davis, 'The "Metropolitan Thesis,"' 98-100. For a study of another external influence, in this case, the activities of the American army, in the growth (and dislocation) of communities on the frontier of the Canadian Northwest, see K.S. Coates and W.R. Morrison, *The Alaska Highway in World War II: The U.S. Army of Occupation in Canada's Northwest* (Toronto 1992), 158-99.

40 Robin, *The Rush for Spoils,* 16.

41 M. Klein, 'The Unfinished Business of American Railroad History,' *Unfinished Business: The Railroad in American Life* (Hanover, ME 1994), 178.

42 Local histories touch on GTP actions in several white communities for which significant company files do not survive. See J.T. Saywell, 'The Bulkley Valley' (Paper prepared for Department of Education, Victoria, 1951); N. Asante, *The History of Terrace* (Terrace 1972); P. Turkki, *Burns Lake and District: A History Formal and Informal* (Burns Lake 1973); J. Glen, Sr., *Where the Rivers Meet: The Story of the Settlement of the Bulkley Valley* (Smithers 1977); M. Wheeler, *The Robson Valley Story* (McBride 1979); L. Hancock, ed., *Vanderhoof: 'The Town That Wouldn't Wait'* (Vanderhoof 1979); R.L. Shervill, *Smithers: From Swamp to Village* (Smithers 1981); Valemount Historic Society, *Yellowhead Pass and Its People* (Valemount 1984); Fraser Lake and District Historical Society, *Deeper Roots and Greener Valleys* (Fraser Lake 1986); and L. Rudland and J. Rudland, *Fort Fraser: Where the Hell's That?* (Cloverdale, BC 1988).

43 In a recent study of the early relations between lawyers and the English railway industry, R.W. Kostal offers a preliminary investigation of the 'pioneering suborganizations,' i.e., the in-house legal departments that some leading companies created during the 1860s. He suggests that the employment of a salaried solicitor and staff played a role in decreasing the overall cost of legal expenditures of the London and Northwestern later that decade. More significant was the new managerial view that 'corporate domestication ... of legal services was good business.' *Law and English Railway Capitalism, 1825-1875* (Oxford 1994), 373, 388

45 K. Lipartito, 'What Have Lawyers Done for American Business? The Case of Baker & Botts of Houston,' *Business History Review* 64 (Autumn 1990):494.

46 K. Lipartito and J. Pratt, *Baker & Botts in the Development of Modern Houston* (Austin, TX 1991), 21-46; K. Lipartito, 'Getting Down to Cases: Baker & Botts and the Texas Railroad Commission,' *Essays in Economic and Business History* 6 (1988):27-36.

47 L. Knafla, 'Richard "Bonfire" Bennett: The Legal Practice of a Prairie Corporate Lawyer, 1898 to 1913,' *Beyond the Law: Lawyers and Business in Canada, 1830 to 1930,* vol. 4 of *Essays in the History of Canadian Law,* ed. C. Wilton (Toronto 1990), 320-76; J. Gray, *R.B. Bennett: The Calgary Years* (Toronto 1991); Regehr, *Canadian Northern,* 44-5. Regehr also suggests that the original company lawyers of the CPR have been forgotten because of the prominence of Stephen and Van Horne in the company's early negotiations. Regehr, '"High Powered Capitalists, Veteran Lobbyists, Cunning Propagandists": Canadian Lawyers and the Beauharnois Scandal,' *Beyond the Law,* 404.

47 NAC, RG 43, Canada, Department of Railways, vol. 307, file 4402-General, L.K. Jones, Secretary, to D. Tate, 27 April 1906.

48 NAC, RG 30, vol. 3437, file 2858, pt. 1, H. Hansard to W.H. Biggar.

49 As a subsidiary of the Grand Trunk, the GTP held shareholders meetings only for company directors and did not publish annual reports. A small, usually uninformative, section of the published Grand Trunk annual reports presented material on the GTP. Little material on GTP expenditures for the Mountain Section remains in the records of the Department of Finance. Some financial data on the GTP can be found in the files of the federal government's

engineer-inspector of the GTP, the Royal Commission on Railways and Transportation (1917), and several reports for the Grand Trunk Arbitration.

50 Even after the manuscript census data for 1911 and 1921 are released, the lack of assessment rolls and city directories will probably compel those who desire to create community studies for these towns to choose a more recent period.

Chapter 2, 'In a Hole': Entry into British Columbia, 1902-12

1 Pacific terminus acquisition played an important role in the development of the other North American transcontinentals, of course, if only because the railway companies usually extracted substantial real estate revenue. The prospect of real estate returns led the Northern Pacific to locate its terminus at Tacoma and construct an expensive main line, misleadingly named the Cascade Branch, across unremunerative territory in Washington to reach it. See J.B. Hedges, *Henry Villard and the Railways of the Northwest* (New Haven 1930); and M. Morgan, *Puget's Sound: A Narrative of Early Tacoma and the Southern Sound* (Seattle 1979).

2 G.R. Stevens, *Towards the Inevitable, 1896-1922*, vol. 2 of *Canadian National Railways* (Toronto 1962), 121-43; R.M. Coutts, 'The Railway Policy of Sir Wilfrid Laurier: The Grand Trunk Pacific – National Transcontinental' (MA thesis, History, University of Toronto, 1968), 1-97. The elements of construction in the contract are set out in Chapter 3.

3 Undoubtedly the most important element in the enlarged project transformed the original proposal for a feeder line from the West for Grand Trunk lines in central Canada into a complete transcontinental that traversed northern Ontario and Quebec and duplicated part of the Intercolonial in the Maritimes.

4 NAC, MG 30 A 18, C.M. Hays Papers, Hays to Rivers Wilson, 14 April 1902; Hays to Grand Trunk Shareholders Meeting, 8 March 1904. K. Bryant, Jr., *History of the Atchison, Topeka, and Santa Fe Railway* (New York 1974), 168-75.

5 Rivers Wilson had first sought to purchase the prairie lines of the Canadian Northern. NAC, Hays Papers, Rivers Wilson to Hays, 24 July 1903, Hays to Rivers Wilson, 12 February 1904.

6 'General Report,' *Reports and Documents in Reference to the Location of the Line and a Western Terminal Harbour, 1878*, ed. S. Fleming (Ottawa 1878), 11; and 'General Report,' *Report and Documents in Reference to the Canadian Pacific Railway, 1880*, ed. S. Fleming (Ottawa 1880), 7. G.M. Dawson, 'Report on ... the Northern Portion of British Columbia,' *Report ... 1880*, 111-28. R.C. Moody, former commander of the Royal Engineers in the province and builder of the Cariboo Road, dismissed the northern route. 'Notes on the Route ... through British Columbia ...,' *Report ... 1880*, 144.

7 Hudson's Bay Company Archives (hereafter HBCA), B 226/b/53.8 R, file 1, R.H. Hall to Commissioner, 20 February 1900.

8 NAC, Hays Papers, Hays to Rivers Wilson, 16 January, 20 September 1904; Special Meeting of the Grand Trunk Shareholders, 8 March 1904. Hays's statement to the shareholders was doubly misleading since the company would take two more years to establish a route across the province.

9 Hays to Rivers Wilson, 24 October 1902. *Trans-Canada Railway Company Prospectus*, undated, submitted to Deputy Minister of Railways on 19 February 1902. Hays sent clippings concerning the Trans-Canada to Rivers Wilson on 22 September 1902. On the Trans-Canada promotion, see Stevens, *Towards the Inevitable*, 122-4, 134-5.

10 NAC, Hays Papers, Grand Trunk Shareholders, Special Meeting, 8 March 1904; MacKay, *Asian Dream*, 103. Hays was not alone in predicting the export of Canadian grain to the Orient, however. See R.J. Gowen, 'Canada and the Myth of the Japan Market, 1896-1911,' *Pacific Historical Review* 39 (February 1970):63-83.

11 *Evening Empire* (Prince Rupert, weekly edition), 1 April 1914. Company publicist F.A. Talbot ascribes the quotation to Hays. On the importance of shipping in bond for the Grand Trunk, see K. Cruikshank, 'Managing a Fragile North American Industry: The Canadian Railway

Problem Revisited' (Paper delivered to Second Business History Conference, University of Victoria, March 1988).

12 A Harriman ally described Hays's resignation from the American concern as 'foolish' and had no difficulty in proposing several able replacements. Professor Maury Klein graciously provided me with a typescript copy of J. Schiff to Harriman, 28 July 1901. The chief engineer of the Southern Pacific later implied that Hays's continued direction of the company would have delayed its development. D. Hofshommer, *The Southern Pacific, 1901-1985* (College Station, TX 1986), 14.

13 BC *Sessional Papers* (hereafter *SP*), 1896, Crown Land Surveys, 1895, 'Northwest Colonization Survey,' 741-810; NAC, Hays Papers, Hays to Rivers Wilson, 16 January 1904.

14 NAC, Hays Papers, Hays to Rivers Wilson, 20 January 1905.

15 NAC, RG 30, vol. 12689, file 1A-1, Ripley to Hays, 7 November 1903, Hays to Ripley, 18 November 1903; vol. 11617, file A-2, W.B. Jansen to H. Philips, 19 July 1907.

16 NAC, RG 30, vol. 12689, file 1-1, H. Emmerson to Hays, 3 December, 27 November 1903

17 Ibid., file 1-2, Memorandum, October 1904.

18 NAC, RG 30, vol. 11617, file A-2, Morse to Hays, 11 November 1907, Hays to Morse, 27 April 1908.

19 For the evolution of GTP townsite policy on the prairies, see J. Gilpin, 'International Perspectives on Railway Townsite Development in Western Canada, 1877-1914,' *Planning Perspectives* 7 (1992):247-62.

20 NAC, Hays Papers, Rivers Wilson to Hays, 17 February 1903, Hays to Rivers Wilson, 20 January 1905.

21 NAC, RG 30, vol. 12746, file 1-44, Biggar to Hays, 23 February 1905; *Canada Gazette*, Letter Patent, 3 August 1906.

22 NAC, Hays Papers, Hays to Rivers Wilson, 13 and 14 February 1903.

23 British Columbia Archives and Records Service (hereafter BCARS), GR 441 (Premiers' Papers), vol. 19, file 126/02, Hays to Prior, 27 December 1902. The Railway Belt became the name for the 40-mile-wide strip of land bracketing the first projected transcontinental railway across the province, which the British Columbia government set aside in 1871 as its share of payment for the railway. After several important adjustments for the CPR shift in route and land already alienated, this belt was transferred to the federal government in 1884 as 14,476,000 acres. The CPR had declined the grant in British Columbia so that it could take the entire grant along its line on the prairies.

24 Like so much of the political history of British Columbia before the McBride era, the role of land grants in maintaining, and land grant scandals in ending, the regime of personal governments – which depended on personal or group loyalties rather than on party political ties – requires a thorough examination.

25 NAC, Hays Papers, Hays to Rivers Wilson, 22 October, 25 November, 15 December 1902.

26 BCARS, GR 441, vol. 19, file 141, Wainwright to Prior, 30 December 1902, Prior to Wainwright, 8 January 1903; *Toronto Star*, 2 February 1903; NAC, Hays Papers, Hays to Rivers Wilson, 6 March 1903.

27 *British Columbia Review*, 28 February 1903; Platform of Conservative Party, 13 September 1902, in *Canadian Annual Review* (hereafter *CAR*), 1903, 218.

28 BC, Minute of Executive Council #396/03, 31 August 1903; BCARS, GR 441, vol. 22, file 8, McBride to Templeman, 31 August 1903.

29 BCARS, GR 441, vol. 159, file 11, Hays to McBride, 27 December 1903, McBride to Hays, 13 January 1904; vol. 386, McBride to Hays, 28 November 1903. NAC, Hays Papers, Hays to Rivers Wilson, 16 January 1904; *CAR*, 1903, 218.

30 BCARS, GR 441, vol. 81, file 4 (8), J.H. Turner to McBride, 25 March 1904.

31 BC, Minute of Executive Council #143/1904, 26 March 1904; BCARS, GR 441, vol. 81, file 1, McBride to Borden, 5 April 1904; vol. 81, file 104/04, McBride to Laurier, 8 April 1904.

32 The Northern Pacific, CPR, and Great Northern acquired most of their holdings in their respective Pacific termini in single transactions with local governments or private landholders. Private donations or transactions followed these major acquisitions. See R.D. Palmer, 'The Northern Pacific Railroad and Its Choice of a Western Terminus, 1869-1887' (MA thesis, History, University of Washington, 1967), 50-1; N. MacDonald, 'The Canadian Pacific Railway Company and Vancouver's Development to 1900,' *BC Studies* 35 (Autumn 1977):3-35; R.W. Hidy, et al., *The Great Northern Railway: A History* (Cambridge, MA 1988), 76-7. Though it required additional land for a ferry terminal, the Canadian Northern acquired its False Creek holdings in Vancouver in one transaction with the city. T.D. Regehr, *The Canadian Northern Railway: Pioneer Road of the Northern Prairies, 1895-1918* (Toronto 1976), 325-31.

33 J.A. Lower, 'The Grand Trunk Pacific Railway and British Columbia' (MA thesis, History, University of British Columbia, 1939), 136-42; B.R.D. Smith, 'Sir Richard McBride: A Study in the Conservative Party of British Columbia, 1903-1916' (MA thesis, History, Queen's University, 1959), 48-52; R.G. Large, *Skeena: River of Destiny* (Vancouver 1957), 121-5; Margaret Ormsby, *British Columbia: A History* (Toronto 1958), 345-6; Stevens, *Towards the Inevitable*, 200-1; Martin Robin, *The Rush for Spoils: The Company Province, 1871-1933* (Toronto 1971), 103. Only P.R. Hunt, 'The Political Career of Sir Richard McBride' (MA thesis, History, University of British Columbia, 1953), 84, 92, realizes that the Kaien Island affair concerned the changing perception of land grants as an incentive for railway construction.

34 The Northern Pacific and Southern Pacific selected Pacific terminus locations on similar grounds. See R.D. Palmer, 'The Northern Pacific Railroad and Its Choice of a Western Terminus, 1869-1887' (MA thesis, History, University of Washington, 1967), 50-1; W.F. Deverell, 'Building an Octopus: Railroads and Society in the Late Nineteenth-Century Far West' (PhD diss., History, Princeton University, 1989), 236-7.

35 NAC, Hays Papers, Hays to Rivers Wilson, 23 October 1903, 20 September 1904. At Port Simpson, land owners demanded $60-200 per acre; at Kitamaat, townsite lots were advertised for $75-350 per lot. C.S. Douglas, Ross, and Co., 'City of Port Simpson,' plan, 30 January 1903; BC Legislative Assembly, Select Committee re Kaien Island Investigation, *Report,* (hereafter *KIIR*), 166, 206-7.

36 NAC, RG 30, vol. 12698, file 1, H. Emmerson to Hays, 3 December 1903. F.A. Talbot, *The Making of a Great Canadian Railway: ... Grand Trunk Pacific Railway ...* (London 1912), 315, claims that the company prepared a 'voluminous report' on the matter.

37 Robin Fisher apparently accepts the pronouncements of the GTP president at face value. He maintains that the GTP was 'more interested in the deep sea harbour than in the land on which the town would be built.' *Duff Pattullo of British Columbia* (Toronto 1991), 96. The master of a coast-wise steamer offered a rather different appraisal. 'In Rupert ... a ship could hardly stay at anchor ... The bottom of the harbour must be all rock because anchors wouldn't hold there ... The railway bought Prince Rupert cheap and then sold their lots at a big price. So I think that's why they picked Prince Rupert. It was going to cost them more money to go into Port Simpson.' *Sound Heritage* 6, 2 (1977):41-2. Only the chart has survived from the Department of the Marine survey in 1906. A recent engineering report noted that the depth of Prince Rupert harbour made the construction of a bulk port near Prince Rupert more expensive than one near Kitimat. It added that the cost of land would also play a role in the decision to locate the terminal. L.R. Stratton, 'Engineering Evaluation of the Most Advantageous Site for a Deep Sea Bulk Cargo Terminal in Northern British Columbia' (typescript 1971).

38 Several sources indicate Bacon's role. Before a royal commission investigating the GTP's preference for American engineers, the harbour engineer himself admitted in July 1904 that he had already inspected the 'terminal at Port Simpson' and 'other ports on the Pacific

Coast.' Canada, Royal Commission in re The Alleged Employment of Aliens ... with the Surveys of the Proposed Grand Trunk Pacific Railway, *Proceedings and Evidence*, 118. Shortly after construction began, an American engineer described Bacon as the 'man who discovered the harbour.' Museum of Northern British Columbia, D.I. McDowell Papers, McDowell to father, 6 December 1908. Two accounts based on the reminiscences of GTP officers maintain that Bacon made the decision. BCARS, G/P/ 93/P 64, R.W. Pillsbury, 'Earliest Days in Prince Rupert'; T.V. Arsdol, 'The Career of C.C. Van Arsdol' (unpublished manuscript). A contemporary journalist claimed that company employees made two independent surveys: Bacon in October 1903; and GTP agent E.G. Russell in January 1904. R.W. Young, 'Prince Rupert: Western Terminus of the Grand Trunk Pacific Railway and Its Wonderful Possibilities,' *British Columbia Magazine* (1908):245.

39 The testimony of James Anderson, the contractor's agent, and E.V. Bodwell, the syndicate's lawyer, suggests that Larsen discovered and promoted Tuck's Inlet independently.

40 It was Bodwell who devised the scheme to block preemptors by including Kaien Island in a land reserve that applied only to the adjacent mainland. The lawyer also suggested how the government could invoke a general provision of the Land Act to justify selling land for the terminus at a very low price, in effect a bonus to the railway company. From this proposition, the lawyer explained, the government would secure two important returns: $10,000 payment for land that would otherwise be worthless, and the automatic reacquisition without cost of one-quarter of the land through the townsite sharing clause in the Land Act when the GTP marketed the townsite. *KIIR*, 123-30, Bodwell to Green, 19 January 1904.

41 *KIIR*, 212.

42 BC, Minute of Executive Council #279/1904, 4 May 1904; NAC, RG 30, vol. 12758, file 13-1, Hays to Green, 19 May 1904. The latter document was not produced at the investigation.

43 NAC, RG 30, vol. 12578, file 13-2, Agreement, 9 July 1904; file 13-4, Agreement, 9 July 1904; file 31-8, Anderson to Larsen, 14 March 1905; vol. 12702, file 25-1, Morse to Philips, 17 March 1906.

44 RG 30, vol. 12758, file 13-3, Agreement, 9 July 1904; 'Map Showing GTP Terminus, 1905.'

45 BCARS, GR 1440, BC, Department of Lands, file 1623/05; CN Real Estate (hereafter CN RE), Prince Rupert, Registration, II, Memo of Agreement, July 1905, H. Philips to G. Ryley, 9 September 1912.

46 G.T. Kane, Statement of Claim, 23 August 1909. Kane argued that he had staked the land before Anderson had.

47 *Victoria Daily Times*, 9 March 1906.

48 *KIIR*, 186-7.

49 C.H. Tupper Papers, UBC, vol. 4, file 3, Tupper to C. Wolley, 31 December 1906.

50 BCARS, GR 441, vol. 81, file 1, McBride to Borden, 5 April 1904; Canada, Senate, *Debates*, 185-6, 27 April 1904.

51 BC, Minute of Executive Council #143/1904, 26 March 1904; BCARS, GR 441, vol. 181, file 104, McBride to Laurier, 8 April 1904.

52 Senate, *Debates*, 576-9, 23 June 1904.

53 Templeman, speech in *Victoria Daily Times* (hereafter *Times*), 22 October 1904; Senate, *Debates*, 4 April 1905.

54 NAC, Hays Papers, Hays to Rivers Wilson, 29 June, 1 July 1904; MG 26 G, W. Laurier Papers, Laurier to Hays, 11 July 1904, Hays to Templeman, draft, with Hays to Laurier, 12 July 1904.

55 *Daily Colonist* (Victoria), 15 July 1904; *Times*, 20 July 1904.

56 *Daily Colonist*, 30 August 1904; *Times*, 22 October 1904.

57 NAC, Hays Papers, Hays to Rivers Wilson, 21 February 1905.

58 BCARS, GR 441, vol. 90, file not numbered, 'An Act to Aid the Construction of the GTPR Co.,' 'An Act in Aid of The GTPR Co.,' undated bills, with annotation, 'draft bills submitted by Mr. Morse.'

59   *Daily Colonist*, 19 February 1905; *Vancouver Daily World*, 24 February 1905.

60   *Daily Colonist*, 26 February, 3 March 1905.

61   Hunt, 'Sir Richard McBride,' 72-3, 76; *World*, 28 February 1905; BCARS, GR 441, vol. 159, file 12, Morse to McBride, 9 March 1905 (quotation).

62   *Daily Colonist*, 10 March 1905; *Vancouver Daily Province*, 11 March 1905.

63   *SP*, 1906, file 18, McBride to Morse, 17 March 1905; *Times*, 17 March 1905; BCARS, GR 441, vol. 159, file 12, Morse to McBride, 20 March 1905; Senate, *Debates*, 205-8, 6 April 1905; NAC, Hays Papers, Hays to Rivers Wilson, 23 March 1905.

64   NAC, RG 30, vol. 12759, file 20-7, Morse and F.G. Vernon, 23 February 1905; file 20-31, An Act Respecting the PNO Ry, n.d.

65   Canada, *Statutes*, 1908, chap. 141; NAC, Laurier Papers, vol. 535, Templeman to Laurier, 23 September 1908; MG 27 II D 8, G.P. Graham Papers, vol. 49, file 435, J. Oliver to Graham, 3 February 1909.

66   Those who have viewed the acquisition in this light include G.A. Shankel, 'The Development of Indian Policy in British Columbia (PhD diss., History, University of Washington, 1945), 214-21; R.E. Cail, *Land, Man, and the Law: The Disposal of Crown Lands in British Columbia, 1871-1913* (Vancouver 1974), 228-9; N.E.G. Stuckey, 'Tsimshian Testimony before the Royal Commission on Indian Affairs for the Province of British Columbia, 1913-1916' (MA thesis, Anthropology, University of Victoria, 1981), 26-7; and E.B. Titley, *A Narrow Vision: Duncan Campbell Scott and the Administration of Indian Affairs in Canada* (Vancouver 1986), 138-9.

67   Students of the GTP have long recognized that the company commenced Pacific construction to acquire the reserve, but they have not examined company actions leading up to this important decision. See Lower, 'Grand Trunk,' 142-4; Large, *Skeena*, 125; Stevens, *Towards the Inevitable*, 201; and P.E. Roy, 'Progress, Prosperity and Politics: The Railway Politics of Richard McBride,' *BC Studies* 47 (Autumn 1980):8.

68   GTP [?], 'Western Terminus of Grand Trunk Pacific: Map of Lima Harbour and Tsimpsean Peninsula' (Chicago 1905); NAC, National map Collection 70959, 'GTPR Plan of Land Required for Terminals on Indian Land near Port Simpson,' 20 May 1904; NAC, RG 30, vol. 3246, file 131, Russell to F. Morse, 11 March 1907.

69   NAC, RG 10, Canada, Department of Indian Affairs, vol. 7675, file 22168, pt. 3, Hays to F. Pedley, Deputy Superintendent General, 1 April 1904, W. Wainwright to Pedley, 26 May 1904.

70   Cail, *Land, Man, and the Law*, 207, 228-43, sets out the legal ground for the British Columbia government's case in the dispute: a dominion order-in-council for a joint allotment commission in 1875, in which the federal government agreed 'that any land taken off a Reserve shall revert to the Province.' He implies, however, that the dispute began only in 1906 with the GTP acquisition of Metlakatla and ended in 1912 with the McKenna-McBride agreement. In 1895, the province asserted its claim of reversionary interest in disputes with the federal government concerning the acquisition of the Songhees Reserve in Victoria and a coal lease on the Nanaimo Reserve. As late as 1917, the provincial government indicated that its reversionary right continued by asserting complete title to the Kitsilano Reserve in Vancouver. See J.L. Kanakos, 'Negotiations to Relocate the Songhees Indians, 1843-1911' (MA thesis, History, Simon Fraser University, 1982), 51-8; and W.J. Zaharoff, 'Success in Struggle: The Squamish People and Kitsilano Indian Reserve No. 6' (MA thesis, History, Carleton University, 1978), 152.

71   Bodwell & Lawson to Chief Commissioner, 21 February 1905, *SP*, 1906, F19.

72   BCARS, GR 1440, file 2204/05, Bodwell to Chief Commissioner, 9 March 1905; McBride to Morse, 17 March 1905, *SP*, 1906, F19; GR 441, vol. 159, file 11, Morse to McBride, 22 March, 26 April, Morse to Green, 19 June, McBride to Morse, 1 August 1905.

73   BCARS, GR 441, vol. 159, file 12, Morse to Green, 19 June, McBride to Morse, 1 August 1905; NAC, RG 10, vol. 7675, file 22168, pt. 3, Wainwright to Pedley, 20 April, 29 April, Pedley,

memo for Minister, 3 August 1905.

74 In April 1907, Russell wrote Morse that 'I am still firmly of the opinion that my course in securing the Indian rights first was the correct course, and the work was done at the right time.' NAC, RG 30, v 3246, file 131.

75 BCARS, GR 441, vol. 159, file 12, Morse to McBride, 22 March 1905. 'The only reason, if I understand correctly, that the Indian Reserve was not included in the original Crown Grant, was you did deemed it desirable to treat the government land and Indian separately.'

76 *Toronto Globe*, 7 August 1905; Canada, House of Commons, 'Papers and Correspondence between the Government of Canada and the Government of British Columbia Relating to the Application of the Grand Trunk Pacific Railway Company to Acquire a Portion of the Metlakatla Indian Reserve' (hereafter Metlakatla Papers) (1908), Pedley to G.W. Morrow, 28 November 1905; NAC, RG 10, vol. 7675, file 22168, pt. 3, Russell to Morrow, 15 January 1906.

77 Historical studies of Native-white relations on the Tsimpsean Peninsula have so far concentrated on the impact of missionaries during the later nineteenth century. Recent examinations include J. Usher, *William Duncan of Metlakatla* (Ottawa 1974); R. Fisher, *Contact and Conflict: Indian and European Relations in British Columbia, 1774-1880* (Vancouver 1977), 125-36; and C. Bolt, *Thomas Crosby and the Tsimshian: Small Shoes for Feet Too Large* (Vancouver 1992). See also E.P. Patterson II, 'A Decade of Change: Origins of the Nishga and Tsimshian Land Protests in the 1880s,' *Journal of Canadian Studies*, 18, 3 (Autumn 1983):40-54. Indian Reserve Commissioner Peter O'Reilly divided IR #2 in 1888 so that the Metlakatla band, with less than a third of the population of Port Simpson, thereafter held 62 per cent of the former joint reserve. The Lax Kw'alaams (Port Simpson) Band Council provided this information.

78 NAC, RG 10, vol. 7675, file 22168, pt. 3, Morrow to Pedley, 8 February, 14 February 1906.

79 NAC, RG 30, vol. 3246, file 131, Tate to Oliver, 28 May 1906, memo in Tate to Morse, 30 May 1906, second of two; Amendment, Sec. 70 of the revised Indian Act.

80 PC 562, 2 April 1906, in Metlakatla Papers, 2-3; *World*, 26 February 1906.

81 BC, Minute of Executive Council #267/06, 7 May 1906, in Metlakatla Papers, 3-4.

82 NAC, RG 30, vol. 3246, file 131, Tate to Oliver, 28 May, Pedley to Tate, 27 June, Memorandum to Minister, 16 February 1909, Tate to Morse, 1 July, 16 July, Morse to Tate, 27 June, 29 June, Tate to Pedley, 17 July 1906, GTP, Undertaking, 24 August 1906; RG 10, vol. 7675, file 22168, pt. 3, Surrender, 17 August 1906, Vowell to Pedley (two letters), 25 August 1906; PC 1859, 21 September 1906; NAC, Hays Papers, Hays to Rivers Wilson, 2 October 1906.

83 NAC, RG 10, vol. 7675, file 22168, pt. 3, S. Stewart, DIA, to Tate, 26 October 1906; RG 30, vol. 3246, file 131, Morse to Tate, 19 November 1906, J.D. McLean, DIA, to Tate, 15 January 1907

84 *Debates*, cols. 2075, 2094-5, 25 January 1907.

85 NAC, RG 10, vol. 7675, file 22168, pt. 3, clipping dated 13 February 1907; BC, Minute of Executive Council #125/07, approved 28 February 1907, in Metlakatla Papers, 17-19, Minute #148/07, 19 March 1907; BCARS, GR 55, BC, Provincial Police, Correspondence Inward, file V-Wd, April 1906-January 1908, R. Vickers to F.W. Hussey, 26 March 1907.

86 NAC, RG 10, vol. 7675, file 22168, pt. 3, Tate to Pedley, 25 March 1907; RG 13, Canada, Department of Justice, file 339/1907, Newcombe to DIA, 12 March, 29 March 1907.

87 NAC, RG 30, vol. 3246, file 131, Russell to Morse, 11 March, Morse to Tate, 7 March 1907.

88 BCARS, GR 441, vol. 87, file 251/07, Morse to McBride, 27 February, McBride to Morse, 26 March 1907, vol. 29, file 56/07, Morse to McBride, 26 Mar, 3 April 1907, vol. 87, file 420/07, McBride to R.G. Tatlow, 30 April 1907. On 23 April, Russell shot himself after writing the following note: 'No one can ever know what I have gone through in the past two months ... The three years with the GTP have worn my nerves out.' GR 55, file V-Wd, April 1906-January 1908, R. Vickers to Hussey, 25 April 1907.

89 NAC, RG 10, vol. 7675, file 22168, pt. 3, Morrow to Pedley, 27 April 1907; Morrow to Vowell, 25 February 1907; Du Vernet to Oliver, 27 April 1907. D.R. Williams, *Trapline Outlaw: Simon*

Peter Gunanoot (Victoria 1982), 75-6, suggests that Capilano expressed concerns about the GTP at a meeting with Laurier in 1908. I have located no sources to support this contention.

90 NAC, RG 30, vol. 3246, file 131, Tate to Pedley, 11 March 1907, Morse to Pedley.
91 BCARS, GR 441, vol. 87, file 420/07, Morse to McBride, 17 April 1907; vol. 89, file 850, F.J. Fulton to McBride, 29 June 1907; NAC, RG 30, vol. 3246, file 131, Tate to Morse, 6 May 1907.
92 BCARS, GR 441, vol. 87, file 420/07, McBride to Tatlow, 30 April 1907.
93 Ibid., Tatlow to McBride, 1 May, 8 May, 13 May, Morse to Tatlow, 8 May, Tatlow to Morse, 15 May 1907. The government had raised the price of third-class land from $1.00 to $2.50 per acre since the Kaien Island purchase.
94 BCARS, GR 441, vol. 89, file 850/07, F. Fulton to McBride, 29 June 1907.
95 NAC, RG 30, vol. 11717, file A-1, Philips, Prospectus, 2nd draft, September 1907, 3rd draft, October 1907. The wildly speculative calculation was never published. The secretary emphasized that he made his estimate 'conservatively,' given the potential of Prince Rupert. It reveals that company officers were convinced that the GTP would make a great profit.
96 BCARS, GR 441, vol. 87, file 420/07, 13 June, McBride to Hays, 7 August, 9 August, 28 August, Hays to McBride, 8 Aug, 19 August 1907.
97 NAC, RG 30, vol. 3246, file 131, Tate to Wainwright, 2 July 1907.
98 NAC, RG 30, vol. 3264, file 364, Tate to Morse, 16 October 1907.
99 NAC, RG 30, vol. 3261, file 267, Tate to Morse, 4 November 1907.
100 Ibid., Tate to Morse, 18 January 1908.
101 BCARS, GR 441, vol. 91, file 606/08, Wainwright to McBride, 18 February 1908; BC, *Statutes*, 1908, chap. 19, 'An Act Respecting the Grand Trunk Pacific Railway'; BC, Legislative Assembly, *Journals*, 6 March 1908.
102 NAC, RG 30, vol. 3266, file 383, Wainwright to Morse, 10 March 1908; BCARS, GR 441, vol. 91, file 420/08, 13 March 1908; file 478/08, 19 March 1908.
103 BCARS, GR 441, vol. 37, file 25, W.E. Bell to Hays, 4 September 1909, Bell to McBride, 23 January 1910, McBride to Hays, 16 May 1910.
104 NAC, RG 30, vol. 3291, file 816, Tate to Chamberlin, 27 January 1909. RG 43, vol. 434, file 11840, Biggar to Jones, 26 February, G. Ruel to Jones, 23 April, Tate to Jones, 14 May, Wainwright to Jones, 26 November 1909; Graham Papers, Graham to Wainwright, 20 September 1909; Regehr, *Canadian Northern*, 289-90; NAC, RG 30, vol. 3305, file 987, Hays to Chamberlin, 29 December 1909; vol. 3305, file 977, Tate to Chamberlin, 19 January, Wainwright to Tate, 27 January 1910.
105 BCARS, GR 441, vol. 107, F. Carter-Cotton to McBride, 11 April 1911; vol. 110, file 933/11, Hays to Norton-Griffiths, 21 October 1910; BC, *Statutes*, 1912, chap. 34, schedule B, GTP and Foley Bros., Welch & Stewart, Agreement, 23 January 1912.
106 The only surviving source concerning the role of the GTP in the creation of the PGE comes from Tate's testimony before a select committee of the British Columbia legislature in 1917. BC, Legislative Assembly, *In re Pacific Great Eastern Railway Company: Proceedings and Evidence*, 513-20, 13 April 1917. On McBride's use of the PGE and other railway projects in the 1912 election, see Roy, 'Progress, Prosperity and Politics,' 15-22.
107 The report of the select committee suggests that the contractors had more interest in looting the line than in completing it. Roy, 'Progress, Prosperity and Politics,' 26, concedes that the investigation provided ample evidence of mismanagement, including Tate's slush fund for the Conservatives. The PGE did not reach Prince George until 1952.
108 BCARS, GR 441, vol. 90, unnumbered file, 'Wainwright's personal memo.'

Chapter 3, 'Banging Right through on a Straight Line': Construction

1 J.A. Ward, *Railroads and the Character of America, 1820-1867* (Knoxville, TN 1986), 12-40, 94-105; J.R. Stilgoe, *Metropolitan Corridor: Railroads and the American Scene* (New Haven 1983), 141-4.

2   F.A. Talbot, *The New Garden of Canada: ... Undeveloped New British Columbia* (London 1911); and *The Making of a Great Canadian Railway: ... Grand Trunk Pacific Railway ...* (London 1912), 183.

3   C.W. Condit, 'The Literature of the Railroad Buff: A Historian's View,' *Railroad History* 142 (Spring 1980):14. The critique concerned Lucius Beebe's celebration of the Southern Pacific.

4   For the seamy side of railway development in British Columbia, see M.B. Cotsworth's two pamphlets, Ministerial Union of the Lower Mainland of B.C., *The Crisis in B.C.* (Vancouver 1915); and, particularly, *Railway Bungling (and Worse) in British Columbia* (Vancouver 1918). The first historical account hostile to the GTP project is H.A. Lovett, *Canada and the Grand Trunk 1829-1932* (Montreal 1924), 141-81. More balanced studies that offer some critical comments on GTP construction include A.W. Currie, *The Grand Trunk Railway of Canada* (Toronto 1957), 400, 407; R.M. Coutts, 'The Railway Policy of Sir Wilfrid Laurier: The Grand Trunk Pacific-National Transcontinental' (MA thesis, History, University of Toronto, 1968), 162-4, 167-70, 190-1, 200-6; and J.A. Eagle, 'Sir Robert Borden and the Railway Problem in Canadian Politics, 1911-1920' (PhD diss., History, University of Toronto, 1972), 33-5, 60.

5   G.C. Backler, 'The CPR's Capacity and Investment Strategy in Rogers Pass, B.C., 1882-1916' (MSc thesis, Business Administration, University of British Columbia, 1981); and Backler and T.D. Heaver, 'The Timing of a Major Investment in Railway Capacity: CPR's 1913 Connaught Tunnel Decision,' *Business History* 24 (1982):300-14.

6   T.D. Regehr, *The Canadian Northern Railway: Pioneer Road of the Northern Prairies, 1895-1918* (Toronto 1976), 159-62.

7   H.A. Innis, 'Government Ownership in Canada,' *Problems of Staple Production* (Toronto 1933), 44, 47.

8   Letter from J.L. Charles to author, 22 July 1983.

9   The revised contract included many paragraphs from the 1903 contract. Canada, *Statutes*, 1903, chap. 71, schedule, 29 July 1903; 1904, chap. 24, schedule, 18 February 1904. GTP preferred stock with a face value of $20 million was never issued. For the Prairie Section, the government three-quarter guarantee was limited to $13,000 per mile. The most important concession the company obtained in 1904 was the elimination of the $30,000 per mile limit on the government three-quarter guarantee of the cost of the Mountain Section. The date for completion was extended to December 1911. The company's estimate of the cost of the Mountain share on which the sale of securities depended is discussed below.

10 Canada, *Statutes*, 1903, chap. 71, schedule, secs. 9, 18; NAC, RG 43, vols. 327 and 4671, Hays to W.S. Fielding, 28 August 1905.

11 NAC, Hays Papers, Grand Trunk Shareholders, Special Meeting, 8 March 1904.

12 Canada, *Statutes*, 1905, chap. 98, schedule A, sec. 4; PC 952, 31 May 1905; NAC, RG 19, vol. 63, file 133-3-14, pt. 1, Hays to Wainwright, 27 June, Hays to Fielding, 28 August 1905.

13 NAC, RG 19, vol. 63, file 133-3-14, pt. 1, Deputy Minister of Finance to Wainwright, 4 July, Fielding to H.R. Emmerson, 29 August 1905. The formal title for the position was Government Consulting Engineer of the Western Division of the National Transcontinental Railway.

14 NAC, RG 19, Canada, Department of Finance, vol. 64, file 133-3-16, G.A. Bell, Memorandum, 1 February 1912.

15 K. Cruikshank, *Close Ties: Railways, Government, and the Board of Railway Commissioners, 1851-1933* (Montreal 1991), 69-79.

16 Canada, *Statutes*, 1903, chap. 71, schedule, sec. 38. Canada, *Statutes*, 1903, chap. 58, Railway Act, sec. 122-3, revised 1906, sec. 157-9.

17 Canada, *Statutes*, 1903, chap. 71, schedule, sec. 11. For a clear statement of the two most expensive elements in the standard, the gradient and curvature, see Canada, National Transcontinental Railway Investigating Commission, *Report* (hereafter NTR IC, *Report*)

(1914), exhibit no. 1, 8, 11, NTR Book of Instructions, January 1907. The standard of the Eastern Division of the NTR followed that of the Western Division, i.e., the GTP.

18 'The Empire's New Highway: Interview with the President of the GTP ...' *National Review* 52 (1908-9):679-81. F.A. Talbot, *The Making of a Great Canadian Railway: ... Grand Trunk Pacific Railway ...* (London 1912), 38.

19 NAC, RG 43, vol. 306, file 4402-General, Schreiber, Estimate, 12 July 1903; *Facts Concerning the Proposed Grand Trunk Pacific Railway* (1903), 15; S.J. McLean, 'Canadian Railroad Expansion,' *Railroad Gazette* 41, 1 (6 July 1906):18.

20 Commons, *Debates*, 8574, 12 August 1903; NTR IC, *Report*, 14-15; A.J. Currie, *The Grand Trunk Railway of Canada* (Toronto 1957), 411.

21 NTR IC, *Report*, 16, 6; Canada, Royal Commission to Inquire into Railways and Transportation, *Report*, 59.

22 This increase accords with the estimate of an engineer for the Grand Trunk Arbitration who argued that the standard increased the cost of the Mountain *and* the less expensive Prairie Section by 20-25 per cent. NAC, RG 36/35, vol. 16, file 5228, J.G. Sullivan, Report on Physical Roadway Section of the GTP, 14 April 1921.

23 NAC, Hays Papers, Hays to Rivers Wilson, 2 February 1905; RG 43, vol. 307, file 4402-TJC, Morse to Schreiber, 11 April 1908. For the higher estimate for the government bond issue, see RG 43, vol. 306, file 4402-General, Schreiber to Emmerson, 22 May 1905. On the securities sold, see Canada, *SP*, 1916, #282, 'Financial Statements Respecting the Grand Trunk Pacific Railway Company,' 8-9. NAC, MG 26 H, R.L. Borden Papers, vol. 25, file OC 143, pt. 2, E.J. Chamberlin to T. White, 6 March 1914. The different estimates determined in large part the disparity between the proportions of the value of securities that the company and government sold. The value of the company bonds clearly signalled the company's expectation of the cost of construction.

24 NTR IC, *Report*, 16.

25 NAC, RG 43, vol. 306, file 4402-General, Schreiber to Emmerson, 1 March 1906; Laurier Papers, Hays to Laurier, 29 January 1907; Talbot, *Making of a Great Canadian Railway*, 170-3.

26 Canada, *Statutes*, 1903, chap. 122, sec. 12.

27 Fielding in Commons, *Debates*, 8575, 12 August 1903; *Debates*, 7682, 30 July 1903.

28 Fraser-Fort George Museum, L.C. Gunn Papers, R.W. Jones, Reconnaissance Report on Proposed Lines, Edmonton to Rocky Mountains, n.d. Gunn's handwritten chronology indicates that the report was made in February or March 1904.

29 NAC Records Centre, Winnipeg, GTP-CN Drawings, GTP, 'Map of part of British Columbia ... showing survey and reconnaissance lines from Edmonton to the Pacific Coast,' 15 March 1905; NAC, Hays Papers, Kelliher to Hays, 16 July 1909, Hays to Rivers Wilson, 25 March 1905.

30 NAC, Hays Papers, Kelliher to Chamberlin, 16 July 1909. Talbot argues that GTP tardiness in the selection of the Yellowhead was part of a plan to throw the rival Canadian Northern off guard. *Making of a Great Canadian Railway*, 171-3.

31 NAC, RG 43, vol. 306, file 4402-EYP pt. 1, Kelliher to Morse, with enclosures, 1 November 1906.

32 J.K.K. Kerry, 'Some Theories upon Railroad Location,' *Transactions of the Canadian Society of Civil Engineers* (March 1903), 283.

33 NAC, RG 43, vol. 306, file 4402-EYP pt. 1, Kelliher to Morse, with enclosures, 1 November 1906.

34 NTR IC, *Exhibits*, H.A. Wood, GTP, to D. Macpherson, 7 August 1905; Backler, 'CPR's Capacity,' 140-1; NAC, Hays Papers, Hays to Rivers Wilson, 13 December 1906.

35 The calculation of excess for the Peace River route was $22 million; for the Wapiti Pass route, $10.5 million. In theory, the allowable margin should not exceed the smallest excess, i.e.,

$10.5 million for the Wapiti Pass. But this route was apparently costed for technical purposes only; the margin used was the excess for the Pine River route, the least expensive practical alternative.

36 Backler, 'CPR's Capacity,' 182-3.
37 NAC, RG 43, vol. 306, file 4402-Route, I, Tate to Schreiber, 20 December 1905, Morse to Schreiber, 20 January 1906; RG 30, vol. 3357, file 1638, Tate to Wainwright, 13 November 1911.
38 S.J. McLean, 'Canadian Railroad Expansion,' *Railroad Gazette* 41, 1 (6 July 1906):18; NAC, RG 43, vol. 306, file 4402-Route, I, Tate to Jones, 3 August, Schreiber to Emmerson, 29 August 1906; file 4402-EYP Location, I, Schreiber to Morse, 9 August, Schreiber to Laurier, 27 August 1906.
39 NAC, RG 30, vol. 2341, file 96, Morse to Tate, 20 September 1906; RG 30, Canadian Northern Legal Series, C 4625, file 1018-63-1, Edmonton, Yukon and Pacific, application, 22 October 1906.
40 NAC, RG 30, vol. 2341, file 96, Morse to Tate, 21 September, Morse to Schreiber, 28 September, Tate to Morse, 28 September 1906.
41 NAC, RG 43, vol. 306, file 4402-EYP Location, I, Morse to Schreiber, 2 November, Schreiber to Emmerson, 8 November 1906.
42 Ibid., Morse to Emmerson, 12 November 1906; PC 2306, 24 November 1906
43 NAC, RG 43, vol. 306, file 4402-EYP Location, I, Schreiber to Emmerson, 24 November, Schreiber to Laurier, 7 December, Morse to Schreiber, 24 December 1906; vol. 3241, file 96, Tate to Morse, 26 November, Tate to Emmerson, 29 November 1906; PC 2452, 8 December 1906. Morse later acknowledged Schreiber's role in passing the order.
44 NAC, RG 43, vol. 306, file 4402-EYP Location, I, Schreiber to G. Ruel, Canadian Northern, 12 December 1906, Schreiber to Emmerson, 31 January 1907; RG 30, C 4625, file 1018-63-1, G. Ruel, memorandum, quoted in Regehr, *Canadian Northern*, 287.
45 NAC, RG 43, vol. 306, file 4402-Route, II, Emmerson to Butler, 2 January 1907; RG 30, vol. 3241, file 96, Tate to Morse, 12 January 1907.
46 NAC, RG 30, C 4625, file 1018-63-1, memoranda dated 31 December 1907; Laurier Papers, 118713-5, Mann to Laurier, 26 January 107.
47 NAC, Laurier Papers, 118716-8, Hays to Laurier, 29 January 1907.
48 Regehr, *Canadian Northern*, 285-8.
49 The most detailed is *Railway and Engineering Journal*, 16 March 1912, 211-35. The many photographs of rock work on the Skeena are more interesting than the text. Articles in the labour press were more critical; they are examined in the following chapter.
50 NAC, Hays Papers, Parker to Hays, 4 July 1909.
51 Ibid., Kelliher to Chamberlin, 16 July 1909.
52 CP Archives, RG 2 (103273), X-1118, T.C. Macnabb, Report on Grand Trunk Pacific Railway, Winnipeg to Prince Rupert, 11 August 1914.
53 NAC, RG 36/35, Berry, vol. 6, 3177-80, 18 March 1921.
54 NAC, RG 43, vol. 306, file 4402-EYP Location, I, Schreiber, Estimate, 5 August 1907, Memorandum RE the division ... (?) August 1907, Schreiber to Morse, 23 August 1907; RG 30, vol. 3262, file 281, Kelliher to Morse, 31 August 1907; vol. 3262, file 281, Kelliher to Schreiber, 12 November 1907; Hays Papers, Kelliher to Chamberlin, 16 July 1909. The Royal Commission valuation for this section was $4,896,000.
55 See Foley Brothers [?], *Seventy Years: The Foley Saga* (Los Angeles 1945); G.W. Taylor, *An Industrial History of British Columbia* (Victoria 1982), 78-82.
56 Minnesota Historical Society, Foley Brothers Records (hereafter FB), file 19-54-a, FWS price list, PR-Copper River, 24 February 1908; RG 30, vol. 12713, file Ry 124-3, GTP-FWS contract, PR-PRE 100 (Copper River), 19 March 1908. On the same day FWS signed another contract for the same prices for work on the Pacific Northern and Omineca Railway, a branch from

Kitimat to Copper River. NAC, RG 30, vol. 3268, file 413, Stewart to Kelliher, 29 April 1908; Overclassification, final estimates.

57 FB, unnumbered file, Stewart to Chamberlin, 11 August 1909

58 Ibid., Welch to T. Foley, 25 August 1909.

59 NAC, RG 30, vol. 12713, file Ry 124-8, GTP-FWS, contract, PRE 100-PRE 236 (Aldermere), 9 November 1909; file Ry 124-7, GTP-FWS, contract, Wolf Creek-Mi. 100, 18 August 1909, extended to Mi. 179, 21 January 1910, backdated to 18 August 1909; Overclassification, Final Estimate; *Vancouver Daily Province,* 6 September 1910.

60 FB, unnumbered file, Stewart to Chamberlin, 11 October 1910.

61 FB, 19-2-a, Stewart to Kelliher, 15 August 1911; NAC, RG 30, file 12713, file 124-3, Hays to Biggar, 19 August, Hays to Schreiber, 21 August, Schreiber to Hays, 21 August 1911. The GTP chief engineer had sounded Schreiber out in the spring of 1911 about such a method of letting the final contract.

62 NAC, RG 30, vol. 3355, file 1622, Memorandum of Agreement, dated 19 August 1911. In this paragraph I have disregarded the dates on the documents, all of which are copies, because they are frequently typed on a different machine, presumably at a later date. If one accepts the dates as precise, then the GTP committed itself to a new form of contract with FWS before it received government sanction. Since Stewart and Chamberlin evidently discussed this matter over several weeks, the provenance that I have suggested seems more probable.

63 Ibid., Tate to Chamberlin, 18 October 1911; RG 30, vol. 3486, file 2382, Kelliher to Hansard, 4 March 1913.

64 See, for example, prices for contractor Duncan Ross, Mile 359-64 PRE, and Stewart Brothers, Mile 364-72 PRE. Some of the members in the latter firm were related to principal contractor J.W. Stewart.

65 NAC, RG 30, vol. 3314, file 1115, Contract, 12 July 1910.

66 NAC, RG 43, vol. 577, file 18464, pt. 1, Kelliher to Schreiber, 17 January 1914, quoted in A.L. Ford, Report on Certain Matters Pertaining to the GTP Ry, 21 May 1917, 15.

67 Ford, Report on Certain Matters, 15-7.

68 NAC, RG 43, vol. 307, file 4402-TJC West, Loc, Tate to Jones, 13 May, 1 October 1909; BRC #7135, 4 June, #8342, 15 October; PC #1451, 21 June, #2232, 8 November 1909.

69 Fraser-Fort George Museum, L.C. Gunn Papers, Gunn to J.C. Callaghan, 5 March, 12 March 1912.

70 NAC, RG 43, vol. 307, file 4402-YHP, C.R. Coutlee, Report on Rival Locations High and Low Line for GTP Ry down Fraser River ... May 1912, 1-2.

71 Ibid., 11.

72 Ibid., Schreiber to Minister, 13 June 1912; Gunn Papers, W. Nor [?] to Gunn, 21 August 1912; CPR Macnabb report, 23.

73 NAC, RG 36/1, vol. 37, file 2216, pt. 1, Kelliher to Chamberlin, 23 April 1914.

74 NAC, RG 36/1, vol. 37, file 2216, pt. 2, W.J. Logan, auditor, to Schreiber, 20 August 1913; pt. 3, Law to Schreiber, 21 August 1912, Kelliher to Schreiber, 25 February 1911.

75 Pt. 1, Kelliher to Chamberlain, 23 April 1914. For the CPR experience, see T.D. Regehr, 'Letters from End of Track,' *The CPR West: The Iron Road and the Making of a Nation* (Vancouver 1984), 43-4.

76 NAC, RG 36/1, vol. 37, file 2216, pt. 3, W.P. Smith to G.L. Law, 14 January, Schreiber to Law, 22 February, Kelliher to Schreiber, 25 February, W.E. Mann to Kelliher, 23 March 1911.

77 Ibid., pt. 1, Schreiber to Reid, 24 April, Kelliher to Chamberlin, 23 April 1914; pt. 3, Law to Schreiber, 15 August 1913.

78 Ibid., pt. 3, Law to Schreiber, 21 August 1912; Ford, Report on Certain Matters, 8.

79 Ibid., pt. 3, Schreiber to Law, 15 October 1912, Schreiber to Law, 27 August 1912.

80 Ibid., pt. 3, Law to Schreiber, 10 January, Schreiber to Law, 16 January, Schreiber to R.K. Chestnut, 14 February 1913.

81 Ibid., pt. 1, F.J. George to Kelliher, 29 January 1913; pt. 2, Kelliher to Schreiber, 8 January 1913.
82 Ibid., pt. 2, Chamberlin to Cochrane, 23 January, Chamberlin to Schreiber, 27 January, 3 February, Schreiber to Chamberlin, 30 January, memo, 5 February 1913.
83 Ibid., pt. 2, Stewart to Kelliher, 5 February 1913; pt. 1, Kelliher to Schreiber, 15 February 1913.
84 PC #367, 31 March 1913; file 2216, pt. 3, Schreiber to Cochrane, 3 April 1913.
85 NAC, RG 36/1, vol. 37, file 2216, pt. 3, Kelliher to Cochrane, 18 June, Logan to Schreiber, 20 August 1913.
86 Pt. 3, Reynolds to Schreiber, 10 July 1913, official and private; PC #1784, 11 July 1913, PC #2276, 5 September 1913.
87 Pt. 3, Law to Schreiber, 25 August, Kelliher to Schreiber, 12 September, 14 October, Schreiber to Kelliher, 9 October 1913.
88 Ford, Report on Certain Matters, 7.
89 NAC, RG 36/1, vol. 37, file 2216, pt. 1, Schreiber to Cochrane, 10 February, Ross to Reynolds, 15 January 1914.
90 PC 1141, 28 April 1914; NAC, RG 36/1, vol. 37, file 2216, pt. 1, Kelliher to Chamberlin, 23 April, Schreiber to Reid, 24 April 1914.
91 Ford, Report on Certain Matters, 9; file 2216, pt. 1, Law to Schreiber, 30 July 1914.
92 NAC, RG 125, vol. 389, file 3827, Supreme Court of Canada, On Appeal, *GTP Ry Co.* v. *British Columbia Express Company,* testimony J.E. Heaman, 246.
93 BC, Department of Highways, file 15, Kelliher to J.E. Griffith, 6 March, 27 March, T. Taylor to Griffith, 4 April 1912; BCARS, GR 1323, Attorney-General, B 2126, file 4969/17 A/15, Griffith to Chamberlin, 4 April 1912.
94 BC, Department of Highways, file 15, Kelliher to Griffith, 16 July, Griffith to Kelliher, 7 August 1913.
95 Ibid., Kelliher to Griffith, 17 February 1914.
96 BCARS, GR 1323, B 2126, file 4969/17 A/15, Griffith to Kelliher, 25 February, Griffith to Kelliher, 2 March 1914; Highways, file 15, Donaldson to Griffith, 8 March 1914.
97 Highways, file 15, Hansard to Taylor, 13 March, Griffith to Donaldson, 18 March, Griffith to E.A. Stone, 21 March, Stone to Griffith, 11 July 1914; BCARS, GR 1323, B 2126, file 4969/17 A/15, Griffith to Hansard, 27 November 1914.
98 BCARS, GR 1323, B 2126, file 4969/17 A/15, Hansard to Griffith, 27 November 1914; Ellis, note, 17 March; Hansard to Bowser, 7 May 1915
99 Ibid., Bowser to Hansard, Hansard to Bowser, 23 August, Hansard to Taylor, 12 June 1916.
100 Ibid., Draft agreement, 13 May; Hansard to King, 27 July 1918.
101 Eagle, 'Sir Robert Borden and the Railway Problem,' 34. *Empire* (Prince Rupert), 19 October 1908. There is no way to discover how much of its material the GTP shipped to Prince Rupert by this route. Exploring the ground and siding of South Hazelton, which the GTP reached only in 1912, the author discovered brackets stamped 'N.S. Steel.'
102 Ford, Report on Certain Matters, 41-2. The valuation was $3,946,987.
103 Regehr, *Canadian Northern,* 354; *Railway Age Gazette* 54, 8 (21 February 1913):17.
104 A government engineer later claimed that the cost increase on standard alone pushed the GTP into receivership. NAC, RG 36/35, vol. 16, file 5228, J.G. Sullivan, Report on Physical Roadway Section of the GTP, 14 April 1921.
105 Hays Papers, Hays to Rivers Wilson, 20 November 1903.
106 'Government Ownership in Canada,' 44, 47; NAC, RG 36/35, vol. 10, 6012-15, J.G. Sullivan, 22 March 1921.

Chapter 4, 'Too Good or Too Fat for the Job': Labour Relations
 1 On the impact of the new machines, see P. O'Bannon, 'Railway Construction in the Early Twentieth Century: The San Diego and Arizona Railway,' *Southern California Quarterly* (1979):255-90.

2   No surviving record provides an estimate of the labour cost in building the GTP line. In Schreiber's breakdown of the first cost of construction in 1916 for the royal commission, the categories of grading, tunnels, bridges (steel and wooden), and maintenance (probably ballasting) appear to embrace most of the construction work. I have subtracted 50 per cent of the value from bridges for imported materials, i.e., steel sections manufactured in Ontario. The combined value of these categories represents 70 per cent of the first cost of the Mountain Section, approximately $50 million of the weighted valuation estimate of the first cost of the British Columbia line. It must be noted that only part of this sum was paid to labourers; the estimate also includes payments to contractors and for other imported materials.

3   For the adoption of these techniques by American railway companies, see H.S. Stromquist, *A Generation of Boomers: The Pattern of Railroad Labor Conflict in Nineteenth-Century America* (Urbana, IL 1987), 226-66. On the CPR innovations, see B. Ramirez, 'Brief Encounters: Italian Immigrant Workers and the CPR, 1900-1930,' *Labour/le Travail* 17 (Spring 1986):9-27. Canadian National Railways, the corporate successor of the GTP, adopted some of these ideas only during the 1920s. A. Seager, 'A New Labour Era?: Canadian National Railways and the Railway Worker, 1919-1929,' *Journal of the Canadian Historical Association* 3 (1992):171-96. For the less enlightened management attitudes toward labour that prevailed on the west coast, see A. Yarmie, 'The Right to Manage: Vancouver Employers' Associations, 1900-1923,' *BC Studies* 90 (Summer 1991):40-74.

4   Important American studies of railway labour include W. Licht, *Working for the Railroad: The Organization of Work in the Nineteenth Century* (Princeton 1983); J.H. Ducker, *Men of the Steel Rails: Workers on the Atchison, Topeka & Santa Fe Railroad, 1869-1900* (Lincoln, NE 1983); and W.T. White, 'A History of Railroad Workers in the Pacific Northwest, 1883-1934' (PhD diss., History, University of Washington, 1981). Recent studies of twentieth-century Canadian railway labour relations include J.H. Tuck, 'The United Brotherhood of Railway Employees in Western Canada, 1898-1905,' *Labour/le Travailleur* 11 (Spring 1983):63-88; Paul Craven, *'An Impartial Umpire': Industrial Relations and the Canadian State, 1900-1911* (Toronto 1980), 318-53; and M. Rosenfeld, '"It Was a Hard Life": Class and Gender in the Work and Rhythms of a Railway Town, 1920-1950,' Canadian Historical Association (hereafter CHA), *Historical Papers* (1988):237-79.

5   Edwin Bradwin used the 'sociological method' for his dissertation, published in 1928 as *The Bunkhouse Man: A Study of Work and Pay in the Camps of Canada, 1903-1914* (2nd ed., Toronto 1972). A.R. McCormack continues this approach in a recent study of those who joined the IWW. See 'Wobblies and Blanketstiffs: The Constituency of the IWW in Western Canada,' *Lectures in Canadian Labour and Working-Class History*, eds. W.J.C. Cherwinski and G.S. Kealey (St. John's 1985), 101-14.

6   B.A. Frederick, 'Construction of the Hudson Bay Railway: A History of the Work and the Workers, 1908-1930' (MA thesis, History, University of Manitoba, 1981), presents much of Bradwin's material concerning the National Transcontinental in northern Ontario during the period before 1914 as a description of conditions on the Hudson Bay Railway in northern Manitoba through the 1920s. G.W. Taylor, *The Railway Contractors: The Story of John W. Stewart, His Enterprises and Associates* (Victoria 1988), 63-4, applies the unusual favourable testimony of a single inspector of camps on the east end of the GTP in Alberta in 1909 to the entire construction project.

7   K. Marx, 'The Eighteenth Brumaire of Louis Bonaparte,' *The Marx-Engels Reader*, 2nd ed., ed. R.C. Tucker (New York 1978), 595.

8   British journalist F.A. Talbot draws on the experiences of his trek along the GTP route in British Columbia during the summer of 1910 to present a rosy corporate view of camp conditions and the work of stationmen in *The New Garden of Canada: ... Undeveloped New British Columbia* (London 1911) and *The Making of a Great Canadian Railway: ... Grand*

Trunk Pacific Railway ... (London 1912). Talbot rehearses some of this material in a third book, *Making Good in Canada* (London 1912), and in innumerable articles in British journals and newspapers to convince navvies to come to Canada to work on the GTP. Taylor's *Railway Contractors* offers only an admiring view of the Canadian partner in the principal contractor of the GTP, J.W. Stewart.

9 A. Laut, 'Revolution Yawns,' *Technical World Magazine* (1912):134-44; A. Laut, *Am I My Brother's Keeper?* (Toronto 1913); P. Foner, *The Industrial Workers of the World, 1905-1917*, vol. 4 of *History of the Labor Movement in the United States* (New York 1965), 227-31; P. Phillips, *No Power Greater: A Century of Labour in British Columbia* (Vancouver 1967), 53-5; S.M. Jamieson, *Times of Trouble: Labour Unrest and Industrial Conflict in Canada, 1900-1966* (Ottawa 1968), 144-6; Jack Scott, *Plunderbund and Proletariat: A History of the IWW in B.C.* (Vancouver 1974), 28-32, 138-41; A.R. McCormack, 'The Industrial Workers of the World in Western Canada: 1905-1914,' CHA, *Historical Papers* (1975):167-90; C. Schwantes, *Radical Heritage: Labor, Socialism, and Reform in Washington and British Columbia, 1885-1917* (Seattle 1979), 186; and M. Leier, *Where the Fraser River Flows: The Industrial Workers of the World in British Columbia* (Vancouver 1990), 45-53.

10 See, for example, P. Turkki, *Burns Lake and District: A History Formal and Informal* (Burns Lake 1973), 16, 24-8; Valemount Historic Society, *Yellowhead Pass and Its People* (Valemount 1984), 14-23, 131-43; R.G. Large, *Skeena: River of Destiny* (Vancouver 1957), 145-6; Large, *Prince Rupert: A Gateway to Alaska and the Pacific* (Vancouver 1960), 34; and F.E. Runnalls, *A History of Prince George* (Vancouver 1946), 102-3, 127-8.

11 Most of the records of the principal contractor, FWS, have been destroyed. Government records such as the provincial sanitary inspectors' reports and the federal fair wage officers' reports have also not survived. The papers of local unions and the Industrial Workers of the World (IWW) in northern British Columbia are sparse because a fire destroyed the Labour Temple in Prince Rupert during the 1930s.

12 Strikers on the west end in 1912 claimed that 10,000 men on the east end came out in sympathy. *International Socialist Review* (October 1912):375. This boast, picked up by Vancouver newspapers, eventually found its way into G.R. Stevens's account of the GTP, *Towards the Inevitable, 1896-1922*, vol. 2 of *Canadian National Railways* (Toronto 1962), 195.

13 NAC, RG 76, Canada, Immigration Branch, file 594511, pt. 3, Kelliher to Chamberlin, 7 November 1910.

14 The GTP payrolls include 166 books for the construction department during the period December 1908 to December 1916 and two books for the engineering department from May 1906 to December 1909. While these books do not encompass the entire company labour force in British Columbia, they do provide pay data on a significant proportion.

15 BCARS, GR 441, vol. 98, file 764/09, Manson to McBride, 30 June 1909; *Vancouver Sun*, 22 August 1912.

16 W.H. Montgomery presented the calculation in his testimony before the British Columbia Royal Commission on Labour in Prince Rupert during the summer of 1913. BCARS, GR 684, Proceedings, file 9-12, 399-400.

17 *Empire* (Prince Rupert), 9 May, 30 May, 27 June, 29 August 1908. Wage rates on the Alaska project averaged $5.00 per day in 1908.

18 It should be noted that these figures did not come from the examination of payrolls but simply from testimony at the hearings. Virtually all the witnesses who discussed wage rates of railway construction were contractors or day labourers for contractors. There is no evidence that employees of the railway company testified.

19 NAC, RG 30, vol. 3355, file 1622, W.P. Hinton to Hansard, 1 March, Hansard to Hinton, 4 March 1913.

20 NAC, MG 30 E 406, LI-RA-MA Collection, vol. 20, Morse to N. Struve, 20 January 1907; BCARS, GR 684, vol. 3, files 13, 55, 155, 171-2; *Industrial Worker* (hereafter *IW*), 8 August

1912; BC, *SP*, Provincial Sanitary Inspector, 'Report, 1912,' M11-12; 'Report, 1913,' F 12-13.

21 BC, Royal Commission on Labour, *Report*, 8; BCARS, GR 684, vol. 3, files 13, 152, 15, 150, vol. 4, file 11, Welch to McNamera, 13 October 1913; Turkki, *Burns Lake*, 16; B. Boyd, 'The Coming of Steel,' *Pioneer Days in British Columbia*, vol. 2, ed. A.G. Downs (Surrey, BC 1975), 97; BCARS, Add Ms. 723, E.H. Allcock, Memoirs, 27. Worker transiency was not unique to the GTP during this period. For the National Transcontinental, see Bradwin, *The Bunkhouse Man*, 146. R.J. Anderson's 'Sharks and Red Herrings: Vancouver's Male Employment Agencies, 1898-1915,' *BC Studies* 98 (Summer 1993):44, notes similar behaviour in the logging industry.

22 All GTP grading contracts with FWS in British Columbia were drawn up on a GTP form. The sections concerning fair wages, working conditions, and liability for injury, sec. 20, 29-30, 48-50, were identical in each contract.

23 NAC, RG 30, vol. 3265, file 376, W.R. Allan to J. Symington, 16 January 1908; *Prince Rupert Optimist* (hereafter *Optimist*), 19 September 1910.

24 NAC, RG 30, vol. 3265, file 376, Mr. Mackenzie, opinion, January 1908; vol. 3304, file 969, Peck & Moore, Prince Rupert to Tate, 20 June 1910.

25 NAC, RG 30, vol. 3266, file 389, Symington to Tate, 13 February, Morse to Tate, 26 March, Tate to Morse, 14 February, Tate to Morse, 25 March 1908.

26 Supreme Court of British Columbia, Prince Rupert, file 42/10, *Malcomson* v. *FWS*.

27 NAC, RG 30, vol. 3265, file 376, Mackenzie, opinion, January 1908. The lawyer's advocacy of contributory negligence to turn away injury litigation followed the practice of many large employers in western North America. See P.N. Limerick, *The Legacy of Conquest: The Unbroken Past of the American West* (New York 1987), 109.

28 NAC, RG 30, vol. 3294, file 868.

29 Supreme Court of British Columbia, Prince Rupert, file 185/12, *Anderson* v. *GTP Ry.*

30 NAC, RG 30, vol. 3266, file 388; vol. 3301, file 928, A.E. McMaster to Dalrymple, 3 December, W. Fisher to McMaster, 17 December 1909; vol. 3323, file 1188, J. McGregor, Report, 15 April, Tate to Patmore, 5 October 1910.

31 NAC, RG 30, vol. 3332, file 1285, Inquest, 1 November 1910, Statements 29 October 1910.

32 Ibid., *passim.*

33 One worker angrily dismissed the protection that the liability laws afforded labour on the GTP as a cruel joke. BCARS, GR 684, vol. 4, file 13, 125.

34 *Empire*, 20 June, 25 July, 24 October, 17 November 1908; NAC, MG 27, II, D 8, Graham Papers, vol. 58, file 495, Schreiber to Graham, 14 December 1908.

35 NAC, RG 76, Immigration Branch, file 594511, pt. 2A, J.B.L. McDonald to Superintendent, 13 April 1909.

36 *Empire*, 8 May, 28 August, 11 September 1909; Anderson, 54; *Ottawa Free Press*, 14 September 1909; NAC, Graham Papers, vol. 58, file 495, Schreiber to Graham, 24 September 1909.

37 NAC, RG 76, file 594511, pt. 2A, Ross to Scott, 3 May, Wainwright to Scott, 18 July 1910. The government relaxed its restrictions the following day, not only for the GTP but also for other railways that had been importuning. See D. Avery, *'Dangerous Foreigners': European Immigrant Workers and Labour Radicalism in Canada, 1896-1932* (Toronto 1979), 28.

38 *Prince Rupert Journal* (hereafter *Journal*), 24 June, 4 August 1910; *Optimist*, 2 July 1910; *Daily Colonist* (Victoria), 24 August 1910.

39 *Journal*, 30 August 1910; *Optimist*, 25 August 1910.

40 *Vancouver Daily Province*, 6 September 1910; *Journal*, 9 September 1910, *Optimist*, 10 September 1910.

41 BCARS, GR 441, vol. 40, file 704/10, Hays to McBride, 16 December 1910; *Optimist*, 25 August, 19 September 1910.

42 *Optimist*, 9 September 1910.

43 Charles Rivers-Wilson at Grand Trunk Railway, Semi-Annual Meeting, 24 April 1909, quoted in A.J. Currie, *The Grand Trunk Railway of Canada* (Toronto 1957), 411; *Empire*, 26 October 1907; *Montreal Herald*, 28 September 1907. On the company's abortive negotiations with the Imperial Russian government for labourers, see D. Davies, 'The Pre-1917 Roots of Canada-Soviet Relations,' *Canadian Historical Review* 70, 2 (June 1989):191-2. Although most Canadians looked to the CPR construction as the precedent for importing Asian labour, the GTP engineering department, hired in large part from the Northern Pacific (NP), may well have suggested to the management that the company should follow the NP's practice of importing Japanese track labourers during the early 1900s. See Y. Ichioka, 'Japanese Immigrant Labor Contractors and the Northern Pacific and the Great Northern Railroad Companies, 1898-1907,' *Labor History* 21, 3 (Summer 1980):325-50.
44 On the objections of the British Columbia government to the Chinese workers who built part of the CPR line during the 1880s, see Patricia E. Roy, 'A Choice between Evils: The Chinese and the Construction of the Canadian Pacific Railway in British Columbia,' *CPR West*, ed. H. Dempsey (Vancouver 1984), 13-36. On the anti-Asian bills of McBride's predecessors, see R.E. Wynne, *Reaction to the Chinese in the Pacific Northwest and British Columbia, 1850-1910* (New York 1979 [PhD diss., 1964]), 382-98. BC, Minute #396/03, approved 28 August 1903; *Daily Colonist*, 1 September 1903. McBride used the request and the federal Liberal rejection of it for his own purposes in the provincial election campaign of 1903. P.E. Roy, *A White Man's Province: British Columbia Politicians and Chinese and Japanese Immigrants, 1858-1914* (Vancouver 1989), 161.
45 BC, Minute #143/04, approved 26 March 1904. The Liberal majority defeated an amendment to ban Asian labour. Commons, *Debates*, 25 May 1904, 3266-82.
46 NAC, RG 30, vol. 3249, file 152, Morse to Tate, 6 November 1906; MG 26 J, W.L.M. King Papers, vol. C 37, file 206, 30042.
47 NAC, MG 26 J, W.L.M. King Papers, vol. C 37, file 206, 29708, 29707; Canada, Royal Commission into ... Oriental Labourers, *Report* (1908), 41.
48 Commons, *Debates*, 23 January 1908, 1745-6. Duncan Ross, Liberal member for Yale-Cariboo and later subcontractor for the GTP, avoided libelling Bowser by implying that someone in the lawyer's office passed him a copy of Russell's statement.
49 *Vancouver Daily Province*, 1 February 1907. Martin Robin views the article as the product of a Tory propaganda machine grown bolder and wilder in its declamations. His explanation of Bowser's discovery of Russell's statement follows the one set out above. *The Rush for Spoils: The Company Province, 1871-1933* (Toronto 1971), 101.
50 BCARS, GR 441, vol. 87, file 420/07, McBride to Tatlow, 30 April 1907; vol. 87, file 251/07, McBride to Morse, 26 March 1907. In April, Morse produced a series of telegrams to prove to McBride that the head office had instructed Russell to stay out of the campaign and that the agent's action did not have the sanction of the GTP. In his admiring study of McBride, B.R.D. Smith evidently accepts the *Vancouver Daily Province* allegations at face value. While noting the two letters above, which cast doubt on the GTP role in the election, he nevertheless concludes that Russell gave full assistance to the provincial Liberals. 'Sir Richard McBride: A Study in the Conservative Party of British Columbia, 1903-1916' (MA thesis, History, Queen's University, 1959), 78.
51 *Victoria Daily Times*, 2 February 1907; Commons, *Debates*, 23 January 1908, 1753 (Ross). Wynne, *Reaction to the Chinese*, 402, describes the article as an irresponsible element of the campaign that many people were willing to believe. Smith, in 'Sir Richard McBride,' 72, mentions it only as a Conservative tactic to make the federal and provincial Liberals hang together. Roy, *White Man's Province*, 167-8, contends that the newspaper claim probably influenced few votes because of its exaggeration and its proximity to election day. She had earlier observed that while McBride might have won the election without the article, it certainly did him no harm. Roy, 'Progress, Prosperity and Politics,' 8.

52 NAC, RG 30, vol. 3280, file 637, Wainwright to McBride, dated 29 February 1908, GTP undertaking, 16 December 1908. The undertaking outside legislation accorded with the interest of the provincial government because it could not be disallowed by the federal government. Roy, *White Man's Province*, 257.

53 *Empire*, 16 November, 30 November 1907.

54 NAC, King Papers, 29704-5; *Empire*, 9 November, 16 November 1907; Royal Commission into ... Oriental Labourers, *Report*, 39, affidavit, 23 November 1907

55 NAC, RG 30, file 225, Tate to Chamberlin, 21 July 1910; *Optimist*, 15 September 1910.

56 For the company's appeal in 1908, see NAC, Graham Papers, vol. 58, file 495, Schreiber to Graham, 30 December 1908; *Empire*, 12 September 1908. For 1909, see *Ottawa Free Press*, 14 September 1909; BCARS, GR 441, vol. 35, file 397/09, Hays to McBride, 16 September, McBride to Hays, 31 September 1909; *Empire*, 30 October 1909. For 1910, see *Optimist*, 1 August 1910; *Daily News-Advertiser* (Vancouver), 11 October 1910; *Journal*, 18 October, 13 September 1910; NAC, Laurier Papers, 174533, Hays to Laurier, 7 September, enclosing *Vancouver Daily Province*, 6 September 1910; NAC, RG 30, vol. 3318, file 1166, Tate to McBride, 14 September 1910; BCARS, GR441, vol. 40, file 664/10, Hays to McBride, 16 October 1910. Roy, *White Man's Province*, 257-9, briefly discusses the GTP campaign.

57 BCARS, GR 441, vol. 47, file 635/12, Chamberlin to McBride, 7 September, McBride to Chamberlin, 10 September 1912.

58 Bradwin, *Bunkhouse Man*, 125; NAC, Graham Papers, vol. 58, file 495, Re *Andrisen et al. v. Peterson*, n.d.; *Empire*, 27 March 1909.

59 *Empire*, 27 March, 3 April, 10 April 1909.

60 Commons, *Debates*, 1909, 3939-41, 5 April; NAC, RG 27, Canada, Department of Labour, Strikes and Lockouts, file 3122, Daly to Department, 8 April 1909.

61 NAC, Graham Papers, vol. 58, file 495, Schreiber to Chamberlin, 29 April, 30 April, 3 May, Chamberlin to Schreiber, 4 May 1909.

62 Ibid., Van Arsdol to Kelliher, 7 May, Stewart to Chamberlin, 7 May 1909, Re *Andrisen et al. v. Peterson*.

63 Ibid., Chamberlin to Schreiber, 25 May 1909; NAC, Laurier Papers, 135717, Schreiber to Laurier, 9 June 1909.

64 NAC, Graham Papers, vol. 62, file 526, Williams and Manson to Templeman, 6 May 1909.

65 Ibid., Templeman to Graham, 25 May 1909.

66 *IW*, 20 May 1909; *Empire*, 6 March 1909.

67 BCARS, GR 441, vol. 98, file 764/09, Manson to McBride, 14 March 1909; *Empire*, 13 March, 20 March 1909; NAC, RG 27, file 3122, clipping dated 24 March.

68 NAC, RG 27, file 3122, Daly to Department, 8 April 1909; Graham Papers, vol. 58, file 495, Chamberlin to Butler, 28 April 1909; *Empire*, 15 May 1909.

69 Prince Rupert Board of Trade Minutes, 2 April, 8 April 1909; *Empire*, 3 April, 10 April, 17 April, 8 May 1909.

70 *Empire*, 6 May, 24 April, 27 March 1909; Daly to Department, 8 April 1909.

71 Graham Papers, vol. 58, file 495, Kelliher to Chamberlin, 26 April 1909.

72 BCARS, GR 441, vol. 34, file 271, Stewart to Kelliher, 27 April, Kelliher to Chamberlin, 6 May 1909.

73 Ibid., McBride to Chamberlin, 17 May, McBride to Manson, 31 May 1909; vol. 98, file 764/09, Manson to McBride, 30 June 1909.

74 BCARS, GR 441, vol. 34, file 271, Chamberlin to McBride, 14 July 1909.

75 *Labour Gazette*, September 1909, 'Wages on Construction of Grand Trunk Pacific R'y,' 323-5. Another version of this report with fewer quotations can be found in Department of Labour, *Annual Report* 1910, 143-6.

76 The findings of the court, of course, were that the strikers alone created the riot.

77 See 'The Battle of Kelly's Cut,' *Sound Heritage* 7, 4 (1978):8-11; P. Phillips, *No Power Greater:*

A Century of Labour in British Columbia (Vancouver 1967), 53-5; K. Luckhardt, 'Prince Rupert: A Tale of Two Cities,' *Sa Ts'e: Historical Perspectives on Northern British Columbia*, ed. T. Thorner (Prince George 1989), 313.

78 *Optimist*, 18 June, 1 August, 27 August 1910.

79 *Optimist*, 9 January 1911.

80 *Optimist*, 13 March 1911. Phillips, *No Power Greater*, 54-5, mistakes desire for action and maintains that the cruiser was used to suppress the strike, a claim that Cook and Brown repeat in their history of Canada for the period. R.C. Brown, and R. Cook, *Canada, 1896-1921: A Nation Transformed* (Toronto 1974), 108-9. Scott, *Plunderbund and Proletariat*, 164, debunks the *Rainbow* episode. *Optimist*, 4 March, 11 March 1911.

81 *Optimist*, 23 March 1911.

82 *Optimist*, 8 April, 6 April 1911; Prince Rupert, Police Detail Book, vol. 2, 6 April 1911.

83 NAC, RG 27, vol. 298, file 3326, W. Davis to King, telegram, 4 p.m., 8 April 1911, and letter, same date. A summary sheet in the file refers to a note of appeal, Morse to King, 8 April, in file 712.3, 'Correspondence RE Riot.' The latter file has not survived.

84 The only reference to the federal inspection by a Dr. Clendennan of the Department of Public Works is found in *IW*, 4 July 1912.

85 *IW*, 1 August 1912.

86 *Vancouver Daily Province*, 25 July 1912; BCARS, GR 56, BC, Provincial Police, vol. 11, file 5, Campbell to Wynn, 23 July, Wynn to Campbell, 26 July, 3 August, 7 August 1912.

87 *Vancouver Sun*, 26 July 1912, *Vancouver Daily Province*, 25 July 1912; BCARS, GR 56, vol. 11, file 5, Wynn to Campbell, 26 July 1912; *IW*, 8 August 1912.

88 BCARS, Add. Ms. 1192, B.M. Martin to Mrs. Medbury, 29 October 1912; *Evening Empire* (Prince Rupert), 30 August 1912.

89 NAC, RG 27, vol. 577, file 3554, V. St. John to Department, 6 August, FWS to Department, 26 August, N. Macintosh to Department, 18 August 1912.

90 *Vancouver Daily Province*, 25 July, 27 July, 1 August, 3 August, *Daily News* (Prince Rupert), 27 July, *BC Federationist*, 10 August, *IW*, 22 August 1912.

91 I have located references to *Bulletin*, no. 6, 28 September, and no. 8, 12 October 1912. Unfortunately, no numbers have survived.

92 *Federationist*, 17 August, *IW*, 8 August, 15 August, 12 September, 19 September 1912.

93 *Federationist*, 10 August, *IW*, 15 August (New Castle, Pennsylvania) *Industrial Solidarity*, 24 August 1912.

94 *Bulletin*, 28 August, reprinted in *Solidarity*, 14 September, *IW*, 19 September 1912.

95 *Solidarity*, 28 September, *IW*, 17 October 1912.

96 *Vancouver Daily Province*, 25 July 1912; *Labour Gazette*, September 1912, 239-40.

97 *Vancouver Daily Province*, 25 July, *Daily Colonist*, 4 August, *Daily News*, 1 August, *Vancouver Sun*, 7 August 1912.

98 *Evening Empire*, 12 August, 13 August, *Journal*, 20 August 1912.

99 *Journal*, 22 August, 23 August, 31 August 1912.

100 *Vancouver Sun*, 22 August *Vancouver Daily World*, 3 August, *Victoria Daily Times*, 5 August, *Evening Empire*, 30 August, 5 September 1912.

101 *Federationist*, 24 August 1912.

102 *Vancouver Sun*, 22 August, 21 August 1912.

103 *Vancouver Sun*, 1 August, 6 August, 23 August 1912.

104 *IW*, 8 August, 15 August 1912.

105 *IW*, 7 November; Avery *'Dangerous Foreigners,'* 29; *Evening Empire*, 5 October 1912.

106 BCARS, GR 684, vol. 4, files 13, 80, 28; NAC, RG 30, vol. 3284, file 690, pt. 2, Mehan to Hansard, 31 May 1913; *IW*, 31 October, 5 December, *Solidarity*, 7 December 1912.

107 *IW*, 14 November, 5 December, *Solidarity*, 7 December 1912.

108 *Solidarity*, 1 February 1913.

109   *Evening Empire*, 5 September 1912.
110   Royal Commission to Inquire into Railways and Transportation, *Report* (1917), xxv, 30; NAC, RG 43, vol. 577, file 18464, pt. 1, A.L. Ford, Report on Certain Matters Pertaining to the GTP Ry, 36. I have used a rate of 4 per cent, rather than 6 per cent, which the commission chose, because the rates on all bonds and loans that supported construction of the Mountain Section after 1905 were 4 per cent or higher. Schreiber allowed $9,882,672 as interest on first cost construction, but neither the government inspector nor the commission explains how this figure was calculated.
111   A.S. Cummings, 'Among the Railroad Builders,' *Christian Guardian*, 2 November 1910.

Chapter 5, 'A Frail Little City': Prince Rupert

1   This pattern obtains for transcontinentals that selected a terminus not yet served by railways and built across unsettled areas of the Pacific slope to reach it. Besides the GTP, the Central Pacific, Northern Pacific, Santa Fe, and CPR fall into this category.
2   W.K. Lamb, *The History of the Canadian Pacific Railway* (New York 1977), 124-6, 149-54, 182-3, 221-2; and J.A. Eagle, *The Canadian Pacific Railway and the Development of Western Canada, 1896-1914* (Montreal 1989), 230-1, offer comments on CPR development of real estate in Vancouver. For CPR actions that hindered the entry of other roads into Vancouver, see T.D. Regehr, *The Canadian Northern Railway: Pioneer Road of the Northern Prairies, 1895-1918* (Toronto 1976), 326-31, 361-3; and P. Veazy, 'John Hendry and the Vancouver, Westminster, and Yukon Railway: "It Would Put Us on Easy Street,"' *BC Studies* 59 (Autumn 1983):44-63.
3   Norbert MacDonald, 'The Canadian Pacific Railway Company and Vancouver's Development to 1900,' *BC Studies* 35 (Autumn 1977):3-35; MacDonald, '"C.P.R. Town": The City Building Process in Vancouver, 1860-1914,' *Shaping the Urban Landscape: Aspects of the City Building Process*, ed. A.F.J. Artibise and G.A. Stelter (Ottawa 1982), 382-412; and MacDonald, *Distant Neighbors: A Comparative History of Seattle and Vancouver* (Lincoln, NE, 1987), 21-43. Other works of urban historians that consider aspects of the CPR activity at its terminus include P.E. Roy, 'Railways, Politicians and the Development of Vancouver as a Metropolitan Centre' (MA thesis, History, University of Toronto, 1963); Roy, *Vancouver: An Illustrated History* (Toronto 1980); and R.A.J. McDonald, 'Business Leaders in Early Vancouver, 1886-1914' (PhD diss., History, University of British Columbia, 1977). For an exception that examines in part the railway role in waterfront development, albeit not on the major harbour, see D.M. Churchill, 'False Creek Development: A Study of the Actions and Interactions of the Three Levels of Government as They Affected the Public and Private Development of the Waterway and Its Land Basin' (MA thesis, Political Science and Sociology, University of British Columbia, 1953).
4   R.C. Nesbit, *'He Built Seattle': A Biography of Judge Thomas Burke* (Seattle 1961), 213-43; F.N. Mellen, 'The Development of the Toronto Waterfront during the Railway Expansion Era, 1850-1912' (PhD diss., Geography, University of Toronto, 1974); E.W. McGahan, *From Confederation to Nationalization 1867-1927*, vol. 1 of *The Port of Saint John* (Saint John 1982).
5   See Chapter 2, pp. 24-5.
6   B. Young, *George-Étienne Cartier: Montreal Bourgeois* (Montreal 1981), 117.
7   H. Kalman, *The Prince Rupert Heritage Inventory and Conservation Programme* (Prince Rupert 1983), 18, 20. In the only analysis of the plan based on primary sources, A.D. Crerar concludes that the scale, land use, and lot size of the design inhibited the growth of the city. 'Prince Rupert, B.C. – the Study of a Port and Its Hinterland' (MA thesis, Geography, University of British Columbia, 1951).
8   G. Hall, 'The Future Prince Rupert as Conceived by Landscape Architects,' *Architectural Record* 26, 2 (August 1909):103-4.

9 N.J. Johnston, 'The Frederick Law Olmsted Plan for Tacoma,' *Pacific Northwest Quarterly* 66, 3 (July 1975), 97-104; J. Reps, *Cities in the American West: A History of Frontier Planning* (Princeton 1979), 565-7. The quotation comes from Hall, 104.

10 Brett, Hall & Co., Report, 14 April 1908, edited version sent to Crerar. In a letter thirty years later to Crerar (8 July 1949), Hall maintains that the architects had allowed twenty-five-foot frontage for lots in the business section but strongly encouraged investors to buy double lots. Adams, *Town Planning and Conservation of Life* 2, 4 (July-September 1916):86; *Town Planning and Conservation of Life* 3, 1 (December 1916):22; M. Simpson, *Thomas Adams and the Modern Planning Movement, Britain, Canada, and the United States, 1900-1940* (London 1985), 88; Crerar, 'Prince Rupert,' 129-30.

11 NAC, RG 30, vol. 3265, file 375, pt. 1, Bacon, memo, n.d. (probably July 1908); file 375, pt. 2, Morse to Tate, 3 June 1908.

12 Ibid., file 375, pt. 2, Morse to Tate, 3 June 1908; pt. 6, Morse to Tate, 19 February 1908; Crerar, 'Prince Rupert,' 126.

13 BC, *Statutes*, 1908, chap. 19, schedule, secs. 4, 5; NAC, RG 30, vol. 3265, file 375, pt. 1, Morse to Tate, 3 June 1908.

14 NAC, RG 30, vol. 3265, file 375, pt. 1, Tate to Morse, 17 June, 19 June, 2 July, 3 July 1908.

15 BCARS, GR 1088, file 136695/12, E.L. James to F.J. Fulton, 23 July 1908; *Empire* (Prince Rupert), 18 July 1908.

16 NAC, RG 30, vol. 3265, file 375, pt. 1, Tate, memo, 27 July, Tate to Morse, telegram, n.d., Morse to Tate, 31 July 1908, Bacon, memo, n.d.; CN Edmonton, Engineering (hereafter CN Eng), file 913, E.A. Woods to H. Hansard, 26 February, Hansard to H. Philips, 15 August 1916.

17 NAC, RG 30, vol. 3265, file 375, pt. 1, Tate to Morse, 1 August, Morse to Tate, 3 August 1908; vol. 121702, file 25-10, Morse to Hays, 22 August 1908; BC, Minute, 512/08, approved 11 August 1908.

18 *Empire*, 27 February 1909.

19 NAC, RG 30, vol. 3278, file 585, lease, 1 May 1908; vol. 3285, file 721, Bacon to Kelliher, 25 April 1909; vol. 3259, file 255, pt. 1, C.E. Dewey, General Freight Agent to Donaldson, 28 November 1912; vol. 3412, file 2454, A. Rosevear to A. Hutcheon, 18 July 1913.

20 NAC, RG 30, vol. 3285, file 721, Tate to Chamberlin, 29 May 1909; vol. 3403, file 2329, pt. 1, Rosevear to McNicholl, 12 August 1914; CN Real Estate, Edmonton (hereafter CN RE), file foreshore, Russell to Morse, 1 March 1907, Ryley to Philips, 26 May, Ryley to Chamberlin, 31 January 1910.

21 NAC, RG 42, Canada, Department of Marine, vol. 159, file 28136, pt. 1, Tate to Brodeur, 3 April, W.P. Anderson to Minister, 9 April 1907, Anderson to Minister, 10 March 1910.

22 NAC, RG 30, vol. 3259, file 255, pt. 1, Kelliher to Tate, 20 March, Tate to Wainwright, 13 April 1910; RG 42, vol. 159, file 28136, pt. 1, Anderson, memo, 20 April, Brodeur, memo, 10 June, Anderson to Minister, 14 July 1910.

23 NAC, RG 30, vol. 3259, file 255, pt. 1, Tate to Wainwright, 28 January 1911; RG 42, vol. 159, file 28136, pt. 1, Tate to A. Johnston, 28 January, Anderson to Minister, 18 February 1911.

24 NAC, RG 42, vol. 159, file 28136, pt. 1, Wainwright to Brodeur, 8 May, Wainwright to A. Johnson, 31 May, 21 June, 15 August, Tate to Brodeur, 8 August 1911; RG 30, vol. 3259, file 255, pt. 1, Tate to Anderson, 2 October 1911.

25 NAC, RG 30, vol. 3259, file 255, pt. 1, Tate to A. Haydon, 5 August, Tate to Chamberlin, 18 September, Tate to Biggar, 2 October 1911; PC 1823, 11 August 1911.

26 NAC, RG 30, vol. 3259, file 255, pt. 1, Tate to Chamberlin, 23 September, Biggar to Tate, 28 September, 28 October 1911 enclosing Tate to Bowser, 23 October 1911, H.H. Hansard to Wainwright, 14 November 1912; RG 13, file 937/1913, E.L. Newcombe to Marine, 25 June 1912.

27 NAC, RG 30, vol. 3259, file 255, pt. 1, Tate to Chamberlin, 18 September 1911; RG 42, vol. 159, file 28136, pt. 1, memo, 2 February, 8 February, H.C. Clements to Minister, 7 February, 15 May 1912, Clements to Wainwright, 15 May, Wainwright to Hunter, 21 May, Clements to Stanton, 2 July 1912.
28 City Council, Minutes, 26 June 1912; NAC, RG 42, vol. 159, file 28136, pt. 1, Clements to Hazen, 26 August, Cochrane to Hazen, 2 October 1912.
29 CN RE, Wainwright to Chamberlin, 11 November 1912; NAC, RG 30, vol. 3259, file 255, pt. 1, Heaman to Hansard, 5 December, Dewey to Donaldson, 28 November, Donaldson to Hansard, 12 December 1912.
30 NAC, RG 42, vol. 159, file 28136, pt. 1, Hull to Lafleur, 12 August 1913, 17 October 1912; RG 30, vol. 3259, file 255, pt. 1, Heaman to Hansard, 5 December, 12 December 1912, Hansard to Donaldson, 17 February 1913.
31 BCARS, GR 1323, file 2977/8/13, Rogers to Bowser, 18 February 1913; NAC, RG 13, vol. 83, file 282/13, Stanton to Newcombe, 19 February, Newcombe to Stanton, 16 April 1913; RG 30, vol. 3259, file 255, pt. 1, Hansard to Biggar, 5 February 1913; PC 1487, 24 June 1913.
32 NAC, RG 30, vol. 3259, file 255, pt. 1, Proposed Settlement, n.d. RG 42, vol. 159, file 28136, pt. 1, Wainwright to Hazen, 14 February 1914; PC 625, 8 April 1914.
33 NAC, RG 30, vol. 3403, file 2329, pt. 1, lease draft, n.d., Hansard to Donaldson, 28 November, Dewey to Donaldson, 15 December 1912.
34 Ibid., Hansard to Donaldson, 22 January, Hansard to Department Minister of Marine, 8 November, Hansard to Stanton, 1 December, Hansard to Biggar, 8 December 1913; PC 661, PC 662, 31 March 1913.
35 NAC, RG 30, vol. 3403, file 2329, pt. 1, Dewey to Donaldson, 15 March 1913, Dewey to Donaldson, 8 March, Hansard to Patmore, 18 March 1914.
36 Ibid., McNicholl to Rosevear, 30 April, F.L. Perry to Dalrymple, 17 September, Hansard to Biggar, 29 September, Dalrymple to Biggar, 28 September 1914; RG 30, vol. 3259, file 255, pt. 1, Clements to McNicholl, 8 September, Rosevear to McNicholl, 12 August 1914.
37 NAC, RG 30, vol. 3403, file 2329, pt. 2, Biggar to Hansard, 3 November 1914, Quit Claim, 24 November 1914, Perry to Dalrymple, 4 February, Hansard to Biggar, 26 April 1915.
38 NAC, RG 30, vol. 3259, file 255, pt. 2, McNicholl to Rosevear, 27 May 1915, Hansard to Mehan, 7 January 1916, Patmore to Hansard, 9 May 1917.
39 See for example Lands, GR 1088, vol. 22, file 59532/12, petition of W.E. Williams et al., to McBride, 20 June 1913, Board of Trade to W.R. Ross, 5 September 1913, Manson to McBride, 22 January 1914, Board of Trade, Report, 10 February 1915, F.S. Wright to D.G. Stewart, 14 September 1915.
40 The name 'Prince Rupert' exceeded the contest limit of ten letters. Stevens, *Towards the Inevitable*, 175; *Canadian Annual Review*, 1906, 242; CN Rail, *Growing with Prince Rupert* (Montreal 1983), 6-7; C. Warman, 'The Grand Trunk Pacific,' *Scribner's Magazine*, 40 (July 1906):83.
41 NAC, RG 30, vol. 11717, file A-1, Philips, Prospectus, 2nd draft, September 1907, 3rd draft, October 1907.
42 Cy Warman, *At the Tip of the Rainbow* (Montreal 1908 [?]), 3, 5.
43 The first edition of the pamphlet (Montreal, January 1909), repeats large passages of Warman's article, 'Prince Rupert,' *Canadian Magazine* 30, 5 (March 1908):395-401, and plagiarizes several pages from T. Major, 'Our New Pacific Port,' *Dominion Magazine* 1, 6 (August 1906):9-13, and Prince Rupert Securities Ltd, *Prince Rupert ...* (Prince Rupert, October 1908). Hays had demanded that the prospectus contain the maps and plan. NAC, RG 30, vol. 11717, file A-1, Philips, memo, 24 October 1907.
44 NAC Records Centre, Winnipeg, CN Prairie and Pacific Regions Real Estate (hereafter PPRE), vol. 77, file O.H. Nelson, Nelson to Ryley, 14 September 1909, Donaldson to Ryley, 2 September 1912.

45 F.A. Talbot, *The Making of a Great Canadian Railway: ... Grand Trunk Pacific Railway ...* (London 1912), 316-17.

46 Corporation of the City of Prince Rupert, *Annual Report for 1916.*

47 NAC, RG 30, vol. 3625, file 375, pt. 1, Hays to Morse, 15 May 1908; vol. 3273, file 514, Bacon to E.B. Mackay, 10 April 1908; BCARS, GR 441, vol. 90, file 113/08, McBride to E.H. Rome, 10 February 1908.

48 CN RE, PR Reg. 3, Ryley to Morse, 23 June 1908; NAC, RG 30, vol. 3625, file 375, pt. 2, Morse to Tate, 3 August, Tate to Morse, 6 August 1908; *Empire,* 15 August 1908.

49 NAC, RG 30, vol. 3625, file 375, pt. 1, Tate to Fulton, 27 July 1908; pt. 2, Fulton to Hays, 16 October 1908; CN RE, PR Reg., file IB, Kelliher to Morse, 18 August 1908.

50 NAC, RG 30, vol. 3625, file 375, pt. 2, Brett & Hall to Tate, 4 February, Hays to Chamberlin, 12 February; pt. 5, Brett to Tate, 16 March, Tate to Ryley, 21 April 1909; RG 30 vol. 3289, file 786, Division of Lots, 1 March 1909.

51 Board of Trade to Hays in *Empire,* 6 March 1909; BCARS, GR 441, vol. 90, file 89/08, Board of Trade to McBride, 1 March 1909; CN RE, PR Reg. 3, Hays to Chamberlin, 24 March, D.H. Hays to Ryley, 20 April 1909; *Empire,* 27 February, 22 May 1909.

52 CN RE, PR Reg. 3, Rand to Ryley, 3 April, 14 April 1909; BCARS, GR 441, vol. 96, file 385/09, Rand to McBride, 17 April, Circular, 21 April 1909; *Empire,* 17 April 1909.

53 CN RE, PR Reg. 3, Rand to Ryley, 1 May 1909; *Empire,* 8 May 1909.

54 BCARS, Add. MS. 3, vol. 3, file 6, T.D. Pattullo to J.B. Pattullo, 26 March, vol. 2, file 14, Pattullo to W.G. Radford, 20 March 1909.

55 Lots 11 and 12, Block 20, Section 1. CN RE, PR Reg. 3, Minutes, 14 May 1909; *Empire,* 29 May 1909; BCARS, GR 1088, vol. 17, file 28281/12, Record of Sale, 28 June 1909; Development Company Statistics, 30 June 1910; GR 441, vol. 101, file 236/10, A.B. Mackenzie to McBride, 4 January, 23 March 1910.

56 BCARS, Add. MS. 3, vol. 3, file 1, A.B. Ballantyne to T.D. Pattullo, 13 September 1909; Crerar, 'Prince Rupert,' *Empire,* 12 June 1909; PR Reg. 3, Ryley to Chamberlin, 13 October 1909.

57 Museum of Northern British Columbia, D.I. McDowell Papers, McDowell to father, 27 March 1913.

58 NAC, RG 30, vol. 3310, file 1057, Hays to Chamberlin, 8 September 1911; PR Reg. 3, Ryley to Chamberlin, 20 July 1912.

59 David Bell, 'A History of Real Estate Development of Prince Rupert' (B. Commerce Essay, University of British Columbia, 1968), 48-9. BCARS, GR 1088, file 28281/12, Record of Sale, 3 January 1913; CN RE, PR Reg. 3, D.H. Hays to Chamberlin, 23 June, Ryley to Chamberlin, 20 July, 16 October 1912, Ryley to Donaldson, 3 July 1914.

60 On 30 June 1912, the GTP Development Company balance sheet showed a profit of $2,338,594.58 on its Prince Rupert property. This calculation rested on deferred payments as well as cash received. NAC, RG 30, vol. 1074. Crerar, 'Prince Rupert,' 129-37.

61 J.R. Stilgoe, *Metropolitan Corridor: Railroads and the American Scene* (New Haven 1983), 38.

62 T. Reksten, *Rattenbury* (Victoria 1978), 87-9; A.A. Barrett and R.W. Liscombe, *Francis Rattenbury and British Columbia: Architecture and Challenge in the Imperial Age* (Vancouver 1983),180-1; *Vancouver Daily Province,* 6 November 1906, cited in Barrett, 363, n. 30.

63 Reksten, *Rattenbury,* 112-13; *Contract Record,* 17 January 1912, 30 July 1913; Barrett and Liscombe, *Francis Rattenbury,* 226, 245; R. Hawker, 'Chateau Prince Rupert: A Forgotten Dream,' *B.C. Historical News* (1987):15-18.

64 For an analysis of the architectural styles incorporated into the design of the three buildings, see Barrett and Liscombe, *Francis Rattenbury,* 338-9.

65 *Canadian Railway and Marine World* (November 1913), 531; NAC, RG 30, vol. 3431, file 2748, Donaldson to Hansard, 15 October 1913; *Evening Empire* (Prince Rupert, weekly edition), 9 December 1914, 15 June 1915.

66 On Bogue's background and the outcome of the Seattle design, see MacDonald, *Distant*

Neighbours, 72-4; Bogue, 'The Development of the Waterfront and Railway Terminals, Prince Rupert, 8 March 1913' (typed volume bound with plans), 7, 12.

67 Bogue, 'Development of the Waterfront,' 35. The calculation is based on rates in the 1910 GTP contract for the extension of the line along the waterfront. NAC, RG 30, vol. 3259, file 255, pt. 2, Biggar to Hansard, 5 December 1914.

68 Bogue, 'Development of the Waterfront,' 39; NAC, RG 30, vol. 3337, file 1346, pt. 1, Woods to Biggar, 9 November, Hansard to Biggar, 1 December 1914.

69 NAC, RG 30, vol. 3371, file 1346, pt. 2, Hays to Biggar, 17 April 1908; *Canada Gazette*, 11 March 1908.

70 NAC, RG 30, vol. 3371, file 1346, pt. 2, Kirby to Hays, 10 May, quoted in Donnelly to Wainwright, 1 July 1910.

71 NAC, RG 11, vol. 4037, file 522-1A, Wainwright to Pugsley, 4 November, Lafleur to Hunter, 22 March 1910, Lafleur to Hunter, 8 July 1911. The company had made a preliminary estimate in October 1909 of $2 million.

72 Ibid., P.C.W. Howe, Report for Director of Naval Service, 8 December 1910, Lafleur to Hunter, 22 December 1910; PC 2250, 2 October 1911.

73 NAC, RG 11, vol. 4037, file 522-1A, Hunter to Lafleur, 11 January, Hunter to Secretary, 20 April; PC 916, 1 May 1911; PC 2250, 2 October 1911; Agreement, GTP and Government of Canada, 30 November 1911. NAC, RG 30, vol. 3371, file 1346, pt. 1, Chamberlin to Tate, 6 February 1912. When the department informed Wainwright of the act's proviso in the summer of 1911, the GTP vice-president glibly replied that the minister would take care of the matter. NAC, RG 11, vol. 4037, file 522-1A, Assistant Deputy Minster to Wainwright, 17 July, Wainwright to Hunter, 14 September 1911.

74 *Canadian Railway and Marine World* (February 1912), 92-6; *Montreal Star*, 10 May 1912.

75 NAC, RG 11, vol. 4037, file 522-B, memo, 18 October 1916; RG 30, vol. 3371, file 1346, pt. 1, Mehan to Hansard, 30 September, Scott to Hansard, 4 November 1913

76 NAC, RG 11, vol. 4037, file 522-1A, G. Brown to R. Desrochers, 27 April, 7 May, Chamberlin to Desrochers, 4 May, Desrochers to M. Donaldson, 18 May, J.D. McNiven, report, 26 May, Donaldson to Desrochers, 3 June 1914; Brown to Deputy Minister, 17 December 1914, Crothers to Rogers, 25 February 1915, Desrochers to Chamberlin, 1 March, with note on Donaldson agreement, 3 March 1915.

77 *Evening Empire* (weekly edition), 2 December 1914, 14 December, 29 December 1915.

78 NAC, Borden Papers, Cotton to Chamberlin, 12 August 1916; RG 11, vol. 4037, file 522-1B, Hull to Lafleur, 10 April 1916.

79 The name of the conflict probably stems from the ancestry of Houston and Police Constable Crippen and Bacon's American habit of labelling those who supported the GTP as white.

80 BCARS, GR 441, vol. 16, file 50, MLAs to Dunsmuir, 1 May 1901. For an examination of Houston's entire career, see P. Wolfe, 'Tramp Printer Extraordinary: British Columbia's John Houston,' *BC Studies* 40 (Winter 1978-9):5-31.

81 *Empire*, 20 July, 3 August, 17 August 1907; BCARS, GR 55, vol. 77, file April 1906-January 1908, U-V, Vickers, 8 September 1907.

82 *Empire*, 7 September, 14 September 1907. *History of Canadian Journalism* (1908).

83 Three accounts of the conflict survive: BCARS, GR 55, vol. 77, file April 1906-January 1908, U-V, L. Crippen, Details, 20 September 1907; Museum of Northern British Columbia, J. Fuller, 'Early Days in Prince Rupert,' 1950; and BCARS, G/P93/P64.2, R.W. Pillsbury 'The War between the Scotch and the Whites.' Pillsbury's account, compiled from his father's notes, appears in P. Bowman, *Land of Liquid Sunshine* (Prince Rupert 1982), 60-1.

84 Crippen, Details; NAC, RG 30, vol. 3261, file 264, J. Houston, permit, 30 September 1907; *Empire*, 28 September, 1907.

85 BCARS, GR 1088, file 136695/12, map drawn by Bacon dated 15 October 1907; NAC, RG 30, vol. 3261, files 264, 300, Pillsbury to Tate, 3 October 1907; *Empire*, 15 December 1907, 4

January, 7 March 1908.

86 *Empire*, 15 February 1908.

87 NAC, RG 30, vol. 3261, file 264, Bacon to McBride, 27 October, Bacon to Tate, 22 October, 30 December 1907; *Empire*, 28 December 1907.

88 *Empire*, 22 February 1908; NAC, RG 30, vol. 3261, file 264, Morse to Tate, 12 March, Bacon to Kelliher, 12 May, Bacon to Fulton, 21 August, 28 August 1908.

89 NAC, RG 30, vol. 3261, file 264, GTP, Government of British Columbia, Agreement, 14 October 1908. During the next session the government would pass legislation to exclude Kaien Island from mining claims.

90 *Empire*, 5 March 1909.

91 *Empire*, 12 June, 15 May 1909.

92 NAC, RG 30, vol. 3258, file 246, Tate to Morse, 11 January 1908; RG 30, vol. 3285, file 720, Tate to McBride, 3 June 1909, Tate to Biggar, 3 February, 17 February, Tate to Chamberlin, 17 February 1910; BC, *Statutes*, 1910, chap. 41, 'An Act to Incorporate the City of Prince Rupert'; *Empire*, 12 June 1909.

93 J.A. Lower, 'The Grand Trunk Pacific Railway and British Columbia' (MA thesis, History, University of British Columbia, 1939), 148-9; R.G. Large, *Skeena: River of Destiny* (Vancouver 1957), 143-4; Robin Fisher, *Duff Pattullo of British Columbia* (Toronto 1991), 95-8.

94 Though the GTP legal department in Winnipeg compiled a thick file on the matter, only a small portion of the file concerning matters long after the dispute was transferred to the National Archives.

95 Pattullo later charged that the official, Arthur Cuthbert, had assessed some GTP Development Company lots for $10 while assessing comparable private lots for $250. *Prince Rupert Optimist* (hereafter *Optimist*), 9 January, 9 May 1911; BCARS, GR 441, vol. 107, file 251/11, Board of Trade to Mayor, 17 September 1910.

96 BCARS, GR 441, vol. 39, file 369/10, Tate to McBride, 1 August 1910; *Optimist*, 2 May, 3 May 1910.

97 BCARS, GR 441, vol. 39, file 369/10, Tate to Chamberlin, 12 May, Tate to McBride, 12 May, 1 August, Chamberlin to Tate, 12 May 1910.

98 BCARS, GR 441, vol. 107, file 251/11, Hays to Stork, 28 June 1910; vol. 104, file 812/10, Hays to McBride, 28 June 1910.

99 BCARS, GR 441, vol. 39, file 369/10, Stork to Hays, 7 July 1910; *Optimist*, 19 July 1910; *Prince Rupert Journal* (hereafter *Journal*), 19 July 1910.

100 BCARS, GR 441, vol. 107, file 251/11, Hays to Stork, 20 July 1910; vol. 103, file 694/10, Hays to McBride, 23 July 1910; file 369/10, Chamberlin to Tate, 27 July, Tate to McBride, 1 August 1910.

101 *Journal*, 30 August, 6 September, 13 September 1910; *Optimist*, 29 August, 6 September 1910.

102 *Journal*, 9 September 1910, *Optimist*, 17 September 1910.

103 *Evening Empire*, 22 September 1910, *Journal*, 30 August, 6 September 1910, *Optimist*, 30 August 1910. On the purchase, see *Optimist*, 22 October 1910, *Journal*, 23 December 1910. Although Pattullo denied that he determined the paper's editorial policy, he had an interest in the company that acquired it. BCARS, Pattullo Papers, vol. 4, file 34, Prince Rupert Publishing Co., 10 shares, 1 November 1910, vol. 5, file 4, Pattullo to Radford, 19 February 1911.

104 *Optimist*, 7 September 1910; BCARS, GR 441, vol. 107, file 251/11, A.J. Morris et al., to Mayor, 17 September 1910.

105 *Evening Empire*, 8 October 1910, *Optimist*, 7 October, 29 December 1910; Corporation of the City of Prince Rupert, Minutes, 3 October, 5 October, 6 October, 7 October, 10 October, 24 October, 21 November 1910; NAC, RG 30, vol. 3323, file 1190, Tate to Chamberlin, 15 October 1910.

106   BCARS, GR 441, vol. 107, file 251/11, Hays to E.A. Woods, 26 October 1910; NAC, RG 30, vol. 3323, file 1209, Tate to Chamberlin, 28 October 1910.
107   *Optimist*, 4 November 1910. The premier's tacit support for the GTP in this dispute may have stemmed from Hays's threat to abandon west end construction or from a desire to discomfit the Liberal council.
108   BCARS, GR 441, vol. 107, file 251/11, Prince Rupert City Council, memo to Tate, 15 December 1910.
109   *Optimist*, 3 January 1911, 8 December 1910.
110   BCARS, GR 441, vol. 107, file 251/11, Tate to McBride, 22 February 1911; *Optimist*, 13 March 1911, *Evening Empire*, 16 March 1911. In exchange for this tax, the council expected the company to transfer land set aside for parks and a 100-foot waterfront.
111   *Daily News* (Prince Rupert), 8 May 1911; BCARS, GR 441, vol. 107, file 251/11, Manson to McBride, 20 March 1911; Minutes, 15 May, 29 May 1911.
112   *Daily News*, 8 June 1911; *Journal*, 20 June 1911.
113   *Evening Empire*, 30 June 1911; *Journal*, 3 September 1911; *Daily News*, 5 September 1911.
114   Because no document survives that indicates the company's expenditure on the works before the halt, one must resort to an estimate. The terminals were started in 1906 and largely completed by 1914. According to the 1917 royal commission's valuation and method of calculation, the GTP had expended at least $900,000 on terminal construction alone by the summer of 1910. With a 3 per cent rate, the interest charge for a nine-month period was more than $60,000. This estimate is probably lower than the actual cost, however, because the company also stopped work on its extension to Block K. It also appears that the halt in Prince Rupert slowed work on GTP main line in the Skeena Valley.
115   NAC, RG 30, vol. 1074, Development Company, Minute Book, Statistics to 30 June 1914. In 1917, the Royal Commission on Railways estimated the first cost of construction of the GTP terminals in Prince Rupert at $1,623,409. *Report*, 53.
116   Mellen, 'Development of the Toronto Waterfront,' 165-81.

Chapter 6, 'A Hold-up Business': Acquisition of Indian Lands

1   While the Department of Indian Affairs formally designated the latter reserve as 'Kitsumkaylum,' this account employs the community's preferred orthography, 'Kitsumkalum.'
2   F.A. Talbot, *The Making of a Great Canadian Railway: ... Grand Trunk Pacific Railway ...* (London 1912), 228-30.
3   See, for example, D. Brown, *Hear That Lonesome Whistle Blow: Railroads in the West* (New York 1977), 85-93; and P. Berton, *The Last Spike: The Great Railway, 1881-1885* (Toronto 1971), 232-7.
4   P.W. Gates, *Fifty Million Acres: Conflicts over Kansas Land Policy, 1854-1890* (Ithaca, NY 1954), 106-52; H.C. Miner, *The Corporation and the Indian: Tribal Sovereignty and Industrial Civilization in Indian Territory, 1865-1907* (Columbia, MS 1976), 1-117; and D.J. Smith, 'Procuring a Right-of-Way: James J. Hill and Indian Reservations, 1886-1888' (Unpublished graduate paper, University of Montana, 1983). W.T. White kindly provided me with a copy of the latter source.
5   D. Clayton categorizes as discourses the documents as well as the geographies of earlier white-Native interactions on the Skeena River. 'Geographies of the Lower Skeena,' *BC Studies* 94 (Summer 1992):29-58.
6   Several Native communities along the GTP line have contemplated or commenced actions against the GTP's corporate successor, CN, or the Canadian government, because it allegedly failed to defend Native interests against the GTP.
7   J.A. McDonald, 'Bleeding Day and Night: The Construction of the Grand Trunk Pacific Railway across Tsimshian Reserve Lands,' *Canadian Journal of Native Studies* 10, 1 (1990):64.

8   *Delgamuukw* v. *British Columbia*, Proceedings, vol. 292, 22001, 6 November 1989.
9   J.A. Lower, 'The Grand Trunk Pacific Railway and British Columbia' (MA thesis, History, University of British Columbia, 1939), 115-16; F.E. Runnalls, 'Boom Days in Prince George,' *British Columbia Historical Quarterly* 8, 4 (October 1944):297-8; W.J. West, 'The "B.X." and the Rush to Fort George,' *British Columbia Historical Quarterly* 13, 3-4 (July-October 1949):175-7; N.B. Holmes, 'The Promotion of Early Growth in the Western Canadian City: A Case Study of Prince George, B.C., 1909-1915' (B.A. thesis, University of British Columbia, 1974), 18-19; M. Whitehead, 'Introduction,' *They Call Me Father: Memoirs of Nicolas Coccola* (Vancouver 1988) 48-50; and B. Christensen, *Prince George: Rivers, Railways, and Timber* (Burlington 1989), 35-6.
10 HBCA, B 280/a/8-9, Journal of Occurrences at Fort George, 1902-11.
11 NAC, RG 10, vol. 4038, file 325224, pt. 1, J. McDougall to Secretary, 25 July 1910; HBCA, B 280/e/3, E.K. Beeston, Inspection Report on Fort George, 13-14 September 1900; BCARS, Morice to Indian Superintendent, Victoria, 26 May 1903; Canada, Royal Commission on Indian Affairs for the Province of British Columbia, Meeting with the Fort George Tribe, 30-1, July 1914. For an account of the missionary impact on the Carrier before the advent of the GTP, see D. Mulhall, *Will to Power: The Missionary Career of Father Morice* (Vancouver 1986).
12 NAC, RG 30, vol. 3268, file 426, Kelliher to F. Morse, n.d. CN RE, file Prince George Reg. 1, Pope to Ryley, 20 May 1909.
13 CN RE, file Prince George Reg. 1, Kelliher to Ryley, 6 October 1909, Kelliher to Morse, 1 April 1908.
14 NAC, RG 30, vol. 3268, file 426, Tate to Morse, 25 April, Kelliher to Tate, 8 May 1908.
15 CN RE, file Prince George Reg. 1, Ryley to Chamberlin, 9 March 1910.
16 NAC, RG 10, vol. 4038, file 325224, pt. 1, Tate to Pedley, 9 May, 9 June, Pedley to Tate, 13 May, 10 June 1908. On the nature and duration of the dispute, see Chapter 2, n. 70.
17 NAC, RG 10, vol. 4038, file 325224, pt. 1, Tate to Pedley, 8 December, Pedley to Tate, 28 December 1908. For an examination of the confusing actions of the provincial and federal governments leading to the McKenna-McBride Agreement of 1912, see R. Galois, 'The Indian Rights Association, Native Protest Activity and the "Land Question" in British Columbia, 1903-1916,' *Native Studies Review* 8, 2 (1992):1-34.
18 NAC, RG 30, vol. 3268, file 426, Morse to Tate, 9 January, Tate to Morse, 12 January 1909.
19 Ibid., Tate to Chamberlin, 17 August, Tate to Wainwright, 7 September, 18 October, Tate to Ryley, 18 October 1909, Wainwright to Tate, 6 September, 23 October, 6 November 1909.
20 Ibid., Chamberlin to Tate, 12 November 1909; NAC, RG 10, vol. 4038, file 325224, pt. 1, Pedley to Oliver, 11 December, Oliver to Pedley, 16 December 1909.
21 NAC, RG 30, vol. 3305, file 987, Hays to Chamberlin, 29 December 1909, Memorandum, n.d.; BCARS, GR 1440, file 359/10, Tate to Ellison, 21 January 1910; RG 30, vol. 3305, file 987, McBride to Tate, 22 February 1910.
22 CN RE, file Prince George Reg. 1, Ryley to Philips, 13 June, Chamberlin to Ryley, 21 June 1910.
23 NAC, RG 10, vol. 4038, file 325224, pt. 1, Millar to Department, 17 August, 22 August, S. Bray, Memorandum, 16 October 1910.
24 F.A. Talbot, *The New Garden of Canada: ... Undeveloped New British Columbia* (London 1911), 161-2.
25 NAC, RG 10, vol. 4038, file 325224, pt. 1, J. McDougall to Secretary, 25 July 1910.
26 Ibid., McDougall to McLean, 20 December 1910, 3 January 1911. Most of the material concerning negotiations with the band has been removed from both the GTP legal and land department files. The relevant DIA file throws some light on GTP strategy during this period, however.
27 Ibid.; *Fort George Tribune*, 3 December 1910; *Tribune*, n.d., reprinted in *Vancouver Daily*

World, 23 December 1910.

28 Oblate Archives, Vancouver, Diocese of Prince George, file 3/14, Coccola to P. Bunoz, 8 February 1911; *Fort George Tribune,* 3 December 1910; *Fort George Herald* (South Fort George), 14 January 1911.

29 NAC, RG 10, vol. 4038, file 325224, pt. 1, Pedley to Wainwright, 11 January, Bellot to Pedley, 14 January, Pedley to Bellot, 16 January 1911.

30 NAC, RG 30, vol. 12704, file 29, Memorandum, 22 February 1911.

31 Ibid., Wainwright to Hays, 22 February 1911; vol. 1073, Chamberlin to Hays, 25 February 1911.

32 NAC, RG 10, vol. 4038, file 325224, pt. 1, Scott to Pedley, 24 February, Pedley to Scott, 25 February, Pedley to Bellot, 26 February 1911.

33 NAC, RG 10, vol. 4038, file 325224, pt. 1, Chamberlin to Wainwright, 12 April 1911, enclosed in McDonald to Secretary, 18 April 1911.

34 *Fort George Herald,* 3 June 1911; NAC, RG 30, vol. 3286, file 426, Tate to Hansard, 12 June 1915, Philips to Biggar, 22 June 1915.

35 Talbot, *Making of a Great Canadian Railway,* 228-30. Talbot sent the book to the publishers in the summer of 1911.

36 NAC, RG 10, vol. 4038, file 325224, pt. 1, Pedley to McAllen, 2 August, Coccola to Pedley, 29 August, McAllan to McLean, 14 September 1911.

37 Whitehead, *They Call Me Father,* 164; Diocese of Prince George, 3/14, Copy of sealed Undertaking of Durnford, 29 August 1911, enclosed in Coccola to Bunoz, 30 August 1911.

38 Although Durnford stayed at the Hudson's Bay post for two weeks, the author of the post journal did not know his employers. HBCA, B 280/a/9, Journal, 28-30 August 1911. In first reporting the sale, both Coccola and the editor of the *Fort George Herald* assumed that Durnford was a GTP agent. Diocese of Prince George, file 3/14, Coccola to Bunoz, 30 August 1911; *Herald,* 2 September 1911.

39 *Herald,* 21 October 1911; NAC, RG 10, vol. 4038, file 325224, pt. 1, McAllan to McLean, 14 September, Coccola to Pedley, 29 August 1911.

40 *Herald,* 28 October 1911; NAC, RG 46, vol. 65, file 146, Hearing, 5 March 1912, 2574.

41 NAC, RG 10, vol. 4038, file 325224, pt. 1, Wainwright to Pedley, 23 September, Pedley to Ramsden, 30 September 1911; BC, Minute of Executive Council #226/11, 10 October 1911.

42 NAC, RG 10, vol. 4038, file 325224, pt. 1, Pedley to Coccola, 2 October 1911; Whitehead, *They Call Me Father,* 164.

43 NAC, RG 10, vol. 4038, file 325224, pt. 1, Rogers to Cory, 28 October, Crawford to Rogers, 30 October 1911, enclosing copy of South Fort George Board of Trade to Burrell.

44 Ibid., Ramsden to McLean, 11 November, Scott to Ramsden, 17 November 1911, Instrument No. R 10675 – Surrender, 18 November 1911.

45 Runnalls, 'Boom Days,' 297-8; West, 'Rush to Fort George,' 175-6. A search of relevant court records in Montreal, Toronto, and Vancouver produced no evidence that a writ had been filed.

46 CN RE, file Prince George Reg. 1, Wainwright to Carruthers, 22 February 1912.

47 Whitehead, *They Call Me Father,* 164; Diocese of Prince George, 3/14, Coccola to Bunoz, 6 October, 26 November 1913; BCARS, GR 1440, file 2436/12, Coccola to Ross, 6 October 1913.

48 NAC, RG 30, vol. 3286, file 426, Hansard to Biggar, 8 June 1915.

49 Whitehead, *They Call Me Father,* 164. The GTP did not receive the patent to the reserve until 8 July 1912.

50 NAC, RG 10, vol. 4038, file 325224, pt. 2, Philips to Wainwright, 15 August, W.J. McAllan to McLean, 22 September 1913. McAllan later described the eviction melodramatically in 'The Moving of the Fort George Indians,' *Cariboo and Northwest Digest* 4, 2 (1948):52-7.

51 NAC, RG 10, vol. 8082, file 984/31-2, E. Lorenz to C.C. Van Arsdol, 14 May 1908.

52 Ibid., Lorenz to Van Arsdol, 1 June 1908; Canada, *Revised Statutes*, 1906, chap. 37, Railway Act, sec. 175; chap. 81, Indian Act, sec. 46; RG 30, vol. 3271, file 487, McLean to Tate, 7 July 1908.

53 NAC, RG 10, vol. 8082, file 984/31-2, Tate to Pedley, 20 January 1909.

54 NAC, RG 10, vol. 1589, R.E. Loring to Vowell, 31 October 1908; McDonald, 'Bleeding Day and Night,' 42-9; McDonald, 'Trying to Make a Life: The Historical Political Economy of Kitsumkalum' (PhD diss., Anthropology, University of British Columbia, 1985), 341, 393-4. For a brief account of similar GTP disputes with Native bands upriver from Kitsumkalum, see R. Galois, 'The History of the Upper Skeena Region, 1850 to 1927,' *Native Studies Review* 9, 2 (1993-4):154-5.

55 CN RE, file 1014/0, Pope to Tate, 1 July 1909; NAC, RG 30, vol. 3755, file BC 616, Permit No. 3417, dated 10 December 1908, in Tate to McLean, 24 August 1909.

56 'The Indian Land Question: Interview with the Land Committee, Naas River,' *Hagaga* (May 1910):1. R. Galois directed me to this source.

57 NAC, RG 10, file 986/31-2-7-1, McLean to Vowell, 25 January, Lorenz to Vowell, 26 April 1909.

58 Ibid., Lorenz to Vowell, 26 April, Tate to McLean, 8 May 1909. The deposit was $1,100 to cover costs on five other reserves as well as Kitsumkalum.

59 Ibid., McLean to Vowell, 14 May, Pope to Lorenz, 13 May 1909, quoted in Lorenz to Vowell, 25 June 1909.

60 Ibid., Johnson to Department, 14 May, Lorenz to Vowell, 19 May 1909.

61 Ibid., McLean to Johnson, 14 June, Lorenz to Vowell, 12 June, McLean to Vowell, 21 June 1909.

62 NAC, RG 30, vol. 3755, file BC 616, Dempster to Pope, quoted in Pope to Chamberlin, 12 July 1909. Perhaps because of the distance between the graveyard and the village, the right-of-way agent described the graveyard as a part of the adjacent reserve along the line, Zimarcord No. 3.

63 CN RE, file 1014/0, Pope to Chamberlin, 2 July 1909; NAC, RG 10, file 986/31-2-7-1, Lorenz to Vowell, 17 July 1909; RG 30, vol. 3755, file BC 616, Chamberlin to W.H. Biggar, 2 July, Tate to McLean, 2 July, McLean to Tate, 7 July 1909.

64 CN RE, file 1014/0, Dempster to Pope, 16 August 1909; NAC, RG 10, file 986/31-2-7-1, Agreement, GTP and Chief Johnson, 10 August, Lorenz to Vowell, 13 August, 17 August 1909.

65 NAC, RG 30, vol. 3755, file BC 616, Chamberlin to Tate, 11 August, Copy of McLean to Vowell, 12 August, Tate to McLean, 13 August, Van Arsdol to Pope quoted in Pope to Tate, 16 August, Tate to Chamberlin, 17 August 1909; RG 10, file 986/31-2-7-1, Vowell to McLean, 19 August 1909.

66 NAC, RG 30, vol. 3755, file BC 616, Tate to Pope, 24 August, Tate to Pedley, 26 August 1909.

67 Ibid., McLean to Tate, 28 August, Tate to McLean, 28 August, Tate to Chamberlin, 28 August 1909; NAC, RG 10, file 986/31-2-7-1, Pedley to Vowell, 21 September 1909.

68 NAC, RG 10, file 986/31-2-7-1, Vowell to McLean, 5 October, Van Arsdol to Vowell, 30 October 1909; PC 2026, 1 October 1909.

69 NAC, RG 10, file 986/31-2-7-1, Tate to McLean, 18 November 1909. Settlements on the Kitsumkalum precedent occurred at the Kitselas, Kitwanga, Andimaul, and Kitseguecla reserves. NAC, RG 10, vol. 8684, file 986/31-2-6-1, R.E. Loring, Indian Agent at Hazelton, to Secretary, 18 July 1910. Royal Commission on Indian Affairs for the Province of British Columbia, Meeting ... with the Port Essington Band or Tribe of Indians, 25 September 1915.

70 Harold Cardinal, *The Unjust Society: The Tragedy of Canada's Indians* (Edmonton 1969).

71 NAC, RG 10, vol. 1583, Kitwanga and Kitwancool to Loring, 18 October 1909.

72   McDonald, the anthropologist of Kitsumkalum, underscores the power of the railway company as well as its contempt for the desires of the Native people. 'Bleeding Day and Night,' *passim*.

Chapter 7, 'In the Hollow of the Corporation's Hand': Prince George

1   F.E. Runnalls, 'Boom Days in Prince George,' *British Columbia Historical Quarterly* 8, 4 (October 1944):281-306; Runnalls, *A History of Prince George* (Vancouver 1946), 78-150; W.J. West, 'The "B.X." and the Rush to Fort George,' *British Columbia Historical Quarterly* 13, 3-4 (July-October 1949):175-82. J.A. Lower, 'The Grand Trunk Pacific Railway and British Columbia' (MA thesis, History, University of British Columbia, 1939), 115-17, disagrees.

2   The most relevant of Artibise's many studies of boosterism is 'In Pursuit of Growth: Municipal Boosterism and Urban Development in the Canadian Prairie West, 1871-1913,' *Shaping the Urban Landscape: Aspects of the Canadian City-Building Process*, eds. G.A. Stelter and A.F.J. Artibise (Ottawa 1982), 116-47. For the application of boosterism to Prince George, see N.B. Holmes, 'The Promotion of Early Growth in the Western Canadian City: A Case Study of Prince George, B.C., 1909-1915' (B.A. thesis, University of British Columbia, 1974). For a contrary view, see F. Leonard, 'Grand Trunk Pacific and the Establishment of the City of Prince George, 1911-1915,' *BC Studies* 63 (Autumn 1984):29-54.

3   *Fort George Herald* (hereafter *Herald*), 22 July 1911.

4   Runnalls, *History of Prince George*, 95-106; and Holmes, 'Promotion of Early Growth,' 12-18.

5   NRS, 'Facts – What British Columbia Offers You,' (1910); NRS, 'Fort George, B.C., A Pictorial and Descriptive Album ...' (1912); Fort George [Townsite] Board of Trade, 'An Introduction to Fort George ...' (1912); *Herald*, 1 June 1912.

6   A. Bumby, 'The Sales Campaign of George J. Hammond and the Natural Resources Security Company,' (Undergraduate paper, History, College of New Caledonia, 1981); NAC, RG 46, vol. 79, file 175, Hearing, 6 May 1913, 3112. The *Herald* and the GTP investigated Hammond in 1912 and 1913 respectively, but neither discovered the holding companies.

7   NRS, 'Facts,' 'Fort George.'

8   HBCA, A 12/L, Misc. 28, J. Thomson to F.C. Ingrams, 7 December 1911.

9   *Saturday Night*, 30 July, 27 August, 3 September, 24 September 1910.

10   NAC, RG 30, vol. 3371, file 1811, NRS, Application to BRC, 17 January 1912, 2-3; RG 46, vol. 65, file 146, 2587, Hearing, 5 March 1912.

11   RG 46, vol. 65, file 146, 2591-92; *Herald*, 20 January 1912.

12   NAC, RG 30, vol. 1074, GTP Development Company, Minute Book, II, Chamberlin to Hays, 25 February 1911, 282-4.

13   Ibid., Hays to Chamberlin, 3 March 1911, 284-6.

14   NAC, RG 46, vol. 65, file 146, 2567-70; NAC, RG 30, vol. 3371, file 1811, NRS, Reply, 22 February 1912, 2.

15   NAC, RG 46, vol. 65, file 146, 2573; RG 30, vol. 3371, file 1811, NRS, Reply, 22 February 1912, 5; BCARS, Department of the Attorney General, GR 1323, file 2919-14-13, NRS, Reply, January 1913. In a telegram to Hammond on 26 June 1911, Hays repeated the demand for cash.

16   NAC, RG 30, vol. 3371, file 1811, NRS, Reply, 22 February 1912, 5-6, reproduces Hammond to Hays, 5 July 1911.

17   NRS, Reply, 22 February 1912, 5, 15-16; NRS, 'Official Location of the GTP Ry Station Grounds and Divisional Yards, Fort George,' September 1911.

18   NRS, Application, 17 January 1912.

19   *Herald*, 20 July 1912, Hays to Daniell, 13 February 1912. Part of the letter was printed earlier, 24 February 1912.

20 NRS, Application, 17 January 1912, Reply, 22 February 1912, GTP, Answer, 17 February 1912, reprinted in GTP, 'Appeal from the Board of Railway Commissioners for Canada ...,' July 1913; NAC, RG 46, vol. 79, file 175, 3168.
21 NAC, RG 46, vol. 65, file 146, 2655–66.
22 *B.C. Saturday Sunset* (Vancouver), 9 March 1912.
23 *Herald*, 18 March 1912, excerpt of Philips to Daniell, n.d.
24 The *Herald* first published a plan of the townsite on 12 April 1913. Precise distances of various station sites appear in RG 46, vol. 79, file 175, 3096.
25 Brett, Hall to editor, not dated, printed in *Prince George Post*, 16 January 1915.
26 The *Herald* first published a plan of the townsite on 12 April 1913. K. Sedgwick, 'The "City Beautiful" Look,' *Prince George Citizen*, 1 June 1985.
27 NAC, RG 46, vol. 79, file 175, 3198; vol. 1432, file 21418, Norton to BRC, 12 June 1915.
28 GTP application, 24 January 1913, BRC, Order No. 18902, 31 March 1913, reprinted (with corrections) in GTP, Appeal, 69.
29 Although the incorrect application and BRC order have been removed, the accompanying GTP right-of-way map with the incorrect mileage remains in the BRC file. See also NAC, RG 46, vol. 79, file 175, 3095–96.
30 NAC, RG 46, vol. 1432, file 21418, Pringle to BRC, 5 April 1912; RG 46, vol. 79, file 175, 3090.
31 NAC, RG 46, vol. 79, file 175, 3188, 3193.
32 NAC, RG 46, vol. 65, file 146, 2653–2665; RG 46, vol. 1432, file 21418, Mountain to Scott, 9 May 1913; BRC, Order No. 19037, 14 May 1913.
33 *Daily News-Advertiser* (Vancouver), 14 May 1913.
34 NAC, RG 30, vol. 3408, file 2438, Hansard to Biggar, 18 May, Biggar to Hansard (telegram and letter), 21 May 1913.
35 *Herald*, 7 June 1913.
36 BC, *Statutes*, 1912, chap. 34.
37 NAC, RG 30, vol. 3420, file 2561, Kelliher to Hansard, 1 April 1913; CN RE, file Prince George Reg. 1, Ryley to M. Donaldson, 14 June, Chamberlin to Donaldson, 23 July, Donaldson to Ryley, 24 July 1913.
38 Talbot, *New Garden*, 160-78; *Making of a Great Canadian Railway*, 228-30; NAC Records Centre, Winnipeg, PPRE, vol. 108, file Auction, Philips to Ryley, 22 July, Ryley to Philips, 9 October 1913.
39 CN RE, file Prince George Reg., 2, Ryley to F. Ellis, n.d.
40 Ryley to Renwick, 12 September 1913; CN Real Estate, Montreal, GTP Development Company file, 'Lot 343' [map], 4 September 1913.
41 NAC, RG 30, vol. 3371, file 1811, Ryley to Philips, 17 November 1913; *Herald*, 20 September 1913; NAC Records Centre, Winnipeg, PPRE, vol. 108, file Fort Rouge Land Co., Bissell to Hansard, 23 August 1919.
42 NAC, RG 30, vol. 3408, file 2438, Hansard to Biggar, 23 June 1913. John Hill, Jr., published a book entitled *Gold Bricks of Speculation ...* (Chicago 1904) concerning the operation of confidence rackets in the American Midwest at the turn of the century in which Hammond is mentioned, 29-35. GTP, Appeal from the Board of Railway Commissioners for Canada (Montreal 1913).
43 NAC, RG 30, vol. 3371, file 1811, Salmon to Hansard, 15 July, 18 July, 2 August, 6 August, 12 August, Hansard to Salmon, 19 July, 30 July, 2 August, 8 August 1913.
44 Ibid., Hansard to Biggar, 22 January 1914; BRC 95, E. Haight to Drayton, 13 November 1913.
45 NAC, RG 30, vol. 3371, file 1811, Hansard to Biggar, 22 January, 26 January 1914.
46 NAC, RG 46, vol. 1432, file 21418, GTP Appeal, 1–3; RG 2/8, vol. 1, file Grand Trunk Pacific, Before the Governor-General in Council, Appeal of the GTP ... 31 January 1914, 28.
47 BCARS, GR 1323, file 2919-14-13, NRS Reply, 1-6.
48 NAC, RG 2/8, vol. 1, Appeal of the GTP ... 31 January 1914, 20.

49   PC 374, 9 February 1914.

50   *B.C. Saturday Sunset*, 1 February 1914; NRS, 'Trains Are Now Running to Fort George' (March [?] 1914); *Fort George Tribune*, Transcontinental Edition (July [?] 1914).

51   NAC, RG 30, vol. 3371, file 1811, Biggar to Hansard, 24 February 1914; NAC, RG 30, vol. 3408, file 2438, Ryley to Hansard, 18 March, 24 March, 26 March, Hansard to Biggar, 21 March 1914.

52   NAC, RG 30, vol. 3408, file 2438, Application of F.L. Murdoff and A.H. Hunter, 2 April 1914, NRS, Answer, 6 May 1914, Fort George Board of Trade, Answer, 7 May 1914.

53   NAC, RG 46, vol. 1432, file 21418, Scott, Decision, 14 May, Haight to Drayton, 31 May, Drayton to Perry, 3 June, Drayton to Kerr, 16 July, Kerr to Drayton, 28 July, Goodeve, Note, 11 August 1914.

54   NAC, RG 30, vol. 3408, file 2438, Hansard to Ryley, 5 September, 5 November, Hansard to Perry, 12 November 1914.

55   NAC, RG 30, vol. 3408, file 2438, Hansard to Biggar, 10 November, Hansard to Armstrong, 10 November 1914.

56   *Herald*, 14 November 1914; *Fort George Tribune*, 14 November 1914; NAC, RG 30, vol. 3408, file 2438, N.E. Brewer to H. McCall (Edson), telegram in code, 16 November 1914.

57   NAC, RG 46, vol. 98, file 212, 5773-74, 5734, 5801.

58   Ibid., 5695, 5838–5843; NAC, RG 46, vol. 1432, file 21418, Scott to Cochrane, 29 December 1914; BRC, Order No. 22995, 17 December, backdated to 23 November 1914. *Herald*, 28 November 1914.

59   NAC, RG 30, vol. 3408, file 2438, Hansard to Woods, 11 January 1915, Hansard to Biggar, 10 November, 24 November, 30 November 1914; NAC, RG 30, vol. 3371, file 1811, Salmon to Hansard, 6 August 1913.

60   NAC, RG 30, vol. 3408, file 2438, Guthrie to Biggar, 30 November, 2 December, 14 December, 15 December, Biggar to Hansard, 1 December, Hansard to Biggar, 4 December 1914.

61   NAC, RG 46, vol. 1432, file 21418, Cartwright to Hansard, 22 January, 13 February, 8 March, Hansard to Cartwright, 9 February 1915; NAC, RG 30, vol. 3408, file 2438, Guthrie to Hansard, 29 January 1915.

62   NAC, RG 30, vol. 3408, file 2438, Biggar to Hansard, 20 April 1915.

63   Ibid., Hansard to Wilson, 17 December 1914.

64   Ibid., Wilson to Hansard, 3 January, Hansard to Donaldson, 15 January, Hansard to McGregor, 23 April 1915.

65   NAC, RG 30, vol. 3408, file 2438, Hansard to Wilson, 26 April 1915; Fort George Board of Trade, Minutes, 19 March 1915.

66   NAC, RG 30, vol. 3371, file 1811, Hansard to Biggar, 7 May 1914; *Fort George Tribune*, 7 November 1914; Hearing, November 1914, 5746.

67   NAC, RG 30, vol. 3371, file 1811, Hansard to Biggar, 7 May 1914; Hearing, November 1914, 5801, 5739.

68   HBCA, A 12/L, Misc. 28, Thomson to Ingrams, 27 April 1915.

69   See, for example, *Herald*, 21 March 1914, which lists the opening of Ford, Massey-Harris, and International Harvester outlets within two blocks of George Street.

70   BCARS, BC, Department of Lands, 2436/12, Fort George Townsite Board of Trade to Ross, June 1914; NAC, RG 46, vol. 1432, file 21418, Moore to Drayton, 31 July 1915.

71   *Fort George Tribune*, 7 November 1914.

72   NAC, RG 46, vol. 1432, file 21418, Norton to Drayton, 28 November 1914, 16 January 1915. Quotations from 1 June 1915.

73   NAC, RG 30, vol. 3371, file 1811, Hearing, November 1914, 5837.

74   NAC, RG 46, vol. 1432, file 21418, BRC, Order No. 30789, 18 March 1921. The construction of the station was completed in February 1922.

75   See Leonard, 'Grand Trunk Pacific and the Establishment,' 48-53.

76 NAC, H.A. Drayton to BRC, 8 March, A. Ferguson to Drayton, 26 July, Hammond to S.J. Crowe, 29 May, Hammond to N.W. Rowell, 30 May 1919, Hammond to A. Meighen, 15 June, Hammond to G.D. Robertson, 17 June, Hammond to T.W. Crothers, 17 June, Hammond to T.A. Crerar, 17 June, Hammond to R. Lemieux, 2 July 1920.

77 Runnalls, *History of Prince George*, 107-9; Holmes, 'Promotion of Early Growth,' 2-12.

78 NAC, RG 30, vol. 3310, file 1060, Martin to D. Tate, 12 April, Tate to G.U. Ryley, 16 April 1910.

79 BCARS, GR 1323, file 2919/14/13, Donaldson to H. Hansard, 6 August, Hansard to W.J. Bowser, 10 August 1914. Donaldson's explanation would apply to the GTP steamship, *Prince George*, christened early in 1910. NAC, RG 30, vol. 3267, file 426, Hays to E.J. Chamberlin, 18 December 1911. B. Christensen, *Prince George: Rivers, Railways, and Timber* (Burlington 1989), 45, suggests that the townsite was named after the youngest son of King George V, but provides no data to support this claim.

80 BCARS, GR 1323, file 2919/14/13, Hansard to Bowser (personal), 10 June, Donaldson to Hansard, 6 August 1914. Although born in Canada, Hammond had gained notoriety through his activities in the confidence rackets of the American Midwest.

81 *Herald*, 11 January 1913; BCARS, GR 1088, file 2436/12, R. Gosnell to Bowser, 3 May 1913; GR 1323, file 2919/14/13, Petition, 14 April 1914, R.S. Lennie to Bowser, 14 April 1914.

82 BCARS, GR 1323, file 11726/13/13, Bowser to Reid, 29 October 1913; file 2919/14/13, Bowser to McKay and O'Brien, 13 April, McKay and O'Brien to Bowser, 26 April 1913; NAC, RG 30, vol. 3267, file 426, Harrington to Tate, 2 February 1912.

83 BCARS, GR 1088, file 2436/12, W.R. Ross to Donaldson, 9 April, R.A. Renwick to Clive Pringle, 3 October, Renwick to Ryley, 9 October 1913, Ross to Clive Pringle, 28 March 1914.

84 NAC Records Centre, Winnipeg, PPRE, vol. 142, file Station Names, Secretary Post Office to Ryley, 14 January, Donaldson, note on Kelliher to Donaldson, 9 April 1914; NAC, RG 30, vol. 3437, file 2858, pt. 1, Ellis to Hansard, 8 August 1914.

85 BCARS, Lands, GR 1088, file 2436/12, G. McGlaughlin to Ross, 8 September 1913; BCARS, GR 1323, file 2919/14/13, Reid to Bowser, 25 February, H.G. Perry to Bowser, 3 March, Bowser to Hansard, 27 May 1914; D. Smelts, comp., *Issues in Townsite Development: Government and Railway Involvement in the Incorporation of Prince George, 1914-1915: A Collection of Documents* (hereafter *Perry Papers*), H.E. Young to Bowser, 10 March, J. Shearer to F. Murdoff, 3 June, Joint Incorporation Committee, Minutes, 8 June, Bowser to Perry, 30 July 1914.

86 NAC, RG 30, vol. 3267, file 426, Hays to Chamberlin, 18 December 1911; vol. 3437, file 2858, pt. 1, Bowser to Hansard, 18 May, Hansard to Bowser, 10 June 1914.

87 NAC, RG 30, vol. 3437, file 2858, pt. 1, Meeting with the Joint Incorporation Committee, Minutes, 8 July 1914.

88 Ibid., Hansard to Perry (draft), n.d., Hansard to Perry (final version), 10 August 1914.

89 Ibid., Hansard to Perry, 13 November 1914; *Fort George Tribune*, 21 November 1914; *Perry Papers*, Joint Incorporation Committee, Minutes, 14 November 1914.

90 *Herald*, 22 August 1914.

91 NAC, RG 30, vol. 3437, file 2858, pt. 1, Hansard to Bowser, 10 November 1914; *Herald*, 28 November, 19 December, 26 December 1914; *Perry Papers*, W.F. Cooke to Perry, 31 December 1914.

92 BCARS, GR 1323, file 2919/14/13, W.G. McMorris to McBride, 16 February 1915. The GTP paid Daniell $1,000 in October 1914 for future advertising space in the *Prince George Post*. Daniell had to print GTP material whenever it was presented. See NAC, RG 30, vol. 3589, file 1707. Descriptions of the two meetings can be found in *Herald*, 16 January, and *Fort George Tribune*, 16 January 1915. BCARS, GR 1323, file 2919/14/13, R. Bradley to Bowser, 15 January 1915.

93 BCARS, GR 1323, file 2919/14/13, Shearer to Bowser, 20 January, Thompson to Bowser, 3

February 1915. Perry realized that the GTP was at the bottom of the unreasonable agitation of the Prince George Townsite members. *Fort George Tribune,* 23 January 1915.

94 BCARS, GR 1323, file 2919/14/13, Thompson to Bowser, 3 February, Prince George Incorporation Committee to Bowser, 16 February, Dearle to McBride, 15 February 1915; file 1726/13/13, A.G. Hamilton to Reid, 20 September 1913.

95 BCARS, GR 1323, file 2919/14/13, Peters to McBride, 19 February, McMorris to McBride, 19 February, Hammond to McBride, 19 February 1915.

96 NAC, RG 30, vol. 3437, file 2858, pt. 1, Hansard to Armstrong, 17 February 1915; Prince George Public Library, Pioneer Tape 18, P.E. Wilson; *Vancouver Daily Province,* 6 March, *Vancouver Sun,* 6 March, *Victoria Daily Times,* 6 March 1915. The *Prince George Post* and *Prince George Herald* (now moved from South Fort George) contain little on the debate. The relevant number of the *Fort George Tribune* has not survived.

97 NAC, RG 30, vol. 3437, file 2858, pt. 1, Hansard to Armstrong, 8 March 1915.

98 NAC, RG 125, vol. 389, file 3827, Supreme Court of Canada, *On Appeal from the Court of Appeal for British Columbia, GTP Ry Co. v. British Columbia Express Company* (printed record), 'Exhibits,' F.W. Aylmer to Chief Engineer, Public Works, 15 February 1912.

99 Ibid., Kelliher to Hansard, 28 April; A. St. Laurent, memorandum, 24 June 1913.

100 Ibid., Millar to Minister of Railways, 6 March 1913; Kelliher to Hansard, 28 April 1913; Hansard to R.C. Desrochers, 31 March 1913.

101 Ibid., C. McElroy to R. Rogers, 2 July 1913; Desrochers to Hansard, 4 July 1913; 'Proceedings,' examination of J.H. Heaman, n.d., 250.

102 Ibid., 'Exhibits,' Wainwright to Desrochers, 25 March 1914 (quotation); Millar to Minister of Public Works, 22 June 1914.

103 Ibid., 'Proceedings,' examination of W.J. West, 25-34; examination of H. McCall, 229-33.

104 Ibid., 'Proceedings,' examination of W.J. West, 29-31; 'Judgments,' Supreme Court of British Columbia, J. Clement, Reasons for Judgement, 26 May 1915, 389; West, 'The "B.X." and the Rush to Fort George,' 209. For a brief account of Lincoln's defence of railroad obstruction of navigable water, see J.P. Frank, *Lincoln as Lawyer* (Urbana, IL 1961), 84-7.

105 NAC, RG 125, vol. 389, file 3827, Supreme Court of Canada, F.W. Tiffin, *Appellant's Factum,* 8 (quotation); Supreme Court of Canada, *On Appeal from the Court of Appeal for British Columbia, GTP Ry Co. v. British Columbia Express Company,* 'Proceedings,' examination of W.J. West, 74 (quotation); *In the Privy Council, On Appeal from the Supreme Court of Canada, British Columbia Express Company v. GTP Ry Co.: Case of the Appellant;* Judicial Committee of the Privy Council, file 111/1917, Judgment, 15 October 1918.

Chapter 8, 'For Pure Spite': Hazelton District

1 Much of this chapter comes from a reworking of F. Leonard, '"To Injure Its Own Interests": The Grand Trunk Pacific Railway Company and the Blighting of Hazelton District, 1910-1918,' *BC Studies* 88 (Winter 1990-1):21-57.

2 Earlier accounts include J.A. Lower, 'The Grand Trunk Pacific Railway and British Columbia' (MA thesis, History, University of British Columbia, 1939), 117-19; Lower, 'The Construction of the Grand Trunk Pacific Railway in British Columbia,' *British Columbia Historical Quarterly* 4, 3 (July 1940):177-8; R.G. Large, *Skeena: River of Destiny* (Vancouver 1957), 129-32, 160; G.R. Stevens, *Towards the Inevitable, 1896-1922,* vol. 2 of *Canadian National Railways* (Toronto 1962), 225-6; R.M. Coutts, 'The Railway Policy of Sir Wilfrid Laurier: The Grand Trunk Pacific-National Transcontinental' (MA thesis, History, University of Toronto, 1968), 194-5; Kitimat-Stikine Regional District, *Hazelton and Vicinity Settlement Plan* (1985), 94-5; D. Abernathy, 'Bioregionalism: A Territorial Approach to Governance and Development of Northwest British Columbia' (MA thesis, Community Planning, University of British Columbia, 1985), 54-6; and G.W. Taylor, *The Railway Contractors: The Story of John W. Stewart, His Enterprises and Associates* (Victoria 1988), 66-9. School Inspector Alex

Lord offers a perceptive appraisal of the competing railway townsites in the district. *Alex Lord's British Columbia: Reflections of a Rural School Inspector, 1915-1936*, ed. J. Calam (Vancouver 1991), 64.

3 Robin's use of the metaphor suggests that the GTP actually secured, rather than merely desired, ill-gotten gains. His inference rests largely on consideration of a single episode of GTP activity in the province, the Kaien Island acquisition discussed in Chapter 2. Robin, *The Rush for Spoils: The Company Province, 1871-1933* (Toronto 1971), 103.

4 F. Valleau, 'Omineca Mining Division,' British Columbia, Department of Mines, *Annual Report* (hereafter Mines, *AR*), 1903, H70.

5 *Omineca Herald* (hereafter *Herald*), 6 March, 17 June 1909.

6 Wolverton & Co., 'Silver Standard,' 5 May 1948; Wolverton & Co., 'Romance of Silver Standard Mine,' 1948 [?]; *Herald*, 19 August, 26 August, 7 October 1911.

7 *Herald*, 10 September, 17 September 1910, 19 August, 30 September, 14 October 1911; Mines, *AR*, 1913, K 107, *AR*, 1914, K 187; NAC, RG 30, vol. 3562, file GR 1586, J. Oppenheimer to Ross, 4 April 1914. BCARS, GR 1438, BC, Company Records, file 44B, 'Butte and Rocher de Boule Copper Company.' The company's complete name never appeared in local newspapers or GTP correspondence.

8 Mines, *AR*, 1911, K 78; *Herald*, 16 April, 19 March, 23 April, 27 August, 15 October, 22 October, 29 October 1910, 14 January 1911; 'New Hazelton' [pamphlet] (1911).

9 Mines, *AR*, 1918, K 111. No explicit table of rates on ore from Rocher de Boule Mine has been located. In July 1914, the president of the mine concern requested that the GTP institute a rate of $3.00 per ton from the railhead to Prince Rupert. *Herald*, 3 July 1914. I have assumed that the GTP set a rate for copper ore similar to that for silver-lead ore in late 1915.

10 For calculations concerning ore value and GTP freight charges for Silver Standard, see Table 9.1.

11 Mines, *AR*, 1918, K 111; *AR*, 1919, N 101.

12 Diocese of Prince George Papers, vol. 3, file 15, Godfroy to Bunoz, 21 September 1911. NAC, RG 46, vol. 62, file 140, Hearing, 19 December 1911, Ryley to Tate, 14 September 1911 (summarized), 9741, 9733; vol. 67, file 151, 5401; vol. 586, file 18787-EX, GTP Development. Co. and W.J. Sanders, 18 November 1911; *Herald*, telegram, 21 October 1911.

13 NAC, RG 46, vol. 1468, file 18787, R. Kelly, Application, 23 November 1911, GTP (W.H. Biggar), Reply, 12 December 1911. *Herald*, 27 October, 24 November, 8 December 1911.

14 NAC, RG 30, vol. 3363, file 1710, Tate to Chamberlin, 9 November 1911; BCARS, GR 1088, file 37246/11, Sanders to Ryley, 27 November, Ryley to Sanders, 27 November, Ross, memorandum, 27 November 1911; BCARS, GR 1088, file 40884/11, Clements to Ross, 20 December 1911; file 37426/11, Summary of Sales, 2 September 1914. (Victoria – 34 lots; Vancouver – 48 lots.)

15 NAC, RG 30, vol. 3366, file 1762, Ryley to Tate, 28 November, Tate to BRC, 7 December 1911; vol. 3363, file 1710, Tate to Chamberlin, 9 December, Chamberlin to Tate, 11 December 1911.

16 NAC, RG 46, vol. 62, file 140, 9731-3, 9737-8, 9744-5, 9746-7.

17 Ibid., 9749-51.

18 *B.C. Saturday Sunset*, 29 December 1911, quoted in *Herald*, 12 January 1912. Clements & Hayward, 'New Hazelton' (full-page ad., which appeared in Vancouver newspaper before 1 January 1912); *Herald*, 22 December, 29 December 1911; *Omineca Miner*, 23 December 1911.

19 NAC, RG 30, vol. 3363, file 1710, Biggar to Tate, 21 December 1911; vol. 11619, file A-67, Hays to Ryley, 27 January, Ryley to Hays, 31 January, Hays to Biggar, 3 February 1912.

20 NAC, RG 46, vol. 1468, file 18787, Mabee to Hays, 3 January 1912; vol. 1429, file 18849, Biggar to Mabee, 10 January, Mabee to Biggar, 15 January 1912; BCARS, GR 1088, file 37426/11, Chamberlin to Ross, 16 January 1912.

21 Petition of the Grand Trunk Pacific Railway ... to rescind Order No. 15727 ... (dated) 17 February 1912.

22 NAC, RG 30, vol. 3363, file 1710, Chamberlin to Ryley, 23 December (copy) in Ryley to Biggar, 23 December 1911.

23 BCARS, GR 1088, file 37426/11, Chamberlin to Tate, 9 January 1912; RG 46, vol. 67, file 151, H.S. Clements, testimony, 4 June 1912.

24 NAC, RG 30, vol. 3363, file 1710, Tate to Biggar, 1 February, 3 February, Petition to the Premier, 7 February, Biggar to Sanders, 13 February, Sanders to Biggar, 20 February 1912; Murray to Aldous, 11 March 1912, reprinted in F.C. McKinnon, letter to editor, *Herald*, 27 September 1912; *Omineca Miner*, 23 March 1912; *Herald*, 24 May 1912.

25 BCARS, GR 1088, file 37426/11, M. Burrell to Ross, 4 May 1912; R.A. Pringle to Ross, 4 May 1912. That this version of the proceedings is accurate is indicated by two fragmentary pieces of evidence. In June, Kelly angrily demanded an explanation from McBride concerning the actions of the government's counsel, R.A. Pringle. To this demand the premier offered the lame response that Pringle only had a watching brief, implying that he realized that the lawyer had done a good deal more than what was normally expected in such a circumstance. BCARS, GR 441, vol. 113, file 778/10, Kelly to McBride, 24 June, McBride to Kelly, 28 June 1912. In a note to Justice Minister C.J. Doherty three days after the appeal, Borden used language that was very close to that in Pringle's report. Canada, Ministry of Justice, file 367/12, Borden to Doherty, 6 May 1912, with Doherty's handwritten note on it.

26 Of the twenty cases appealed from the BRC to the cabinet between 1904 and March 1917, the GTP Hazelton appeal was the only one allowed. Canada, *Sessional Papers*, No. 20c, 1918, 99.

27 *Monetary Times*, 23 May, 1 June, quoted in *Herald*, 14 June 1912.

28 NAC, RG 46, vol. 586, file 18787-EX, affidavits.

29 Ibid.

30 NAC, RG 46, vol. 67, file 151, Hearing, 4-6 June 1912, 172-3, 203, 5413-16.

31 Ibid., 5259, 5252, 5400-1, 5440-8; NAC, RG 46, vol. 586, file 18787-EX, photograph titled 'Hazelton – the Old and the New.'

32 NAC, RG 46, vol. 67, file 151, 5247, 5217-8, 5259, 5303.

33 Ibid., 5325, 5403.

34 NAC, RG 30, vol. 3363, file 1710, McLean, Judgment, 10 June 1912; BRC, Order #16891. A technicality in the language of this order led to its repeal and the issue of another order with the same intent, BRC, Order # 16987, 12 July 1912.

35 *Omineca Miner*, 29 June 1912.

36 Ibid., clipping, dated 21 June 1912; *Herald*, 28 June 1912.

37 BCARS, GR 441, vol. 115, file 1148/12, Clements to McBride, 3 July, 10 August 1912; *Omineca Miner*, 24 August, 21 September 1912; *Herald*, 20 September 1912.

38 NAC, RG 30, vol. 3366, file 1762, Donaldson to Hansard, 18 July 1912.

39 BCARS, GR 1088, file 37426/11, Ross to Chamberlin, 25 July, Chamberlin to Ross, 26 August, Renwick to Ross, 10 September, Ross, Notice, 22 November 1912, List of Lot Purchasers on GTP Property, May 1913.

40 NAC, RG 46, vol. 1429, file 18849, A.J. Nixon, G. Mountain, memo, 25 September 1912, 'Hazelton' telegrams, 26 September 1912, McLean, Judgment, 2 October 1912

41 Ibid., McLean, memo, 11 October, Biggar to Cartwright, 15 October, Sanders to Goodeve, 16 October, Biggar to Cartwright, 21 October, Hazelton Board of Trade to BRC, 23 October, F. McKinnon to Pringle and Guthrie, 24 October, Secretary, Board of Trade, to BRC, 25 October 1912.

42 Ibid., McLean, Judgment, 30 October 1912, BRC Order, #17905, 31 October 1912.

43 *Omineca Miner*, 14 December, 7 December 1912; *GTP South Hazelton: Northern Interior Metropolis* (Vancouver 1913 [?]).

44 NAC, RG 46, vol. 1468, file 18787, C. Harvey to Clements, December 1912; A. Lord, *Alex Lord's British Columbia*, 64.
45 BCARS, GR 1088, file 61426/12, Sanders and Kelly, agreement, 13 July 1913.
46 BCARS, GR 1088, file 37426/11, Du Vernet to Renwick, 3 April 1914, Superintendent, circular letter, 29 August 1913. The letter of Emily Carr to Superintendent, 8 September 1913, implies that the company would not provide refunds.
47 *Herald*, 28 March 1913.
48 BRC, Order #17769, 14 October 1912; NAC, RG 46, vol. 1468, file 18787, McLean to Scott, 15 November 1912; *Herald*, 22 November, 29 November 1912.
49 NAC, RG 46, vol. 1468, file 18787, Chamberlin to Biggar, 26 November, Scott to Biggar, 28 November 1912; *Herald*, 6 December, 13 December 1913.
50 NAC, RG 30, vol. 3366, file 1762, Donaldson to Hansard, 13 February, Ryley to Hansard, 27 February 1913.
51 *Herald*, 20 December 1912, 3 January 1913; NAC, RG 30, vol. 3394, file 2150, Drayton to Hansard, 6 January, Hansard to Drayton, 17 January 1913; vol. 3363, file 1710, Hansard to Donaldson, 17 December 1912.
52 *Herald*, 17 January 1913.
53 Ibid., 17 January, 24 January 1913.
54 *Vancouver Sun*, 19 February 1913; *Herald*, 7 February, 2 April, 9 May 1913.
55 *Herald*, 13 June 1913, 25 September, 9 October 1914; NAC, RG 46, vol. 1468, file 18787, M.J. McCaul to G. Spencer, 22 December 1915.
56 *Herald*, 2 January 1914.
57 Bulkley Valley Museum, James Cronin Papers, file Babine Data 2, 'Silver Lead Mining in British Columbia,' 'Description of Babine Bonanza,' undated memoranda (1921 [?]). In the calculation of limits for the operation of a profitable silver-lead mine, the first document assigns a proportion of 36 per cent of the assay value of ore to four factors in the cost of production: milling (concentrating), smelting, freight charges from railhead to smelter, and, presumably, hauling ore to the railhead. But the memorandum suggests no way to disaggregate these costs. Scribbled hurriedly in pencil with several erasures, some of the calculations also appear to be based on a higher ore value than the one stated in the memorandum. In the second document concerning the operation of Babine Bonanza during 1921, Cronin disaggregates costs in part by calculating that the combined cost of two factors, freight charges (railhead to smelter) and smelting, represents 19 per cent of the assay value of the mine's ore. I have assigned a proportion to freight charges from railhead to smelter alone according to a San Francisco smelter's settlement sheet for Cronin's mine in late 1917 where the ratio of freight charges (19 per cent of assay value) to basic smelting charges (13 per cent of the assay value) for a shipment of silver-lead ore was 3:2. That freight charges of 19 per cent ore value made Cronin's mine operation unprofitable is indicated by the fact that the mine shipped no ore during the following year. See file 1918, 'Confidential Report.'
58 *Herald*, 20 June, 8 August 1913.
59 Traffic agreements and government regulations provided that the GTP share this revenue with other lines that hauled the ore, of course.
60 Mines, *AR*, 1919, N101.
61 NAC, RG 30, vol. 3453, file 3115, Mehan to Donaldson, 1 June, Hansard to Donaldson, with enclosures, 17 June 1915.
62 Ibid., Mehan to Hansard, 14 July, Hansard to Mehan, 17 July, Donaldson to Hansard, 23 July 1915.
63 Ibid., J.S. Swalwell, auditor's reports, New Hazelton and South Hazelton.
64 NAC, RG 46, vol. 1468, file 18787, Clements to Drayton, 7 December 1915.
65 Ibid., 'Protest,' n.d.
66 Ibid., Hansard to BRC, 19 November, New Hazelton Citizens' Association to BRC, 10

December, McCaul to Spencer, 22 December 1915, Spencer to Drayton, 6 January 1916, McCaul to G. Spencer, 1 December 1915, Drayton, Judgment, 12 January 1916.
67 NAC, RG 30, vol. 3453, file 3115, Mehan to Hansard, 27 February 1916.
68 The BRC decided on the first advance; the cabinet on the second. A report of the railway companies' applications for a general increase in rates in 1917 ('15 per cent' case) can be found in 22 *Canadian Railway Cases* (1918):49-84. The GTP application to the BRC on this matter has not survived. The order-in-council for the second increase ('25 per cent' case), P.C. 1863, 27 July 1918, is published in *Canadian Railway and Marine World* (October 1918):446. For a general discussion of these complex changes in rates, see K. Cruikshank, *Close Ties: Railways, Government, and the Board of Railway Commissioners, 1851-1933* (Montreal 1991), 127-55. For tables setting out the impact of the two increases on the standard classification for British Columbia, see H.W. Hewetson, 'The Railway Rate Problems of Western Canada with Particular Reference to British Columbia' (MA thesis, Political Economy, University of British Columbia, 1925), 105-6. Although Hewetson provides a few examples of how the increases affected the cost of forwarding particular commodities on the CPR and the Canadian Northern, he does not discuss the GTP. Neither the surviving GTP legal files nor BRC records contain material on the GTP's actions in the cases, unfortunately.
69 NAC, RG 30, vol. 3478, file 3661, BRC hearing, 28 November 1919, 12388. The *Herald* does not discuss the closure of the Silver Standard in 1918. For the role of the GTP, one must rely on the admittedly partisan claim of the Silver Standard agent in late 1919. It is significant, however, that the GTP general freight agent who was present at the hearing did not dispute the claim. That Cronin's freight-charges limit of 12 per cent for the profitable operation of a mine applies in this case is suggested by the fact that the Silver Standard installed an ore concentrator in late 1917 to reduce freight charges of 14.65 per cent ore value during that year. Without the waybill advance, freight charges for 1918 would have returned to the level of 10 per cent for the years 1913-16. See Table 8.1.
70 NAC, RG 30, vol. 3593, file GR1797, Rosevear to Hansard, 20 July 1915; *AR*, 1916, K 107; *Herald*, 23 June, 18 August 1916; *Evening Empire* (Prince Rupert, weekly edition), 21 June, 5 July, 25 October 1916. There are no documents in the surviving files of the BRC concerning this complaint.
71 *Herald*, 10 November, 1 December, 8 December 1916; *Evening Empire* (weekly edition), 13 September 1916;
72 NAC, RG 30, vol. 3458, file 3237, Mehan to Hansard, 29 June 1916; *Evening Empire* (weekly edition), 25 October 1916.
73 NAC, RG 30, vol. 3458, file 3237, Donaldson to Hansard, 5 July 1916.
74 Ibid., BRC Order #25439, 19 September 1916; *Mining and Engineering Record* (August 1917):247.
75 Stevens, *Towards the Inevitable*, 206-7.
76 After its criticism of the GTP treatment of the Rocher de Boule Mine noted above, the *Mining and Engineering Record* (August 1917), 248, concluded that the GTP 'as a development road has been a failure.'
77 H.A. Innis, *A History of the Canadian Pacific Railway* (Toronto 1923), 140-2. Compare Cole Harris's conclusion concerning Innis's ideas in 'Industry and the Good Life around Idaho Peak,' *Canadian Historical Review* 66, 3 (September 1985):343.
78 H.A. Innis, *Settlement and the Mining Frontier* (Toronto 1936), 398.

Chapter 9, 'Grand Trafficker of Promises': Operations, 1914-19
1 On these events, see J.A. Eagle, *The Canadian Pacific Railway and the Development of Western Canada, 1896-1914* (Montreal 1989), 437-511; Eagle, 'Monopoly or Competition: The Nationalization of the Grand Trunk Railway,' *Canadian Historical Review* 62, 1 (March 1981):3-30; A.J. Currie, *The Grand Trunk Railway of Canada* (Toronto 1957), 432-60; G.R.

Stevens, *Towards the Inevitable, 1896-1922,* vol. 2 of *Canadian National Railways* (Toronto 1962), 455-508; and T.D. Regehr, *The Canadian Northern Railway: Pioneer Road of the Northern Prairies, 1895-1918* (Toronto 1976), 385-437.

2 Regehr, *Canadian Northern,* 397-8; J.A. Lower, 'The Grand Trunk Pacific Railway and British Columbia' (MA thesis, History, University of British Columbia, 1939), 181-2; A.D. Crerar, 'Prince Rupert, B.C. – the Study of a Port and Its Hinterland' (MA thesis, Geography, University of British Columbia, 1951), 148-51; Stevens, *Towards the Inevitable,* 204; and D. MacKay, *Asian Dream: The Pacific Rim and Canada's National Railway* (Vancouver 1986), 118-19.

3 *Grand Trunk Pacific Railway, Plateau and Valley Lands in British Columbia: General Information for the Intending Settler,* 5th ed. (Winnipeg 1915), 3, 9, and *passim.*

4 *Chicago Record-Herald,* 9 September 1911, reprinted in *Evening Empire* (Prince Rupert), 23 September 1911. See, for example, Chamberlin's remarks in *Fort George Herald,* 14 October 1911.

5 NAC, RG 30, vol. 10712, Smithers to Chamberlin, 18 October 1912.

6 Ibid., Smithers to Chamberlin, 24 November 1914. Smithers points out but does not explain the decrease in rate of growth of gross earnings after 1918.

7 NAC, Hays Papers, Parker to Hays, 4 July 1909.

8 Ibid., Kelliher to E.J. Chamberlin, 16 July 1909.

9 *Fort George Herald,* 23 March 1911.

10 *Daily News* (Prince Rupert), 21 February 1912; *Evening Empire,* 31 January 1912.

11 'The Grand Trunk, GTP and Trans-Continental,' *Canadian Annual Review* (1914), 733-4.

12 NAC, RG 30, vol. 5567, file 1919, R.C. Lett to W.P. Hinton, 8 December 1919.

13 For the years 1914-19, the unpublished GTP annual reports to the department are located in NAC, RG 46, vols. 927-8. Selected data for the GTP and other railways were published in Canada, *Sessional Papers,* Railway Statistics, 1915-20. Unpublished returns exist for the fiscal years 1911-13, but they contain few data.

14 Until 1916, returns for the main line included the Lake Superior Branch. Completed in 1908, the company relinquished operation and returns of the branch to the federal government in 1915 for a rent of $600,000 per annum. See NAC, RG 36, series 35, vol. 27, file 6, 'The Grand Trunk Pacific Railway Company' (1920 [?]), 1-2. Since this section provides estimates of *ceilings* of the volume of traffic on a part of the main line, the assumption that aggregate freight totals apply to the main line from Prince Rupert to Winnipeg only increases, in theory, the freight on each part of the line.

15 Stevens, *Towards the Inevitable,* 207.

16 J.C. Lawrence, 'Markets and Capital: A History of the Lumber Industry of British Columbia, 1778-1952' (MA thesis, History, University of British Columbia, 1957), 54-63; G. Hak, 'Prairie Capital, Prairie Markets, and Prairie Labour: The Forest Industry in the Prince George District, British Columbia, 1910-1930,' *Prairie Forum* 14 (1989):9-22.

17 NAC, RG 30, vol. 5567, file 1919, R.C. Lett to W.P. Hinton, 8 December 1919.

18 Minnesota Historical Society, Northern Pacific President, Subjects, file 892-I, JGW, 7 February 1914; *Pacific Fisherman* (October 1914).

19 NAC, RG 23, file 728-2-4, pt. 1, Fisheries Committee, Prince Rupert Board of Trade, to Hazen, 27 November 1914; PC 468, 9 March 1915; *Seattle Times,* 4 May 1915.

20 NAC, RG 23, vol. 1166, file 724-3-2, pt. 19, D.C. Reid to W.A. Found, 19 March 1919; pt. 1, Memorandum, Re Transportation of Fresh Fish by Express, n.d.

21 A GTP publicity photograph of the first fish express is reproduced in P. Bowman, *Whistling through the West* (Prince Rupert 1980), 67.

22 NAC, RG 23, vol. 1166, file 724-3-2, pt. 24, D.J. Hanna to E. Hawken, 27 December 1920; pt. 1, Desbarats to P. Godrath, 31 October 1914; pt. 23, Prince Rupert Branch of the Canadian Fisheries Association to Association, 13 July 1920; Canadian Express Company, Minute

Book, AR 1917. The company responded to the complaints in 1920, but the record of the BRC hearing does not survive. NAC, RG 30, vol. 3481, file 3695.

23 Canada, *Sessional Papers*, Report of the Department of Customs, 1914-20.

24 NAC, RG 36, series 35, vol. 17, file 5232, G. Somers, Traffic Report GTPR, 14-15. Asian traffic via Vancouver included cotton and tobacco from the Southern states and iron and machinery from Pennsylvania and Ohio.

25 *Evening Empire*, 26 September 1914; *Daily News*, 26 September 1914; NAC, RG 36, series 35, vol. 17, file 5232, Traffic Report, 20.

26 Canadian National, Vancouver, file 2123-4, 'Movement of Grain through Prince Rupert: Grain Concerns and Steamship Lines Interested in Grain Export from Vancouver.' (Undated memorandum attached to L. McCutcheon to W. Manders, 12 January 1926.)

27 NAC, Borden Papers, vol. 25, file OC 143, pt. 6, W.P. Hinton to J.S. Gibson, 16 February 1916.

28 UBC Library, Special Collections, CNR, 'Data Requested by the Province of British Columbia' (typescript, 1925), Q. 7 and 8.

29 Railway Commission, 'Standard Freight Mileage Tariff, Grand Trunk Pacific Railway,' *Canada Gazette*, vol. 48, 15 August 1914, 539-40.

30 W.T. Jackman, *Economics of Transportation* (Toronto 1926), 306-7.

31 The population of districts and communities adjacent to and north of the GTP British Columbia line was 26,685 in 1911; 38,131 in 1921. The largest community, Prince Rupert, had a population of 4,184 in 1911 and 6,393 in 1921. See Dominion Bureau of Statistics, *Sixth Census of Canada* (1921), I, 215-16.

32 Grand Trunk Pacific Railway, *Employees' Timetable No. 11*, 3 January 1915, Mountain Division (Prince Rupert to Prince George), and *Employees' Timetable No. 16*, 3 January 1915, Prairie and Mountain divisions (Winnipeg to Prince George), appended to C. Schreiber to R. Borden, 25 January 1915, Borden Papers, vol. 25, file OC 143, pt. 4, 9045-47.

33 NAC, RG 36, series 35, vol. 17, file 5232, G. Somers, Traffic Report GTPR.

34 This estimate probably exaggerates the percentage of ton miles generated on the British Columbia line since the calculations concerning fish and lumber products entail freight hauled to the end of the calendar year 1919 while the main line total extends only to end of June 1919.

35 One can find some detailed estimates of traffic on the GTP Mountain Section, *east* of Red Pass Junction, in the papers of Alex Ferguson, the government engineer who supervised the effective merging of the GTP and Canadian Northern lines over some 170 miles between Red Pass and Imre to provide track for the front in France. During 1918, the number of GTP freight *and* passenger trains that traversed this joint section per week (in both directions) ranged from 14 to 36. While Ferguson claims that these numbers excluded trains on the GTP Alberta Coal Branch, they apparently included trains on the main line travelling to and from the Coal Branch. The heavier weight of trains travelling east supports this inference. NAC, MG 30 B118, vol. 2, file 25.

36 Figures from the 1917 Royal Commission suggest that the British Columbia line cost between $63 million and $70 million. The first cost of the entire main line was $109,828,588.

37 A brief account of the government's track removal in 1917 to provide rails for France can be found in L. Kozma, 'Senseless Duplication: A Brief Case History of the Development and Demise of the CNoR and GTP Mainlines from Edmonton to Red Pass' (Unpublished paper, 1978). On GTP protests against the track removal and sharing the Canadian Northern line, see NAC, RG 30, vol. 3463, file 3323. For a perceptive account of the maintenance problem and its consequences, see A. Lord, *Alex Lord's British Columbia: Recollections of a Rural School Inspector*, ed. J. Calam (Vancouver 1991), 61-8.

38 NAC, Borden Papers, vol. 175, pt. 2, file RLB, 265 (1), Borden to Biggar, 6 August 1914, Donnelly to Chamberlin, 18 February 1915; Borden to Chamberlin, 5 March 1915.

39 *Evening Empire* (weekly edition), 16 February 1916; Borden Papers, McCaffery to Borden, 31

March, Merryfield to Borden, 22 March, Resolutions, 29 March 1916.

40 NAC, RG 11, vol. 4037, file 522-1A, Chamberlin to Hunter, 12 May, 19 April, Chamberlin to McCaffery, 8 April 1916.

41 NAC, RG 30, vol. 3371, file 1346, pt. I, Hansard to Donaldson, 7 June 1916; Borden Papers, Cotton to Chamberlin, 19 August 1916.

42 *Evening Empire* (weekly edition), 29 April, 27 September 1916; NAC, RG 11, vol. 4037, file 522-1A, Hull to Lafleur, 13 June, 8 August 1916; Borden Papers, Rogers to Borden, 21 August 1916.

43 *Evening Empire* (weekly edition), 19 September, 4 October, 11 October, 27 October 1916.

44 NAC, RG 11, vol. 4037, file 522-1A, Donnelly to Lafleur, 17 January 1917, Wood to Admiralty Superintendent, 18 September 1916, Desbarats to Deputy Minister, 5 October, Chamberlin to Desrochers, 28 November 1916; RG 24, vol. 3591, file 44-2-2, Admiralty to Kingsmill, 28 January 1917.

45 NAC, Borden Papers, vol. 219, pt. 2, Smithers to Chamberlin, 31 January, Chamberlin to Smithers, 1 February 1917; NAC, RG 24, vol. 3591, file 44-2-2, Donaldson to Kingsmill, 3 January, Donaldson to Kingsmill, 22 February, Admiralty to Kingsmill, 11 April 1917.

46 NAC, RG 24, vol. 3591, file 44-2-2, Kingsmill to Admiralty, 20 February 1917, Pillsbury to Superintendent, 2 April 1918; Borden Papers, Oliver to Borden, 28 March (2), Borden to Oliver, 28 March, 29 March, Nelson to Borden, 2 April 1918.

47 NAC, Borden Papers, vol. 219, pt. 2, E. Fitzgerald to Borden, 26 June, T.A. Russell to Chairman, 25 July, Flavelle to Borden, 27 July, W.E. Williams to Borden, 31 July 1917.

48 Merchants Association to Chamberlin, 9 January, Chamberlin to Merchants Association, 24 January 1917, printed in *Prince Rupert Journal* (hereafter *Journal*), 7 February 1917.

49 Minutes, 6 February 1917 in *Journal*, 7 February 1917, *Journal*, 15 February 1917.

50 NAC, Borden Papers, Fitzgerald to Smithers, 21 June, Chamberlin to Union Iron Works, 22 June, Snyder to Chamberlin, 6 July, Borden to Chamberlin, 10 July, Board to Mortimer, 18 July 1917. When a Norwegian concern expressed interest in construction ships in August 1917, Flavelle discouraged the application stating it would be better not to disturb the 'already highly excited labour market' through the placement of new orders. Flavelle to Borden, 3 September 1917.

51 NAC, RG 11, vol. 4037, file 522-1B, Lafleur to Hunter, 11 March, Assistant Secretary, Memo, Pringle and Guthrie to Public Works, 2 August, Newcombe to Secretary, 21 August 1918; PC 2203, 12 September 1918.

52 NAC, RG 30, vol. 3619, file 3182, *Prince Rupert Dry Dock et al.*, v. *W.E. Williams et al.*, Mullen, affidavit, 4, 7-8; RG 11, vol. 4037, file 522-1B, GTP and J.L. Mullen, Agreement, 1 August, Hansard to Hunter, 4 September, Newcombe to Secretary, 5 November 1918; *Evening Empire* (weekly edition), 8 January 1919.

53 As part of a refinancing scheme, E.E. Loomis and J. Platten prepared a report on the future traffic and earning potential of the Canadian Northern in 1916-17. See Regehr, *Canadian Northern*, 417-20. Because the Canadian Northern filed the first application for a general increase in rates in June 1917, its application has been preserved and is considered in some detail in the BRC judgment of the '15 per cent case.' NAC, RG 46, vol. 609, file 27840, Application of the Canadian Northern Railway Company, 16 June 1917. Board of Railway Commissioners, *AR 1917*, 'In re Increase in Passenger and Freight Tolls,' 70-104.

54 CP Archives, RG 2 (103273), X-1118, T.C. Macnabb, Report on Grand Trunk Pacific Railway, Winnipeg to Prince Rupert, 11 August 1914.

55 *The Railway Transportation Problem in Canada* (n.p., 1921).

56 Royal Commission to Inquire into Railways and Transportation in Canada, *Report* (Ottawa 1917), Examination of E.J. Chamberlin, 24 February 1917, 76, 78. For discussions of the royal commission, see Stevens, *Towards the Inevitable*, 470-7; Eagle, *Canadian Pacific Railway*, 315-70; and Regehr, *Canadian Northern*, 413-32.

57 Royal Commission to Inquire into Railways, *Report*, xcvi.

58 Ibid., xxv, xxxii.
59 Canada, *Sessional Papers*, 1922, no. 20, Department of Railways, 'Grand Trunk Arbitration,' 184.
60 Ibid., 175.
61 Ibid.

Chapter 10, Conclusion: 'The Tenderloin and the Hook'

1 Michael Bliss contends that 'the otherwise solvent' parent Grand Trunk was dragged down by its obligations to cover only its share of the cost of GTP construction. He castigates Hays as 'the man most responsible for getting the Grand Trunk into this situation.' For Bliss, the 'worst-located of the prairie and mountain main lines' made the GTP 'a doomed company.' *Northern Enterprise: Five Centuries of Canadian Business* (Toronto 1987), 376.

2 Julius Grodinsky, *Transcontinental Railroad Strategy, 1869-93: A Study of Businessmen* (Philadelphia 1962), 425, 423. Of the six major transcontinental systems constructed during the nineteenth century, the Union Pacific, Northern Pacific, the first Canadian Pacific, and the Santa Fe failed. The Central Pacific-Southern Pacific escaped only by absorbing parts of a projected seventh transcontinental, the failed Texas & Pacific. As a transcontinental, only the Great Northern did not fail. Its unusual performance rested in large part on the losses of the original investors in the major predecessor company, the St. Paul & Pacific. L.J. Mercer, *Railroads and Land Grant Policy: A Study in Government Intervention* (New York 1982).

3 M. Klein proposes this grouping. *The Rebirth 1894-1969*, vol. 2 of *Union Pacific* (New York 1990), 168. On the Chicago, Milwaukee & St. Paul, see S. McCarter, *Guide to the Milwaukee Road in Montana* (Helena 1992); and C.A. Schwantes, *Railroad Signatures across the Pacific Northwest* (Seattle 1993), 149-54. On the Western Pacific, the most useful work remains W.C. Odisho, 'Salt Lake City to Oakland: The Western Pacific Link in the Continental Railroad System' (PhD diss., History, University of California, 1941). On the Canadian Northern, see T.D. Regehr, *The Canadian Northern Railway: Pioneer Road of the Northern Prairies, 1895-1918* (Toronto 1976).

4 H.R. Grant suggests this counterfactual argument in a discussion of one of the Milwaukee's rivals. 'Seeking the Pacific: The Chicago & North Western's Plans to Reach the West Coast,' *Pacific North West Quarterly* (April 1990):67-73.

5 Resistance to what appears to be common sense was not the sole preserve of the GTP, of course. For a provocative discussion of managerial resistance to applying business principles to railroad product costing, see G.L. Thompson, 'Myth and Rationality in Management Decision-Making: The Evolution of American Railroad Product Costing, 1870-1970,' *Journal of Transport History* 12, 1 (1991):1-10.

6 In his statements to shareholders' meetings for 1900-2, CPR president T.G. Shaughnessy emphasized this traffic and the returns it produced as the most important element in his company's strong financial position.

7 The exception was the Central Pacific, the west end of the first transcontinental, because it was able to haul some ore from Nevada silver mines before connection with the east end Union Pacific.

8 On the Great Northern investigations, see R.W. Hidy, et al., *The Great Northern Railway: A History* (Cambridge, MA 1988), 110. For more detailed accounts of CPR investigations, see F.D. Lewis and D.R. Robinson, 'The Timing of Railway Construction on the Canadian Prairies,' *Canadian Journal of Economics* 17, 2 (May 1984):340-52; and, in British Columbia, G.C. Backler, 'The CPR's Capacity and Investment Strategy in Rogers Pass, B.C., 1882-1916' (MSc thesis, Business Administration, University of British Columbia, 1981). While L.D. Mercer, *Railroads and Land Grant Policy*, offers estimates of promoters' *ex ante* calculations for undertaking transcontinentals, he presents little on the methods the promoters used to make these calculations.

9 N. Knight, 'Mega-Project Planning and Economic Welfare: A Case Study of British

Columbia's North East Coal Project' (PhD diss., Community and Regional Planning, University of British Columbia, 1990), 1.

10 BCARS, GR 441, vol. 123, file 1756/13, Matters and Things, Speech before the Vancouver Progress Club, 4 June 1913 (typed copy).

11 P.N. Limerick, *The Legacy of Conquest: The Unbroken Past of the American West* (New York 1987), 42-4.

12 NAC, MG 30 A 93, A.W. Smithers Papers, file 4, C. Rivers Wilson, 1909, Visit to Canada, 29 September 1909. This 'strictly confidential' memorandum was privately printed for distribution to the Grand Trunk London Board.

13 Olivier Zunz uses the first label in his brief to enhance the significance of the activities middle-level executives of the Chicago, Burlington & Quincy. *Making America Corporate, 1870-1920* (Chicago 1990), 40. O.D. Skelton, *Life and Letters of Sir Wilfrid Laurier*, II (Toronto 1921), 417.

14 R. Overton, *Burlington West: A Colonization History of the Burlington Railroad* (Cambridge, MA 1941); K. Bryant, Jr., *History of the Atchison, Topeka, and Santa Fe Railway* (New York 1974); Hidy, *Great Northern Railway*; W.K. Lamb, *The History of the Canadian Pacific Railway* (New York 1977), 219-21; Max Foran, 'The CPR and the Urban West, 1880-1930,' *The CPR West: The Iron Road and the Making of a Nation*, ed. H. Dempsey (Vancouver 1984), 89-105; Regehr, *Canadian Northern*, 225-33, 240-1.

15 S.G. Marks, *The Road to Power: The Trans-Siberian Railroad and the Colonization of Asian Russia, 1850-1917* (Ithaca, NY 1991), 191.

16 NAC, A.W. Smithers Papers, file 4, Visit to Canada, 29 September 1909.

17 Such an attitude, perhaps less warmly expressed, was probably not foreign to the legal offices of the CPR and the Canadian Northern. Charges that these companies also behaved in a predatory manner were, after all, not infrequent.

18 J.E. Dalrymple in *Omineca Herald*, 9 May 1913; *Evening Empire* (Prince Rupert, weekly edition), 25 October 1916.

19 NAC, RG 30, vol. 2858, pt. I, Hansard to Biggar, 16 March 1915.

20 *Vancouver Daily World*, 3 April 1913. A. Martin, *Enterprise Denied: The Origins of the Decline of American Railroads, 1897-1917* (New York 1971), 80.

21 Stephen Leacock, *My Discovery of the West: A Discussion of East and West in Canada* (Boston 1937), 224.

22 On the mapping of capital to illuminate an urban hierarchy and the extent of a metropolis's hinterland, see W. Cronon, *Nature's Metropolis: Chicago and the Great West* (New York 1991), 263-95.

23 The ratios resting on extant figures are Prince Rupert assessment/GTP expenditure: .25; Vancouver assessment (1893)/CPR expenditure: .86. The Vancouver/CPR ratio is skewed upward, however, because the CPR built a shorter main line in the province. The CPR expenditure total also does not include the Port Moody to Vancouver extension, railway terminals in Vancouver, and snowsheds in the Selkirks to allow year-round operation. Nevertheless, after one makes allowances for these factors, the difference in the terminus assessment/expenditure ratios remains striking. Corporation of the City of Prince Rupert, *Annual Report*, 1917. For the calculation of GTP expenditure from Schreiber's final estimate of the Mountain Section, see Chapter 3. Corporation of the City of Vancouver, *Annual Report*, 1900, 32. Canada, *Sessional Papers*, 1886, no. 35, 155-6, CPR Estimate, 11 December 1885; and NAC, RG 43, vol. 306, file 4402-General, Schreiber, Estimate, 12 July 1903.

24 The quotation comes from the poem, 'The Grand Trunk Pacific,' which is reproduced at the beginning of Chapter 1 of this study. S. Tomblin, 'In Defense of Territory: Province Building under W.A.C. Bennett' (PhD diss., Political Science, University of British Columbia, 1985), 57, argues that the territorial (spatial) characteristics of the Pacific Great Eastern Railway reflected the aspirations and fears of the 'province-building' premier who extended it.

SELECT BIBLIOGRAPHY

The major source for this work, the records of the GTP legal department branch office in Winnipeg, is reviewed in the introduction. Additional GTP material includes the Hays-Rivers Wilson correspondence, the A.W. Smithers Papers, the relevant files of the office of land commissioner (land department), the corporate records, and scattered files of the secretary and the engineering department. Some GTP material is also located in the records of the parent concern, the Grand Trunk Railway Company of Canada. The surviving records of the GTP land commissioner concerning British Columbia are divided between CN Edmonton and the NAC Records Centre, Winnipeg. Some structure (bridge) files of the engineering department are located at CN Edmonton. The other company material is deposited in the National Archives. Unfortunately, the records of two important departments have not survived. Most disappointing is the lack of records from the freight department, which might illuminate traffic levels after completion. Another important gap is the industrial department, which apparently encouraged enterprises that could provide freight for the line.

More data on construction and labour relations on the British Columbia line come from the records of the federal Department of Railways, the Consulting Engineer, the Royal Commission on Railways, and the papers of Liberal railways minister George Graham. One can find limited material on operation and traffic after completion in the records of the Grand Trunk Arbitration. On the activities of the GTP in railway townsites, the correspondence and proceedings of the Board of Railway Commissioners for Canada (BRC) frequently illuminate both the origins and the consequences of actions undertaken by the company's legal department. There is also valuable material on several aspects of GTP activity in British Columbia in the Laurier and Borden Papers.

Because the GTP was an enterprise largely funded and supervised by the federal government, the British Columbia government evinced only sporadic interest in the company's activities after it compelled the GTP to make a general settlement concerning Prince Rupert Townsite and right-of-way across the province in 1908. Before the settlement, however, the Premiers' (McBride) Papers provide essential, if incomplete, information on the company's early attempts to secure a land grant. The records of the Department of Lands illuminate the activities of the company throughout the province. Provincial Police files provide some details of GTP actions in Prince Rupert before incorporation in 1910. The records of the Department of the Attorney General yield useful files on Prince George Townsite after 1911. Before that year, unfortunately, a different organization system did not usually group related individual documents as files. The provincial Department of Railways holds no material on the GTP.

For GTP activities in the communities of Prince Rupert, Prince George, and in the Hazelton district, I have examined local newspapers and the minutes of city councils and boards of trade to complement material in the company and government files. Indian Affairs files, of course, throw light on company relations with Native people.

Archival Sources
National Archives of Canada, Ottawa
R.L. Borden Papers, MG 26 H
Canadian National Railways, RG 30
Canadian Transport Commission, Board of Railway Commissioners for Canada, RG 46
Finance, RG 19
Fisheries and Oceans, RG 23
Government Consulting Engineer, National Transcontinental Railway, RG 36/1
G.P. Graham Papers, MG 27 II D 8
Grand Trunk Railway Arbitration, RG 36/35
C.M. Hays Papers, MG 30 A 18
Immigration Branch, RG 76
Indian Affairs, RG 10
Justice, RG 13
W.L.M. King Papers, MG 26 J
Labour, Strike and Lockout Files, RG 27
W. Laurier Papers, MG 26 G
Marine, RG 42
Public Works, RG 11
Railways and Canals, RG 43
Royal Commission on Railways and Transportation, RG 33/12
A.W. Smithers Papers, MG 30 A 93
Transport, RG 12

British Columbia Archives and Records Service, Victoria
Attorney General, GR 1323
Lands, GR 1088, 1440
Pacific Great Eastern Railway, GR 818
T.D. Pattullo Papers, Add. Ms. 3
R.W. Pillsbury Papers, G P 93
Premiers' [McBride] Papers, GR 441
Provincial Police, GR 55, 56
Royal Commission on Labour, GR 684

Canadian National, Edmonton
Real Estate
Engineering

NAC Records Centre, Winnipeg
CN Records, 1905-20

Canadian National Headquarters, Montreal
Corporate Archives

Canadian Railway Historical Association Museum, Montreal
C.M. Hays Papers

CP Rail System, Montreal
Corporate Archives

Minnesota Historical Society, St. Paul
Foley Brothers Papers

Hudson's Bay Company Archives, Winnipeg
British Columbia District Manager's Correspondence, Fort George, HBC Reserve

Oblate House, Vancouver
Diocese of Prince George Papers

University of British Columbia Library, Special Collections, Vancouver
Charles Hibbert Tupper Papers
IWW Papers

Corporation of the City of Prince Rupert, Prince Rupert
Minutes, 1910-19

Prince Rupert Chamber of Commerce
Minutes, 1908-19

Museum of Northern British Columbia, Prince Rupert
D.I. McDowell Papers

Corporation of the City of Prince George, Prince George
Minutes, 1915

Prince George Chamber of Commerce
Minutes, 1915-19

Fraser-Fort George Museum, Prince George
L.C. Gunn Papers

Bulkley Valley Museum, Smithers
James Cronin Papers

Government Publications
British Columbia. Legislative Assembly. *Journals of the Legislative Assembly.* 1902-19
——. Select Committee re Kaien Island Investigation. *Report.* 1906
——. *Sessional Papers.* Annual Reports. Commissioner of Lands, 1891-1910. Department of
    Lands, 1911-20. Department of Railways, 1911-17. Department of Mines, 1903-20
——. *Statutes.* 1889-1915.
Canada. Parliament. House of Commons. *Debates.* 1903-19
——. *Papers and Correspondence between the Government of Canada and the Government of
    British Columbia relating to the Application of the Grand Trunk Pacific Railway Company
    to Acquire a Portion of the Metlakatla Indian Reserve ....* 1908.
——. Parliament. National Transcontinental Railway Investigating Commission. *Report.* 1914
——. Parliament. Royal Commission on Railways and Transportation. *Report.* 1917
——. Parliament. Senate. *Debates.* 1903-5
——. Parliament. *Sessional Papers.* Annual Reports. Department of Railways and Canals,
    1903-22. Board of Railway Commissioners for Canada, 1908-20. Superintendent of
    Indian Affairs, 1906-13
——. *Statutes.* 1903-19

Selected Newspapers and Journals
B.C. Saturday Sunset, Vancouver, 1910-15 (title varies slightly)
Canadian Annual Review, Toronto, 1902-19
Canadian Railway and Marine World, Toronto, 1902-19 (title varies)
Daily Colonist, Victoria, 1902-8
Daily News, Prince Rupert, 1911-19
Fort George Herald, South Fort George, 1910-15
Fort George Tribune, 1909-15
Industrial Worker, Spokane, 1909-13

Omineca Herald, Hazelton and New Hazelton, 1908-19
Omineca Miner, Hazelton, 1912-17
Poor's Manual of Railroads, New York, 1902-20
Prince George Post, 1914-15
Empire, Prince Rupert, 1907-19 (also *Evening Empire* and *Evening Empire* weekly edition)
Prince Rupert Journal, 1910-17 (title varies slightly)
Prince Rupert Optimist, 1909-11
Railroad Gazette, New York, 1902-19 (title varies)
Saturday Night, Toronto, 1910
Vancouver Daily Province, 1902-8
Victoria Daily Times, 1902-8

Books, Articles, Pamphlets

Anderson, R.J. 'Sharks and Red Herrings: Vancouver's Male Employment Agencies, 1898-1915.' *BC Studies* 98 (Summer 1993):43-84
Andreassen, J.C.L. 'Canadian National Railway Records.' *Business History Review* 39 (Spring 1965):115-19
Armstrong, C., and H.V. Nelles. *Monopoly's Moment: The Organization and Regulation of Canadian Utilities, 1830-1930.* Philadelphia 1986
——. 'The Rise of Civic Populism in Toronto.' In *Forging a Consensus: Historical Essays on Toronto.* Ed. V.L. Russell, 192-237. Toronto 1984
——. *Southern Exposure: Canadian Promoters in Latin America and the Caribbean, 1896-1930.* Toronto 1988
Artibise, A.F.J., ed. *Town and City: Aspects of Western Canadian Urban Development.* Regina 1981
——. *Winnipeg: A Social History of Urban Growth, 1874-1914.* Montreal 1975
Artibise, A.F.J., and P.-A. Linteau., eds. *The Usable Urban Past: Planning and Politics in the Modern Canadian City.* Toronto 1979
Asante, N. *The History of Terrace.* Terrace 1972
Athearn, R.G. *The Denver and Rio Grande Western Railroad: Rebel of the Rockies.* 2nd ed. Lincoln, NE 1977
Avery, D. 'Canadian Immigration Policy and the "Foreign" Navvy, 1896-1914.' Canadian Historical Association. *Historical Papers* (1972):135-56
——. *'Dangerous Foreigners': European Immigrant Workers and Labour Radicalism in Canada, 1896-1932.* Toronto 1979
Backler, G.C., and T.D. Heaver. 'The Timing of a Major Investment in Railway Capacity: CPR's 1913 Connaught Tunnel Decision.' *Business History* 24 (1982):300-14
Barman, J. *The West beyond the West: A History of British Columbia.* Toronto 1991
Barrett, A.A., and R.W. Liscombe. *Francis Rattenbury and British Columbia: Architecture and Challenge in the Imperial Age.* Vancouver 1983
Baskerville, P.A. 'On the Rails: Trends in Canadian Railway Historiography.' *American Review of Canadian Studies* 9, 1 (Spring 1979):63-72
——. 'Professional vs Proprietor: Power Distribution in the Railroad World of Upper Canada/Ontario, 1851-1881.' Canadian Historical Association. *Historical Papers* (1978):47-63
Bersohn, Ken. *Cutting Up the North: The History of the Forest Industry in the Northern Interior.* Vancouver 1981
Berton, P. *The National Dream: The Great Railway, 1871-1881.* Toronto 1970
——. *The Last Spike: The Great Railway, 1881-1885.* Toronto 1971
Bickersteth, B. *The Land of Open Doors: Being Letters from Western Canada, 1911-1913.* 2nd ed. Toronto 1976

Bliss, M. *A Canadian Millionaire: The Life and Times of Sir Joseph Flavelle, Bart., 1858-1939.* Toronto 1978
——. *Northern Enterprise: Five Centuries of Canadian Business.* Toronto 1987
Bolt, C. *Thomas Crosby and the Tsimshian: Small Shoes for Feet Too Large.* Vancouver 1992
Borak, A.M. 'The Chicago, Milwaukee and St. Paul Railroad: Recent History of the Last Transcontinental.' *Journal of Economic and Business History* 3, 1 (November 1930):81-117
Bowman, P. *Land of Liquid Sunshine.* Prince Rupert 1982
——. *Muskeg, Rocks and Rain!* Prince Rupert 1973
——. *Whistling through the West.* Prince Rupert 1980
Bradwin, E.W. *The Bunkhouse Man.* 2nd ed. Toronto 1972
Brown, D. *Hear That Lonesome Whistle Blow: Railroads in the West.* New York 1977
Brown, R.C. *Robert Laird Borden: A Biography.* 2 vols. Toronto 1975, 1980
Brown, R.C., and R. Cook. *Canada, 1896-1921: A Nation Transformed.* Toronto 1974
Bryant, Jr., K., ed. *Encyclopedia of American Business History and Biography: Railroads in the Age of Regulation, 1900-1980.* New York 1988
Bryant, Jr., K. *History of the Atchison, Topeka and Santa Fe Railway.* New York 1974
Buckley, K. *Capital Formation in Canada.* Toronto 1955
Cail, R.E. *Land, Man and the Law: The Disposal of Crown Lands in British Columbia, 1871-1913.* Vancouver 1974
Calam, J., ed. *Alex Lord's British Columbia: Reflections of a Rural School Inspector, 1915-1936.* Vancouver 1991
Canada. Department of Trade and Commerce. *Bibliographical List of References to Canadian Railways, 1829-1938.* Ottawa 1938
Canadian Liberal Party. *Railway Question in Canada.* Ottawa, 1915
Chandler, Jr., A.D. 'The Railroads: Pioneers in Corporate Management.' *Business History Review* 39 (Spring 1965):16-40
——. *The Railroads: The Nation's First Big Business.* New York 1965
——. *Strategy and Structure: Chapters in the History of the American Industrial Enterprise.* Cambridge, MA 1964
——. *The Visible Hand: The Managerial Revolution in American Business.* Cambridge, MA 1977
Chandler, Jr., A.D., and S. Salsbury. 'The Railroads: Innovators in Modern Business Administration.' In *Railroads and the Space Program: An Exploration in Historical Analogy.* Ed. B. Mazlish, 127-162. Cambridge, MA 1965
Christensen, B. *Prince George: Rivers, Railways, and Timber.* Burlington, ON 1989
Clayton, D. 'Geographies of the Lower Skeena.' *BC Studies* 94 (Summer 1992):29-58
CN Rail. *Growing with Prince Rupert.* Montreal 1983
Coates, K.S., and W.R. Morrison. *The Alaska Highway in World War II: The U.S. Army of Occupation in Canada's Northwest.* Toronto 1992
Cochran, J.S. 'Economic Importance of Early Transcontinental Railroads: Pacific Northwest.' *Oregon Historical Quarterly* 71 (March 1970):27-98
Cochran, T. *Business Leaders, 1845-1890: The Business Mind in Action.* Cambridge, MA 1953
Condit, C.W. 'The Literature of the Railroad Buff: A Historian's View.' *Railroad History* 142 (Spring 1980):7-26
Cotsworth, M.B. *Railway Bungling (and Worse) in British Columbia.* Vancouver 1918
Craven, Paul. *'An Impartial Umpire': Industrial Relations and the Canadian State, 1900-1911.* Toronto 1980
Craven, Paul, and T. Traves. 'Dimensions of Paternalism: Discipline and Culture in Canadian Railway Operations in the 1850s.' In *On the Job: Confronting the Labour Process in Canada.* Eds. C. Heron and R. Storey, 47-74. Montreal 1986
Cronon, W. *Nature's Metropolis: Chicago and the Great West.* New York 1991
Cruikshank, K. *Close Ties: Railways, Government, and the Board of Railway Commissioners,*

1851-1933. Montreal 1991

——. 'The Intercolonial Railway, Freight Rates and the Maritime Economy.' *Acadiensis* 22, 1 (Autumn 1992):87-110

——. 'The Transportation Revolution and Its Consequences: The Railway Freight Rate Controversy in the Nineteenth Century.' CHA. *Historical Papers* (1987):112-38

Currie, A.W. *The Grand Trunk Railway of Canada.* Toronto 1957

Cruise, D., and A. Griffiths. *Lords of the Line: The Men Who Built the CPR.* Toronto 1988

Daggett, S. *Principles of Inland Transportation.* 2nd ed. New York 1934

——. *Railroad Consolidation West of the Mississippi River.* Berkeley 1932

——. *Railroad Reorganization.* Cambridge, MA 1908

Davies, D. 'The Pre-1917 Roots of Canada-Soviet Relations.' *Canadian Historical Review* 70, 2 (June 1989):180-205

Davis, D.F. 'The "Metropolitan Thesis" and the Writing of Canadian History.' *Urban History Review* 14, 2 (October 1985):95-114

Dechief, H., comp. *A Bibliography of Published Material and Theses on Canadian Railways.* Montreal 1980

Dempsey, H., ed. *The CPR West: The Iron Road and the Making of a Nation.* Vancouver 1984

den Otter, A.A. *Civilizing the West: The Galts and the Development of Western Canada.* Edmonton 1982

——. 'Railways and Alberta's Coal Problem, 1880-1960.' In *Western Canada: Past and Present.* Ed. A.A. Rasporich, 84-98. Calgary 1975

Deverell, William. *Railroad Crossing: Californians and the Railroad, 1850-1910.* Berkeley 1994

Dorman, R., comp. *Statutory History of the Steam and Electric Railways of Canada, 1836-1937.* Ottawa 1938

Eagle, J.A. *The Canadian Pacific Railway and the Development of Western Canada, 1896-1914.* Montreal 1989

——. 'Monopoly or Competition: The Nationalization of the Grand Trunk Railway.' *Canadian Historical Review* 62, 1 (March 1981):3-30

——. 'Railways and Canadian Development.' *Acadiensis,* 7, 2 (1978):159-64

Easterbrook, W.H. 'Uncertainty and Economic Change.' *Journal of Economic History* 14 (1954):346-60

Fahey, J. *Inland Empire: D.C. Corbin and Spokane.* Seattle 1965

Fisher, R. *Contact and Conflict: Indian and European Relations in British Columbia, 1774-1880.* 2nd ed. Vancouver 1992

——. *Duff Pattullo of British Columbia.* Toronto 1991

——. 'T.D. Pattullo and the North: The Significance of the Periphery in British Columbia Politics.' *Pacific Northwest Quarterly* 81, 3 (July 1990):101-11

Fleming, R.B. *The Railway King of Canada: Sir William Mackenzie, 1849-1923.* Vancouver 1991

Fogel, R.W. *Railroads and American Economic Growth: Essays in Econometric History.* Baltimore 1964

——. *The Union Pacific Railroad: A Case in Premature Enterprise.* Baltimore 1960

Foner, P.S. *The Industrial Workers of the World, 1905-1917.* Vol. 4 of *History of the Labor Movement in the United States.* New York 1965

Fournier, L. *Railway Nationalization in Canada.* Toronto 1935

Frank, T. 'The Leviathan with Tentacles of Steel: Railroads in the Minds of Kansas Populists.' *Western Historical Quarterly* (February 1989):37-54

Fraser Lake and District Historical Society. *Deeper Roots and Greener Valleys.* Fraser Lake 1986

Galois, R. 'The History of the Upper Skeena Region, 1850 to 1927.' *Native Studies Review* 9, 2 (1993-4):113-83

——. 'The Indian Rights Association, Native Protest Activity and the "Land Question" in

British Columbia, 1903-1916.' *Native Studies Review* 8, 2 (1992):1-34

Gates, P.W. *Fifty Million Acres: Conflicts over Kansas Land Policy, 1854-1890*. Ithaca, NY 1954

George, P.J. *Government Subsidies and the Construction of the Canadian Pacific Railway*. New York 1981 (PhD dissertation, 1967)

Gilpin, J. 'International Perspectives on Railway Townsite Development in Western Canada, 1877-1914.' *Planning Perspectives* 7 (1992):247-62

——. 'The Poor Relation Has Come into Her Fortune: The British Investment Boom in Canada, 1905-1915.' *Canada House Lecture Series* 53. London 1992

——. 'Urban Land Speculation in the Development of Strathcona (South Edmonton), 1891-1912.' In *The Developing West: Essays in Honour of Lewis H. Thomas*. Ed. J.E. Foster, 179-200. Edmonton 1983

Glazebrook, G.P. de T. *A History of Transportation in Canada*. Toronto 1938

Glen, Sr., J. *Where the Rivers Meet: The Story of the Settlement of the Bulkley Valley*. Smithers 1977

Gowen, R.J. 'Canada and the Myth of the Japan Market, 1896-1911.' *Pacific Historical Review* 39 (February 1970):63-83

Grand Trunk Pacific: A Transcontinental Line. Pamphlet. 1904

Grand Trunk Pacific Railway Company. *The Grand Trunk Pacific: Canada's National Transcontinental Railway*. Pamphlet, 10 eds. 1905-12

——. *Prince Rupert, British Columbia: The Pacific Coast Terminus*. Pamphlet, 6 eds. 1909-12

——. *Plateau and Valley Lands of the Central Interior*. Pamphlet, 8 eds. 1911-19

Grand Trunk Railway Company of Canada. *Annual Reports*. 1902-19

– [?]. *Facts Concerning the Proposed Grand Trunk Pacific Railway*. Pamphlet. 1903

——. Grant, H.R. 'Guest Editorial: Railroad History as Seen by Railroaders.' *Railroad History* 158 (Spring 1988):9-12

——. 'Seeking the Pacific: The Chicago & North Western's Plans to Reach the West Coast.' *Pacific North West Quarterly* (April 1990):67-73

Gray, J. *R.B. Bennett: The Calgary Years*. Toronto 1991

Gresko, J., and R. Howard, eds. *Fraser Port: Freightway to the Pacific, 1858-1985*. Victoria 1986

Grodinsky, J. *Transcontinental Railway Strategy, 1869-93: A Study of Businessmen*. Philadelphia 1962

Hak, G. 'Prairie Capital, Prairie Markets, and Prairie Labour: The Forest Industry in the Prince George District, British Columbia, 1910-1930.' *Prairie Forum* 14 (1989):9-22

——. 'The Socialist and Labourist Impulse in Small-Town British Columbia: Port Alberni and Prince George, 1911-1933.' *Canadian Historical Review* 70, 4 (December 1989):519-42

Hale, L.L., and J. Barman, comps. *British Columbia Local Histories: A Bibliography*. Victoria 1991

Hall, D.J. *A Lonely Eminence, 1901-1929*. Vol. 2 of *Clifford Sifton*. Vancouver 1985

Harris, R.C. 'Moving amid the Mountains, 1870-1913.' *BC Studies* 58 (Summer 1983):3-39

Harvey, T. 'Railroad Towns: Urban Form on the Prairie.' *Landscape* 27 (1983):26-34

Hawker, R. 'Chateau Prince Rupert: A Forgotten Dream.' *B.C. Historical News* 20 (1987):15-17

Hedges, J.B. *Building the Canadian West: The Land and Colonization Policies of the Canadian Pacific Railway*. New York 1939

——. *Henry Villard and the Railways of the Northwest*. New Haven 1930

Henry, R.A.C. *Railway Freight Rates in Canada: A Study Prepared for the Royal Commission on Dominion-Provincial Relations*. Ottawa 1939

Hidy, R.W., et al. *The Great Northern Railway: A History*. Cambridge, MA 1988

Hofsommer, D. *The Southern Pacific, 1901-1985*. College Station, TX 1986

Hopper, A.B., and T. Kearney. *Canadian National Railways: Synoptical History of Organization, Capital Stock, Funded Debt, and Other Information*. Montreal 1962

Human Rights Commission (Prince George) Summer Program. *Indian Issues, Yesterday and*

Today. Prince George 1972

Ichioka, Y. 'Japanese Immigrant Labor Contractors and the Northern Pacific and the Great Northern Railroad Companies, 1898-1907.' *Labor History* 21, 3 (Summer 1980):325-50

Innis, H.A. *Essays in Canadian Economic History.* Ed. M.Q. Innis. Toronto 1956

——. *A History of the Canadian Pacific Railway.* 2nd ed. Toronto 1971

——. *Problems of Staple Production.* Toronto 1933

——. *Settlement and the Mining Frontier.* Toronto 1936

Jackman, W.T. *Economics of Transportation.* Toronto 1926

Jacoby, S.M. *Employing Bureaucracy: Managers, Unions and the Transformation of Work in American Industry, 1900-1945.* New York 1985

Johnston, N.J. 'The Frederick Law Olmsted Plan for Tacoma.' *Pacific Northwest Quarterly* 66, 3 (July 1975):97-104

Kellett, J.R. *The Impact of Railways on Victorian Cities.* London 1969

Klein, M. *The Life and Legend of Jay Gould.* Baltimore 1986

——. *Unfinished Business: The Railroad in American Life.* Hanover, ME 1994

——. *Birth of a Railroad, 1862-1893.* Vol. 1 of *Union Pacific.* New York 1987

——. *The Rebirth 1894-1969.* Vol. 2 of *Union Pacific.* New York 1990

Knafla, L., ed. *Law and Justice in a New Land: Essays in Western Canadian Legal History.* Toronto 1986

Kostal, R.W. *Law and English Railway Capitalism, 1825-1875.* Oxford 1994

Lamb, W.K. *History of the Canadian Pacific Railway.* New York 1977

Large, R.G. *Prince Rupert: A Gateway to Alaska and the Pacific.* Vancouver 1960

——. *Skeena: River of Destiny.* Vancouver 1957

Larson, J.L. *Bonds of Enterprise: John Murray Forbes and Western Development in America's Railway Age.* Cambridge, MA 1984

Laut, A.C. *Am I My Brother's Keeper?* Toronto 1913

——. 'Revolution Yawns.' *Technical World Magazine* (1912):134-44

Lavallée, O. 'The Grand Trunk Railway of Canada: An Overview.' *Railroad History* 147 (Autumn 1982):12-18

Lavis, F. *Railway Estimates: Design, Quantities and Costs.* New York 1917

Leacock, S. *My Discovery of the West: A Discussion of East and West in Canada.* Boston 1937

Leier, M. *Where the Fraser River Flows: The Industrial Workers of the World in British Columbia.* Vancouver 1990

Lee, D. 'Chinese Construction Workers on the Canadian Pacific.' *Railroad History* 148 (Spring 1983):43-57

Leonard, F. 'Grand Trunk Pacific and the Establishment of the City of Prince George, 1911-1915.' *BC Studies* 63 (Autumn 1984):29-54

——. 'John Houston.' *Dictionary of Canadian Biography.* Vol. 13, 480-1. Toronto 1966-

——. '"To Injure Its Own Interests": The Grand Trunk Pacific Railway Company and the Blighting of Hazelton District, 1910-1918.' *BC Studies* 88 (Winter 1990-1):21-57

Lewis, F.D., and M. MacKinnon. 'Government Loan Guarantees and the Failure of the Canadian Northern Railway.' *Journal of Economic History* 47, 1 (March 1987):175-96

Lewis, F.D., and D.R. Robinson. 'The Timing of Railway Construction on the Canadian Prairies.' *Canadian Journal of Economics* 17, 2 (May 1984):340-52

Licht, W. *Working for the Railroad: The Organization of Work in the Nineteenth Century.* Princeton 1983

Limerick, P.N. *The Legacy of Conquest: The Unbroken Past of the American West.* New York 1987

Lipartito, K. 'Getting Down to Cases: Baker & Botts and the Texas Railroad Commission.' *Essays in Economic and Business History* 6 (1988):27-36

——. 'What Have Lawyers Done for American Business? The Case of Baker & Botts of

Houston.' *Business History Review* 64 (Autumn 1990):489-526

Lipartito, K., and J. Pratt. *Baker & Botts in the Development of Modern Houston*. Austin, TX 1991

Lovett, H.A. *Canada and the Grand Trunk, 1829-1924*. Montreal 1924

Lowe, J.N. 'Canada's Third Transcontinental Railway: The Grand Trunk Pacific/National Transcontinental Railways.' *Journal of the West* 13 (1978):52-61

Lowe, G.S. '"The Enormous File": The Evolution of the Modern Office in Early Twentieth-Century Canada.' *Archivaria* 19 (Winter 1984-5):137-51

Lower, J.A. 'The Construction of the Grand Trunk Pacific Railway in British Columbia.' *British Columbia Historical Quarterly* 4, 3 (July 1940):163-81

Lucas, R.A. *Minetown, Milltown, Railtown: Life in Communities of Single Industry*. Toronto 1972

Lugrin, C.H. 'Economic History.' In *The Pacific Province*. Vol. 21 of *Canada and Its Provinces*. Eds. A. Shortt and A.G. Doughty, 241-82. Toronto 1914

Lyman, E.L. 'Outmaneuvering the Octopus: Atchison, Topeka and Santa Fe.' *California History* (June 1988):95-107, 145-6

McCann, L.D. 'Heartland and Hinterland: A Framework for Regional Analysis.' In *Heartland and Hinterland: A Geography of Canada*. Ed. L.D. McCann, 2-35. Toronto 1982

McCarter, S. *Guide to the Milwaukee Road in Montana*. Helena, MO 1992

McCormack, A.R. *The Blanketstiffs: Itinerant Railway Construction Workers, 1896-1914*. Ottawa 1974

——. 'The Industrial Workers of the World in Western Canada: 1905-1914.' CHA, *Historical Papers* (1975):167-90

——. *Reformers, Rebels, and Revolutionaries: The Western Canada Radical Movement, 1899-1919*. Toronto 1977

——. 'Wobblies and Blanketstiffs: The Constituency of the IWW in Western Canada.' *Lectures in Canadian and Working-Class History*. Eds. W.J.C. Cherwinski and G. Kealey, 101-14. St. John's 1985

McDonald, J.A. 'Bleeding Day and Night: The Construction of the Grand Trunk Pacific Railway across Tsimshian Reserve Lands.' *Canadian Journal of Native Studies* 10, 1 (1990):33-69

MacDonald, N. 'CPR Town: The City Building Process in Vancouver, 1860-1914.' In *Shaping the Urban Landscape*. Eds. A.F.J. Artibise and G.A. Stelter, 382-412. Ottawa 1982

——. 'The Canadian Pacific Railway and Vancouver's Development to 1900.' *BC Studies* 35 (Autumn 1977):3-35

——. *Distant Neighbors: A Comparative History of Seattle and Vancouver*. Lincoln, NE 1987

McDonald, R.A.J. 'The Business Elite and Municipal Politics in Vancouver 1886-1914.' *Urban History Review* 11, 3 (February 1983):1-14

——. '"Holy Retreat" or "Practical Breathing Spot"? Class Perceptions of Vancouver's Stanley Park, 1910-1913.' *Canadian Historical Review* 65, 2 (June 1984):127-53

——. 'Working Class Vancouver 1886-1914: Urbanism and Class in British Columbia.' *BC Studies* 69/70 (Spring/Summer 1986):33-69.

McGahan, E.W. *From Confederation to Nationalization, 1867-1927*. Vol. 1 of *The Port of Saint John*. Saint John 1982

MacKay, D. *The Asian Dream: The Pacific Rim and Canada's National Railway*. Vancouver 1986

——. *The People's Railway: A History of Canadian National*. Vancouver 1992

Maclean, E. *The Far Land*. Prince George 1933

McLean, S.J. 'National Highways Overland.' In *The Dominion Industrial Expansion*, pt. 2. Vol. 10 of *Canada and Its Provinces*. Eds. A. Shortt and A.G. Doughty, 359-66. Toronto 1914

Marks, S.G. *The Road to Power: The Trans-Siberian Railroad and the Colonization of Asian*

Russia, 1850-1917. Ithaca, NY 1991

Martin, A. *Enterprise Denied: Origins of the Decline of American Railroads, 1897-1917.* New York 1971

——. *James J. Hill and the Opening of the Northwest.* New York 1976

——. 'Light at the End of a Very Long Tunnel: The Railroads and the Historians.' *Railroad History* 155 (Fall 1986):15-33

Mercer, L.J. *Railroads and Land Grant Policy: A Study in Government Intervention.* New York 1982

Meyer, R.H., comp. *Railroading in British Columbia: A Bibliography.* 2nd ed. Vancouver 1993

Miner, H.C. *The Corporation and the Indian: Tribal Sovereignty and Industrial Civilization in Indian Territory, 1865-1907.* Columbia, MS 1976

——. *The St. Louis-San Francisco Transcontinental Railroad: The Thirty-Fifth Parallel Project, 1853-1890.* Lawrence, KS 1972

Ministerial Union of ... B.C. [M.B. Cotsworth.] *The Crisis in B.C.: An Appeal for Investigation.* Vancouver 1915

Minter, R. *The White Pass: Gateway to the Klondike.* Toronto 1987

Morgan, M. *Puget's Sound: A Narrative of Early Tacoma and the Southern Sound.* Seattle 1979

Morris, R. *Railroad Administration.* New York 1915

Mouat, J. 'Creating a New Staple: Capital, Technology, and Monopoly in British Columbia's Resource Sector, 1901-1925.' *Journal of the Canadian Historical Association* 1 (1990):215-38

Mulhall, D. *Will to Power: The Missionary Career of Father A.G. Morice.* Vancouver 1986

Murphy, G. 'Canada's Forgotten Railway Tycoon.' *The Beaver* 73, 6 (December 1993-January 1994):29-36

Naylor, R.T. *The History of Canadian Business, 1867-1914.* 2 vols. Toronto 1975

Nelles, H.V. 'Looking Backward: Interpreting Canadian Economic Development.' In *Se Connaître: Politics and Culture in Canada.* Ed. J. Lennox, 17-44. Toronto 1985

——. *The Politics of Development: Forests, Mines, and Hydro-Electric Power in Ontario, 1849-1941.* Toronto 1974

Nesbit, R.C. *'He Built Seattle': A Biography of Judge Thomas Burke.* Seattle 1961

O'Bannon, P. 'Railway Construction in the Early Twentieth Century: The San Diego and Arizona Railway.' *Southern California Quarterly* (1979):255-90

O'Brien, Patrick. *The New Economic History of Railways.* New York 1977

Ormsby, M.A. *British Columbia: A History.* 2nd ed. Toronto 1971

Overton, R. *Burlington West: A Colonization History of the Burlington Railroad.* Cambridge, MA 1941

Patterson II, E.P. 'A Decade of Change: Origins of the Nishga and Tsimshian Land Protests in the 1880s.' *Journal of Canadian Studies* 18, 3 (Fall 1983):40-54

Perl, A. 'Public Enterprise as an Expression of Sovereignty: Reconsidering the Origin of Canadian National Railways.' *Canadian Journal of Political Science* 27, 1 (March 1994):23-52

Phillips, P.A. *No Power Greater: A Century of Labour in British Columbia.* Vancouver 1967

Ramirez, B. 'Brief Encounters: Italian Immigrant Workers and the CPR, 1900-1930.' *Labour/le Travail* 17 (Spring 1986):9-27

Ramsey, B. *PGE: Railway to the North.* Vancouver 1962

Regehr, T.D. *The Canadian Northern Railway: Pioneer Road of the Northern Prairies, 1895-1918.* Toronto 1976

Renz, L.T. *The History of the Northern Pacific Railroad.* Fairfield, WA 1980

Reps, J. *Cities of the American West: A History of Frontier Urban Planning.* Princeton 1979

Ripley, W.Z. *Railroads: Finance and Organization.* New York 1915

Rivers Wilson, C. *Chapters from My Official Life.* London 1916

Robin, M. *The Rush for Spoils: The Company Province, 1871-1933.* Toronto 1971

Rolfe, C. 'A British Artist and the Romance of Canada's Railways.' *British Journal of Canadian Studies* 8, 1 (1993):42-52

Rosenfeld, M. '"It Was a Hard Life": Class and Gender in the Work and Rhythms of a Railway Town, 1920-1950.' CHA, *Historical Papers* (1988):237-79

Ross, T. *Oh, the Coal Branch.* Edmonton 1976

Roy, P.E. 'Direct Management from Abroad: The Formative Years of the British Columbia Electric Railway.' In *Enterprise and Development: Essays in Canadian Business and Economic History.* Ed. G. Porter and R. Cuff, 101-21. Toronto 1973

—. 'The Fine Arts of Lobbying and Persuading: The Case of the B.C. Electric Railway, 1897-1917.' In *Canadian Business History.* Ed. D. Macmillan, 239-54. Toronto 1972

—. 'Progress, Prosperity and Politics: The Railway Politics of Richard McBride.' *BC Studies* 47 (Fall 1980):3-28

—. *Vancouver: An Illustrated History.* Toronto: Lorimer1980

—. *A White Man's Province: British Columbia Politicians and Chinese and Japanese Immigrants, 1858-1914.* Vancouver 1989

Rudland, L., and J. Rudland. *Fort Fraser: Where the Hell's That?* Cloverdale, BC 1988

Runnalls, F.E. *A History of Prince George.* Vancouver 1946

—. 'Boom Days in Prince George.' *British Columbia Historical Quarterly* 8, 4 (October 1944):281-306

Sarty, Roger. '"There Will be Trouble in the North Pacific": The Defence of British Columbia in the Early Twentieth Century.' *BC Studies* 61 (Spring 1984):3-29

Scholefield, E.O.S., and R.E. Gosnell. *A History of British Columbia.* Vancouver-Victoria 1913

Schull, J. *Laurier: The First Canadian.* Toronto 1965

Schwantes, C.A. 'The Milwaukee Road's Pacific Extension, 1902-1929.' *Pacific Northwest Quarterly* 72 (January 1981):30-40

—. *The Pacific Northwest: An Interpretative History.* Lincoln, NE 1989

—. 'Perceptions of Violence on the Wageworkers' Frontier.' *Pacific Northwest Quarterly* 77 (1986):52-7

—. *Radical Heritage: Labor, Socialism, and Reform in Washington and British Columbia, 1885-1917.* Seattle 1979

—. *Railroad Signatures across the Pacific Northwest.* Seattle 1993

Scott, J. *Plunderbund and Proletariat: A History of the IWW in B.C.* Vancouver 1974

Scott, R.V. *Railroad Development Programs in the Twentieth Century.* Des Moines 1985

Seager, A. 'A New Labour Era?: Canadian National Railways and the Railway Worker, 1919-1929.' *Journal of the Canadian Historical Association* 3 (1992):171-96

Sedgwick, J.K. 'The "City Beautiful" Look.' *Prince George Citizen*, 1 June 1985

Shervill, R.L. *Smithers: From Swamp to Village.* Smithers 1981

Shortt, A. 'Railroad Construction and National Prosperity: An Historic Parallel.' *Transactions of the Royal Society of Canada* (1914):295-303

Simmons, J. *The Railway in Town and Country.* London 1986

Simpson, M. *Thomas Adams and the Modern Planning Movement: Britain, Canada and the United States, 1900-1940.* London 1985

—. 'Thomas Adams in Canada, 1914-1930.' *Urban History Review* 2, 2 (October 1982):1-15

Skelton, O.D. *Life and Letters of Sir Wilfrid Laurier.* 2 vols. Toronto 1921

—. *The Railway Builders: A Chronicle of Overland Highways.* Toronto 1916

Smedley-L'Heureux, A., ed. *Settlement Begins, 1905-1914.* Vol. 3 of *From Trail to Rail.* Vanderhoof, BC 1989

Smelts, D., comp. *Issues in Townsite Development: Government and Railway Involvement in the Incorporation of Prince George, 1914-1915: A Collection of Documents.* Prince George 1981

Stelter, G.A. 'A Regional Framework for Urban History.' *Urban History Review* 13, 3

(February 1985):193-206

Stelter, G.A., and A.F.J. Artibise. 'Canadian Resource Towns in Historical Perspective.' *Plan Canada* 18, 1 (March 1978):7-16

——, eds. *Power and Place: Canadian Urban Development in the North American Context.* Vancouver 1986

Stevens, G.R. *Towards the Inevitable, 1896-1922.* Vol. 2 of *Canadian National Railways.* Toronto 1962

——. *History of the Canadian National Railways.* New York 1973

Stewart, J. 'The Canadian Northern Strike of 1912.' *Labour History* 3, 1 (1981):8-10

Stilgoe, J.R. *Metropolitan Corridor: Railroads and the American Scene.* New Haven 1983

Stromquist, H.S. *A Generation of Boomers: The Pattern of Railroad Labor Conflict in Nineteenth-Century America.* Urbana, IL 1987

Talbot, F.A. *Making Good in Canada.* London 1912

——. *The Making of a Great Canadian Railway: ... Grand Trunk Pacific Railway ....* London 1912

——. *The New Garden of Canada: ... Undeveloped New British Columbia.* London 1911

Taylor, G.D., and P. Baskerville. *A Concise History of Business in Canada.* Toronto 1994

Taylor, G.W. *Builders of British Columbia: An Industrial History.* Victoria 1982

——. *The Railway Contractors: The Story of John W. Stewart, His Enterprises and Associates.* Victoria 1988

Thomson, L.R. *The Canadian Railway Problem: Some Aspects of Canadian Transportation and a Suggested Solution for the Railway Problem.* Toronto 1938

Thompson, G.L. 'Myth and Rationality in Management Decision-Making: The Evolution of American Railroad Product Costing, 1870-1970.' *Journal of Transport History* 12, 1 (1991):1-10

Thompson, N., and J.H. Edgar. *Canadian Railway Development from the Earliest Times.* Toronto 1933

Thorner, T., ed. *Sa Ts'e: Historical Perspectives on Northern British Columbia.* Prince George 1989

Titley, E.B. *A Narrow Vision: Duncan Campbell Scott and the Administration of Indian Affairs in Canada.* Vancouver 1986

Tomblin, S. 'The Pacific Great Eastern Railway and W.A.C. Bennett's Defense of the North.' *Journal of Canadian Studies* 24, 4 (Winter 1989-90):29-40

——. 'W.A.C. Bennett and Province Building in British Columbia,' *BC Studies* 85 (Spring 1990):45-61

Traves, T. 'Business-Government Relations in Canada.' *History and Social Studies Teacher* 18, 2 (December 1982):75-82

——. *The State and Enterprise: Canadian Manufacturers and the Federal Government, 1917-1931.* Toronto 1979

Tuck, J.H. 'Canadian Railways and the Unions in the Running Trades, 1865-1914.' *Industrial Relations* 36 (1981):106-31

——. 'Union Authority, Corporate Obstinacy, and the Grand Trunk Strike of 1910.' CHA, *Historical Papers* (1976):175-92

——. 'The United Brotherhood of Railway Employees in Western Canada, 1898-1905.' *Labour/le Travailleur* 2 (Spring 1983):63-88

Turkki, P. *Burns Lake and District: A History Formal and Informal.* Burns Lake, BC 1973

Turner, R.D. *West of the Great Divide: An Illustrated History of the Canadian Pacific Railway in British Columbia, 1880-1986.* Victoria 1986

Usher, J. *William Duncan of Metlakatla: A Victorian Missionary in British Columbia.* Ottawa 1974

Valemount Historic Society. *Yellowhead Pass and Its People.* Valemount, BC 1984

Van Cleef, E. 'Prince Rupert – An Error in Location.' *Journal of Geography* 58 (March 1959):127-32

Veazey, P. 'John Hendry and the Vancouver Westminster and Yukon Railway: "It Would Put Us on Easy Street."' *BC Studies* 59 (Autumn 1983):44-63

Voisey, P. 'The Urbanization of the Canadian Prairies, 1871-1916.' *Histoire sociale/Social History* 15 (May 1975):77-101

——. *Vulcan: The Making of a Prairie Community.* Toronto 1988

Waiser, W.A. 'A Willing Scapegoat: John Macoun and the Route of the CPR.' *Prairie Forum* 31, 1 (Spring 1985):65-87

Walsh, M. 'By Packtrain and Steamer: The Hudson's Bay Company's British Columbia District Manager's Correspondence, 1897-1920.' *Archivaria* 20 (Summer 1985):127-35

Ward, J.H. *Railroads and the Character of America, 1820-67.* Knoxville, TN 1985

Ward, W.P. *White Canada Forever: Popular Attitudes and Public Policy toward Orientals in British Columbia.* Montreal 1978

Washburn, S. *Trails, Trappers and Tenderfeet in the New Empire of Western Canada.* Toronto 1913

Wellington, A.M. *The Economic Theory of the Location of Railways.* New York 1877

West, W.J. 'The "B.X." and the Rush to Fort George.' *British Columbia Historical Quarterly* 13, 3-4 (July-October 1949):129-230

Wheeler, M.J., ed. *The Robson Valley Story.* McBride, BC 1979

White, W.T. 'Race, Ethnicity, and Gender in the Railroad Work Force: The Case of the Far Northwest, 1883-1918.' *Western Historical Quarterly* 16 (July 1985):265-83

——. 'Railroad Labor Protests, 1894-1917.' *Pacific Northwest Quarterly* 75 (January 1984):13-21

——. 'The War of the Railroad Kings: Great Northern-Northern Pacific Rivalry in Montana, 1881-1896.' In *Montana and the West: Essays in Honor of K. Ross Toole.* Eds. R.C. Meyers and H.W. Fritz. Boulder, CO 1984

Whitehead, M., ed. *They Call Me Father: Memoirs of Father Nicolas Coccola.* Vancouver 1988

Wicks, W. *Memories of the Skeena.* Saanichton 1976

Williams, D.R. *Duff: A Life in the Law.* Vancouver 1984

——. *Trapline Outlaw: Simon Peter Gunanoot.* Victoria 1982

Williams, W.H. *Railroad Correspondence File.* 2nd ed. New York 1910 [typescript copy, 1936]

Wilson, W.H. 'How Seattle Lost the Bogue Plan.' *Pacific Northwest Quarterly* (October 1984):171-80

Wilton, C., ed. *Beyond the Law: Lawyers and Business in Canada, 1830 to 1930.* Vol. 4 of *Essays in the History of Canadian Law.* Toronto 1990

Wolfe, P. 'Tramp Printer Extraordinary: British Columbia's John "Truth" Houston.' *BC Studies* 40 (Winter 1978-9):5-31

Woods, J., and J.S. Marsh. *Snow War: An Illustrated History of Rogers Pass and Glacier National Park.* Ottawa 1985

Wynne, R.E. *Reaction to the Chinese in the Pacific Northwest and British Columbia, 1850-1910.* New York 1979

Yarmie, A. 'The Right to Manage: Vancouver Employers' Associations, 1900-1923.' *BC Studies* 90 (Summer 1991):40-74

Yates, J. *Control through Communication: The Rise of System in American Management.* Baltimore 1989

Young, B. *George-Étienne Cartier: Montreal Bourgeois.* Montreal 1981

——. *Promoters and Politicians: The North-Shore Railways in the History of Quebec, 1854-1885.* Toronto 1978

Zaslow, Morris. *The Opening of the Canadian North, 1870-1914.* Toronto 1971

Zunz, O. *Making America Corporate, 1870-1920.* Chicago 1990

Theses and Manuscripts

Backler, G.C. 'The CPR's Capacity and Investment Strategy in Rogers Pass, B.C., 1882-1916.' MSc thesis, Business Administration, University of British Columbia, 1981

Barman, J. 'Writing the History of Northern British Columbia.' Manuscript chapter in forthcoming *Historiography of the Provincial Norths*. Eds. W.R. Morrison and K. Coates

Bell, D.S. 'A History of Real Estate Development in Prince Rupert.' B.Comm. Essay, Commerce, University of British Columbia, 1968

Bumby, A. 'The Sales Campaign of George J. Hammond and the Natural Resources Security Company.' Undergraduate paper, History, College of New Caledonia, 1981

Churchill, D.M. 'False Creek Development: A Study of ... the Public and Private Development of the Waterway and Its Land Basin.' MA thesis, Economics, Political Science, and Sociology, University of British Columbia, 1953

Clayton, D. 'Geographies of the Lower Skeena, 1830-1920.' MA thesis, Geography, University of British Columbia, 1989

Coutts, R.M. 'The Railway Policy of Sir Wilfrid Laurier: The Grand Trunk Pacific-National Transcontinental.' MA thesis, History, University of Toronto, 1968

Crerar, A.D. 'Prince Rupert, B.C. – A Study of a Port and Its Hinterland.' MA thesis, Geography, University of British Columbia, 1951

Cross, P. 'Persistence and Change: The Demographic and Cultural Reasons for Acceptance and Rejection of Economic Development on the Skeena and Nass Rivers of British Columbia, 1831-1916.' MA thesis, History, University of Victoria, 1992

Cruikshank, K. 'Managing a Fragile North American Industry: The Canadian Railway Problem Revisited.' Paper presented to the Second Canadian Business History Conference, University of Victoria, BC, March 1988

Dwyer, M.J. 'Laurier and the British Columbia Liberal Party, 1896-1911: A Study in Federal-Provincial Party Relations.' MA thesis, History, University of British Columbia, 1961

Eagle, J.A. 'Sir Robert Borden and the Railway Problem in Canadian Politics, 1911-1920.' PhD diss., History, University of Toronto, 1972

Frederick, B.A. 'Construction of the Hudson Bay Railway: A History of the Work and the Workers, 1908-1930.' MA thesis, History, University of Manitoba, 1981

Gilpin, J. 'The Canadian Agency and British Investment in Western Canadian Land, 1905-1915.' PhD diss., History, University of Leicester, 1992

Hak, G.H. 'On the Fringes: Capital and Labour in the Forest Economies of the Port Alberni and Prince George Districts, British Columbia, 1910-1939.' PhD diss., History, Simon Fraser University, 1986

Harvey, N. 'History and Finances of the Pacific Great Eastern Railway.' BA thesis, Commerce, University of British Columbia, 1935

Hewetson, H.W. 'The Railway Rate Problems of Western Canada with Particular Reference to British Columbia.' MA thesis, Political Economy, University of British Columbia, 1925

Holmes, N.B. 'The Promotion of Early Growth in the Western Canadian City: A Case Study of Prince George, B.C., 1909-1915.' BA thesis, History, University of British Columbia, 1974

Hunt, P.R. 'The Political Career of Sir Richard McBride.' MA thesis, History, University of British Columbia, 1953

Johnson, A.J. 'The Canadian Pacific Railway and British Columbia, 1871-1886.' MA thesis, History, University of British Columbia, 1936

Kanakos, J.L. 'Negotiations to Relocate the Songhees Indians, 1843-1911.' MA thesis, History, Simon Fraser University, 1982

Kellogg, J.E. 'The Impact of the Railroad upon a Frontier Region: The Case of Alaska and the Yukon.' PhD diss., Geography, University of Indiana, 1975

Knight, N. 'Mega-Project Planning and Economic Welfare: A Case Study of British Columbia's North East Coal Project.' PhD diss., Community and Regional Planning, University of British Columbia, 1990

Lawrence, J.C. 'Markets and Capital: A History of the Lumber Industry of British Columbia, 1778-1952.' MA thesis, History, University of British Columbia, 1957

Lower, J.A. 'The Grand Trunk Pacific Railway and British Columbia.' MA thesis, History, University of British Columbia, 1939

McDonald, J.A. 'Trying to Make a Life: The Historical Political Economy of Kitsumkalum.' PhD diss., Anthropology, University of British Columbia, 1985

McDonald, R.A.J. 'Business Leaders in Early Vancouver, 1886-1914.' PhD diss., History, University of British Columbia, 1977

Mellen, F.N. 'The Development of the Toronto Waterfront during the Railway Expansion Era, 1850-1912.' PhD diss., Geography, University of Toronto, 1974

Meyer, R. 'The Evolution of Railways in the Kootenays.' MA thesis, Geography, University of British Columbia, 1970

Odisho, W.C. 'Salt Lake City to Oakland: The Western Pacific Link in the Continental Railroad System.' PhD diss., History, University of California, 1941

Palmer, R.D. 'The Northern Pacific Railroad and Its Choice of a Western Terminus, 1869-1887.' MA thesis, History, University of Washington, 1967

Roy, P.E. 'Railways, Politicians, and the Development of the City of Vancouver as a Metropolitan Centre, 1886-1929.' MA thesis, History, University of Toronto, 1963

Saywell, J.T. 'The Bulkley Valley.' Paper prepared for Department of Education, Victoria, 1951

Shankel, G.E. 'The Development of Indian Policy in British Columbia.' PhD diss., History, University of Washington, 1945

Smith, B.R.D. 'Sir Richard McBride: A Study in the Conservative Party of British Columbia, 1903-1916.' MA thesis, History, Queen's University, 1959

Smith, D.J. 'Procuring a Right-of-Way: James J. Hill and Indian Reservations, 1886-1888.' Graduate paper, University of Montana, 1983

Tomblin, S. 'In Defense of Territory: Province Building under W.A.C. Bennett.' PhD diss., Political Science, University of British Columbia, 1985

Van Arsdol, T. 'The Career of C.C. Van Arsdol.' Unpublished manuscript, 1987

White, W.T. 'A History of Railroad Workers in the Pacific Northwest, 1883-1934.' PhD diss., History, University of Washington, 1981

Williams, J.D. 'A History of the Edmonton, Dunvegan, and British Columbia Railway, 1907-1929.' MA thesis, History, University of Alberta, 1956

Wogin, G. 'The Wealth Maximizing Behaviour of the Canadian Pacific Railway: Lands, Freight Rates, and the Crow's Nest Pass Agreement.' PhD diss., Economics, Carleton University, 1981

Yerburgh, R.E.M. 'The Pacific Great Eastern Railway: An Account of Its History, the Question of Its Future, with an Attempted Solution to the Problem.' BA thesis, Economics, University of British Columbia, 1928

Zaharoff, W.H. 'Success in Struggle: The Squamish People and Kitsilano Indian Reserve No. 6.' MA thesis, History, Carleton University, 1978

INDEX